LABORATORIES OF DEMOCRACY

LABORATORIES OF DEMOCRACY

by

DAVID OSBORNE

Harvard Business School Press
Boston, Massachusetts

Printed in the United States of America

92 91 90 89 88   5 4 3 2

Portions of chapters 1, 2, 5, and 6 appeared in *Economic Competitiveness: The States Take the Lead*, published by the Economic Policy Institute, November 1987.

Portions of the Introduction and chapters 2 and 5 appeared in *Best of Business Quarterly*, Spring 1988.

Portions of the Introduction and chapter 4 appeared in *The Washington Monthly*, February 1988.

Portions of the Introduction and chapters 5 and 10 appeared in *Dissent*, Winter 1988.

Library of Congress Cataloging-in-Publication Data

Osborne, David (David E.)
    Laboratories of democracy / by David Osborne.
        p.   cm.
    Includes index.
    ISBN 0-87584-192-9
    1. Industry and state—United States—States.   2. Economic
development projects—United States—States.   3. Technological
innovations—Economic aspects—United States—States.
4. Competition, International.   5. Governors—United States.
6. United States—Politics and government—1981–   I. Title.
HD3616.U46083 1988
338.973—dc19   88-5895
                                                                         CIP

For Rose

"There must be power in the States and the Nation to remould, through experimentation, our economic practices and institutions to meet changing social and economic needs. . . . Denial of the right to experiment may be fraught with serious consequences to the Nation. It is one of the happy incidents of the federal system that a single courageous State may, if its citizens choose, serve as a laboratory; and try novel social and economic experiments without risk to the rest of the country."

Supreme Court Justice Louis Brandeis
New State Ice Co. v. Liebmann,
Dissenting Opinion, 1932.

CONTENTS

Acknowledgments   ix
Introduction   1

PART I   THE LABORATORIES

1   The Class of '74: The Roots of a New Paradigm   21
2   Pennsylvania: The Economic Development Model   43
3   Arkansas: The Education Model   83
4   Arizona: Protecting the Environment, Rethinking Social
    Services   111
5   Michigan: Creating the Factory of the Future   145
6   Massachusetts: Redistributing Economic Growth   175
7   New York: Housing the Poor   211

PART II   THE LESSONS

8   The First Agenda: Creating Economic Growth   249
9   The Second Agenda: Bringing the Poor into the Growth
    Process   289

PART III   THE POLITICS

10   The Emerging Political Paradigm   319
Notes   339
List of Abbreviations   365
Index   368

ACKNOWLEDGMENTS

Reading other books, I have always puzzled about authors who describe their works as collaborations, given the lonely process that is writing. Now I understand. This book could not have been written without the generous assistance of dozens of people. I am grateful to the hundreds of people I interviewed. I am deeply indebted to a smaller group of people who spent countless hours, over the course of three years, sharing their work and their perspectives, steering me to others, offering advice, reading drafts, and providing support in what at times felt like an endless and impossible task.

Bill Schweke and Bob Friedman, at the Corporation for Enterprise Development, were invaluable from the first day to the last. Michael Barker, Pete Plastrik, and Walt Plosila were also immensely helpful. Bob Kuttner and Bob Reich offered support throughout—moral, critical, and financial (through the Economic Policy Institute). John Judis was enormously helpful with the final rewrite. All read drafts and offered constructive criticism.

Various chapters and drafts also benefited from readings by Fred Strebeigh, John Junkerman, Gerald Benjamin, Bob Thompson, Beth Siegel, Belden Daniels, Brad Kirkman-Liff, Kathleen Ferris, Peter Cove, Lee Bowes, and Carol VanDeusen Lukas. Mary Houghton and Ron Grzywinski taught me a great deal and offered valuable insights on relevant portions of the manuscript. Others who were enormously generous with their time and efforts included Bob Coy, Steve Schlesinger, Bill Eimicke, Allison Thomas, Jack Russell, Lou Glazer, Joan Roberts, Bob Nash, Bob Wise, Lucy Gorham, and Barbara Dyer. I do not have the space to mention the countless others who shared their thoughts and work with me.

Richard Taub, DeWitt John, Scott Fosler, Carol Steinbach, Stewart Perry, Diane Blair, Larry Landry, Doug Henton, and Steve Waldhorn generously allowed me to read their manuscripts before publication. Jeff Faux and Roger Hickey, at the Economic Policy Institute, provided valuable financial assistance and published a study based on part of the book. Sheila Leahy and Craig Kennedy at the Joyce Foundation offered a critical research grant. George Gendron, Steve Pearlstein, and Steve Solomon at *Inc.*

magazine provided assignments that made important portions of my research possible.

Special thanks must go to Kristine Dahl, who was, as always, the perfect agent, and to my editor at Harvard Business School Press, Barbara Ankeny, who was a joy to work with. I also want to extend long overdue thanks to two people who got me started as a writer, Doug Davis and Stanley Goldstein. Robert Wright, who flew in and offered his help at a critical moment, proved once again that no one could ask for a better friend.

Finally, I want to thank my family. Bill and Eileen Wolf went out of their way to help when deadlines loomed. My parents provided support throughout, as they always have; words cannot express how much I owe them. My wife and children, whose everyday love and support got me through the final year's rush to meet deadlines, deserve the biggest thanks. Rose put up with a husband who worked too many hours and whose mind stayed with the book even when he wasn't working; without her care, support, and tolerance, I could never have finished. My children put up with a father who had to work even on Father's Day. They, in turn, made every day special.

Boston, Massachusetts   David Osborne
January 1988

LABORATORIES OF DEMOCRACY

INTRODUCTION

Franklin Roosevelt once said of the New Deal, "Practically all the things we've done in the federal government are like things Al Smith did as governor of New York."[1] There was surprising honesty in Roosevelt's remark, though he might have credited other states as well. Many of FDR's initiatives—including unemployment compensation, massive public works programs, deposit insurance, and social security—were modeled on successful state programs.[2] The groundwork for much of the New Deal social agenda was laid in the states during the Progressive Era.

A similar process is under way today, particularly in the economic arena. The 1980s have been a decade of enormous innovation at the state level. For those unfamiliar with state politics—and given the media's relentless focus on Washington, that includes most Americans—the specifics are often startling. While the Reagan administration was denouncing government intervention in the marketplace, governors of both parties were embracing an unprecedented role as economic activists. Over the past decade, they have created well over 100 public investment funds, to make loans to and investments in businesses. Half the states have set up public venture capital funds; others have invested public money in the creation of private financial institutions. At least 40 states have created programs to stimulate technological innovation, which now number at least 200. Dozens of states have overhauled their public education systems. Tripartite business-labor-government boards have sprung up, often with the purpose of financing local committees dedicated to restructuring labor-management relations. A few states have even launched cooperative efforts with management and labor to revitalize regional industries.

Why this sudden burst of innovation at the state level? Just 25 years ago, state governments were widely regarded as the enemies of change, their resistance symbolized by George Wallace in the schoolhouse door. The answer has to do with the profound and wrenching economic transition the United States has experienced over the past two decades. In the 1980s, a fundamentally new economy has been born. With it has come a series of new problems, new opportunities, and new challenges. In the states, government has responded.

The notion that America has left the industrial era behind is now commonplace. Some call the new age the "postindustrial era," some the "information age," others the "era of human capital." But most agree that the fundamental organization of the American and international economies that prevailed for three decades after World War II has changed. The United States has evolved from an industrial economy built upon assembly-line manufacturing in large, stable firms to a rapidly changing, knowledge-intensive economy built upon technological innovation.

The most obvious symptoms of this transition are idle factories, dislocated workers, and depressed manufacturing regions. Less obvious are the problems that inhibit our ability to innovate: a poorly educated and trained work force; adversarial relations between labor and management; inadequate supplies of risk capital; and corporate institutions that lag behind their foreign competitors in the speed with which they commercialize the fruits of their research, adopt new production technologies, and exploit foreign markets.

Jimmy Carter was elected just as the public began to sense that something had gone wrong with the American economy. Like other national politicians of his day, he only dimly perceived the emerging realities of the new economy. Ronald Reagan owed his election to the deepening economic crisis, but his solution was to reach back to the free-market myths of the preindustrial era. He had the luxury to do so because he governed an enormously diverse nation, in which rapid growth along both coasts balanced the pain experienced in the industrial and agricultural heartland.

Most governors have not had that luxury. When unemployment approached 13 percent in Massachusetts, or 15 percent in Pennsylvania, or 18 percent in Michigan, governors had to respond. They could not afford to wait for the next recovery, or to evoke the nostrums of free-market theory.

The same dynamic occurred during the last great economic transformation: the birth of our industrial economy. The Progressive movement, which originated at the state and local level, grew up in response to the new problems created by rapid industrialization: the explosion of the cities, the emergence of massive corporate trusts, the growth of urban political machines, the exploitation of industrial labor. Many Progressive reforms introduced in the cities or states were gradually institutionalized at the federal level—culminating in the New Deal.

This reality led Supreme Court Justice Louis Brandeis to coin his famous phrase, "laboratories of democracy." One of America's leading Progressive activists during the early decades of the twentieth century, Brandeis viewed the states as laboratories in which the Progressives could experiment with new solutions to social and economic problems. Those that worked could be applied nationally; those that failed could be discarded.

Brandeis's phrase captured the peculiar, pragmatic genius of the federal system. As one approach to government—one political paradigm—wears thin, its successor is molded in the states, piece by piece. The process has little to do with ideology and everything to do with trial-and-error, seat-of-the-pants pragmatism. Part of the beauty, as Brandeis pointed out, is that new ideas can be tested on a limited scale—to see if they work, and to see if they sell—before they are imposed on the entire nation.

Today, at both the state and local levels, we are in the midst of a new progressive era. Just as the state and local Progressivism of Brandeis's day foreshadowed the New Deal, the state and local experimentation of the 1980s may foreshadow a new national agenda. Already the issues that have dominated state politics in the 1980s—economic competitiveness and excellence in education—are emerging as major themes in the 1988 presidential election.

The New Economy

Two forces above all others have transformed our economy: technological advance and global competition. At the root of both was the invention of the computer, which triggered the microelectronic revolution. "The transformation of industry by the microprocessor may well constitute a tumultuous advance comparable in magnitude to but far more compact in time than the great divides of steam and electrical power," writes Jack Russell, father of an economic development program called the Michigan Modernization Service.[3]

The spread of microelectronic technology has so transformed our economy that the most accurate label for the new era might be the "microelectronic age." As computer technology has worked its way through the economy, factories have been automated; rapid technological change has become the norm; the number of workers who process "information" has skyrocketed; and the economies of scale in much of the business world have reversed, favoring decentralization rather than centralization. The symptoms of these changes are everywhere. Only 9 percent of American workers still labor in factories.[4] The number of Americans who run businesses or work for themselves now equals the number who belong to unions.[5] Since 1980, America's five hundred largest companies have lost almost three million jobs, while small businesses—those with one hundred employees or fewer—have created ten million.[6]

Global communications made possible by the microelectronic revolution, when combined with rapid growth in Asia and Europe, have ushered in a new era of international competition. In 1960, only 20 percent of goods produced in the United States were in active competition with foreign products; by 1980, a full *70 percent* were.[7] In 1970, imports accounted for 9 percent of all goods purchased by Americans; just ten years later, they accounted for 22 percent.[8] Today our manufacturers must compete against labor forces paid one-tenth of what American workers receive. In this context, our competitive advantage no longer lies in products that can be manufactured on traditional assembly lines. It lies instead in sophisticated new products and services that depend on advanced technologies and skilled workers.

The microelectronic revolution and the global market have altered the very elements necessary to produce economic growth. During the industrial era, manufacturers looked for raw materials, abundant low-cost labor, cheap power, and good transportation to markets. *Physical* infrastructure was the key. Today they look for educated workers, outstanding research universities, entrepreneurial climates, and an attractive quality of life. Good roads and airports are still important, but *intellectual* infrastructure is the key. Manufacturing muscle has been replaced by industrial intelligence.

"Comparative economic advantage has taken on new meaning," writes John Wilson, chief economist at the Bank of America. Today it means "human creative power, a highly educated work force, organizational talent, the ability to choose, the ability to adapt. Moreover, these attributes are not conceived of as natural endowments but as qualities achieved through public policies such as education, organized research, and investment in social overhead capital."[9]

In a world awash in low-wage labor, our future rests upon our ability to make research breakthroughs in the laboratory, to translate those breakthroughs into new products and processes, and to manufacture the results using the kind of technological sophistication and skilled labor that is still rare in the developing nations. In a nutshell, our future rests upon our ability to innovate.

With fierce competition not only from the Third World but from Western Europe and Japan as well, we must innovate with blinding speed. During the industrial era, the average time lag between a research breakthrough and its commercial application was 15 years; by the mid-1970s, it was three to four years.[10] The average life span of a new product was once measured in decades; today, in electronics, it is three to five years.[11] During the industrial era, stability was an important element of economic growth: corporations strove to create stable markets and work forces, while governments strove to create stable environments for corporations. In the new economy, rapid change is the norm, and flexibility—not stability—is the key to success.

The First Agenda: Creating Economic Growth

To stimulate growth in this new environment, we must create a context in which innovation flourishes as a continuous, everyday process. Government's primary role is to nourish the elements that make innovation possible: a vibrant intellectual infrastructure; a skilled, educated work force; an attractive quality of life; an entrepreneurial climate; a sufficient supply of risk capital; a healthy market for new products and processes; a commitment to industrial modernization; an industrial culture built on cooperation and flexibility; and a social system that supports innovation and change. Virtually every state initiative to create economic development falls within one of these nine categories.

The intellectual infrastructure. In today's economy, rapid growth tends to cluster in areas that have quality universities, top-flight research laboratories, and sophisticated networks of investors and entrepreneurs who turn innovative ideas into new or improved products and services. The Boston area, for instance, has long had an inadequate physical infrastructure: its highways are choked, its airport is overburdened, its harbor is the most polluted in the nation. But because it boasts the most concentrated intellectual infrastructure in the nation, it has spawned what we now call the Massachusetts miracle. To improve their intellectual infrastructures, state governments have poured money into their universities, funded new research institutes, opened university research parks, and created programs to bring academic and business researchers together.

A skilled, educated work force. Nothing is more important, in the long run, than the skills and capacity of our work force—what some call our human capital. New technologies can be copied by other nations, even exploited before we have a chance to get them to market. Virtually anything that can be reduced to a blueprint can be sent overseas. But unlike financial capital and technological expertise, human capital is largely immobile. If our work force is better educated, more skilled, and more creative than those of other nations, we have a competitive advantage that cannot be taken from us. This is particularly true in an age when our competitive edge depends upon our use of computerized production technologies and "flexible manufacturing"—the production of specialty items in limited quantities, which are less susceptible to competition from foreign assembly lines. Both of these arenas require workers who can adapt to new technologies, learn new skills on the job, and find new solutions as problems emerge.

The connection between growth rates and education levels could not be clearer if the statistics had been doctored. In the 1980 census, the states with the highest percentages of college graduates read like a list of states that were succeeding in the new economy: Massachusetts, Connecticut, Maryland, Virginia, Colorado, California, Utah, Hawaii, and Alaska.[12] A recent study of nine major cities found that in each one, industries whose average worker had not graduated from high school were losing jobs, whereas those whose average workers had graduated were gaining jobs.[13]

State governments have put an enormous amount of energy and money into improving their education systems during the 1980s. Because the goal has been economic competitiveness, the push for reform has come almost exclusively from political leaders, often with strong support from business. "It did not start with teachers, it did not start with parents, it did not start with students," says Emily Feistritzer, director of the National Center for Education Information. "It started at the top. The decisions have really moved out of the arena of the traditional educational establishment, and that is a significant policy change in this nation."

The states have done less well on job training. The main reason is that state governments have long been responsible for education, while the federal government has funded the majority of public-sector training programs. As federal money for training has dwindled, however, the states have begun to respond with new efforts.

An attractive quality of life. In addition to its intellectual infrastructure, the Boston region was blessed with a quality of life its educated work force found attractive. The city was a cultural center; it had managed to preserve its charm and its sense of history; and it was blessed with the many attractions of New England, all within a few hours' drive. People who flocked to the area for college or graduate school stayed for the quality of life. One survey found that over 90 percent of the electrical engineers who graduated from New England institutions remained in the region.[14]

"Unlike smokestack industries that need access to raw materials, energy, and transportation, high-tech plants locate where the quality of life is high enough to draw a skilled work force," says James Howell, chief economist at the Bank of Boston. "You don't locate plants for cheap labor or even taxes. You locate where people want to live."[15] Most academic studies confirm the point.[16]

Given that the physical environment is one ingredient of a high quality of life, environmental protection can no longer be viewed simply as a hindrance to growth.[17] In many areas, it is now a critical element of growth. This helps explain why Japan continues to grow at a rapid clip, despite its strict environmental regulations. It also explains why the governors of so many growth states in the 1980s, from Massachusetts to New Jersey to Arizona, have been ardent environmentalists.

An entrepreneurial climate. Many areas with major universities and attractive qualities of life have not experienced significant growth, because they do not have entrepreneurial climates. They lack whatever it is that encourages people to start new companies and pursue new ventures: the support networks, the role models, the risk capital, the technical assistance, and the incubator institutions (whether academic institutions or businesses) from which entrepreneurs spring. Often their economies are dominated by large corporations that fail to nurture entrepreneurial behavior within their own ranks and discourage spin-offs by employees.

Pittsburgh is a classic example. Prior to 1980, Pittsburgh boasted two major universities, a series of major corporate headquarters, and some of the nation's largest banks—but no entrepreneurial climate. Since 1980 local public and private-sector leaders—aided by state government—have begun a concerted effort to create such a climate. In Pennsylvania and in dozens of other states, governments have created business assistance centers, small-business incubators, financing programs for new and small businesses, even tax and regulatory reforms designed to encourage entrepreneurs.

Risk capital. One essential element of an entrepreneurial climate is a supply of risk capital, to finance innovative ventures. Growing economies require a wide variety of financial institutions capable of providing an array of investments: seed capital; venture capital; loans to small businesses; long-term debt for growing firms; creative combinations of debt and equity for mature firms that are struggling to turn themselves around. Capital markets dominated by a few large financial institutions often fail to provide this array, because large banks and institutional investors tend to become bureaucratized. To improve their capital markets, many state governments have set up public or quasi-public venture capital pools and loan funds. More important, they have worked to create new financial institutions in the private sector. They have directed portions of their employees' pension funds to venture capital investments or small-business loans. And most important of all, they have changed the rules governing the private marketplace, to encourage more venturesome investment behavior.

A market for new products and processes. An early market is a critical element in the survival of any innovative venture. Often new technology companies spring up around large, existing firms, which buy their products and services. Occasionally an entire industry emerges because government has created a demand for its products; the microelectronic revolution, which was driven almost exclusively by the Pentagon and the National Aeronautics and Space Administration (NASA), is the classic example.[18] The states have tried a number of methods to help their smaller businesses find markets. They have set up procurement assistance programs, to help them tap the federal market. They have helped small firms find work as subcontractors for larger firms in the state. And they have helped firms sell their goods abroad.

A commitment to industrial modernization. If we are to be competitive in the new economy, innovation cannot be limited to new enterprises. Our mature industries must also embrace innovation and flexibility, by modernizing their manufacturing technologies and adopting production meth-

ods that allow them to adjust to rapidly changing markets. To help their
mature manufacturing firms make this transition the states have set up a
variety of "industrial extension" systems. These services typically provide
consultants who help firms analyze their needs, choose the automated
equipment they need to remain competitive, and train their work force to
use it. Generally they work with smaller firms, which often find it difficult
to negotiate the complexities of the microelectronic age on their own. A
few states have begun to experiment with loan funds to help mature firms
restructure. Several have also bought management and labor from an entire industrial sector together to work out modernization strategies.

A new industrial culture. The process of continual innovation necessitates
a fundamental change in the culture of industry, from hierarchical, adversarial relations between labor and management to cooperative systems in
which responsibility and rewards are far more equally shared. Corporations can continually improve and change their products and processes
only if their workers buy into that process: if they are willing to try new
methods, to come up with new ideas, and to troubleshoot when problems
develop. To make this happen, explains Robert Reich, author of several
penetrating works on economic competitiveness, firms must push "responsibility down to production workers and to lower-level service workers, because they have a greater degree of day-to-day understanding of
what can be improved, what small incremental steps need to be taken to
improve products and processes."[19]

State governments have begun to encourage this process by funding
local labor-management committees and by providing technical assistance
to companies and unions that are working to change their internal cultures. A few states have launched efforts to help workers buy out firms
that are closing and run them as employee-owned enterprises.

Better social organization. In an economy undergoing a transformation as
fundamental as that we have experienced over the past 15 years, economic
growth requires social reorganization. A society that asks its people to
embrace continual innovation, for instance, must ensure that they are not
victimized by the changes that result. Yet our social welfare system is built
on assumptions of stability, rather than change. A product of the industrial
era, it assumes that most workers will spend their entire careers in the
same type of job; hence the few training programs we have created are
designed to train people once, for a specific job built on a specific technology. It assumes that those who lose their jobs need to be helped only
through a temporary period of unemployment; hence we provide unemployment insurance but forbid the unemployed (in many states) to enroll
in training programs while collecting it. It assumes that married women do
not work outside the home; hence we have not bothered with publicly
sponsored child care.

In today's world, these assumptions are obsolete. Because they still define our social systems, they inhibit innovation and change. Workers who know that they will not be retrained and reemployed at skilled jobs, with decent wages, resist the introduction of automated equipment. People who know that there are no financial systems in place to help them get further education or training resist career changes. Women who fear they will not be able to find affordable child care shy away from productive, full-time careers.

State governments have begun to respond to these problems by transforming their social welfare systems into social adjustment systems. They have begun to revamp their vocational-technical education systems and to create new programs designed to retrain people as technologies change. They have begun to provide subsidies for child care and to work with the private sector to expand the availability of child care. And they have set up programs to respond to plant closings and major layoffs with counseling, job training, and relocation assistance.

While the states have concentrated on *microeconomic* concerns, such as new business formation, regional capital markets, and labor-management relations, the federal government has remained preoccupied with *macroeconomic* issues: monetary policy, fiscal policy, and tax policy. During the depression the federal government embraced microeconomic intervention, through the National Labor Relations Act, the Agricultural Adjustment Administration, the Reconstruction Finance Corporation, and similar efforts. But the United States emerged from World War II with the only intact industrial economy in the world. Because our economy was so much stronger than those of our competitors, economists gradually came to believe that they could fine tune it into full production simply by adjusting the macroeconomic aggregates—interest rates, budget deficits, and tax rates. Microeconomic policy was largely forgotten, and the few microeconomic initiatives undertaken by the Small Business Administration, the Economic Development Administration, and other federal institutions were as flawed as they were marginal.

In an economy under siege by foreign competition, macroeconomic adjustments are simply not enough. Competitiveness has become a function of qualitative as well as quantitative factors: not just how much we produce, but how we produce it; not just how much capital is available, but what kind of capital; not just how much research we do, but how fast it is commercialized; not just how many workers we have and at what wages, but how well they are prepared and how well they work together.

This is not to say that macroeconomic policy is no longer important. Indeed, the economic problems of the past decade have stemmed in part from inappropriate macroeconomic policy. While it is important that we fashion new microeconomic tools with which to heighten our competitiveness, these tools will not work unless we also correct our macroeconomic mistakes. If federal policies drive the dollar to record levels, as they did in the early 1980s, programs to stimulate manufacturing modernization will be overwhelmed by an avalanche of inexpensive imports. If prices rise unpredictably, as they did in the late 1970s, efforts to encourage investments in innovation will be undercut as investors flee into real estate, gold, and other hedges against inflation.

To compete with Japan, West Germany, and the rest of the world's advanced economies, we must concentrate on both macro- and microeconomic policy. Whereas most state initiatives of recent years should remain in state hands—a subject I shall return to in Part II of this book—other microeconomic problems will require federal solutions.

A debate over federal microeconomic policy began during the early 1980s, under the rubric of "industrial policy." Unfortunately, this term meant different things to different people. Some used it to describe policies to aid specific industries. Others used it to describe policies designed to revitalize industry in general. Still others equated it with government attempts to "pick winners" by investing in particular products or technologies, in hopes of ensuring their success on world markets.

The third interpretation became widespread, in large part because some of the better-known proponents of industrial policy made their central recommendation a new Reconstruction Finance Corporation, to make large federal investments in targeted industries.[20] Though many industrial policy advocates disliked the notion, the RFC proposal served as a lightning rod for critics, who argued that government could neither predict what would succeed in the marketplace nor keep political considerations out of its investment decisions.

While the debate in Washington aborted, governors of both parties began to craft programs to improve the competitiveness of their economies—which, after all, was the point of industrial policy. Some call these efforts industrial policies, others prefer the label industrial strategies or competitiveness strategies. Whatever the label, these programs seldom attempt to pick winners, in the sense of investing large public sums in specific firms, industries, or technologies to ensure their success in the marketplace. State experience has demonstrated that the common notion that government has two choices—to "pick winners" or to respect the free market—is simply wrong. To frame the debate in this way is to profoundly misunderstand the issue—and to foreclose a constructive role for government.

The real question is how government can reshape (or perfect, to use a term more palatable to conservatives) the market so as to ensure that more American winners emerge in global competition. Rather than targeting specific industries or products, most states are targeting *processes*: technological innovation, capital formation, new business formation, the commercialization of research, and the adoption of new manufacturing technologies. Even when they have begun to work with specific industries, their role has been to facilitate the process of innovation and revitalization, rather than to give a particular product or technology a leg up in the marketplace. They are not trying to *plan* economic activity, but to quicken the pace of innovation, to sharpen our ability to bring new ideas to market, to increase the technological sophistication with which we manufacture. When they do invest directly in firms, states normally do so to fill gaps left by private financial markets—such as small-business lending or early-stage venture capital—rather than to ensure the success of a particular industry or technology.

The issue of government's proper role in the marketplace is not a simple one. Every time a government decides to fund research or provide a loan, it must make judgments about which areas show the most potential for success. The Japanese have had considerable success in subsidizing particular industries, such as robotics, to propel them to world dominance. Other governments have had less success: the British and French with the Concorde; the U.S. with synthetic fuels. But while the issue of picking winners may be crucial at some future stage, at this point the United States lacks the public-sector capacity to contemplate such activity. For the foreseeable future, our federal government will have its hands full simply keeping up with the states.

The Second Agenda: Bringing the Poor into the Growth Process

During the industrial era, wages made up the bulk of most manufacturers' costs. All other things being equal, the lower they could be held, the more competitive the corporation's products would be. Within this context, poverty had a clear function: it depressed wages by ensuring that there would always be plenty of people ready to take even the lowest-paid job away from a worker, or group of workers, who demanded higher pay. But in an age of global competition and technological revolution, low wages and social inequality no longer make America more competitive. Even if we cut all American wages in half, they would still be extravagant by global standards. For many American manufacturers, particularly those who have embraced automation, labor is no longer their major cost. Where it is, most corporate managers have given up trying to compete and have simply shipped their low-wage manufacturing overseas.

In the new economy, poverty, low wages, and social inequality hurt many American corporations more than they help. If their workers are illiterate, American corporations will lose out to their Japanese and European competitors. If their workers are paid a fraction of what their managers earn, distrust and resentment will mar their relations and productivity will suffer. If the social pathology of the cities in which they operate makes them expensive and inconvenient places to do business, they will lose out to competitors elsewhere. There are obviously limits to what American workers can be paid, but if we are to remain competitive in the new economy, there are also limits to how much social inequality we can tolerate. In the postindustrial era, the developed nations with the most competitive economies are also those with the least social inequality.[21]

Few governors have grasped this new reality. Development programs designed to combat poverty remain a poor stepchild of broader economic development. But a few of the more liberal governors, such as Michael Dukakis and Mario Cuomo, have begun to pioneer a development agenda in poor communities. Unlike the 1960s, when the primary focus was on bringing the poor into the *political* process—through civil rights legislation, community organizing, and federal efforts like the Community Action Program—today's efforts focus primarily on bringing them into the *economic* process. Whereas liberals in the 1960s thought primarily in terms of increasing the *incomes* of the poor, governors such as Dukakis and Cuomo have sought to increase their *economic activity*—through education, training, employment, and investment.

This agenda consists primarily of two strategies: efforts to bring down the barriers that keep people out of the mainstream economy; and efforts to create a growth dynamic in poor communities.

Bringing down the barriers. For some Americans, barriers to participation in the mainstream economy are very real. These include racial and sexual discrimination; poor schools; illiteracy; government regulations that limit access to the marketplace (such as ceilings on the number of taxi drivers in a city); welfare systems that encourage dependency; and the tangle of social pathologies we call the culture of poverty. The states have begun to attack a few of these problems, including illiteracy, the schools, and the welfare system. They have created welfare programs that channel people into education and training programs and then help them find jobs. They have worked to upgrade their schools and to keep disadvantaged youths in school—or, failing that, to provide them with alternative experiences such as conservation corps. And they have poured new money into adult literacy programs.

Creating a growth dynamic in poor communities. During the industrial era, revitalization strategies in poor communities focused on tearing down slums and building "urban renewal" projects. These efforts created the appearance of growth, rather than the process of growth. More often than not, they did more harm than good. For these reasons—and because the states cannot afford such megaprojects any longer—the governors are beginning to work out small-scale, decentralized revitalization strategies, which seek to build the capacities of community development organizations in poor areas. For instance, a handful of states have created programs to nurture the growth of community development corporations (CDCs), particularly as developers of low- and moderate-income housing. Though still very rudimentary, such efforts point in the right direction.

New Mechanisms to Deliver Government Services

CDCs are one example of a trend evident under both agendas: the use of institutions that operate in neither the traditional public sector nor the traditional private sector. These institutions exist to solve social problems, as government does, but they use methods more characteristic of the private sector. Whether for-profit or non-profit, many of them are at risk in the marketplace. They will go out of business if they make poor investments—in businesses, in housing developments, or in people. They are therefore driven to invest in those with the capacity to succeed in the marketplace, in a way that government seldom is. But because they are partially subsidized by government, they can reach segments of the market that are not profitable enough for the private sector. These institutions constitute a "third sector" between government and business.

During the industrial era, government created large public bureaucracies, such as welfare departments and unemployment offices, to deliver services. Alternatively, it reimbursed private corporations for delivering services—as in the medicare and medicaid programs, and in many low- and moderate-income housing programs. Today those very delivery systems are often the problem. The Public Policy Center of the Stanford Research Institute put it well, in a monograph called *Redesigning Social and Economic Problem-Solving*. "In some ways," the authors said, "the current situation is analogous to that of the 1920s, when the challenge was to develop 'good government' and professional standards of public service in well-designed programs. The 'evils' that were being avoided then were those of political machines that organized government services on the basis of party loyalty and thus distributed benefits and service inequitably, and welfare programs that depended on non-professional efforts and distributed benefits on the basis of arbitrary factors (e.g., religions, being 'deserving'). In the 1980s and 1990s, the task is to develop new community-based approaches to social and economic problems. The 'evils' that need to be avoided today are bureaucratic and inflexible programs that (by and large inadequately) compensate victims instead of solving problems."[22]

The Emerging Political Paradigm

Just as fundamental economic transitions demand new roles for government, those new roles demand new ideologies. The last two decades have been a period of ideological interregnum, in which neither party, nor any coherent ideology, has established its dominance. But if one looks closely, one can see a new political paradigm evolving in America's state capitols. In the same way that Progressivism foreshadowed New Deal liberalism, the politics evident at the state (and local) level today may well foreshadow the next phase of national politics.

A political paradigm is a set of assumptions about the world—about which issues are important, what responses to those issues are possible, and what role government can play in the process. These assumptions define the context within which different ideologies compete for ascendancy. The transition to an industrial economy, around the turn of the century, brought forth the rough outlines of a new paradigm, but no dominant national ideology. In contrast, the maturation and crisis of the industrial economy brought forth a new paradigm and an ideology that dominated within it, New Deal liberalism.

By its very success in responding to the new realities of the mature industrial era, New Deal liberalism ensured its own demise. After three decades of rapid economic growth, a host of problems never imagined by New Deal liberals had emerged: stagflation, fierce global competition, the decline of traditional manufacturing, the challenge of Third World nationalism.

Today, if one looks at the broad spectrum of efforts across several dozen states, one can see the rough outlines of a post-New Deal paradigm. That paradigm is built around new roles for government in the economy and new partnerships between the public and private sectors. In the 1980s, governors of both parties have attacked problems by using the public sector—in partnership with business, academia and labor—to reshape the marketplace. This is an activist role, but one that takes the form of intervention in the marketplace more often than increased spending by public bureaucracies.

One can begin to see glimmerings of this paradigm on the national level as well. If they come to fruition, our national politics will also come to focus on government's role in restructuring the marketplace to solve our problems. We will come to understand our core problem not as too little or too much government—as we have understood it in recent decades—but as America's changing role in the global economy. We will come to see the core solutions not in new spending programs (or spending cuts), but in new relationships—new *partnerships*—between the public and private sectors.

Few governors think in such conceptual terms; most are too busy responding to their constituents to philosophize about the next political paradigm. But it is precisely their executive responsibility, their direct accountability for the health of their states, that has forced them to adapt their politics. And it is precisely this adaptation that distinguishes them from their counterparts in Washington. "Washington has a way of dealing with yesterday's issues," says Michigan Governor James Blanchard, who served in Congress for eight years. "If you are a U.S. senator, you can give an ideological response to a serious problem and probably never be held accountable for it. Whereas the governors are dealing with the real world— they have to run things, to make them work."

The paradigm taking shape at the state level is still new enough that even those who think of it as a paradigm have yet to come up with a name. Some of the national Democrats who fit the pattern have been labeled neoliberals. But neoliberalism has been defined largely by segments of the Washington press, rather than by the political process. The definition differs according to who is writing, and the focus has been almost entirely on national issues. For both of these reasons, the term neoliberal does not do justice to what is happening at the state level. Governors such as Michael Dukakis of Massachusetts, Bill Clinton of Arkansas, and former Republican Governor Richard Thornburgh of Pennsylvania are all acting within the new paradigm, for instance, but none is widely viewed as a neoliberal. Given the historical parallels to the Progressive Era, the better description might be *neoprogressive.*

During his 1984 presidential campaign, Gary Hart struck a chord with many voters when he called for a "new generation of leadership" in Washington. For anyone visiting the state capitols, Hart's cliche springs to life. Most of the more innovative governors are in their forties, and most were inspired to go into politics by John F. Kennedy's New Frontier. Virtually all of their key staff people—the brains behind the new programs—were still in their twenties or thirties when they made their major contributions. Typically, these people came of age during the 1960s, saw the debacle of McGovernism, and began to rethink traditional liberalism. They are neither Great Society liberals nor Reagan conservatives. They do not operate by the old rules. They *are* the next generation of leadership in American politics.

In the chapters that follow, I will use the personal stories of these new leaders to tell the larger story of economic and political evolution in America's laboratories of democracy. But this book is not about individuals. The people I describe have played critical roles, for history moves through individuals. But had they not been in the right place at the right time, history would have found others through which to move. Fundamentally, what has happened in America's state capitols is the product, not of individual creativity, but of economic transformation. This transformation will remake national policy and politics as inevitably as it remade state policy and politics—regardless of the individuals history chooses as its actors.

I have chosen six states as the major vehicles for my story. I chose these states for a variety of reasons, chief among them their geographical diversity, their political diversity, and their degree of innovation. I found myself writing about five Democratic governors and one Republican, in part because at the time I started this research—in early 1985—Democratic governors outnumbered Republicans by 34 to 16. The Democrats were also further along the innovation curve, no doubt because their reigning ideology had become obsolete a decade earlier, just as the reigning Republican ideology began its rise to power. Thus while Democrats were rethinking, many Republican governors were swept up in the antigovernment rhetoric of Ronald Reagan. As I write today, however, the Democratic governors outnumber their Republican counterparts by only 26 to 24, and several Republican governors other than Thornburgh—including Thomas Kean in New Jersey and Robert Orr in Indiana—have embraced the economic activism formerly more characteristic of Democrats.

In each of the six state chapters, I have offered comments evaluating the performance of the governor. These evaluations must, at bottom, be subjective. There is simply no way to apply "objective" criteria to the records of six different governors in six very different states. As a general rule, I have asked the following basic question: What were the core problems facing the state, and how well did the governor address those problems? In this sense, I might find a great deal to applaud in the record of a governor who was less active than his colleagues on most fronts, because he successfully attacked the single most fundamental problem facing his state. I have also tried to judge the accomplishments of each governor within the context of his own state. If a governor operated within a state with a small public sector and a conservative political environment, I have not measured his achievements by the same yardstick I might apply in a state with a tradition of larger, more activist government.

The fundamental issues of the 1990s will be economic. Will the United States slip quietly into the ranks of former economic powers, as Great Britain did half a century ago? Or will we adapt to the realities of the new era, retool our economy, and restore our competitive strength? The answer to this question will depend upon both our economic and our social policies—but more fundamentally, it will depend upon our politics.

For nearly 20 years, we have been lost in an ideological interregnum.

This period will end only when one (or both) of the major parties comes to grips with the realities of the new economy, fashions a new role for government, and articulates a new politics. The election of 1988 may determine which party that is—or it may simply prolong the interregnum. But if the stirrings in America's laboratories of democracy are any indication, the question is not whether we will embrace a new national agenda, but when.

PART I

THE LABORATORIES

1
THE CLASS OF '74: THE ROOTS OF A NEW PARADIGM

On election day 1974, a new age dawned in American politics. It was a unique moment: in 1972, the McGovern debacle had discredited liberal Democratic politics; by 1974, Watergate had discredited the Republicans. Democrats were almost a shoo-in in 1974, as long as they were not Great Society Democrats. "You could not run for office in 1974 or 1976 without getting the message," remembers Gary Hart, who first ran for the Senate in 1974. "We're tired of big government, we're tired of regulations, we're tired of high taxes—that's all I heard in Colorado."

The result was a generation of governors and congressmen with a distinct profile: liberal on social issues but moderate to conservative on fiscal policy. The names are familiar: Paul Tsongas, Gary Hart, Tim Wirth, Chris Dodd, Jim Blanchard, Dick Lamm, Michael Dukakis, Ella Grasso, Jerry Brown, even Bruce Babbitt, who first ran for attorney general in Arizona in 1974, then became governor in 1978.

Tim Wirth, now the Democratic senator from Colorado, describes how different the congressional class of '74 was from its predecessors. "We were the children of Vietnam, not the children of World War II," he says. "We were products of television, not of print. We were products of computer politics, not courthouse politics. And we were reflections of JFK as president, not FDR. We were the first class that was like that, and now the whole place is."[1] Because of the seniority system, the class of '74 in Congress still awaits real legislative power. In the states their counterparts took immediate control.

Just as the new breed of governors took office, in January 1975, the worst recession since the 1930s set in. Suddenly they were under intense pressure to respond to a problem they had never encountered in political life: 8 percent unemployment. Most governors failed the test. But a few began to grapple with the issues raised by America's rude awakening to the new realities of the global economy. In Massachusetts, Michael Dukakis created a series of quasi-public finance agencies to provide capital to new firms, growing technology firms, and firms in poor communities. In California, Jerry Brown pushed through new job-training programs, "Adjustment Teams" to respond to plant closings, a new research and development program, and a variety of efforts to give new and small businesses better access to capital. Several southern governors backed comprehensive education reform. Slowly a new economic development strategy began to take shape—and with it a new political paradigm. These developments would not come to fruition until the 1980s. But the seeds were planted by the class of '74.

Massachusetts: The First Dukakis Administration

Of all the new governors elected in 1974, Michael Dukakis was perhaps the most liberal—and, ultimately, the most successful. As such, his journey, which has taken him from the antibusiness liberalism of his first term to an embrace of public-private partnerships, tax cuts, and economic growth, has been the most revealing.

Michael Dukakis was a classic post-Watergate Democrat: socially liberal, fiscally moderate, and squeaky clean. He believed, as he said at a 1975 National Democratic Issues Convention, that "much of what government has tried to do over the past 15 years has failed."[2] As a brash young state representative from Brookline, an affluent suburb surrounded on three sides by Boston, his electoral base had always been among the educated middle class. He did not care deeply about issues that moved union members or the poor, but about those embraced by the educated liberals who had formed the backbone of McGovern's "new politics"—issues like no-fault auto insurance, environmental protection, urban revitalization, and governmental reform.

Cool, reserved, and intensely rational, Dukakis was the antithesis of the backslapping Boston pol. He was elected as Mr. Clean, dedicated to sweeping away the state's entrenched patronage system and tightening up its antiquated and often corrupt management. Like Jimmy Carter and Jerry Brown, he had no use for the trappings of government: he shopped at Filene's Basement, the famous discount store; he rode the subway to work; and he carried his lunch in a brown bag. During the 1974 campaign, he gave a "lead-pipe" guarantee not to raise taxes.

Upon taking office, Dukakis discovered a deficit of close to $600 million—somewhere around 17 percent of total state revenues. As a percentage of the budget, this was roughly equivalent to the 1986 federal deficit. But because the state was legally required to balance its budget, Dukakis had to deal with it immediately. "I remember my first cabinet meeting," says Frank Keefe, then director of the Office of State Planning. "The welfare commissioner came in with shoe boxes of unpaid welfare bills dating back to 1968. The unraveling of that fiscal crisis was just mind-boggling, and it was a shock to the governor—one he continues to remember."

Breaking his lead-pipe guarantee, Dukakis pushed through the largest tax increase in the state's history. He raised sales taxes, income taxes, alcohol taxes—"just about every tax he could raise," according to Keefe. He floated a $450-million bond issue. He cut personnel, froze salaries, and took a "meat cleaver"—Dukakis's words—to social programs.[3] Between 1975 and 1979, overall state spending grew only 5.5 percent in inflation-adjusted dollars; between 1970 and 1974, under liberal Republican Frank Sargent, it had grown 23.5 percent. Subtracting debt service, payments to the pension system, and aid to localities, Dukakis actually cut state spending by five percent during his first term.[4]

Dukakis's Democratic opponent in 1978, Ed King, used his tax increases to defeat him. The experience reinforced Dukakis's fiscal instincts and made him gun-shy—like every governor burned by the tax revolt—on tax issues. Though hardly a fiscal conservative, Dukakis has been very careful since then not to get on the wrong side of public opinion on the issue.

The other major chapter in the education of Michael Dukakis involved his attitude toward business. When he took office, says Howard Smith, secretary of economic affairs during the first Dukakis administration, "Mike didn't really understand businessmen very well. He had a typical liberal Democratic perspective—businessmen were greedy, they had no social responsibility. He didn't know where jobs came from, and I had to teach him—they come from businessmen who want to invest."

Smith was a businessman, but Dukakis's other cabinet members dealing with economic issues were liberal reformers like himself. They cared little about overall economic growth; their passion was revitalizing the dying cities of Massachusetts. In 1975, Dukakis pulled them together in a "Development Cabinet" and put Frank Keefe, a 28-year-old former planning director from Lowell, in charge. Using the Development Cabinet as a whip to force other departments into line, Dukakis and Keefe gradually forced the state bureaucracy to give priority in every area—transportation, housing, job training, even education—to declining urban centers. They targeted federal highway and sewer money to existing urban areas rather than new suburban developments. They "broke arms" to put a new community college campus in Roxbury, Boston's black ghetto, and to convince the North Shore Community College to build a new campus in downtown Lynn, rather than along the suburban beltway, Route 128. And they developed the most aggressive antiredlining policies of any state.

The flagship of Dukakis's urban development policy was Lowell. Dukakis had first noticed Keefe, in fact, when Keefe and Pat Mogan, the director of Lowell's Model Cities program, wrote a paper calling for a state Heritage Park, a historic park to preserve Lowell's old mills and canals and tell the story of the birth of America's industrial revolution. In 1975, Lowell had an unemployment rate of 16 percent. "It was like pictures right out of 1933," says Keefe. *"The Wall Street Journal* called it the bleakest industrial city in America." Dukakis spent $10 million in state money to establish the nation's first urban Heritage Park, and another $20 million on new highways to get people there. He supported Sen. Paul Tsongas's efforts to make the site a national park, a decision that brought in another $40 million. He also backed the creation and expansion of the University of Lowell, a state institution that has emerged as a respected technology-oriented university.

In 1977, after the city and state had committed themselves to the revitalization effort, An Wang decided to build the first of three Wang Laboratories office towers in Lowell. By the mid-1980s Wang employed some nine thousand people there, the unemployment rate hovered just over 3 percent, and Lowell was making headlines as the most dramatic urban comeback story in America.[5]

The zeal with which Dukakis and his young reformers tried to force private investment into urban centers brought them into repeated conflict with business. In western Massachusetts, for instance, Dukakis tried to force a developer to put his mall in downtown Pittsfield rather than outside town—where it would have pulled shoppers away from downtown. When the developer refused, the governor minced no words. "There will be no access to the state highway," he declared. "Forget about your development. We just won't permit it."[6] Keefe's office even worked up a policy to block the construction of all suburban shopping malls, although Dukakis discarded the plan as the Pittsfield incident and others brought business anger to a boil.[7]

"Many of us had the kind of disdain for business that young, policy-oriented people often have," says Michael Barker, then a deputy to Keefe in the planning office. "We thought we knew more. Here we were, people whose largest personal expenditures had been on stereo systems, pronouncing where and why and when shopping centers could be built in the state."

Ultimately, the economy forced a change in the administration's priorities. As the 1975 recession deepened, unemployment topped 12 percent—higher than in any other industrial state. New England's textile mills and shoe factories had long since moved away; defense spending had dried up as the Vietnam War wound down; and in a region dependent on imported oil, the OPEC price increases had hit with particular force.

Within this context, Dukakis's antigrowth and antibusiness image was extremely damaging. When he and Keefe finally realized the extent of the damage, "they turned around almost on a dime," in Barker's words. They produced a document called *An Economic Development Program for Massachusetts*, which Keefe's office published in August 1976. "What Massachusetts needs is a vigorous economic development program to bring balance to the social programs of the sixties and the environmental program of the early seventies," it said. "We must acknowledge that more jobs and higher incomes are prerequisites to the improvement of the public welfare and the enjoyment of our rich natural and man-made environment."[8]

The most important elements of Dukakis's subsequent economic development program did not come from Keefe's office, however. They came from the Task Force on Capital Formation, authorized by Dukakis in 1976. The task force story runs parallel to the story of Keefe's Development Cabinet, and it contains the same elements: activist liberals gradually moving from a focus on poor, urban communities to a broader concern for economic growth.

The tale begins with the demise of a proposed network of highways through the heart of Boston. As a state legislator, Dukakis had been among the leaders of the antihighway coalition. During the late sixties and early seventies, this was the classic urban battle: community groups and liberal activists fighting to keep their neighborhoods from being torn apart for highways, and other monuments of "urban renewal."

When the key battle was won in Boston, a three-and-a-half mile swath called the Southwest Corridor had already been cleared. Now it stood empty, an eyesore that had torn the heart out of a series of neighborhoods—black, white, and Hispanic. As part of the political settlement, a coalition of grass-roots organizations demanded control over development along the corridor, and state transportation officials agreed. Mel King, a black state legislator who had led the fight (and who would in 1983 be runner-up for mayor of Boston), decided the community would need access to capital if that promise was to mean anything. King convened a small group of left-wing activists and intellectuals with a promise of his own: if you'll show up every Wednesday morning at 7:30 to help work out a program, I'll cook breakfast. Few events have proven more important in the history of state economic development.

Like many activists of the 1960s, the members of the Wednesday Morning Breakfast Group were in the midst of a transition from protest to development, from a focus on stopping or changing government policies to a focus on creating new programs to invest in poor communities. Besides King, the group's original members included Elbert Bishop, a black attorney who was director of the Southwest Corridor Coalition; David Smith, a professor of economics at the University of Massachusetts and a consultant on community economic development (who later became a key aide to Sen. Ted Kennedy); and Belden Daniels, a community development consultant, attorney, and lecturer at Harvard.

Daniels's résumé included five years as an investment banker in Asia and three years as director of the commonwealth's own war on poverty. In Japan, Hong Kong, and elsewhere, Daniels had watched systems of business-government collaboration in action and concluded that they were "much more conducive to economic innovation than our own." In Massachusetts he had been in on the invention of community development corporations (CDCs), the grass-roots organizations that later became a mainstay of the federal Office of Economic Opportunity (OEO). In 1972 he had received a grant from the OEO-funded Center for Community Economic Development, to study the potential role state governments could play in financing economic development in poor communities.

King's initial purpose in convening the Wednesday morning group had been to create a development bank to invest in the rebirth of the Southwest Corridor. But as their discussions broadened, the Wednesday morning group focused increasingly on the more fundamental problem: flaws in the marketplace that left poor communities starved for capital. They believed that those making decisions at financial institutions were both ignorant of the realities in poor communities and unwilling to take risks there. They also believed there were potential investments that might not make sense to a private investor concerned only with profits, but would make sense from a public perspective because of the "social return" from tax revenues, lower welfare caseloads, and decreased crime rates. To bring capital back into poor communities, they decided, government would have to begin making public investments and steering private capital, as Daniels had witnessed in Asia. With this insight they were to revolutionize state development policy.

The group decided to focus its initial efforts on one institution—"a state institution better than anything OEO ever had," in Daniels's words. It would be a public capital fund to invest in businesses sponsored by CDCs in poor communities, a "third-sector" institution with the policy perspective of government but the marketplace orientation of business. Its board would be publicly appointed but independent, free to move quickly. "It was intended to be a market-sensitive reaction to the failed history of OEO," Daniels explains. "It sounded like a wild idea, but we knew, given time, it would work."

Ten days before the 1974 gubernatorial election, Dukakis came to a Wednesday morning breakfast, ate fish and grits, and agreed to back a $10 million Community Development Finance Corporation (CDFC). On December 31, 1975, five minutes before midnight, the bill finally passed the state legislature—although no money was provided until several years later.

While pushing the bill through the legislature, the Wednesday morning group continued to refine its ideas. Its members realized that no economic development strategy would pass if it were targeted entirely at poor communities. In December 1975, at the height of the recession, Daniels visited the commissioner of commerce and development and urged him to create a Capital Formation Task Force, to design a strategy to fill other "capital gaps" in the state. Daniels's agenda was to pull key business, labor, and political leaders together, to sell them on the Wednesday morning group's ideas, and to use their support to generate political legitimacy.

At the time, because of the severe recession, many governors were looking for ways to create jobs. During the decades of postwar prosperity, most states had not had to worry a great deal about economic development. Some used tax-exempt bonds to help finance new plants and equipment, and most promoted tourism, but their priorities were elsewhere. When unemployment hit 8 percent, they were suddenly under tremendous pressure to do something—*anything*. Most states responded with conventional medicine: they cut taxes and offered large firms in other states a host of tax and financial incentives to open new plants across state lines. The practice became known as smokestack chasing, and by the late seventies it was a spectacle to behold, as firms learned that they could play one state off against another until they got their dream deal.

In reality, state taxes were too minor a factor to change the economics of many plant location decisions, as study after study would demonstrate. Outside the South, which had low *wages* to offer, smokestack chasing was a dismal failure. Even there, it created jobs but rarely kicked off the kind of chain reaction that leads to economic growth. No one symbolized the failure of smokestack chasing better than Ohio's Republican Governor James Rhodes, whose aides spent so much time in other states recruiting plants that they became known as Rhodes' Raiders. Under Rhodes, Ohio and its cities offered so many tax abatements that by 1978 public schools were closing in April for lack of money.

Massachusetts was lucky, because the secretary of economic affairs, Howard Smith, understood the futility of smokestack chasing. "I knew it by instinct," Smith says. "I was a businessman." Smokestack chasing "was mostly showboating. In truth, jobs are homegrown. You grow them by nurturing your own firms, watering them, fertilizing them." Just to make certain, Smith commissioned a study of firms moving from Massachusetts to New Hampshire, which was celebrated for its low taxes. "It was minimal," he found. "This specter of New Hampshire sucking the lifeblood out of the Massachusetts economy was just that, a specter."

Smith first convinced Dukakis of this truth, then set about trying to help businesses already in Massachusetts. He turned his department into an ombudsman for business, with a representative assigned to sit down with every firm in every district and help resolve their problems with government. He set up a "one-stop shopping" system for permits. He fought with more liberal members of the Development Cabinet, taking the business side on most issues. And when Belden Daniels argued that small firms and entrepreneurs with new ideas were having trouble attracting capital in Massachusetts, Smith hired him to put together the Capital Formation Task Force.

Daniels hired David Smith as a consultant and carefully picked a group of business executives who might be supportive of the Wednesday Morning Breakfast Group's plans. The task force also included labor leaders, community activists, and representatives of government. It concluded that there were three critical capital gaps in Massachusetts. Businesses in poor communities had trouble getting capital. (This was the gap already addressed by the Community Development Finance Corporation [CDFC].) Small businesses had trouble getting long-term loans. And the venture capital market for young, growing firms—a market that had been born in Massachusetts and had propelled its crucial high-tech sector—had all but dried up. The task force recommended funding for CDFC and the creation of two new capital institutions to fill the other gaps: the Massachusetts Industrial Finance Authority (MIFA), to sell tax-exempt bonds for business loans; and the Massachusetts Technology Development Corporation (MTDC), to provide early-stage venture capital to new technology companies. All three institutions would be overseen by a Massachusetts Industrial Development Authority (MIDA).

To satisfy its business members, the task force also argued in no uncertain terms that state taxes were too high. "The Task Force is *emphatic* in stating that these short-term recommendations [the new capital institutions] are limited in their long-run capability to stimulate jobs and revenue creation, *unless* there is fundamental tax reform and expenditure control," the report said.[9] When Dukakis gave this conclusion short shrift—and spent a cursory few minutes at the task force's final meeting, where the report was presented to him—several leading business executives were so angry that they decided to create the Massachusetts High Technology Council, now the most aggressive business lobby in the state.

MIDA was never set up, principally because Mel King and other advocates of CDFC did not want a superagency telling CDFC what to do. But MIFA, MTDC, and a $10-million bond issue for CDFC were all enacted by the legislature. MIFA and MTDC have both performed well. (CDFC will be discussed at length in chapter 6.) MIFA was the first state industrial development bond (IDB) agency to restrict its bonds for commercial projects to urban business districts, giving a boost to downtown redevelopment and avoiding some of the abuses common in other states, such as the use of tax-exempt bonds for golf courses and suburban shopping malls. When the federal government restricted the use of tax-exempt bonds in 1985 and 1986, in part because of such abuses, MIFA issued the first *taxable* bonds to finance pools of small-business loans ever sold in the United States.[10]

MTDC was the second public venture capital fund created by a state government. (The first, the Connecticut Product Development Corporation, was set up in the mid-1970s and was something of a model for the Capital Formation Task Force.) MTDC makes small ($100,000 to $250,000), early-stage loans and equity investments in technology companies that have been unable to secure sufficient capital from conventional sources. Run by a board that includes three members of the administration and seven private business people, it had invested $7.4 million by mid-1986 and registered a profit of roughly $4 million.[11] With investments in only 29 active companies, however, it could hardly be judged to have had a significant impact on the Massachusetts economy. Its creators could not foresee that in 1978, just as they legislated MTDC into being, a nationwide boom in venture capital investment would begin—triggered by a cut in the capital gains tax rate and a move into venture capital by pension funds and other institutional investors. Net new funds committed to venture capital would rise from $39 million in 1977 to $4.5 billion in 1983.[12]

In response, MTDC adjusted its strategy by concentrating more on helping firms land private capital. It launched programs to help entrepreneurs draw up business plans, identify the likeliest sources of private (or public) money, and make their cases to investors. For its own investments, it targeted start-up companies that would not normally get venture capital. (Most private venture capital firms want companies that can provide profits within about five years and have potential annual sales of $100 million or more.) In the process, it discovered that although investors were reluctant to take the time required to investigate and package less-promising ventures, they would often invest after MTDC had done the spadework. In this way MTDC not only fills a small capital gap itself but also encourages the private sector to do so.

The most significant of the new agencies created in 1978 was not a quasi-public agency but the private-sector Massachusetts Capital Resource Company. MCRC did not come out of the Capital Formation Task Force. Indeed, Daniels testifies that it was deliberately kept out of the package because it was too controversial.

The MCRC story goes back to the early 1970s, when the Massachusetts legislature slapped a one percent tax on the life insurance industry's gross income (as opposed to profits). The legislature had acted in retaliation for the industry's role in financing a campaign to defeat a graduated income tax proposal. Since then, industry representatives had complained repeatedly that the tax put them at a disadvantage when competing against companies in other states.

Keefe's staff agreed. But thanks to a study by the New England Regional Commission, they knew that the life insurance industry, a huge source of investment capital, was investing very little in the high-tech firms that were so critical to the state's economic future. Keefe decided to ask for a quid-pro-quo. If you put $100 million into a new Massachusetts Capital Resource Company and use the money to make unsecured loans to businesses that cannot get affordable money elsewhere, he told the industry, we'll bring your taxes back into line with your competitors. (Unsecured loans are those in which no collateral is promised in case of default.)

The tax cut would be phased in over five years—but only if MCRC met certain targets for jobs created and loans granted each year. The bill also established strict investment criteria regarding company size, geographic location, and ownership (a certain percentage had to be in distressed areas, another percentage owned by minorities, and so on). If the fund failed to meet its targets, the tax cut could be rescinded and the insurance companies would be required to pay back taxes. Hence, the insurance companies could not do what many recipients of tax-exempt bonds or state loans have done: promise hundreds or thousands of new jobs, but deliver far fewer.

Industry executives were not pleased. Most believed MCRC would fail; they saw it as the price they had to pay for a tax break. Foster Aborn of John Hancock, who chaired MCRC's finance committee for its first nine years, still calls the tactic "high-level bribery." But he also calls MCRC "an outstanding success." By 1986, it had loaned over $140 million to more than one hundred companies. By a conservative formula the state uses to count jobs created, which ignores the ripple effect of a growing company on suppliers and service businesses in the area, it had created more than eight thousand jobs.[13]

Perhaps the most notable example of MCRC's impact was one of its first loans, to Wang Laboratories. In 1978, Wang was not yet the giant company it is today. Its sales were $198 million a year, and the office word-processing systems that would make Wang a household name had been on the market only a year. The potential for expansion was tremendous—the company would more than quintuple its sales in the next five years—but the capital necessary to finance that expansion was scarce. The banks had refused to give the firm long-term loans, leaving it dependent on short-term, revolving credit lines. Its primary bank, the Bank of Boston, was threatening to call in a major loan. "At that point, Wang's product cycle was obsolescing every three years," explains Aborn. "It was very hard for a banker to look into the future and see whether long-term debt could be paid off by operations, because operations were changing too rapidly."

MCRC stepped into the breach. It gave Wang a ten-year, $5-million "subordinated" loan—meaning that if the company went bankrupt, MCRC would be repaid only after all other lenders had been repaid. Thus protected, Wang's banks came forward with another $20 million in long-term debt. The MCRC loan was not the only factor in their decision. "This company was moving, and the banks could see the handwriting on the wall," says Wang Assistant Treasurer Martin Miller. "But there's no question that the MCRC loan helped. When you can come in on top of some of that subordinated debt, you've got to believe you're more comfortable."

As interest rates hit 16 and 18 percent in the next few years, Wang's $25 million in fixed-rate capital looked better and better. "The MCRC loan was very important to the company," says Miller. "We were a small company. When you can get somebody not only to give you long-term debt but to give it to you on a subordinated basis—that's very hard to get at that stage in your growth."

Wang is now one of the nation's two hundred largest businesses, with sales in some 150 countries. In 1986 its sales were $2.6 billion, 13 times the 1978 figure.[14] Even after cutbacks in 1985 and 1986, its work force had grown from four thousand in 1978 (roughly half in Massachusetts) to 30,000 in 1987 (roughly 14,000 in Massachusetts).[15]

Wang is a dramatic example, but the process has been repeated on a smaller scale more than 150 times. Not all have been success stories; as of 1986 MCRC had written off $8 million in loans. But enough have been successful to generate a small profit for MCRC's investors, the life insurance companies.[16] In the process, MCRC has helped those companies (and the banks) invest in riskier firms.

State economic development officials believe MCRC has not taken enough risks in its lending. From their perspective, which puts a premium on high-risk investments in poor communities, they have a point. But Aborn argues that a conventional lender in the insurance industry would be fired for loans as risky as those in the MCRC portfolio. "We have responsibly loaned over $140 million, and we still have most of our capital in place to do it again," he points out. "We have done it at close to marketplace terms, so we have not taken business away from tax-paying companies like banks. There is no other organization in the state which has done anything like this."

MCRC's contribution cost the state nothing other than a tax break that its economic development staff felt was justified anyway. Had the state tried to do the same thing itself, it would have found it impossible to raise $100 million ($10 million for CDFC was a struggle). More important, a state loan program would have had little impact on the investment behavior of the private sector. MCRC, in contrast, has helped change the investment patterns of an entire industry. Today Massachusetts life insurance companies routinely invest in the previously shunned high-tech sector—so routinely, in fact, that MCRC has shifted more than half of its capital into basic industries such as textiles, paper, and fish processing, where long-term subordinated debt and equity are harder to come by.[17] MCRC cannot claim all—or even most—of the credit for the change of heart in the life insurance business. But according to Aborn and others, its success was one of many factors that convinced the insurance executives that they could profitably invest in companies like Wang.

The principle involved here—that it is far more effective to change private investment patterns than simply to make public loans—has since become a centerpiece of economic development thinking. The experts call it wholesaling, to distinguish it from retailing, or providing direct public investments. Not all capital gaps can be filled this way; some areas are simply too risky for all but the public sector and a few hardy private investors. But as MCRC has demonstrated, wholesaling can be extremely effective under the right conditions. The impact of a reshaped private marketplace, with its billions of dollars of capital, can dwarf the impact of a few million dollars in public loans.

Looking back after a decade of imitation, several of the original development institutions in Massachusetts appear rudimentary. But when they were formed, they were the state-of-the-art, and in the intervening years the third-sector model has had a tremendous impact on other states. The principles upon which that model was built—public-private partnership, a strategy of targeting capital gaps, a focus on new and growing technology companies, and an emphasis on wholesaling—are today the central elements of many state economic development efforts.

Unfortunately for Dukakis when he ran for reelection in 1978 his new development institutions were not yet up and running. And while he had toned down his rhetoric, he continued to stress that economic growth was not an end in itself, but only a means to achieve more important social goals. "Mike Dukakis is so preoccupied with slow growth, managed growth, and steady growth that he is forgetting a major point," shot back Ed King, the conservative Democrat who challenged him. "What does this type of growth mean to 160,000 unemployed persons in this state? I am for full growth, period."[18]

At war with business, with public employees, and with much of the liberal community (which ran a protest candidate against him), Dukakis lost to King by 51 to 42 percent. In the wake of California's Proposition 13, the tax issue blindsided him. Only days after Proposition 13 passed, King began hammering his opponent for his failure to reduce Massachusetts' heavy property tax burden—and promised to do so himself. A month before the election, the highest property tax bills in state history went out. Having alienated the left with his fiscal conservatism and the right with his antibusiness image, Dukakis now lost much of his base in the middle. He would have four years on the sidelines to ponder his errors.

The Intellectual Revolution

The spread of new ideas is seldom easy to track with any precision, but in this case history has obliged us. Four months before Dukakis lost to

King, Michael Barker, then only 26, left Keefe's office to work for the Council of State Planning Agencies, in Washington. Affiliated with the National Governors Association (NGA), CSPA was a small, one-man operation whose members consisted largely of mid level state planning officials.

Barker had become disenchanted with the Dukakis administration's preoccupation with redistributing growth rather than rekindling it, as well as its tendency to focus on individual projects rather than more structural intervention, such as that pushed by the Capital Formation Task Force. He brought a new agenda to CSPA, and he quickly sold it to his new boss, Robert Wise. Wise had received a $250,000 Economic Development Administration (EDA) grant to fund a series of pamphlets. Barker convinced Pat Choate, the EDA official who had made the grant (himself a former state development official) to let CSPA alter its use. Barker wanted to use the money for a series of books on what his experience in Massachusetts told him were the key issues in state economic policy: public financial institutions, venture capital, banking, small business, pension funds, tax policy, the working poor, and so on. "People in positions like I'd been in needed to learn lots very quickly, and to understand better how various issues fit together," Barker says today. "Those books were meant to do that." As authors, he hired Belden Daniels, two of Daniels's former associates, Michael Kieschnick and Lawrence Litvak, and others who shared his approach to economic development.

While Barker's authors were at work, MIT economist David Birch completed a study called "The Job Generation Process." Birch and his research team had spent five years examining Dun and Bradstreet data on 5.6 million American firms, which represented 82 percent of all private-sector employment. Their study revealed that the difference between a growing region and a stagnating region was not how many jobs they lost but how many they created. All areas—North and South, cities and suburbs—lost about 8 percent of their jobs every year. Virtually all these losses were from firms shrinking or dying, not moving elsewhere. By implication, this meant state economic policy makers should target the creation of new jobs in home-grown businesses, and here Birch produced his most surprising results: 52 percent of all new jobs were created in independent firms with 20 or fewer employees, and *80 percent* of all new jobs were created by firms four years old or younger. While governors were busy chasing smokestacks, the real job-creators were the small, young, dynamic firms that survived the intensely competitive and risky early years. Not only were these companies generally ignored by state government, they were precisely "the kind of firm that banks feel very uncomfortable about."

On a Saturday morning in 1979 Birch sat down at a typewriter and knocked out a first draft, which he sent to about ten people who had expressed interest. Those ten copies hit the world of development policy like a bomb. "There's a network of several thousand people out there who care vitally about this," Birch says. "And they started copying this thing—I mean, there must be ten thousand copies of those original texts. It was very embarrassing, because it was full of typos. It was just a rough draft. The small-business part was an afterthought."

The small-business emphasis has since become something of an albatross around Birch's neck. Small-business advocates have pushed the study so hard that it has become identified with the thesis that small business is the key to economic development. In reality, as Birch himself has often stressed, the real lesson is that innovation, which often happens in young, growing firms, is the key to economic growth. Most small firms are irrelevant; they feed off growth, rather than creating it.

Barker had been aware of Birch's preliminary findings while still in Massachusetts. He promoted the Birch study and made his authors at CSPA integrate Birch's findings into their own analyses. Arguing that smokestack chasing was a waste of time and cutting taxes would do little to stimulate business, the CSPA team hammered out what was in essence a new thesis of economic development. The goal of state policy, they believed, should be the stimulation of technological innovation, particularly in new and small businesses. That meant stimulating research and development; it meant reducing regulatory barriers to investment in such companies; and it meant perfecting the marketplace by encouraging banks and pension funds and other financial institutions to invest in the small, growing, risky firms that Birch had found to be so important. The CSPA books discussed public capital institutions, particularly those in Massachusetts, at length. Several CSPA authors focused on poor communities, arguing that third-sector capital institutions could be used to bring them into the development process.

The new CSPA publications had a tremendous impact. Roger Vaughan's book on tax policy alerted state policy makers to the futility of smokestack chasing.[19] Michael Kieschnick's follow-up study on taxes landed on the front page of the *New York Times*[20] (whereupon the director of Ohio's Washington office tried to have Barker's boss fired). *America in Ruins*, by Pat Choate and CSPA staffer Susan Walter, almost single-handedly catapulted the infrastructure crisis into the national consciousness.

Barker promoted the books relentlessly. He and his two principal authors, Kieschnick and Vaughan, held sessions at National Governors Association meetings, gave traveling seminars to state development officials, and began consulting with governors and their staffs on new economic programs. For the first time, governors had an organized, national network of technical experts, including those at CSPA and at Belden Daniels's firm, on which to draw.

While Barker was transforming CSPA, the remnants of the New Left were also contributing to the stream of new ideas. In 1975 Lee Webb, a former national secretary of Students for a Democratic Society (SDS), had founded the Conference on Alternative State and Local Policies, which brought together the network of sixties activists who had turned to local government and dug in for the long haul. Webb organized a series of conferences, and in between he pumped out a stack of studies, proposals, and reports on new programs. Several years before Barker arrived at CSPA, the conference had launched an assault on smokestack chasing and begun to spread the word about public development banks and public pension funds. Because its members were on the left, however, its impact was more limited than that of CSPA, which had the ears of governors and their staffs.

California, where Tom Hayden had founded the Campaign for Economic Democracy, was home to a good many of the conference members. In the late seventies two of them, CED activists Fred Branfman and Nathan Gardels, went to work for Jerry Brown. Branfman subsequently recruited Michael Kieschnick. When Brown returned from his ill-fated 1980 presidential campaign and decided to put together his own state reindustrialization strategy, the core of his brains trust was in place, and the locus of innovation moved west.

California: The Jerry Brown Years

Jerry Brown, perhaps the most outspoken member of the class of '74, epitomized its new attitudes. His father, governor of California from 1958 to 1966, had epitomized traditional liberalism. What Nelson Rockefeller did in New York, Pat Brown matched in California. He initiated the construction of one thousand miles of freeway, three entire university campuses, six state colleges, and the $1.75-billion California Water Project. In eight years, Brown doubled state expenditures and increased the state work force by 50 percent.[21] "Under Pat Brown," wrote Joel Kotkin and Paul Grabowicz in *California Inc.*, "California had its New Deal, Fair Deal, Square Deal, New Frontier and Great Society all rolled into one."[22]

Jerry Brown watched the "master builder" at work and, for whatever reasons—psychological, political, or generational—rejected the model. He quickly became wildly popular—more popular than any California governor had ever been, according to the polls—by ruthlessly questioning government spending and baiting the bureaucracy. His irreverence, his fiscal conservatism, and his antibureaucratic forays fit the national mood perfectly, as his late string of victories in the 1976 presidential primaries would show.

"What I was trying to get at," Brown explained a decade later, "is that we've got big spending on all sides, privately and publicly, and we're not looking at the future. I started out more with the sense of government getting out of hand. I saw a mismatch between government's generally self-congratulatory tone and its mismanagement. The first process was to challenge: Why are you doing it this way? I wanted no sacred cows."

Brown developed a reputation as an innovator, with his efforts to support the fledgling wind and solar industries, his Office of Appropriate Technology, and his California Conservation Corps, which put youths to work in the national forests and in similar projects. But he did share one blind spot with many traditional liberals: he was indifferent toward, and at times contemptuous of, economic growth. Indeed, it was Jerry Brown who popularized the phrases "era of limits" and "small is beautiful."

All that changed on January 19, 1977, when Dow Chemical Company announced it was abandoning plans to build a petrochemical refinery north of San Francisco, ostensibly because the process of obtaining state permits had become prohibitively expensive and time consuming. Unemployment was over 9 percent at the time, well above the national average. (Like Massachusetts, California had tasted the good life of high-technology growth, only to be set back by the end of the Apollo space program and the Vietnam War.) Business and labor leaders seized on Dow's decision to unleash a furious assault on Brown, whom they labeled a "no-growther."

Brown responded almost immediately. In retrospect, says Nathan Gardels, the Dow incident was a watershed between two distinct eras in the Brown administration: "recognizing the era of limits, and trying to find ways to transcend those limits." Brown instructed his Office of Planning and Research to develop a streamlined permit process for industrial sites. He began meeting with the state's high-tech leaders. He took a highly publicized trip to Japan, trying to convince its auto makers to build a plant in California. He abolished the state tax on business inventory. He had thousands of California Means Business buttons printed, and wore one on his lapel throughout his entire 1978 reelection campaign. And he created a job-training program under which the state trained workers specifically for firms that were expanding or opening new plants.

Just as it took Michael Dukakis several years to reorient his economic policies, so it took Jerry Brown several years to think through the economic issues. His new conceptual framework emerged in a series of speeches before and during the 1980 presidential campaign. He spoke of an American economy in transition from industrial technologies aimed largely at a domestic market to computerized, information technologies produced for a global—and very competitive—market. He described the growing importance of research and development, of a skilled work force, and of energy efficiency. And he advocated new forms of cooperation between government, business, and labor to drive America into the new age. These themes have since become commonplace in American politics, but Jerry Brown was the first politician of national significance to articulate them.

Once Ted Kennedy entered the 1980 presidential race, there was little room left for Brown. After several early primary defeats, he returned to California bent on turning his dreams of "an industrial-economic strategy for the 1980s" into concrete programs.[23] Always disdainful of hierarchy, he gradually fashioned a shadow cabinet made up of five young, second-level staff people with a penchant for new ideas: Branfman, his director of research; Gardels, who was in charge of pension fund reform; Kieschnick, who directed his Office of Economic Policy; Roger Carrick, who worked for Branfman; and Allison Thomas, a young ex-Carter aide Brown hired to develop public support for his economic program. Brown set up a series of task forces, on research and development, new business development, pension funds, and securities reform, which his shadow cabinet staffed. Kieschnick drafted a memo with 20 ideas. Branfman came up with two themes from a CSPA paper: "investment in economic strength" and "investment in people." Together they set about creating what Branfman calls "a comprehensive post–New Deal economic and social program."

Brown's "investment in people" program focused on education reform and job training. California pumped $25 million into education reform, established a network of centers to train teachers in the use of computers, upgraded the state engineering schools, and proposed stricter standards for high school curricula and university admissions. On the job-training side, Brown proposed an Employment Training Panel to retrain workers who had lost their jobs or were in danger of losing them because of economic or technological change. Now considered a national model, the program is funded by diverting a small portion of the unemployment tax paid by employers. This marks the first time unemployment taxes have been used to finance retraining, rather than unemployment checks. Brown also set up the nation's first Adjustment Teams to respond to plant closings, a model copied by dozens of other states.

Brown's "investment in economic strength" program did not fare as well; the legislature had little idea what Brown was talking about and even less interest. Of the few economic initiatives that passed, perhaps the most successful was the Microelectronics Innovation and Computer Research Opportunities (MICRO) program, dreamed up by Carrick and Kieschnick. The United States has traditionally been a world leader in basic research, but in recent years other nations have proven more adept at bringing the fruits of their (and our) research to the marketplace. Part of the problem is the chasm that separates academia, where most basic research is done, and business, where new products are created. Occasionally that chasm is bridged, as when researchers from MIT and Stanford set up their own companies and triggered the sudden growth of the computer and semiconductor industries, in the 1950s and '60s. But too often business remains ignorant of research advances at universities, and academic researchers remain ignorant of business needs.

MICRO was designed to bridge this gulf—to get university researchers working more closely with business on applied research that might lead to new products. As an incentive to get researchers out beating the bushes for businesses interested in their work, and vice versa, MICRO offered to match any microelectronics research grant made by a California business to a University of California faculty member. A model of simplicity and reliance on the marketplace rather than the bureaucracy, MICRO has grown from a budget of $1 million to $4.4 million a year—generating $7.5 million in corporate research grants.[24]

A second successful economic experiment was pioneered by Brown's chief deputy superintendent of banking, Derek "Pete" Hansen—another CSPA author. Hansen knew that small-business people who wanted to expand complained bitterly about the difficulty they had raising capital. Few small companies can attract venture capital, and banks consider loans to small businesses risky, time consuming, and not terribly rewarding, compared to their other lending opportunities. As a result, most small businesses have to either put up the owners' home as collateral or settle for high-interest, 90-day loans and hope to keep rolling them over. Neither is a good way to grow a company.

The federal Small Business Administration (SBA) has long tried to remedy this problem by guaranteeing up to 90 percent of some loans, making them virtually risk free for the banks. But because SBA-guaranteed loans involve a great deal of research and paper work, banks have not been terribly enthusiastic about the SBA program.

Hansen's solution was simple: he drew up a bill authorizing a new class of investment bank—the Business and Industrial Development Corporation (BIDCO). Because BIDCOs do not have depositors—they are instead capitalized by investors—they can take greater risks with their money than banks. Because they are regulated by the state, they can participate in SBA programs.

In California, BIDCOs have concentrated largely on SBA loans. By specializing, they have become more efficient in dealing with the SBA bureaucracy than bank officers, who only process an SBA loan occasionally. With the SBA guaranteeing 80 or 90 percent of most loans, BIDCOs can also resell them to institutional investors such as insurance companies. Thus, a BIDCO that invests $1 million can actually make $9 or $10 million in loans, selling off the guaranteed $8 to $9 million to institutional investors. By 1984, the average BIDCO loaned as much SBA-guaranteed money as 50 banks, and institutional investors were eager to buy their loans.[25]

Brown also set up a state-owned BIDCO to invest in alternative energy and conservation technologies, called SAFE-BIDCO. Though its loan portfolio took a beating when oil prices fell, SAFE-BIDCO has been politically popular. "People see it as self-supporting and nonbureaucratic," says Mark

Braly, its first president. "It is not part of the bureaucracy, its people are not civil servants, it operates primarily in the private sector, and it is self-supporting. But it operates under a public mandate to accomplish something in particular. There's a lot of interest in that as a type of public policy innovation." Though he does not use the phrase, Braly is talking about the third-sector model.

Yet another of Brown's successful efforts was his Pension Fund Investment Unit, set up to encourage the state's public pension funds—which hold the retirement money of public employees—to diversify their investments into areas that would help the state grow. Under Nathan Gardels' leadership, fund managers committed almost $1 billion of their $30 billion in assets to housing mortgages and small-business loans in California, in just two years.[26] Gardels's unit also drafted a constitutional amendment softening the restrictions on public pension funds investments, which passed on its second try. Before passage, the funds were allowed to buy stock only in the safest firms, which included only five of the nation's one hundred fastest growing corporations. After passage, the stock portfolio of the state's largest fund quickly grew from fewer than one hundred companies to one thousand, and other funds began to follow suit—gradually making more investment capital available to America's growth firms.[27]

To provide seed capital for technology start-ups, Brown created a small Corporation for Innovation Development, similar to the Technology Development Corporation in Massachusetts. To stimulate private investment in small but growing firms, he partially deregulated securities, making it less costly and less time consuming for California firms to issue stock. He also repealed the state capital gains tax on productive investments in small California companies, while increasing it a commensurate amount on speculative investments such as gold, antiques, and art.

In 1981, to create a political constituency for more far-reaching economic strategies, Brown appointed a California Commission on Industrial Innovation, which included bankers, labor leaders, and high-tech businessmen such as Steve Jobs, of Apple Computer, and David Packard, of Hewlett-Packard. Motivated by the deepest recession in 40 years, the commission grappled seriously with the question of government's role in the marketplace. "We went through the whole industrial policy debate two years before they did in Washington," says its staff director, Allison Thomas. Because the Japanese were making serious inroads in high technology, the group fastened on one question above all others: Should state government make low-cost capital available to industries targeted by the Japanese? By a narrow margin, its answer was no. Instead, it recommended the path since taken by most states: targeting activities, such as research and development, technological innovation, and venture capital, rather than industries.

Because of Brown's failings as a politician, the commission's work came to naught. By 1981, Brown's eccentric personal style, his two presidential campaigns, and his perceived failure in the state's "fruit fly" crisis had alienated the legislature and destroyed his once-staggering 80 percent approval rating. As with Dukakis during his first term, by the time Brown established a core philosophy built around economic growth, no one was listening.

Jerry Brown originally caught the public eye with his ideas, however, not his accomplishments. Even today, when asked about his lasting contributions, he talks about "the amount of time I spent in conceptualizing initiatives and bringing people together." Despite his fall from public favor, those ideas had an impact far beyond California's borders. Brown sponsored the first National Governors Association task force and conference on technological innovation—in the process stimulating Michigan Governor William Milliken, his cochair, to launch his own economic development effort. Brown's staff put together the first NGA book cataloging all state efforts to spur technological innovation. The shadow cabinet pumped hundreds of copies of its proposals out to people in other states. California's pension fund research helped convince other states to reform their own systems. And the tide of innovation moved on.

While Michael Kieschnick took the CSPA agenda to California, Roger Vaughan did the same in New York, where he served in Gov. Hugh Carey's Office of Development Planning. Republican governors were also beginning to embrace the new economic development agenda. In Michigan, Pennsylvania, and Indiana, Republican governors embraced activist economics.[28] "Our thinking [used to be] that the best thing we could do for business was to stay out of the way," said Lt. Gov. John Mutz, the moving force behind Orr's new agenda. "But we couldn't sit on our hands any longer. We needed to become competitive and we did."[29]

In the South, most governors understood that they had to begin at a more basic level. Realizing that states with high illiteracy rates or work forces that could not adapt to computerized technologies might be left behind, southern governors began to focus on education reform. North Carolina's James Hunt raised teacher salaries, put an aide in every elementary school classroom, set up an annual testing program for students, and required that students pass a final competency test before graduating from high school. He created two Governor's Schools for talented children and instituted an Adopt-a-School program, under which businesses would volunteer to strengthen a school's curriculum and teaching corps. Hunt also pumped money into higher education and research—constructing, for instance, a $43-million Microelectronics Center to support advanced semiconductor research at five universities and to attract corporate research projects to North Carolina's Research Triangle Park. Though the Hunt administration continued to chase smokestacks, in 1983 Hunt created a Technology Development Authority that included a small-business incubator program and an Innovation Research Fund to make seed grants to small companies for research and development.[30]

Arkansas Governor Bill Clinton, elected in 1978, stressed education reform and relied heavily on CSPA for his economic development agenda, which sought to turn Arkansas away from smokestack chasing toward a grow-your-own strategy. Mississippi Governor William Winter, South Carolina Governor Richard Riley, and Tennessee Governor Lamar Alexander also sponsored comprehensive education reform programs.

By 1982, when the recession hit, the groundwork had been laid for new strategies in virtually every area—as well as for a new set of politics that combined the activism of traditional liberals with the fiscal moderation of traditional conservatives. The antibusiness tenor of many liberals in the early 1970s, including Dukakis and Brown, had given way to an urgency about job creation shared by Democrats and Republicans alike. A network of increasingly sophisticated, experienced economic consultants was available to the new governors, including the new Corporation for Enterprise Development, a Washington-based nonprofit that published a comprehensive volume touching on virtually all aspects of the new development model, *Expanding the Opportunity to Produce*.[31] Dozens of state task forces had trooped to Route 128 and the Silicon Valley to discover the secrets of their success. And the national debate over industrial policy had created greater awareness that the era of international competition required new relationships between the public and private sectors, to sharpen America's ability to compete, and between business and labor, to heighten American productivity.

"With Reagan's coming, with the cutbacks in federal programs, and with the severe recession, a lot of states were hurting," says William Schweke of the Corporation for Enterprise Development (CfED). "Given how politics works, I don't think a governor in that kind of situation could afford to say, 'Hey, the market will take care of it, we're just going to wait.' "

"If you follow the innovation geographically," adds CfED founder Bob Friedman, "it does track where the shoe started pinching. It started in New England, which first felt the impact of our entry into a global economy, with textiles and the shoe industry." (California, which appears to be an exception, may be explained by Jerry Brown's passion for new ideas and the post-Vietnam cutbacks in defense spending, which in the mid-1970s suddenly turned a boom state into a high-unemployment area.) "Then it shifted to the Midwest, with the 1982 recession's severity in the rust belt.

Now it's moving to the Southeast, which is losing a lot of those same textile plants that left Massachusetts in the 1950s. And you're just beginning to see it in the Southwest, which has been hit hard by the falling price of oil."

The next six chapters follow the new agenda as it unfolded across America, in rough chronological order. The first three chapters, on Pennsylvania, Arkansas, and Arizona, chronicle administrations that began in 1978 and '79. The last three, on Michigan, Massachusetts, and New York, cover governors who took office in 1983. While these six states provide a good sampling of the new strategies being tested in the laboratories of democracy, they are hardly alone. Ohio, Indiana, and New Jersey have all created broad new economic development systems, and at least a dozen other states have embraced parts of the new economic agenda. An equal number have undertaken comprehensive education reform initiatives. Indeed, by 1988 the activism described in this book has become the norm, rather than the exception.

2
PENNSYLVANIA: THE ECONOMIC DEVELOPMENT MODEL

It has been a long time since Pennsylvania was known as an entrepreneurial state: one has to go back almost to the days of Ben Franklin. For the last century, the state's bread and butter has been basic industry: coal, steel, and heavy manufacturing.

During the 1980s, a new Pennsylvania began to emerge—a Pennsylvania of new firms and advanced technologies. Ron Thomas, the founder of a Bethlehem firm called Polar Materials, Inc., is one of the pioneers of that Pennsylvania.

Five years ago, Thomas worked at Pfizer, Inc., the giant pharmaceutical manufacturer. Before Pfizer, he had put in 15 years at Xerox. But when Pfizer announced major layoffs, in 1983, Thomas was on the list. He and one of his colleagues decided to start a company of their own. While still collecting severance pay from Pfizer, they set up shop in Thomas's home.

Thomas was an expert in plasma coatings: ultrathin coatings originally developed for use on computer chips. Applied in vacuum chambers by forcing a gas to solidify on an object, plasma coatings provided a more even, durable surface than liquid coatings. Thomas saw almost an infinite number of potential applications outside the computer world: on nuts and bolts, machinery, even cars, to prevent corrosion; on rubber products and cutting tools, to cut down on wear; on fabrics, to enhance soil resistance; on silk ties, to allow washing.

One day a representative of a new state economic development program came to speak at Pfizer. The program was called the Ben Franklin Partnership; its purpose was to create a more entrepreneurial economy, principally by stimulating the commercialization of academic research. The spokesman described the research grants the Partnership would make and the building it planned to use as a small-business incubator in Bethlehem.

Thomas was intrigued. He set up a breakfast meeting with the Ben Franklin representative. By that afternoon, he had signed up for space in the incubator, which offered labs and offices at less than half the market rate and $5,000 to get under way. The incubator provided a free conference room, free computer and computer-aided design facilities, shared secretarial services, a Xerox machine, and access to free legal, accounting, financial, marketing, and insurance services. "It was a major factor in how fast we progressed," says Thomas. "Within six months of founding the company—and within three months of moving into the incubator—we raised $600,000 from two private investors. Without the incubator facilities, the impressive site, we'd have had a tough time doing that. And initially, the fact that we were part of the Ben Franklin program was extremely helpful in convincing bankers, accountants, and professors that we were a serious entity."

Thomas also applied for research grants from the Partnership. By 1987, Polar Materials and the academic researchers it hired had received some $365,000 from the state. By then it had moved to a building with 30,000 square feet; it had 14 employees and annual sales of over $1 million; and it had raised several million dollars of venture capital. Thomas predicted that sales would triple every year for the next five years, with the work force expanding from 14 to perhaps a hundred.

"Damage to American industry from corrosion alone is considered to be around $20 billion a year," he explained. "While this doesn't mean plasma coating is a $20-billion industry, it at least has a multibillion-dollar potential. We're on the edge of a new industry, and we hope to be one of the leaders. We're taking a high technology into basic industry."[1]

The man who created the Ben Franklin Partnership was Richard Thornburgh, Pennsylvania's governor from 1979 through 1986. Thornburgh was a former U.S. attorney who had earned high marks for prosecuting organized crime and public corruption in western Pennsylvania. A Republican, he won an upset victory in 1978, largely on the corruption issue and the disastrous state of Pennsylvania's finances. Five cabinet officers in the administration of Democratic Governor Milton Shapp had been convicted, and the state was almost bankrupt. Its bonds had the lowest ratings in the country. Its highway department, a particularly virulent nest of patronage, was so broke it had virtually shut down.

Thornburgh tackled these problems with the same hardheaded rationality he had displayed as a prosecutor. Crisp, businesslike, and articulate, he immediately froze state expenditures and new hiring, imposed a new code of conduct for state officials, and empaneled the first statewide investigating grand jury to probe corruption and organized crime. He removed highway maintenance from the old patronage system—outraging his own Republican county chairmen, who lost their power to reward party workers with highway jobs. At the Department of Transportation, he appointed an inspector general to investigate corruption, trimmed the staff from 15,000 to 12,400, and pushed through five tax and fee increases to pay for highway repairs.

Overall, Thornburgh squeezed more than 14,000 jobs out of the state bureaucracy; when he left office, only Florida had fewer state employees per capita.[2] He kept spending almost level with inflation, increasing it only for items such as highways, prisons, economic development, and education. Time and again he vetoed bills for social programs. Pennsylvania had the nation's most liberal General Assistance program (welfare for single people without children); Thornburgh took 60,000 able-bodied adults off the rolls. In real dollars, he cut welfare spending by over a third.[3] Though he raised taxes in 1983 to deal with a recession-induced deficit, he then cut taxes by over $1 billion in his last three years.

Thornburgh had been elected as a moderate Republican. But his relentless effort to reduce spending and taxes, combined with his take-no-prisoners style, convinced the public that he was a staunch Reaganite. For those on the other side of Pennsylvania's bitter partisan divide, he was an inaccessible, unforgiving adversary. "His doors are closed," said Pennsylvania AFL-CIO chief Julius Uehlein. "He's a prosecuting attorney by background. Their training is not talking to other people: you study a case and then you prosecute."

The Pennsylvania Economy

Although Thornburgh devoted his first years in office to cleaning up the fiscal mess, Pennsylvania's fundamental problem was its economy. Like Massachusetts before it, Pennsylvania was in the throes of a painful transition from an industrial to a postindustrial economy.

A century ago, Pennsylvania was the nation's foundry. Immigrants poured into the coal towns around Scranton and Wilkes-Barre, the smaller mining towns of Appalachian Pennsylvania, and the booming steel towns of Pittsburgh and its environs. After New York, Pennsylvania was the nation's largest state—and it was growing rapidly.

The boom years ended with the depression. After World War II, coal lost markets to oil, and a long, slow decline began in the anthracite belt and the Appalachians. Twenty years later, the competition began to eat away at Pennsylvania's manufacturing muscle as well. Looking back, one can date the decline from 1965, when Pennsylvania's share of national manufacturing employment began to fall.[4] In the two decades that followed, Pennsylvania manufacturers lost 400,000 jobs, nearly two-thirds of them in primary metals (principally steel), textiles, and apparel.[5]

By the time Thornburgh took office, Pennsylvania's unemployment rate was already the ninth highest in the nation. Then the economy fell off a cliff. Between 1979 and 1985, 21.5 percent of all manufacturing jobs in Pennsylvania disappeared.[6] The state's 40 largest corporations were literally cut in half, as their total employment fell from 1.2 million in 1979 to 600,000 in 1986.[7] Unemployment peaked at 14.9 percent. When *Inc.* magazine ranked American cities by their growth in jobs and business start-ups between 1981 and 1985, Pennsylvania had *six* cities in the bottom 20.[8]

The economic crisis created tremendous pressure on Thornburgh. Pennsylvania is one of the most bitterly partisan of all the states, and the Pennsylvania Democrats villified Thornburgh for what they perceived as a failure to respond. Their approach to economic development was the traditional one: smokestack chasing and social welfare spending. Their model was the Shapp administration, which had won the premier smokestack-chasing prize of the seventies, a Volkswagen Rabbit plant. Though Shapp called it the crowning achievement of his administration, the deal was a classic example of the failings of smokestack chasing.[9] For its $40 million in 1.75 percent loans (on which Volkswagen did not have to begin paying until 1998), $25 million in highway and rail construction, $3 million in training subsidies, and five years of local tax abatements, Pennsylvania got only half the five thousand jobs Volkswagen had promised and perhaps 10 percent of the spin-off jobs Shapp had predicted.[10] In 1987, just nine years after the plant had opened, Volkswagen announced that it was closing.

Thornburgh wanted nothing to do with expensive subsidies or social welfare programs. Instead, he decided to commission an in-depth study of the state's economy. Called *Choices for Pennsylvanians*, it took almost three years to complete and solicited input from public meetings throughout the state. It then served as the "polar star," in Thornburgh's words, around which all of his efforts revolved.

As the recession deepened, the Democrats pounded Thornburgh unmercifully for his failure to act. Thornburgh and his top staff, who were known for their conservativism and their palace guard mentality, pounded back. The combination of the Democrats' severe pressure to act and Thornburgh's fiscal restraint and market orientation eventually produced perhaps the best economic development system in the country. But listening to the rhetorical bombshells, the public concluded that Thornburgh was a typical Reaganite who thought government was the problem, not the solution. Even when he embraced an activist economic agenda, the image stuck. Thornburgh's actual performance was a vivid illustration of the growing divergence between the national Republican party and its governors. But because he adopted the rhetoric of Reaganism, the public never noticed.

The driving force behind Thornburgh's economic development program was Walt Plosila, a young midwesterner who ran his Office of Policy and Planning, then moved over to the Commerce Department to implement the new initiatives he had conceived. Descended from Finnish immigrants who spent their best years unloading ore for U.S. Steel on the shores of Lake Erie, Plosila was the first in his immediate family to go past high school. A broad man with a wide face and a shock of brown hair that constantly falls over his forehead, he looks like a pulling guard for the Pittsburgh Steelers. He acts like it as well. Leaning forward, elbows on his desk, he wades right into the topic at hand. The flat midwestern vowels come rapid-fire, studded with phrases that would sound more at home in a small-town bar than in a governor's office.

Despite the lack of polish, however, Plosila's creativity and blunt persistence earned him respect from both sides of the aisle, something extremely rare in Pennsylvania's legislature. "I got in trouble when I was first here, because I never realized you weren't supposed to work with the other side of the aisle," Plosila recalls. "But I didn't pay any attention anyhow. I play it down the middle. I've gone from Goldwater Republican to McGovern liberal to the middle of the road. I'm a good old Ripon Society Republican is what I am, a neoliberal Republican. I like the *Washington Monthly*—that's what kind of neoliberal I am."

Early in Thornburgh's first term, Plosila wrote a speech for the governor in which he called for "compassionate pragmatism." When Thornburgh's top staff found out—after the governor had delivered the speech—the alarm bells went off. Plosila was never again invited to write a speech.

As Thornburgh's point man with the National Governors Association, Plosila met Michael Barker and his colleagues at the Council of State Planning Agencies. In 1982, he served as president of CSPA. "To some extent, Walt played a role of legitimizing this new school of state economic development policy," recalls David Arnold, who served on the NGA staff in the early 1980s and is now with the Ford Foundation. "It was one thing for people like Michael Barker to be spinning out these theories about what the new paradigm ought to be. It was something else for somebody to take their ideas and actually test them out in a state that was having serious economic difficulties, and that had a fairly traditional political environment."

Through CSPA, Plosila heard about David Birch's research on the role of new and small businesses in job creation. When he checked the data for Pennsylvania, he found that large corporations were contracting so rapidly that *all* net new jobs in the state were being created by small firms. Relying on Birch's evidence, the *Choices* report rejected smokestack chasing and stressed the importance of new and small businesses. It recommended that Pennsylvania seek to modernize its existing manufacturing base and diversify its economy, particularly through the growth of innovative, advanced technology companies. It also called for new partnerships between the public and private sectors, as well as between state and local governments.

Like Dukakis, Thornburgh created an Economic Development Committee of the Cabinet, with its own staff, to force his bureaucracy to buy into his new priorities. When the biggest smokestack-chasing prize of the 1980s came along—GM's Saturn plant—Thornburgh said, "I'd rather have 50 new plants with a hundred employees apiece in different industries than five thousand new jobs in a one-industry operation." His first wave of efforts focused on small business. He cut their taxes, set up a Small Business Action Center to help them deal with red tape and bureaucracy, put up a small matching grant to secure 13 of the SBA's new Small Business Development Centers, to provide technical and management assistance, and amended the lending powers of the Pennsylvania Industrial Development Authority (PIDA). Once devoted almost exclusively to large manufacturers, by 1984 PIDA directed half of its loans to businesses with 50 or fewer employees.

The Ben Franklin Partnership

Among Pennsylvania's greatest strengths, the *Choices* report pointed out, were its universities and its reservoir of technological expertise—its intellectual infrastructure. Pennsylvania graduated more engineers than all but two other states. It had four universities among the nation's top 50 graduate research institutions, with expertise in robotics, computer-assisted design and manufacturing, electronics, computer science, and advanced materials. It ranked fifth among the states on three related measures: the number of scientists and engineers in the state, the number of workers employed in advanced technology industry, and the amount spent on research and development.[11] Yet Pennsylvania had failed to capitalize on these intellectual resources. The kind of interaction between business and academic institutions that had kicked off explosive growth in Massachusetts and the Silicon Valley was absent. Thornburgh and Plosila made the creation of that environment their primary goal.

While finishing *Choices*, the governor had commissioned a study of how to rejuvenate the state Science and Engineering Foundation, which dated from the 1960s. Out of both studies grew the idea of a partnership between the universities and industry to stimulate the rapid commercialization of research advances. Plosila drafted a bill, and in a stroke of public relations genius, Thornburgh suggested the name. "We're trying to include entrepreneurs, scientists, innovators, and bring them all together," he said. "Why not name it after Ben Franklin?"[12]

Unlike many state technology programs, which pour money into new buildings and institutes, the Ben Franklin Partnership is essentially a matching grant program. The heart of the program offers "challenge grants" to university-based projects—primarily applied research projects—funded by businesses. As with California's MICRO program, the idea is to provide a carrot to get industry and academia interested in working together on research that might result in a marketable (or improved) product or process.

Several years ago, for instance, a professor of biochemistry and biophysics at the University of Pennsylvania, Britten Chance, developed a new type of nuclear magnetic resonance machine that performed a specialized form of brain and body scan. It could measure the brain metabolism of premature infants; it could diagnose peripheral vascular disease (such as hardening of the arteries) in adults; it could even evaluate the level of physical conditioning achieved by an athlete. Chance launched a company and poured a significant amount of his own money into it, but finally reached his financial limits. He then applied to the Ben Franklin Partnership, which responded with $330,000 in research grants over three years. In 1986 the firm, Phospho-Energetics, Inc., raised $4 million in venture capital. "In five years' time," said its president, Roger Wheatley, "we would hope to be a $100-million medical instrument company. Without the Ben Franklin Partnership, this company would not have been commercialized. It's the perfect example—this technology exists at the university, and the state provides some money to get that technology out of the university, into the marketplace."

Although the majority of the research projects involve young, entrepreneurial companies, many also fund efforts to help older firms adopt new technologies in order to remain competitive. When the Partnership was created, a debate raged among advocates of industrial policy over the wisdom of targeting sunrise versus sunset industries. Wisely, Plosila and Thornburgh chose to target both. To underscore their commitment, they adopted the term *advanced technology* rather than *high technology*. "What we see in advanced technology is not simply another Silicon Valley," said Thornburgh. "We see new technology clusters emerging; but of equal importance, we see the spinning in of new technology into our traditional industries."

In addition to research, the Partnership also awards challenge grants for education and training programs and for entrepreneurial development activities, again requiring a private-sector match. Examples of the former include programs to help public school teachers achieve computer literacy; a center to train industry personnel in computer-assisted design; and internships in industry for vocational education instructors. Examples of the latter include feasibility studies for small-business incubators; technical assistance for small businesses; and efforts to start "enterprise forums," in which local venture capitalists meet regularly with entrepreneurs who need risk capital.

The program is operated through four Advanced Technology Centers (ATCs), each in a different region of the state. Each center is affiliated with a major university or universities, but every higher education institution in the region is eligible for grants. Each center focuses on two to four technology areas, depending upon the economic strengths of local universities and the region. They include robotics; advanced materials; computer-aided design and computer-aided manufacturing (CAD/CAM); microelectronics; biotechnology; biomedical technologies; sensor technologies; manufacturing in space; food and plant production and processing; and coal and mineral production and processing. A board made up of regional leaders from academia, business, government, and economic development organizations oversees a staff of 10 to 20 at each center.

Rather than imposing a model on each region, the state allowed each board to craft its own design. Predictably, several of the universities assumed that they could use the money as they would any other research dollars: to finance basic research of interest to their faculty. During the first year, the central Ben Franklin board rejected both Penn State's and the Philadelphia center's proposals and sent them back to the drawing board— whereupon a state legislator from the Penn State area tried to have Plosila fired. To force the centers to focus on projects of value to business, the board decided to make them compete with one another for funding, based on the commercial potential of their projects.

The process works like this. Every spring, each center submits a package of applications for challenge grants. The state board rates each project according to criteria such as potential commercial application; number of jobs created; size of the company (there is a bias toward small firms, on the theory that large corporations do not need as much state help); and quantity and quality of the private-sector match. It also ranks each center according to how well its past projects have done on measures such as job creation, corporate match, and attraction of venture capital. Centers with higher average ratings get more money. They can then divide their allocation up as they wish—providing smaller grants for some projects than originally proposed, for instance, to make the money go further.

In its first four years the Partnership funded close to 1,500 projects, which involved 128 of the state's 135 higher education institutions and 2,500 private firms. With its $77 million in challenge grants, the state claimed to have leveraged $281 million in other investments, the majority of them from private industry.[13]

Although challenge grants remain the heart of the Partnership, Thornburgh and Plosila gradually added a series of other programs. To make sure that even the smallest companies could take advantage of the program, they introduced small research grants of up to $35,000 a year for businesses that could not afford the time and money required by a joint business-academic project. To stimulate the growth of small-business incubators, they set up a separate fund to make loans and grants to those creating incubators.

Early experience with the Partnership and the incubators underlined how little venture capital, particularly seed capital, was available in Pennsylvania. To address this problem, the state put together six pots of $750,000 and offered them to private venture capitalists. To get the money, they had to come up with at least $2,250,000 of their own and use the total to create a seed venture fund, which would make small investments in young firms that were not yet ready to go to market.

Another program provided $3 million for new equipment in engineering schools. And in 1986, the administration began setting aside several million dollars a year to fund applied research facilities that were consistent with the goals of the Ben Franklin Partnership. The first $4 million went to help match National Science Foundation grants for new Engineering Research Centers won by Lehigh and Carnegie-Mellon universities.

The North East Tier Advanced Technology Center

Perhaps the best way to understand the Ben Franklin Partnership is to take a close look at several of its centers. The North East Tier Advanced Technology Center, anchored at Lehigh University, is often considered the best of the four. With a strong engineering school, Lehigh has long encouraged professors to work with local businesses, even to start their own companies. In the 1980s it has spawned a series of interdisciplinary programs designed to respond to industry's changing needs, and it has become a driving force in the region's revitalization. By reinventing itself as the economy around it changed, Lehigh has become a good example of what some call the postindustrial university.

Lehigh's location is also apt. The Lehigh Valley, which comprises Bethlehem, Easton, and Allentown, was once a booming center of coal mining and steel production. It is the home of Bethlehem Steel; indeed, the company's former research facility, itself the size of a small university campus, sits atop a mountain overlooking Bethlehem, a stone's throw from Lehigh. But for more than 20 years, the region's 500,000 residents have watched their manufacturing might gradually wither. Between 1980 and 1986, manufacturing employment in the valley dwindled from 107,000 to 78,000.[14]

When the Ben Franklin Partnership came along, university leaders quickly grasped its significance and made it the core of their entire effort to work with industry. "Our first priority is to help existing industries be competitive," said Mike Bolton, who moved over from his position as director of development at Lehigh to run the new center. "That's why we call our program advanced technology, not high technology. We think the biggest users are going to be traditional firms."[15]

The leading actor in that strategy is Lehigh's Computer Integrated Manufacturing (CIM) Laboratory, which works with some 25 companies a year
on Partnership-funded projects. The CIM Lab sponsors short courses for
industry people—intensive, five-day seminars on new production technologies, for instance. But most of its Ben Franklin projects send teams of
faculty and students into plants to examine production processes and help
companies adopt new technologies.

These range from efforts to create networks through which all the
computer-driven machines in a plant can communicate, to complex, year-
long campaigns to redesign entire factory floors. According to lab director
Emory Zimmers, a Lehigh engineering professor, most large companies
can afford these services on their own. But with matching grants from the
Ben Franklin Partnership, small and medium-sized companies can afford
the lab's services as well.

One client makes a sensing device used to measure pressure or meter
the flow of material in a manufacturing process. Over seven years its plant
had shrunk from 3,500 employees to about seven hundred, as foreign
competition ate into its markets. To keep the plant open, the firm desperately needed to get its costs down. With a $200,000-Ben Franklin grant
paying for about half of the research and development work, the CIM Lab
sent a team of people in to design a new production process with 18 robot
cells (each cell consisting of one or more robots, plus attached equipment),
all linked by computers. The CIM engineers tested the design of the robot
cells, as well as the design of the entire factory, through graphic simulation
on computers. By the time half the robot cells had been installed, the firm
had driven its cost per unit below those of its competitors.[16]

These projects not only help individual companies, they also help the
engineers involved advance the frontiers of factory automation. "Without
these applied research projects," says Zimmers, "there's no proving
ground for new, innovative ideas. We really do both at the same time—
when we're doing the short-term project, we are also interacting with the
factory and creating new ideas about how factories should run. The factory
is our laboratory."

Mature industries are also the targets of many of the Lehigh center's
applied research projects. Examples have included projects to develop software for automated manufacturing, a new process for recycling tires, a
new design that allows industrial furnaces to burn high-sulfur coal, and a
computer-aided design process for cosmetic bottles.

Despite this emphasis on mature manufacturers, the Lehigh center also
works with small, entrepreneurial firms. Its staff played a role in creating
the region's new seed capital fund, which is now housed in its building.
The Partnership provides partial support for four Small Business Development Centers in the region. It funds feasibility studies for incubators. And

it actually runs an incubator—the one in which Ron Thomas launched Polar Materials.

The incubator takes up one building in Bethlehem Steel's former Homer Research Laboratories, a vast complex Lehigh recently purchased, with $10 million in state aid, from the company. It has offices and laboratories jammed into every conceivable space. (Thornburgh loves to tell the story of the time he toured the building and discovered one company operating out of a former storage closet.) A Partnership staff member, who has several decades of experience in business, has an office in the building and provides technical assistance to the tenants.

The Homer Research facility is one of the country's only "product development" incubators—meaning that it is limited to start-up firms which are creating new products. Its first generation of tenants spanned a fascinating spectrum of advanced technologies. Two wrote computer programs for industrial clients. Another developed the first nontoxic paint stripper on the market. A fourth developed a new trap for bag worms, which are difficult to eliminate with chemical pesticides.

A fifth does contract research on advanced materials—metals, ceramics, and polymers—for manufacturing firms. Called Innovare, Inc., it was founded by Al Austen, a former research engineer at beleaguered Bethlehem Steel. In 1983, when he heard about the new incubator, Austen leapt at the chance to go out on his own. His company uses supercold processing of metal powders to create alloys with qualities that cannot be obtained under traditional hot processes—a combination of strength and flexibility, for instance, or resistance to corrosion, or conductivity. With ceramics, Austen works with high temperatures and pressures to produce superior products. In the course of his research, he and his team have developed a programmable, computer-controlled hydraulic press, to extrude (shape) both hot and cold materials. Innovare began selling small versions of the press in 1987, while developing a marketing plan to sell to large manufacturers.

"Our market niche is to serve the sophisticated, rapidly solidified, powdered metallurgy industry—composites, new deformable ceramics, and so on," Austen says. "For those operations you need a new generation of processing equipment, and that's what we see our role as providing." Because this niche is on the cutting edge of new technologies, Innovare has little competition and boundless potential. In 1987 it had six employees. "We could be three or four times as big today if over the last six months I'd been three or four people and been able to simply answer requests," Austen said. If he succeeds in selling large hydraulic presses to industry, the company will set up production facilities.

By 1987, Innovare had received two Ben Franklin seed grants of $35,000 each. Researchers at Lehigh with whom Austen had contracted had received close to $80,000 in challenge grants. (Austen matched those grants with about $250,000 of Innovare money and equipment.) Without the Ben Franklin money, Austen says, he would not have undertaken the joint research projects with Lehigh: "It wouldn't be affordable. That's part of the purpose of this program—to make technology affordable to the small company."

For the company's first three years, the incubator provided inexpensive space, the flexibility to expand into additional space, shared facilities, and "a community in which you are able to talk to other people who are in your same position." Part of it was moral support, but Austen also learned about conferences, training programs, and the like through colleagues. In addition, the Partnership staff referred him to the right researchers at Lehigh, sponsored a workshop on product liability insurance, and held regular sessions with a committee of finance, venture capital, and marketing people to critique company business plans.

Austen lavishes praise on the Partnership staff. "Their enthusiasm rubs off not only on the people in the program but on the people who can cooperate with it, whether they're bankers or large companies or whoever," he says. "I guess I would have gone into business sooner or later, but this program made it sooner. I was drawn in because of the benefits I saw, and what I've experienced has been even better than I expected."

Like Austen, Ron Thomas got an invaluable boost from the incubator and the Ben Franklin Partnership. But Thomas also points out the program's limitations. Although the Lehigh center was instrumental in his research and start-up phase, it was not terribly helpful when it came to teaching a scientist how to manage a rapidly growing business. "We were very naive as businessmen," Thomas says. "And the kind of problems that come up in all these companies are very similar. You're dealing with very, very bright people, who are technically trained but who don't understand the business side." Because the center relied primarily on academic people for technical assistance, it was of little help. Thomas's solution was to bring in a partner with a strong business background.

The Western Pennsylvania Advanced Technology Center

The Western Pennsylvania center, in Pittsburgh, has developed an interesting solution to the problem Thomas describes. It subsidizes several institutions that provide people like Thomas and Austen with intensive business assistance. One, called the Enterprise Corporation, has four senior staff people with graduate degrees and extensive business experience. They sort through 150-odd business plans every year, pick ten to 15 of the most promising, and go to work—teaching entrepreneurs how to restructure their business plans, raise venture capital, find partners for joint ventures, do market research, and so on. Typically, they spend six months to a year working closely with a company—and some firms come back later for another round.

The Enterprise Corporation does this work for free. Occasionally, to make sure a firm genuinely needs its help, it asks for a small equity stake in the company. The firms are generally too young to afford any other form of payment. "No one could make a living doing what we do for fees," says Thomas Canfield, president and CEO of the corporation. "We figured out one year that the average salary of the heads of the companies we had helped was $14,000."

Canfield and his colleagues also created a bimonthly forum where firms can present their business plans to venture capitalists. Every three months they sponsor a Software Entrepreneurs Forum, which brings representatives of 120 software firms together to address issues specific to their industry. They hold conferences, seminars, and an annual venture capital fair, which attracts dozens of venture firms from outside the region. In 1985, they put together the Pittsburgh Seed Fund, one of the regional seed funds that received money from the state.

Another local organization partially funded by the Partnership is the Pittsburgh High Technology Council (PHTC). The council sponsors publications and studies to document the growing high-tech presence in Pittsburgh, as well as conferences and meetings to build the network. It runs a CEO Network, for instance, through which local CEOs act as mentors for start-up firms. That group has in turn created a $10-million CEO Venture Fund, for second-stage venture capital, and a seed capital fund, which received Ben Franklin money.

Until the 1980s, Pittsburgh was the antithesis of the entrepreneurial city. The first major city in the nation's interior, it was dominated for a century by giant corporations such as U.S. Steel, Gulf Oil, and the Mellon Bank. Even today it hosts more major corporate headquarters—including those of 15 *Fortune* 500 firms—than all but two other American cities.

"In the Pittsburgh area, you had large corporations and large unions," says State Representative Tom Murphy, a Democrat who sits on the Partnership board. "Typically what happens is you graduate from high school, or quit high school, and go to work in the mill and make enough to raise a family. That's my family's tradition, and most of the people I know, that was their tradition. The sense of risk taking that is important in the kind of society we're living in today was really eliminated in the Pittsburgh area, largely because of the security. There was no venture capital, and there were no entrepreneurs."

In the '80s, an entrepreneurial, high-tech economy finally began to emerge out of Carnegie-Mellon University's expertise in computer science and robotics, the University of Pittsburgh's medical center, and the growing interest of firms such as Alcoa in advanced materials. A 1986 survey found 639 high-tech firms employing 66,000 people—more than double the number left in steel. It was a small core, but it was growing at four times the rate of the regional economy.[17]

Those who run the Western Pennsylvania center have done everything in their power to nurture this emerging high-tech economy. They do fund some efforts aimed at mature industries, but in Pittsburgh the steel industry collapsed so thoroughly and so rapidly that the region's future clearly rests on the vigor of its sunrise industries. Like the other centers, the Pittsburgh center puts 60 to 70 percent of its money into applied research projects, most of which spring out of Carnegie-Mellon or the University of Pittsburgh. This money has helped a spate of new technology firms get started. "Without Ben Franklin money, a lot of companies we work with might not be around," says Canfield. "The Ben Franklin Partnership has significantly manufactured this climate for entrepreneurship. Without their money we'd be doing a hell of a lot less."

"The cumulative effect is to make people believe that Southwest Pennsylvania can be a technology leader," adds Tim Parks, executive director of the High Tech Council. "It changes the way you think of Pennsylvania, the way Pennsylvanians think of themselves."

Perhaps the Partnership's most important contribution in Pittsburgh has been to teach the business and political leadership that economic development is more than knocking down old steel mills and building industrial parks. Pittsburgh already had an extremely active private sector and a tradition of public-private partnership, but those efforts had always focused on the physical rehabilitation of the city. "The great strength of the Ben Franklin Partnership was that it understood that the key to economic development is now intellectual infrastructure, not physical infrastructure. It's research and technology and innovation, not real estate projects," says Tom Cox, director of an economic development organization on Pittsburgh's North Side. As an accepted member of the economic development community, the Partnership has brought that message home.

Evaluating the Ben Franklin Partnership

The Ben Franklin Partnership is probably the most comprehensive economic development institution in the country. If an entrepreneur needs inexpensive start-up space, Pennsylvania has 30 incubators—more than any other state. If he or she needs technical assistance, each center offers several options. If research is the problem, challenge and seed grants are available, or the local Ben Franklin staff can help the firm apply for a federal grant. If capital is the problem, both seed and traditional venture capital funds are available. If the company needs loans rather than equity, the staff can refer it to local bankers who specialize in its area, or to the right state or regional loan fund. If an older company needs new technology to survive, teams of experts are available to help. "One thing leads to another," says Walt Plosila. "We're trying to build the kind of informal network you see in places like Route 128 and the Silicon Valley."

Equally important, these services are available *locally*. A business person does not have to travel to Harrisburg to deal with any of them. In fact, a business person is hardly aware that he is dealing with a state program. Most of the services—the research, the technical assistance, the analyses of production processes, the venture capital—are *not* provided by state programs. The state simply offers a carrot, a matching grant, to encourage business people to use academic resources, or to create seed funds, or to finance incubators, or to provide technical assistance. Once those resources are in place, the centers operate sophisticated referral services. The object, as it should be, is to change private-sector behavior in ways that stimulate innovation and productivity.

The Partnership would have been even stronger had the legislature passed a Technology Assessment Program proposed by Thornburgh in 1986. The idea was to provide more money—$6.25 million in the first year—for the kind of work Emory Zimmers's laboratory does with Lehigh Valley manufacturers. Pennsylvania already had a program, called PENNTAP, through which eight "technical specialists" at Penn State campuses helped small businesses with technical information and referrals to university or private-sector consultants. But Thornburgh's new Technology Assessment Program would have gone much further. It would have provided on-site consulting, low-interest loans for the purchase of new equipment, and hands-on assistance in integrating that equipment into production lines and training workers to use it.

Supporters of the Partnership argue that the proof of its value is the amount of money that business has put into its projects. In the program's fourth year of operation, private corporations matched $26.45 million in challenge grants with roughly $20 million in cash and $48 million in equipment, laboratories, and staff time.[18] (Another $40 million came from other sources, including the universities, the federal government, and foundations.) "Those folks wouldn't be putting their money on the table if it wasn't working for them," says Peter Likins, president of Lehigh University.

Partnership enthusiasts also note that firms receiving grants attracted $61.4 million in private venture capital during the program's first four years.[19] "This is not something we thought about that much when we designed the program," says Plosila. "But a lot of venture capitalists see us as an imprimatur, because we're turning down three projects for every one we fund, and we have review committees at each of the centers. It's a fairly selective process, so we're doing some of the weeding and screening for the venture people. You have to look at this in perspective. In 1983, there was $31 million raised in Pennsylvania in its entirety for venture capital, and I'm sure most of it went out of state. Then along comes Ben Franklin, and we've got $61 million in our projects from venture firms all across the nation, all in Pennsylvania."

The Partnership is not designed only to help business, however. It is also designed to change academia. "The program is a success as a culture transformer," says Likins. "It creates a different kind of environment in universities. The state money is not coming in here to finance a faculty member's exploration of the inner workings of their personal curiosity. It's coming in here to finance a faculty member's pursuit of a concern that has its roots in some company."

Initially, adds Emory Zimmers, some professors at Lehigh feared that the program would move academic research "too much from the 'R' to the 'D.' But in reality it helps to focus the research on more critical issues, both long and short term. People that don't have any contact with industry tend to create a cure for no known disease. They mask that by saying, 'Well, I'm 20 years ahead of my time.' In reality, their time never comes. Academia is inbred, and this program opens it up a little."

Another intangible factor is the program's role in mobilizing local business, academic, and government people to work together in new ways. By requiring the involvement of many players in local boards and consortia, the state has attempted to generate a process that will gather momentum on its own. Because it has allowed these local players to shape each center to fit the region, it has succeeded in very different environments.

The program is not perfect. Not all the centers are equally vital, for instance. Because of the rural nature of its territory and its lack of historic orientation toward the private sector, the Penn State center has lagged visibly behind the others. Conversely, the other centers could profitably use double the money they now get, because they each turn down as many solid proposals as they accept.

Critics argue that some of the centers have become too dominated by the universities. Ron Thomas, who now sits on the local board that oversees the Lehigh center, feels that Lehigh University has gained effective control of the program. As a result, he says, the research money is too directed toward academic interests, and participating businesses are suffocating in red tape and bureaucracy. "Right now I've got one grant, and if I want to expend over $100, I have to have five signatures," Thomas says. "That would take me at least six weeks to two months. You fall into the bureaucracy of the university, and it prohibits you from accomplishing anything."

Thomas also points out that the universities have refused to give up their patent rights on any research their professors conduct. Companies sponsoring the research have to sign licenses to use the results. Because of this, "as soon as a company like ours gets into any kind of position of financial strength, it cuts off that university research, because they're not about to share their patents with a university researcher."

Thomas believes the Partnership would have more impact if 73 percent of its funds went to businesses and 27 percent to academics, rather than the other way around. He points to the incubators and programs like the Enterprise Corporation as the real Ben Franklin success stories.

Others, such as Peter Likins, disagree with Thomas. But even Likins agrees that the program has one weakness: its use of the number of jobs created by each project as a major determinant of funding. The Ben Franklin Partnership is not designed to create jobs in the short run; it is designed to create new products and processes, to heighten productivity, and to increase the number of start-up companies spun off by Pennsylvania universities. If those goals are met, jobs will follow—in the long run. Yet funding is partially determined by short-term job creation, and the public is told that the Partnership is a jobs program.

"I think it is dangerous to put the centers in the position in which they have the impression that the more jobs they report creating—or worse, saving—the more money they get," says Likins. "Because these things are very difficult to document accurately and honestly."

Walt Plosila and the state board recognized these problems, but believed that job-creation figures were necessary to get support from the legislature. Plosila also argued that the use of job-creation figures forced the universities to concentrate on projects with commercial potential. He insisted that the program erred on the conservative side in counting jobs, if it erred anywhere. Still, virtually the only negative publicity the Partnership has received came when the *Philadelphia Inquirer* traced down two cases of exaggerated job claims, in an early press release.[20]

Despite these quibbles, the Ben Franklin Partnership is a model program—and it is recognized as such throughout the nation. It is comprehensive; it is decentralized; it catalyzes significant private investment in important economic activities; and it has mobilized major local players in new ways. It is also focused on important targets: the commercialization of research, the transfer of technology from academia to industry, the generation of risk capital, the birth of new firms, and the integration of advanced technology into mature industries. Its continued success will depend upon the ability of the state board to resist the constant pressure from the universities to use the money for basic research, new buildings, and other academic priorities. But the anecdotal evidence suggests that, to a surprising degree, the board has done so. The result is arguably the best state economic development program in the country.

The Regional Enterprise Development Program

Although faculty at almost all of Pennsylvania's colleges have received Ben Franklin grants, the program's real impact has been, and will continue to be, in areas with major universities. For outlying areas, the Thornburgh administration created a second regional economic development system.

In 1981, the Reagan administration tried to do away with the Appalachian Regional Commission (ARC) and the Economic Development Administration (EDA), which together funded seven Local Development Districts in Pennsylvania—regional organizations encompassing 52 of the state's 67 counties. These organizations, which were essentially consortia of local governments, existed to tap federal grant money. Generally held in low regard by economic development experts, they spent most of their federal money on highway construction and social service programs.

Budget Director David Stockman's attacks on ARC and EDA got Plosila and his staff thinking about the Local Development Districts. It was clear that even if Congress saved the programs, their budgets would dwindle. "We decided that if these things were going to survive, they were going to have to be more self-sustaining," Plosila remembers. "We decided either we would make them action oriented in economic development or get rid of them."

Plosila decided to focus the Local Development Districts on helping small manufacturers, initially by creating a Pennsylvania Capital Loan Fund to offer low-interest loans of up to $50,000 for businesses with 50 or fewer employees. He and his staff looked for models all across the country on which to build the new loan program. They settled on the Al Tech Fund in Jamestown, New York, a successful revolving loan fund set up in the 1970s. The basic idea was to create a source of "gap financing"—money that could be tapped when traditional bank loans, SBA-guaranteed loans, and state loans were not quite enough to make a deal go.

Plosila sent one of his deputies, Ivan Tylawsky, over to the Commerce Department to manage the effort. "I remember sitting across from somebody at ARC in Washington who basically turned white when I explained what we wanted to do," Tylawsky chuckles. The Local Development District staffs were equally apprehensive. "They were scared as hell. What do you mean development? What do you mean loans?"

Over its first five years, the Pennsylvania Capital Loan Fund received roughly $8 million in federal money and almost $30 million in state funds. As with the Ben Franklin Partnership, the state divided up the money among the local districts in part based on their performance. It also encouraged them to create revolving loan funds of their own, using local government funds, federal block grant money, and the like. Some districts now have as many as eight revolving funds, divided between business and housing loans. Finally, the state helped them secure designation from the Small Business Administration to offer financing through a key SBA program. With all these financing tools available, the Local Development Districts often play the lead role in putting together financial packages for local businesses.

The next step was a program to help businesses tap the nation's largest single market: purchases by the federal government. Then came an export assistance program. Meanwhile, the district staffs, some of which are as large as 50, were developing the expertise to provide more general management assistance.

The district staffs also refer companies to the Ben Franklin Partnership, help write their grant proposals, and at times receive Partnership grants themselves. Most of the districts have helped create small-business incubators. Several of them function as Service Delivery Administrators under the Job Training Partnership Act, and some have initiated local and regional labor-management committees. Several have also been instrumental in saving local rail lines abandoned by Conrail. One of the districts bought and rehabilitated 80 lines of rail, created an independent Rail Authority, and contracted with a short-line railroad company to operate trains on the line. Another helped a private firm buy one hundred miles of abandoned lines, which it now operates profitably.

The performance of Pennsylvania's Local Development Districts is mixed. Some have large, professional staffs and have earned the respect of business people in their regions. Others are still struggling to make the transition from social services to economic development. Some of their loans go to companies that could not get capital elsewhere; others are simply exploited by firms with plenty of access to private capital, because they want 6 percent interest rates.

Tylawsky points out, however, that the loan funds act as a carrot; they give the districts credibility and bring business people in to see them. Once a relationship is established, the staff can help in more important ways, with exports or federal procurement or management consulting.

Tylawsky believes that the most important thing about the system is precisely that it is a *system*, rather than a single program. Like the Ben Franklin Partnership, the districts provide a wide range of services at the regional level.

And unlike most state bureaucracies, the Local Development Districts are hands-on organizations, whose staff members can make quick decisions. They operate as intermediaries between the state and local businesses, delivering services funded by the state but maintaining the flexibility of local institutions. In effect, they play the role of local public-sector entrepreneurs, just as the Ben Franklin centers do. This is a role missing in all too many state economic development efforts.

The 1982 Election and the Pennsylvania Economic Revitalization Fund

In 1982, unemployment in some Pennsylvania communities—particularly the steel towns and manufacturing centers of western Pennsylvania—approached depression levels. Thornburgh had given priority to distressed communities in a number of existing state programs, but he had not created new programs or new funding for those areas. "If I had come into office and made my first priority the areas of high unemployment," he later argued, "we would be nowhere today. First we had to get the fiscal situation straightened out, then we had to develop an intelligent overall economic development program. It was tough. We had no economic development strategy in place until '82—arguably '83—because we took the time to do this *Choices* process and put something together that was not off the shelf and was not just one more glitzy incentive package."

In retrospect, the care with which Thornburgh approached the task is laudable. ("It was worth every day," he says.) But at the time it was an enormous risk. As the recession deepened, the Democrats chafed at Thornburgh's inaction. When the bill creating the Ben Franklin Partnership passed in 1982, it went virtually unnoticed; most legislators saw it as an insignificant academic research program. Clamoring for action on economic development, they reduced Thornburgh's appropriation from $3 million to $1 million. Most Democrats still equated economic development with smokestack chasing, and by that measure, Thornburgh was not even in the ball game.

Thornburgh and his political staff compounded the problem by refusing to talk about economic development. By late 1981, the governor had a commanding lead in the polls over his potential Democratic opponents, based on his success in straightening out the state's finances, weeding out corruption, and tackling the state's massive road repair problems. Thornburgh's staff decided to keep the focus on those issues. When the Pennsylvania Manufacturers Association attacked *Choices* because it downplayed smokestack chasing, the staff decided to bury the report. The public—even the legislature—was never told that the governor had developed a comprehensive economic development plan.

As the recession deepened, however, the economy became the key issue. Fearing Thornburgh's lead in the polls, the strongest Democratic candidates had chosen not to run. Allen Ertel, a little-known congressman from central Pennsylvania, won the nomination. Though he was able to raise little money, Ertel went on the attack on bread and butter issues. "Ertel was hitting Thornburgh over the head with campaign commercials asking where the state's economy was and where it was going," remembers Plosila. "Thornburgh's strategy was to focus on the basics of government—integrity, balancing the budget, road building—with very little attention to what he was going to do on economic development." Thornburgh even refused to debate Ertel. Hence, the public never understood that Thornburgh was willing to go beyond Reagan's stance of "let the market take its course."

When Thornburgh cut 60,000 people from welfare while statewide unemployment approached 15 percent, the debate became shrill. Welfare activists camped out in the Statehouse, and residents of North Philadelphia threw eggs at the governor as he campaigned for reelection. In a surprisingly close election, Thornburgh squeaked by with only a 100,000-vote margin.

At this point, Democratic leaders in the House decided to take matters into their own hands. They hired Gail Garfield Schwartz, an economic development consultant and coauthor, with Pat Choate, of *Being Number One: Rebuilding the U.S. Economy*, to study the state economy. Her report reached conclusions very similar to those of the *Choices* study. "While traditional industries will still be large employers," she wrote, "the long run job security and expansion will be in emerging industries. Therefore, Pennsylvania must encourage firm formations, expansion in existing industries, new enterprise, innovation, retooling, and new product development."[21]

The House Democrats then put together a $910-million proposal, to be financed by a temporary increase in personal income taxes. They called it PennPRIDE: the Pennsylvania Program for Recovery, Investment, Development, and Education. In roughly equal proportions, the new money would have created economic development programs, closed the state budget deficit, and funded relief efforts aimed at distressed communities and the unemployed. Though it had some merits, PennPRIDE was the kind of program one gets when ten politicians sit down together to divvy up $1 billion: relatively unsophisticated, untargeted, and focused more on temporary relief than long-term structural change.

Thornburgh ridiculed the plan as a traditional Democratic tax-and-spend approach. It cost too much, it wasted too much money on "welfare-type programs," and it failed to leverage private-sector action, he argued. "That philosophical collision was very, very vivid," Thornburgh says in retrospect. "I think it was acknowledged by all observers as a gunfight at the OK Corral between the old Democratic way of doing things and what we were trying to do."

The showdown dragged on for 19 days beyond the deadline for passing the budget. When the General Assembly sent Thornburgh a budget that was $1 billion out of balance—because it included many of the PennPRIDE initiatives but not the taxes needed to pay for them—the governor retaliated by line-item vetoing $1 billion of spending, including the entire budget for the General Assembly. In subsequent negotiations, his veto of the PennPRIDE proposals stuck.

When it was finally over and tempers had cooled, the public pressure to do something about the economy remained. Thornburgh's aides sat down with the Democratic leadership and crafted a compromise: a $190-million bond issue that adopted some of the PennPRIDE initiatives and pumped new money into some of Thornburgh's initiatives. Called the Pennsylvania Economic Revitalization Fund (PERF), the three-year program was passed by voters in April 1984. The amended PennPRIDE initiatives included:

•$20 million for small-business incubators and seed capital funds;
•$50 million for infrastructure projects needed by businesses (highways, access roads, and the like);
•$27 million to upgrade equipment in the state vocational-technical schools and community colleges;
•$15 million to create a Youth Conservation Corps to employ young Pennsylvanians in projects designed to improve public facilities and parks; and
•$10 million to provide loan guarantees and interest deferrals on bank loans to family farmers.

Other programs, some of which have been mentioned earlier, included:

•$15 million in new money for the Pennsylvania Capital Loan Fund, administered by the Local Development Districts;
•$15 million for loans to employee and community buy-outs;
•$3 million for new engineering equipment at universities;
•$30 million for parks and public recreation facilities; and
•$5 million in new money for the Minority Business Development Authority, which has provided over $20 million in loans and surety bonds to minority businesses since its inception in 1974.

The results of PERF have been mixed. Most of the new money was put to good use, but the legislature's regulations governing the incubator and employee buy-out programs restricted their use considerably. In addition, interest rates on loans were tied to interest rates on the bonds, which kept them relatively high. As a result, the Thornburgh administration later financed the last $105 million of PERF spending with general revenues, and in 1986 it convinced the legislature to amend some of the programs and divert some of the unused funds to other purposes. Overall, the PERF initiative was far more useful for traditional kinds of programs—infrastructure, education, parks, and youth employment—than for more pioneering economic development efforts. Like PennPRIDE, the program was characterized more by legislative consensus than by original thinking.

Enterprise Zones

In 1983, while Thornburgh was still fighting with the Democrats over PennPRIDE, he finally created his first new program to target distressed communities: enterprise zones. Popularized by Republican Congressman Jack Kemp and enthusiastically supported by President Reagan, enterprise zones have been adopted in some form by at least 32 states.[22] Most of the state programs rely primarily on the Kemp formula: tax breaks to induce companies to locate in poor communities.

There are a number of problems with this approach. Most analyses suggest that tax breaks are not powerful enough to overcome the disadvantages of locating in the inner city, including crime and poor transportation. In addition, most federal and state tax breaks are useless to new firms, because new firms generally do not earn profits that can be taxed during their first few years. (This is less true of property tax abatements.) And, like most tax inducements, those in enterprise zones go to companies regardless of whether they would have located in the target area anyway and regardless of whether they need them; hence they waste money. In many zones, businesses are not required to hire even a percentage of zone residents. Even if the tax breaks did work, zone residents might get the increased congestion associated with new businesses, but few of the jobs. (In the worst case, they might be displaced by rising rents.) Finally, the Kemp formula ignores the complex web of realities—the lack of education and training, the social pathologies, the dearth of entrepreneurial capacity—that keeps poor communities poor.

Enterprise zones remain popular with politicians, because they are easy to pass and administer, and they provide the appearance of doing something. Appearances do affect reality, and some evaluations suggest that the establishment of an enterprise zone can change attitudes toward investment in a poor community. But sophisticated economic development practitioners long ago concluded that if enterprise zones were really to work, government would have to build comprehensive local economic development networks in poor communities, tied to broader state and federal resources. In a sense, poor communities need their own versions of Pennsylvania's Local Development Districts, designed to work closely with businesses to ensure their survival and growth and to provide extensive education, training, and placement services to poor residents in the area.

It is ironic that while many Democratic governors have created traditional enterprise zone programs, Governor Thornburgh, a Republican, rejected the tax incentive model. Thornburgh and his staff were convinced by the *Choices* experience that taxes were not major factors in most corporate relocations, and that most new jobs came from new and small businesses, not from relocations or branch plants. Rather than relying on tax breaks, they tried to build local economic development partnerships. Some tax abatements are provided by local governments, and in 1986 Thornburgh set aside $7 million for tax incentives. But they are not the heart of the program.

Under the program, communities applying for designation as enterprise zones must put together Enterprise Zone Coordinating Committees, with public and private-sector involvement and local funding for proposed projects (revolving loan funds, incubators, economic development staffs, etc.). Usually the committees involve representatives from local government, the local redevelopment authority, the financial community, community-based organizations, and in some cases local labor and religious groups. During the planning stages (usually about two years), they receive $50,000 "planning grants." Once their plan is in operation, they receive annual $250,000 "development grants." The state then gives the zones priority in a series of other programs, from loans to infrastructure grants to highway funds. It also allows tax-exempt bonds to finance commercial and retail projects, like shopping malls, only in enterprise zones— a policy copied from Massachusetts.

Each year new communities compete for designation. They are judged according to the quality of their local committees, proposals, and matching funds. By 1986–1987, the state was dividing $6.25 million among thirty-four zones, and it claimed to have pumped $200 million in other grants (some of which would no doubt have been awarded regardless of the program) into the zones.[23]

Most observers agree that the success of the program depends entirely upon the strength of the local coalition or organization in charge. If the public and private partners in a zone are active and have a competent staff, they can use the state program to bring significant public investments into the community—in turn catalyzing significant private investments. If they are not well organized, the program means little more than an extra $250,000 to spread around on a few projects.

One of the best zone programs is run by the North Side Civic Development Council, in Pittsburgh. The North Side is a large, relatively poor area made up of perhaps ten different neighborhoods. Back in 1953, merchants from the area created the North Side CDC to help stimulate area businesses. When the Thornburgh administration announced the enterprise zones program, the North Side CDC saw an opportunity to bring new state resources into the neighborhood. But according to Tom Cox, its director, city officials considered the program's $250,000 annual grants too small to be worth pursuing. Cox and his council convinced the city to pursue a grant and to contract with North Side CDC to administer it.

The first thing Cox did was set up a state-certified Industrial Development Corporation and apply for a state loan for a light industrial building. Because the building was in an enterprise zone, the state granted the loan even though the building would not normally have qualified. Over the next three years the state loaned $1 million to three different North Side CDC real estate projects. Cox also received $800,000 in state money for a small-business incubator and state help in securing jobs for local residents on a major highway project. He and the council have put most of their annual grant money into a seed capital fund, to invest in start-ups locating in the district. "We believe the North Side has to be part of the business development that is technology-driven or we'll just get bypassed," Cox explains. "Because our money is so flexible and so early stage, everybody wants it. So we're part of the venture capital network here in Pittsburgh. Even if we lose all our money—and so far the jury is out—it's a wonderful marketing tool for the neighborhood."

By 1987, the North Side CDC had developed close to a dozen commercial real estate ventures, including a small hotel, a restaurant, two buildings housing light industry, a brewery, the incubator, a commercial and office complex, and a minority-owned retail center. It was one of the lead developers of a large light industry and office complex being built on Herr's Island, where the city had spent $10 million to raze old stockyards and slaughterhouses.

Despite North Side CDC's track record, Cox admits that it has not created a tremendous number of jobs—certainly nowhere near the number needed by area residents. Though Thornburgh's model is clearly superior to the average enterprise zone program, even his best zones are limited in their impact. Experience suggests that development in many poor communities, particularly in the inner city, requires comprehensive institutions with access to significant capital resources.

This suggests that Pennsylvania's program might benefit from adding an entirely new dimension. Certainly larger grants for weak zones would be a waste of money. But for those zones in which strong organizations or coalitions are in place, the state might consider creating a special fund from which it could provide significant matching dollars, on the order of $5 to $10 million per zone, to capitalize comprehensive new "third-sector" development banks. I will discuss the kind of programs that might make sense in chapter 9.

The Renaissance Communities Program

Pennsylvania's most distressed communities are the cities and towns where large steel mills or manufacturing plants have closed down. What Lowell was to Massachusetts 15 years ago, the Monongahela Valley and Beaver Valley are to Pennsylvania today. Until his last year in office, Thornburgh virtually ignored their problems.

The American steel industry got its start in western Pennsylvania, in the mill towns that hug the mountainsides along the Monongahela and Allegheny and Ohio rivers. In the 1940s and 1950s, these river valleys were filled with the smoke of dozens of huge steel mills. Nearly half the region's employees worked in manufacturing, nearly half of them in steel. Only Detroit was more dependent on one industry. Pittsburgh was the city of "midnight at midday," its air so dirty that corporate executives brought two shirts to work—because by noon the first was already covered with soot. As late as the 1970s, even as the region lost its dominant position in world markets, the United Steel Workers won contracts that pushed per capita income in the region up faster than in all but three other metropolitan areas: Houston, Dallas, and Anaheim.[24]

Then the bottom dropped out. Between 1979 and 1984, roughly seven of every ten steel jobs in the region disappeared. By 1984, only one of every five area workers was in manufacturing; more people labored in corporate headquarters than on the production line.[25] "Pittsburgh was once the mightiest industrial power on the planet," says Tom Cox. "It went from being an international power to one that is barely of regional importance, in just 20 years."

Today the Pittsburgh region stands as a graphic symbol of the end of the industrial era. The silent, deserted steel mills line the rivers: miles-long, rusting hulks that once lit the night sky. The names evoke an entire era: the Homestead Works, the Duquesne Works, the Wheeling-Pittsburgh Works. Of the dozen or more plants that once made steel in the valley, only two still operate.

The small cities that cluster around these plants are now eerily quiet. Once muscular, shot-and-beer towns, they are slowly collapsing in on themselves. The row houses are weathered and aging, their brick faded, their asbestos shingles unchanged since the 1940s. The downtowns are pockmarked by empty storefronts; the roads need repair. There are no shopping malls, no new homes, virtually no sign of new investment in the past two decades. It is as if time were frozen. Even the fast-food places date from the pre-McDonald's era.

Of the 72 separate municipalities in the Mon Valley, well over half are classified as distressed by the federal government.[26] Unofficial estimates of unemployment, counting those who have quit looking for work or are underemployed, range from 20 to 30 percent. Monessen, a major city in the Mid Mon Valley, has lost over a quarter of its population since 1970.[27] The older workers have retired on their pensions; the younger workers have moved away. Those in between, with families to support and homes they cannot sell, struggle along with part-time jobs, or look for work in Pittsburgh.

When Thornburgh focused his economic development efforts on advanced technology and the universities, people in the Mon and Beaver valleys felt abandoned. In 1985, he pushed through a $25-million tax credit for new investments by mature industries, widely known as the steel tax credit. But it was too late for places like the Mon Valley. In frustration, legislators from the Mid Mon Valley finally introduced a resolution of no-confidence in the Commerce Department. Though it never passed, it led to discussions between the legislators and the Commerce Department, and finally to a Renaissance Communities program.

The new effort, passed in Thornburgh's last year in office, involved three approaches: heightened targeting of state grant programs to distressed communities; partial state funding for several big projects in the Pittsburgh area, including a new terminal at the airport and a university research park built on the site of an old steel plant; and what Thornburgh has described as "super enterprise zones" in the Mon Valley, the Beaver Valley, and the Shenango Valley (the Sharon area, about 80 miles north of Pittsburgh). The third effort, the heart of the program, involved $1-million grants to public-private economic development coalitions in four areas (the Mon Valley was divided into two regions). As in enterprise zones, the grants were designed to stimulate the formation of areawide organizations, to help them hire staff, and to support their strategies for revival. In addition, the state promised to expedite all applications for specific project grants from these organizations.

Walt Plosila designed the program on the same basic model he had used for the Ben Franklin Partnership, the Regional Economic Development Program, and enterprise zones. "We're trying to do a grass-roots-up effort," he explained. "Self-help is what it comes down to—getting the community together, through a council that's an umbrella agency, representing labor, business, and local economic development groups, to develop a long-term strategy and then work with us on a day-to-day basis to help implement it. We've said we would give priority in all our state monies, across the board, to that area, if they could identify projects. This approach is better than us trying to solve all their problems for them, because we can't. We're not going to have the resources to deliver."

Another goal was to overcome the local tradition of every town for itself. Set alone down in a bend of the river or a cleft in the hills, each valley town was a world unto itself, its identity securely tied to its steel mill or manufacturing plant. "A lot of people never had to think beyond their city," says Jim Schucolsky, coordinator of the Mid Mon Revitalization Commission. "It was a company town mentality. Now everyone is saying that we've got some problems here, and that we're going to have to work together."

Each of the four areas has taken a different approach. The first to develop its strategy was the Mid Mon Valley, where the Mid Mon Valley Progress Council pulled 16 area organizations together into a Revitalization Commission. Projects funded by the commission during its first year included an incubator; a successful effort to get three enterprise zones established in the area; a labor-management committee; and feasibility studies looking at the potential reuse of the two largest area plants that have closed in recent years. In one of these cases, a huge Wheeling-Pittsburgh integrated steel mill, the commission worked hard to find a new buyer who might operate a slimmed-down operation. In this effort, however, it was hampered by the absence of any state program to help in the restructuring of mature industries. Its other major priority, a new expressway to connect the area to Pittsburgh by limited access highway, also awaits a major state investment.

The expressway symbolizes the real function of the Renaissance Communities program: to help the steel valleys organize themselves to seize what opportunities appear as the new Pittsburgh economy gains momentum. Lowell succeeded in Massachusetts in large measure because local leaders were organized and able to sell their city to the state, the federal government, and private corporations. Like Lowell, the Mon and Beaver valleys will survive according to their capacity to exploit whatever growth the regional economy can produce. "It's sort of like getting organized on both sides of a bridge, and making sure the bridge is in place," says Ivan Tylawsky, who oversees the effort in the Commerce Department. "Then the traffic will come across."

The Renaissance Communities program does not involve a great deal of new money. "The big myth about a lot of these economic development stimuli is that you can measure the commitment in terms of what public dollars are appropriated," argues Thornburgh. "What really needs to be done is not just throwing money at these problems, but developing some very careful, fine-tuned strategies that are responsive to the needs and capitalize on the resources of those communities."

Thornburgh is correct, but when he left office in January 1987, those fine-tuned strategies had yet to be revved up. To be truly effective, the Renaissance Communities program, like the enterprise zone effort, will probably have to be given a new dimension. One million dollars a year in "glue money" is a start, but to make a real dent, the targeted regions will need more powerful development institutions. In a sense, these areas need their own equivalent of the Ben Franklin centers: major, long-term, comprehensive institutions designed to address the problems of mature industries and distressed communities, while building a new entrepreneurial base.

The Culture of Industry

While Thornburgh came late to the problems of Pennsylvania's distressed regions, he virtually ignored the issue that lay behind their distress: the failure of mature industries to restructure so as to remain competitive in the new economy. Part of the problem, particularly in Pennsylvania, has been a tradition of extremely adversarial labor-management relations. Despite Thornburgh's lack of attention, Pennsylvania has made significant progress in this area.

In 1978, leaders of the state AFL-CIO and the Chamber of Commerce sat down to discuss Pennsylvania's problem. Out of those discussions grew a proposal for a business-labor-government council, funded by the legislature, to work on improving both the state's labor climate and its overall economy. They called it the MILRITE Council, an acronym for "Make Industry and Labor Right in Today's Economy" and a spin on *millwright*, the term for those who built America's mills.

The MILRITE Council began by working to form labor-management committees around the state, with the help of $500,000 a year in matching grants provided by the legislature. The committees were designed to improve cooperation between labor and management, to heighten labor's role in decision making, and to increase productivity. By mid-1987 there were 14 areawide committees in the state, which had helped launch some 50 in-plant committees.[28]

Perhaps the most successful of the 14 areawide committees is in Scranton. Ed Dulworth, one of its two cochairmen, is vice-president for manufacturing at Topps Chewing Gum. Dulworth admires Thornburgh's efforts to stimulate technological innovation, but he is skeptical that new technologies alone will solve America's manufacturing problems. "Technology is important, but it's overplayed," he argues. "The people side—what and how people work together—that is where the greatest problems are and the biggest opportunities lie."

Dulworth's views grow out of his three decades as an engineer and plant manager with Ford, General Foods, and Topps. As an engineer with Ford and General Foods, he learned that technology cannot stand alone. "I can remember vividly having to face up to the fact that what I considered to be excellent systems did not work," he says. "As I got into it and learned more, I found it was the people—it was a lack of ownership. I've seen it over and over."

At General Foods, Dulworth put his new insight to work. Gradually he developed a reputation as the best engineer in the company. "It wasn't because I was the best, it was because things I worked on worked. It was execution. And that was because I was paying attention to getting involvement and commitment and ideas from people doing the actual production work. It was a lot of stuff that was soft—but in fact was critical to the end product."

In the late 1960s, General Foods asked Dulworth to help design and run a new Gaines Pet Food plant around his emerging philosophy. Set in the wheat fields of Kansas, it was the equivalent of the General Motors Saturn plant today—and in its time it got almost as much publicity. The plant used the latest technology, and it revolutionized the world of work. "It was highly participative and lean as hell in management," says Dulworth. "Everything was organized around the work, with tremendous responsibility and power within the work teams that operated the plant."

The work teams selected their own team leaders, established their own work rules, interviewed and hired replacements, and disciplined their members. All production workers shared the same job classification, and all employees—workers and management—used the same parking lot, the same cafeteria, and the same lounge. Each worker was encouraged to learn every job on his team. When his team members decided he had mastered every job, he got a raise, moved to a new team, and began learning its jobs. This not only minimized boredom, it assured that if anyone was sick others could fill in for him, and that if something went wrong any team member could troubleshoot.[29]

The system worked. Absenteeism was one-half of one percent, compared to 10 percent in much of industry.[30] "Over about four or five years," says Dulworth, "we took the output of that plant about 50 percent higher than it had been designed for, without spending any major money. We had state-of-the-art technology, but the people operating it constantly came up with all kinds of small improvements. We were doing things with equipment that the people who built the stuff were amazed by. It was all fine tuning, neat little inventions." The result was higher quality and 30 to 40 percent greater productivity than another General Foods plant making the same product (Gravy Train dog food). "It was the number one plant at General Foods every year."

The plant was also a threat to other managers at General Foods. "It threatened top management," Dulworth says, "because you can't dictate from the top in the same way—some of the asinine things that come from the top just don't work in those kinds of systems. The distribution of power is very different." And it threatened other plant managers because Dulworth and his colleagues were overly enthusiastic. "We were pretty charged up. It was fun, it was exciting, it was very unusual. None of us had ever experienced anything like it. We were evangelistic, and we found ourselves becoming outsiders in the company. There were words like *communist cell* thrown around, and *country club*, and *soft and mushy*."

Eventually, Dulworth and his colleagues wore out their welcome, and they were invited to leave. Dulworth moved to Topps and began doing the same things, if at a slower pace. He cut management by two-thirds, pushed the distribution of power down through the company, and brought the union leadership in even on decisions about which products should be manufactured in-house and which should be purchased elsewhere. Again the result was a 30 to 40 percent improvement in productivity and quality.

As at General Foods, Dulworth broke down the rigid separation between production workers and the technical staff. One of his electricians, for instance, liked to tinker with computers. "Today that guy does everything: he designs our computer-controlled manufacturing systems, he selects hardware and software, he programs, he implements—the whole shebang. He has no formal degree, he just came out of our organization. And we have a fair amount of that. We have machinists who can build machines from nothing, from sketches. They have the skills, and they work with our computer guy. They get involved in new products, new processes, they work hand in hand with our research arm. We've been able to do some things that are either considered to be impossible, or they're not available on the market. We have some products that were impossible to make in the past that we can now make with this technology. And by experimenting on-stream, we're saving a lot of time and effort, we're doing stuff that might take months or years if we went outside the company for the expertise. The benefits to the company are immense. And people get such a kick out of the innovations. I mean to see 'em and feel 'em, to know where they came from—it's creation, it's growth, it's success."

Soon after he arrived in Scranton, Dulworth began talking with other area business people and labor leaders about creating an area labor-management committee to spread the gospel. The committee formed in 1978, but it took four years before it began to jell. The turning point came in 1982, when the region's Local Development District got a federal grant that allowed the committee to hire a staff person. The next year, the MILRITE Council took over the funding. "Without that," says Dulworth, "we couldn't have done what we've done." The committee has spawned 15 in-plant labor-management committees—in businesses, in school districts, even in city governments.

Labor-management committees date from as far back as the turn of the century. During World War II, when they were widely used to push production to maximum levels, some five thousand of them were registered with the War Production Board.[31] But after the war most disappeared. Their revival stems from the early 1970s, when Stan Lundine, then the mayor of Jamestown, New York (now lieutenant governor of New York), pulled together local union and corporate leaders to form a committee. As a congressman, Lundine later sponsored the Javits-Lundine Act on labor-management cooperation, which created a small federal grant program for areawide and in-plant committees. By 1987 there were some one hundred area labor-management committees nationwide. They had created their own national association, and several states had followed Pennsylvania's lead in supporting them.

The movement began with the simple idea of resolving labor disputes, improving communication, and preventing strikes. In-plant committees focused on the most obvious problems and achieved some early success. But gradually these islands of cooperation bumped up against the reality of adversarial relations built into top-down corporate organizations. "There is growing evidence that in-plant committees either stagnate or fail after about three to five years of success," says Robert Coy, who served as executive director of the MILRITE Council until 1987, when he moved over to run the secretary of labor and industry's policy office under Democratic Governor Robert Casey. "Middle managers often sabotage the cooperative activities, fearing a loss of authority and responsibility. Unions often withdraw support, fearing that worker ideas for improving productivity are costing them their jobs. Many business, labor, and academic leaders have come to the conclusion that in-plant labor-management cooperation cannot be institutionalized in the absence of fundamental changes in corporate cultures—the organization of work, reward systems, work rules, job security, and the roles and responsibilities of labor and management."

This is particularly true in industries that are trying to stay alive by adopting advanced production technologies. A recent study by a National Academy of Sciences committee found that firms have been unable to get the productivity they expect out of advanced manufacturing technologies unless they thoroughly redesign social relations in the plant. The electromechanical technologies developed a century ago required only that workers be cogs on an assembly line. But the microelectronic technologies used today—robots, computer-controlled machining centers, and so on—take workers away from physical labor and put a priority on their ability to think, to operate computers, to adjust to change, and to troubleshoot. As the Japanese have demonstrated, this kind of manufacturing requires a work force that is highly skilled and flexible; an organizational chart in which work rules and job classifications are kept to a minimum, so workers can handle many different problems as they erupt; and a corporate ethic of partnership between labor and management. It also requires a corporate organization capable of rapid change. And as organizational behavior expert Warren Bennis once wrote, "Democracy is the only system of organization which is compatible with perpetual change."[32]

Major American corporations that have bought into this philosophy include Westinghouse, Procter & Gamble, Cummins Engine, General Electric, IBM, Xerox, and Polaroid.[33] Most of Pennsylvania's labor-management committees have not broached fundamental restructuring of the kind seen at these corporations. But there are exceptions, and the MILRITE Council is trying its best to encourage them. It has begun to sponsor training programs for area labor-management committees, union staff people, and corporate managers, for instance—programs that, in Coy's words, "go beyond how we improve labor-management relationships to how we use the process to restructure the corporation."

Coy is particularly excited about the training program for union staffs, which began with the United Steel Workers. "The idea is to create a group of union leaders who understand the concepts and also know how to install them in a way that doesn't threaten the interests of the unions," he says. "If we become known as the state where union leaders are actively involved in installing these kinds of participative, shared-authority, employment-security systems—not just in dividing up the pie—we'll have the Japanese beating our doors down."

According to Coy, even most of the avant-garde corporations have ignored one of the most fundamental issues: employment security. Workers understand that heightened productivity often translates into fewer workers, so they hold back their ideas for fear that they will eventually destroy their own jobs. The solution is a system of job guarantees, in which companies avoid short-term layoffs during recessions by shifting surplus workers to problem-solving activities that can increase the overall efficiency of the organization.

Sidney Rubinstein, a consultant who works with corporations and labor unions to design cooperative systems, points out that "employment security has a double-edged effect." It reassures workers, thus encouraging them to help the firm increase its productivity. But it also forces management to look at its workers differently. If they must be kept on even during recessions, they must be viewed, not as replaceable parts, but as resources. Management must begin to look at ways to capitalize on their intelligence, to train them for more than one job, to exploit their troubleshooting abilities. This is how management has traditionally looked at salaried employees, Rubinstein points out; employment guarantees for production workers simply extend the principle. To encourage firms to move in this direction, the MILRITE Council has proposed that the state offer partial subsidies, in the area of $50,000, to help firms design employment security systems.

Notions such as employment security suggest that if Pennsylvania—or any other state—wants to get serious about changing the culture of industry, it must attack the problem at higher levels than the area labor-management committees. "If you're talking about restructuring," says Ben Fischer, a former United Steel Worker economist who now teaches labor relations at Carnegie-Mellon University, "then that's way beyond the people you're dealing with in a labor-management committee. That's not their thing—you can't have a steward in a plant concerned with the future of the industry. You need people with more power. It would be useful if the governor convened the major actors and began to encourage them to develop strategies. Government can provide leadership, because essentially what you're dealing with is how you get a society to change its approach and its thinking." To move in this direction, the MILRITE Council has proposed that Casey sponsor an annual Governor's Conference on Labor-Management Cooperation.

Public Pension Fund Reform

Unlike the handful of labor-management programs in other states, the MILRITE Council does far more than work with labor-management committees. Indeed, it is one of the few state programs that actively involves labor in broader economic development issues. It played a role, for instance, in the creation of the Ben Franklin Partnership.

Perhaps the council's greatest success has come in the area of public pension fund reform. In late 1981, the council hired Michael Barker, who had just left CSPA, and Lawrence Litvak, one of Barker's CSPA authors and consultants, to study Pennsylvania's capital markets. After discussions with a wide variety of bankers, venture capitalists, and others, Barker and Litvak concluded that financing was difficult to get in Pennsylvania in two areas: venture capital (particularly seed capital and funds to purchase and turn around mature firms) and long-term, fixed-rate debt for established manufacturing firms. The attorney general subsequently ruled that the pension funds did not have the right to make venture capital investments, so the MILRITE Council worked out legislation with the administration that allowed one percent of pension fund assets to be invested in venture capital.

With MILRITE's help, the two statewide public pension funds had by late 1987 approved the investment of $155 million in private venture capital funds.[34] The strategy had three parts. First, the pension funds invested in a series of private venture funds with particular experience in Pennsylvania, each of which agreed to a goal of investing half the money in the state. Second, the pension funds invested in the regional seed venture funds created to tie into the Ben Franklin Partnership. Third, the pension funds uood $10 million as bait to convince a major national venture firm to create a new Pennsylvania Venture Capital Fund (also with a goal of investing 50 percent of the funds in Pennsylvania).

Although Pennsylvania was not the first state to invest pension funds in venture capital, MILRITE's other initiative to fill the state's capital gaps was unique. It has convinced a group of public- and private-sector pension funds to put $63 million into a "private placement separate account," to be managed by Cigna Corporation, a large insurance company. Private place ment separate accounts are often set up by insurance companies for tax-exempt organizations. In this case, the money will be used to make long-term (up to 15-year) loans of $500,000 to $3 million, at fixed interest rates, to manufacturing firms with sales in the area of $20 million a year. Most of the money will go to firms whose credit ratings are not quite good enough to get long-term, fixed-rate loans from banks or insurance companies.

The MILRITE Council also focused on plant closings. After a careful study of the issue, it put together legislation to create a $500,000 revolving loan fund to help workers study the feasibility of buying their plants. The House Democrats expanded the proposal into a $15-million program, which included financing for feasibility studies and buy-out loans for both employee and community groups. In hindsight, they picked the wrong strategy. In part because employee buy-outs need equity rather than debt, and in part because the regulations have scared off many investors by requiring that employees have the right to vote their stock within five years, the money was barely tapped. In 1986, the administration and legislature diverted all but $500,000 of the money (which is now available only for feasibility studies and technical assistance) to other purposes.

Evaluating Pennsylvania's Economic Development Efforts

Not all of Thornburgh's efforts have been chronicled above. He successfully pushed into place a fairly comprehensive education reform agenda; he pushed through a bill allowing Pennsylvania banks to open branches throughout the state; and he created a customized job-training program to help companies train people for open jobs and upgrade the skills of their employees.

As with any economic development program—particularly one that has been in place only five years—it is difficult to measure the precise impact of Thornburgh's programs. Pennsylvania's economy is clearly moving in the directions sought by the Thornburgh administration. The economy is diversifying away from its former reliance on heavy manufacturing, which left it extremely vulnerable to foreign competition. Services have passed manufacturing as the leading category of employment, and employment in computer-related industries is growing rapidly.[35] The state's birthrate for new firms, which until 1985 was only about half the national average, has also begun to rise; in 1986, it grew twice as fast as the national average.[36] Also in 1986, unemployment fell below the national average—for the first time since the early 1970s—and stayed there.

How much Thornburgh's efforts have contributed to these developments is impossible to say. As a politician, Thornburgh likes to paint such statistics as the "full flowering" of his programs. Perhaps the best antidote to such claims is a 1984 essay he wrote describing his economic development strategy. In the introduction, he discussed an analogy drawn by Dr. Allan Meltzer of Carnegie-Mellon University: "Dr. Meltzer refers to state government's role in the economy as that of the skipper of a rowboat on a stream. The skipper cannot change the direction of the river's current; nor can he, except perhaps in a Don Quixote fashion, attempt to move up river against that current. What the skipper can do is assure that the rowboat is moving on as straight a course down the stream as possible, rather than towards one shoreline or the other. He also can row the boat slower or faster. In other words, state governments, on their own, cannot move against the currents of national and international economic forces, but they can attempt to steer the ship of the state on a narrow, steady and straight course, taking maximum advantage of these national and international economic forces as they affect the currents."[37]

That is perhaps the best description of what Thornburgh has done. The Ben Franklin Partnership, for instance, is an excellent program, but its role is to accelerate developments already under way in the marketplace. Even in that role, its impact will only become clear over a 10- to 20-year period. Pennsylvania is much better positioned for the 1990s than it was for the 1980s, and programs like the Ben Franklin Partnership have certainly pushed that adjustment along—both economically and psychologically. Even Pittsburgh, which has been hit so hard by the decline of the steel industry, is remarkably well positioned—thanks largely to local public- and private-sector leadership over the last two decades, but with an intelligent assist from the Thornburgh administration.

The unsolved problems remain the urban ghettos and the many towns that once lived off steel, coal, or a single manufacturer. Thornburgh's enterprise zones and Renaissance Communities program need to be brought up to scale. In addition, a development bank designed to help manufacturers restructure might have helped a few more plants survive, or helped a few more steel plants carve out profitable niches as minimills.

The major criticism leveled by Thornburgh's opposition had to do with his fiscal conservatism. He was too cautious, critics argue, too slow to make major investments in social programs, in major redevelopment projects, and in efforts to help the state's beleaguered manufacturers. "Certainly in

Thornburgh's first term it was critical that he be very tight with the purse strings, because our state had a terrible reputation; it was poorly run," says Rep. Tom Murphy, not one of Thornburgh's harsher critics. "But I think in his second four years he probably could have become a little more of a risk taker. While I think we've made enormous improvements in the last five years, there was never the sense of urgency that there could have been from the Thornburgh administration."

Thornburgh's response is simple. "The key thing in most of what we're doing is leveraging private-sector investment," he argues. "It goes back to two things we have always accepted as givens. One, you're not going to solve these problems by throwing money at them; your resources are limited. And two, the key decisions are going to be made by the private sector."

There is truth in both arguments. Thornburgh's economic programs were intelligently devised to change private-sector investment patterns, and they appear to have succeeded. With programs such as the Ben Franklin Partnership or the Local Development Districts, it is probably better to go slowly and to make sure they are working properly, as Thornburgh did, than to invest too much money too quickly. Indeed, too much money too soon sometimes enables communities to avoid the difficult tasks of building local capacity and changing private-sector behavior.

But in other areas—distressed communities, dislocated workers, and mature industries—Thornburgh's fiscal conservatism did hurt. Democratic spending proposals such as PennPRIDE, on the other hand, would not have produced the necessary long-term change. Pennsylvania is probably a rare case in which the bitter battles between two partisan political parties produced better results than either party could have produced on its own. Constant pressure from the Democrats pushed Thornburgh to do more than he might otherwise have done. But his fiscal conservatism and emphasis on the private sector ensured that the Democrats' initiatives were pared down to manageable size and intelligent design.

The Politics of Economic Development

Thornburgh did not get a lot of credit for his economic development work. It is very difficult to translate economic development programs into political capital. The public tends to judge a governor based on the performance of the economy, not on his or her attempt to affect that performance. And through most of Thornburgh's term, Pennsylvania's economy was in trouble.

By naming his major program after Ben Franklin, Thornburgh did create an effective symbol of what he was trying to do. But its power was limited to a fairly elite constituency. To most voters the Ben Franklin Partnership remained an abstraction. To Pennsylvania's huge blue-collar constituency, it was a symbol of their abandonment. State Rep. Tom Murphy, who sits on the Partnership board, is routinely attacked by other Democrats for his involvement with the program. "In the kind of districts most of us represent in Pittsburgh, technology in some ways is a threat," he explains. "It causes antagonism. It's killing jobs. I have ten to 15 people a day coming to my office looking for jobs. They don't want to hear that four years from now there's going to be a wonderful software industry in Pittsburgh. Both of my Democratic opponents in the last election used the technology issue as a criticism of me. They would say I spend too much time worrying about technology, that I should be more interested in creating more traditional jobs."

The lesson here is that economic development efforts alone are not enough to create a broad-based political coalition. They must be complemented by programs designed specifically to bring the poor, the disadvantaged, and the dislocated into the growth process. Thornburgh not only failed to do this, he deliberately cultivated an image which alienated these constituencies.

This leads to the second lesson of Thornburgh's experience: it is virtually impossible to communicate an activist economic agenda if one's dominant message is antigovernment. Thornburgh was elected as a moderate Republican, but his priorities were cutting spending, cutting taxes, and cutting down the size of government. After Reagan's election, he supported the president down the line. As a result, when Thornburgh finally began to talk about economic development in 1983 and 1984, it so contradicted his image as a Reaganite that the media and the public virtually ignored it.

"If you listened to Thornburgh's political rhetoric, you reached one conclusion," says Robert Coy. "But if you looked at what he did, you reached another conclusion. I think when you get right down to it, he is simply a pragmatic guy, who had no choice but to deal with the economy."

Thornburgh himself bears this analysis out. He defends the Reagan record on cutting taxes and spending, but argues that Republicans must now move beyond that to a more proactive agenda. "I'm an activist in a way that does not involve the classic tax-spend-borrow cycle," he says. "I think government has a role as a partner and a facilitator. Decisions made by private investors and employers are going to create economic growth, but government can be a catalytic agent that can provide the tip-over component in a particular decision. That's where the real interplay between business and government ought to be."

Thornburgh admits that this view puts him in close company with many Democratic governors. (And, he adds, their fiscal moderation puts them in close company with him.) He also acknowledges that his views put some distance between himself and the conservatives who captured the Republican party in 1980. "It is far easier to dramatize a political ideology or a set of principles in vivid terms—cut out this agency, slash that tax, toss out those regulations," he says. "That is the Reagan revolution, stage one, and I think the argument can well be made that it has run its course. Now you have to get beyond that, and begin to fine tune the message and build on those successes. 'More of the same' is not a credible platform for any Republican candidate in 1988. That doesn't mean repudiating, discrediting, turning your back on what the president has accomplished. It just means realizing that you can never put your foot in the same river twice."

ARKANSAS: THE EDUCATION MODEL

It is October 1986, two weeks before election day, and Arkansas's favorite form of entertainment is in full swing. Six hundred Washington County Democrats have turned out for barbecued chicken, baked beans, and an evening of politics in the Springdale Rodeo Association Hall. Television cameras crowd the entryway, which is lined with photos of the Rodeo Association's past chairmen in their western shirts and cowboy hats. But inside there are no cameras. Stepping inside the cavernous hall is like stepping back 30 years, back into a time before television changed American politics. Hundreds of people mill about, their chests covered with campaign buttons. Candidates work the crowd, shaking hands and asking after relatives. The noise is terrific.

After everyone gets their chicken and beans, the speeches begin. The lost art of political oratory is alive and well in the rural South, and here in Washington County the crowd is looking forward to two of the best: Gov. Bill Clinton and Sen. Dale Bumpers. But first they have to listen to the amateurs, the Democratic candidates for sheriff and judge and half a dozen other open slots. They wait patiently, sitting for hours after the chicken gets cold.

Bill Clinton is a large man, two inches over six feet and a solid two hundred pounds. The first baby boomer to serve as a governor, he was originally elected in 1978, at the tender age of 32. But tonight he is 40, well seasoned by his four previous campaigns for governor. His hair is flecked with gray, and the wrinkles that crease his eyes when he smiles are beginning to look permanent.

Clinton's topic this night, as it has been throughout the campaign, is economics and education. Arkansas is caught in the midst of a swirl of changes sweeping through the international economy, he tells his listeners. In areas where foreign competition is no threat, the state is experiencing dramatic job growth. ("So far the Japanese have not figured out how to import chickens into Arkansas.") But "the people in our state whose livelihoods are subject to foreign competition and who can't compete are really suffering"—those who work in the timber industry, the paper plants, the cut-and-sew shops, and of course the farmers.

"I submit to you that the job of the governor of this state—not me, any governor—would be to try to make those changes which will open up opportunity and beat back those problems," Clinton says. "And I believe there are only two ways to do that. First, we have to create a nationally competitive system of education—and that is what we're trying to do. When you strip away all the controversy and all the people who don't agree with me about teacher testing, and you get everybody down to the lick log and ask everybody what they really think is true, even the people who don't agree with me will have to admit that in the last three years there have been dramatic improvements in education. . . . There is a whole new atmosphere about education sweeping this state."

He accelerates now, his voice raised, his fist poised to pound the podium. "Do you think it's an accident that we've got 87 percent of the schools with computer classes? Do you think it's an accident that 85 percent of the schools already offer 38 units? Do you think it's an accident that you've got more foreign language and science and math and music and art than you had before?

"No! It was because it was required and there was a deadline and we were moving forward!" The crowd roars.

Clinton goes on to talk about the poor, rural school districts that have raised their property taxes and hired more teachers to teach more subjects, to meet his education standards. He talks about the shortage of state revenues caused by economic problems on the farm and in the oil fields, but he promises to find more money next year.

Again his voice picks up: "I have been attacked all over this state because we gave 24 cents on the dollar, 24 cents off the sales tax dollar, to higher education, community colleges, and vo-tech schools! And I plead guilty. I plead guilty!" (Roar.)

"In the 1980 census Arkansas had only 9.7 percent of its people over 25 with four-year college degrees." He is riled up now, speaking rapidly, banging the podium. "It was the lowest in the country. The next lowest was Kentucky with 11.1 percent. And the plain evidence in every state in this country is that you must have a higher threshold of people with college degrees if you want low unemployment—not because most of the new jobs in the economy will require college degrees; most of 'em won't. But because most of them will be created by entrepreneurs who have that kind of education.

"So I plead guilty. I want more kids coming to the University of Arkansas! I want more people going to West Arkansas Community College in Fort Smith! I want more people flooding into this vo-tech school in Springdale that's done a brilliant job of training people for the modern economy! That's what I want, and I plead guilty of putting money into it, and the Arkansas economy is benefiting because of it! So if you think that we ought to choke the life out of every other kind of education, then you ought to support my opponent. But if you want to keep going like we're going, if you like that engineering school down there in Fayetteville that I've been attacked for funding, if you like this new truck-driving program we put in here at the vo-tech school that's already getting two hundred people guaranteed jobs a year from J.B. Hunt alone—one company [bang!]—then support me, and we'll keep 'em goin'!"

The crowd is with him every step of the way, and when he finally finishes, it rewards him with a standing ovation. It is an amazing sight—amazing, not that Bill Clinton can bring a crowd to its feet, but that he can do so by talking about education. This is the stuff of Rotary Club luncheons. It is the kind of material that, in normal times, when spoken by normal politicians, puts people to sleep. But Bill Clinton has pounded the podium and raised his voice and brought the crowd roaring to its feet. Welcome to southern politics in the 1980s.

The Arkansas Context

To understand Arkansas politics, it helps to start with the basics. This is a poor, rural state. In per capita income, it bounces around between 47th and 49th, competing with Mississippi and West Virginia. Nearly half of its 2.3 million people live in towns of 2,500 people or less.[1] Over 40 percent of the adult population has never graduated from high school.[2]

You feel this in Arkansas within hours of arriving. Little Rock, the capital city, has only 180,000 people, yet it is more than double the size of the next-largest city, Fort Smith. To an outsider, Little Rock is a small, sleepy town. It takes five minutes to drive in from the airport, another five to drive across downtown. Although the residents focus on the new construction and bright future, I noticed the vacant lots and old buildings, and felt like I had stepped into the past.

State government gives one the same feeling. The Statehouse is a smaller replica of the Capitol in Washington, but it faces no sweeping vista, just a vacant lot and an old building that evokes the 1930s. State legislators are paid only $7,500 a year. They meet in regular session only once every two years, for a month or two (though special sessions have become common in between). The governor, who was until 1986 elected to two-year terms, earns only $35,000 a year. (Before 1975, the figure was $10,000.) The bureaucracy, too, is a throwback. The Department of Finance and Administration does not even have the capacity to estimate lost revenues from tax breaks, which the legislature hands out like candy.[3]

Like Ireland, Arkansas exports much of its talent. But in politics, its best and brightest find considerable outlets at home. "People in Arkansas love politics," explains John Ward, former Gov. Winthrop Rockefeller's public relations director and biographer. "They love a fight. We still have political fish fries and chicken cookouts and you go speak at picnics. It's still pretty old-fashioned—you almost get up on a stump in your shirtsleeves. And people like that stuff."

Perhaps because there are so few other outlets for those with talent and ambition, Arkansas has produced some first-rate politicians over the years. Sen. William Fulbright was a giant. Dale Bumpers, who defeated him, is considered by many the best speaker in the Senate. Clinton, a former Rhodes scholar, has been touted as presidential material ever since his election at age thirty-two.

Arkansas is not a traditional deep South state. It has always been more populist on economic issues than much of the South, no doubt because its economy was dominated more by small farms than by plantations. And despite Gov. Orval Faubus's confrontation with President Eisenhower over desegregation, Arkansas made an earlier break with segregationist politics than most southern states. The man responsible was Winthrop Rockefeller, who beat Faubus in 1966 to become the first Republican governor since Reconstruction.

Rockefeller, who moved to Arkansas in 1953 after a messy divorce, once described what he found as "a massive inferiority complex."[4] He ran in 1966 as a progressive, an integrationist, and a reformer, and he spent enough of his own money to win. Ironically, his two victories did less to create a Republican party than to reform the Democratic party.

Before Rockefeller's election, explains Ward, "the Democratic party was controlled by good ol' boys whose fortune depended upon being in some control of state affairs. The great thing Winthrop Rockefeller did was he had the prestige and the leadership and the wealth to break down the system. He starved the good ol' boys away." By defeating the Democratic segregationists, Rockefeller also paved the way for a Democrat who favored integration, Dale Bumpers.

Bumpers's emergence was startling. An unknown country lawyer, his only previous elected position had been on the local school board. Until the final weeks of the primary campaign, he was at 2 to 3 percent in the polls. But he borrowed some money, sold some cattle, and used the funds to buy television time. "He'd hop up on a stool with a yellow note pad and tape a 15-minute talk," remembers Ernest Dumas, an editorial writer and columnist for the *Arkansas Gazette*. "Nothing was ever redone, but he was just very, very good. He talked about bringing our people together, healing their wounds." In the primary he came in second to Faubus, who was attempting a comeback; in the runoff he demolished Faubus, and he has never been beaten since. As governor, he pushed through a tremendous amount of progressive legislation, much of it originally proposed by Rockefeller.

Like Bumpers, Bill Clinton was an instant star. Brilliant, gregarious, and a natural leader, he had always known he was headed for politics. He had attended Georgetown University in Washington, D.C., where he worked as an intern on Fulbright's staff. From there he went to Oxford as a Rhodes scholar, then to Yale Law School. In 1972, while still a law student, Clinton ran George McGovern's campaign in Texas. A committed, antiwar liberal who had supported McGovern long before he won the nomination, Clinton nevertheless realized that the McGovernites had lost touch with the American people. "What was so disturbing to the average American voter was not that he seemed so liberal on the war, but that the entire movement seemed unstable, irrational," he told *Washington Post* columnist David Broder. "The average person watching it on television in some small town in Arkansas, the kind of person who is the backbone of my support there, had the unsettling feeling that this campaign and this man did not have a core, a center, that was common to the great majority of the country."[5]

In 1973, Clinton returned home to teach law school at the University of Arkansas, and within a year he was running for Congress. Backed by a cadre of young liberals and labor activists, he almost defeated Republican Congressman John Paul Hammerschmidt, who had not had a tough race since his election in 1966. "Clinton was kind of the boy wonder that year," remembers Dumas. "John Paul Hammerschmidt was considered unbeatable, and this guy almost did it. That's what we all wrote about—Bill Clinton, here's the man to watch, the rising star."

Two years later Clinton easily won election as attorney general. After two years as an activist defender of consumer interests against the utilities, he walked into the governor's mansion. His youth was never a problem, says Dumas: "Here was this brilliant young man, Rhodes scholar, remarkable speaker, articulate, very warm. People thought this would be a feather in our cap."

Clinton was immediately touted by the national press, just as he had been in 1974 by the state press. One of the most intellectual of the governors, he can talk in depth on almost any issue. "Pity the poor devil who gets into a debate with Bill Clinton," wrote Arkansas columnist Frank Fallone after a 1984 interview with Clinton. "The governor would have Walter Mondale and Ronald Reagan cowering in fear after the first 15 minutes."[6]

Perhaps Clinton's greatest asset, however, is that he is a born politician. He thrives on the handshaking and elbow-rubbing that are the backbone of politics in Arkansas, and people bask in his warmth. Rather than wearing him down, the personal contact seems to rev him up. He is as comfortable and natural telling jokes with the good ol' boys as discussing international economic problems with a group of professors. Among governors today, he is virtually unparalleled at either.

The First Term

During Clinton's first term, in 1979 and 1980, he was in many ways the epitome of the crusading young liberal. He brought in a team of youthful activists and introduced a blizzard of new legislation.

Clinton's first priority, as in his later terms, was education. In a poor state like Arkansas, the low education levels of the work force are perhaps the biggest stumbling block to economic growth. In the past, when the state was dependent upon agriculture, timber, and manufacturing plants brought in from the North, education was not so important. But in the information age, when innovation is the key to economic growth, quality educational institutions are critical. As former banking commissioner Marlin Jackson puts it: "You can't have a bunch of uneducated, illiterate people running a bunch of high-tech companies and high-tech farms."

When Clinton came into office, Arkansas was last in the nation in education spending per child, in teacher salaries, and in percentage of college graduates.[7] This reflected its state and local tax burden, which, per capita, was also the lowest in the nation.[8] "From an educational standpoint, the average child in Arkansas would be much better off attending the public schools of almost any other state in the country," reported a public education commission established by the legislature.[9]

Clinton pushed through budget increases of 40 percent over two years for elementary and secondary education, the largest in the state's history. (Economic problems forced some cuts in the second year.) He raised teacher salaries by almost $2,000, required applicants for teacher certification to pass the National Teacher Exam, and created a summer residence school for gifted children, at which he and his wife taught. Finally, he introduced standardized tests to measure the performance of public school students, to see just how bad the problems were.[10]

Clinton also tackled economic development. Since the 1950s, when Governor Faubus created the Arkansas Industrial Development Commission (AIDC), Arkansas had been a national leader in smokestack chasing. Winthrop Rockefeller, who served as the first chairman of AIDC, used his own money to supplement salaries and brought in some of the best talent in the country. With its low wages, low taxes, and pioneering use of development and revenue bonds, Arkansas was successful in luring textile plants, metal shops, and other branch plants from the North.

By the late seventies, however, these same plants were beginning to pick up and head overseas. Soon after Clinton's primary victory in May

1978, Steve Smith, his policy aide in charge of economic development, got to know Michael Barker and Robert Wise at CSPA. They fed him the early results of David Birch's work, as well as their evolving grow-your-own notions about economic development. Soon Arkansas had become something of a laboratory for CSPA, and Clinton had become Wise and Barker's chief sponsor at the National Governors Association, which housed CSPA and was still dominated by smokestack-chasing governors.

Clinton and Smith viewed the AIDC recruitment staff as little more than "entertainment directors for visiting industrialists," Smith remembers. "They had these nice cars and jobs and expense accounts, and they liked taking the boys out to the bars and tellin' 'em why they ought to come to Arkansas." Clinton changed the name of AIDC to the Department of Economic Development and downgraded the recruitment effort. He set up a small-business division to provide consulting for entrepreneurs, an agriculture division to fund small farm projects and promote agricultural exports, and a community development division to help local communities organize themselves and promote their own economic development. He forced Local Development Districts funded by the Economic Development Administration and Ozark Regional Commission to use their money to help new and small businesses, as Pennsylvania later did. He deposited state funds in banks according to a new formula that encouraged lending in Arkansas. And he tried unsuccessfully to get the state's public pension fund managers interested in investing in Arkansas businesses."

Clinton's strategy was extremely controversial. The veterans at AIDC and their constituents out in the local Chambers of Commerce were furious. In 1980, they supported Clinton's Republican opponent, who hammered the governor for ignoring industrial recruitment. "This is a state that's still very paranoid about its share of industrial development," says Rob Middleton, who directs the AIDC Community Development Division today. "That's just a very powerful and popular notion. It bombed real bad when he was perceived to discount all that."

Education and economic development were not the only targets for Clinton and his band of reformers, however. They cracked down on welfare cheaters, reformed the food stamp program, and used the money they saved to expand services for children and the elderly. They instituted an aggressive program to encourage energy conservation and the development of renewable resources. They continued to ride herd on utility rates, as Clinton had during his two years as attorney general. And they set up a network of rural health clinics around the state.[12]

Politically, Clinton was too aggressive for his own good. By the end of his first term, he had managed to offend virtually every major business interest in the state. The local Chambers of Commerce were angry about his reorientation of AIDC. The doctors were angry about his rural health

initiative, which largely bypassed them. The trucking and poultry industries were angry about the higher taxes he had imposed on trucking to pay
for road repairs. The timber industry was furious about hearings he held
on clear-cutting.

Part of the problem was simply the youth and inexperience of Clinton's
staff. "He had a staff that was literally out to see where they could pick a
fight, and see who they could make mad," says Tom McRae, former chief
of staff to Governor Bumpers, now president of the Winthrop Rockefeller
Foundation. "There were a whole lot of things they did that were dumb,
and insensitive."

Smith agrees: "We probably did too much head bashing in the first
term. Part of it was that people like me on the staff were sort of smart-ass,
and angered a lot of people. We were after every dragon in the land." Both
McRae and Smith cite the hearings on clear-cutting as an example. "I used
language like 'corporate criminals,'" says Smith, "which did not really
endear the governor to the timber companies."

Another problem, again stemming partly from inexperience, was Clinton's inclination to put good policy over good politics. The classic example
was a major highway repair program he pushed through, financed by
raising the gas and tire taxes, increasing vehicle license taxes, and raising
the title-transfer fee paid when people bought a car. The biggest part of the
package was the license tax, which virtually doubled for most people—
from about $15 to $30.

The increase did not appear terribly controversial at the time. But in
Arkansas, the "car tag" tax is an object of hatred. Every year car owners
must go down to the courthouse, prove that they have had their car in-
spected in the previous 30 days, prove that they have paid their personal
property tax for the previous year, submit an assessment of their current
personal property, and—finally—pay their license tax. "It's a nightmare—
you stand in line forever," explains Dumas. "People in the countryside
were outraged when they'd finally get to the end of the line and be hit with
this increase. That's all anybody talked about for a year, in the countryside." Particularly in poor, rural areas, people drove old cars and pickup
trucks, which got the stiffest increases because of their weight. To make
matters worse, the title-transfer fee hit the rural poor hardest, because they
often bought an old car, drove it until it broke down, and then bought
another one.

As the anger built, there was loud talk of repeal. But Clinton stood firm.
Jodie Mahony, a state legislator from El Dorado, Arkansas, remembers a
scene from the 1980 campaign, when Clinton came to talk at the local
electricians' hall. "He was explaining how the license increase would save
the working man money, as opposed to the gas tax increase," Mahony
remembers. "And they said, 'Governor, we know all that, but we told you

we didn't want it.' He wanted to do what was best, not what people wanted."

Clinton's Republican opponent, businessman Frank White, blasted Clinton for the car tag and title-transfer taxes. He also hit him for not bringing enough plants to Arkansas. And he blamed Clinton, who was publicly close to President Carter, for the fact that Carter put thousands of Cuban refugees from the Mariel boatlift at Fort Chafee, Arkansas. When the Cubans broke out and rioted in the streets, White put the footage in his campaign ads and hammered Clinton for not standing up to the president.

The campaign subtext was equally important. White painted Clinton as too young, too liberal, and too big for his britches. He criticized him for bringing eastern liberals in to run his administration and charged that he was only using Arkansas as a stepping-stone to national office. He exploited the symbolism of Clinton's administration: his youthful, bearded aides, and the fact that his wife had kept her maiden name. "It was ridiculous," says Mahony, "but those were the burning issues of 1980: Cubans, car tags, and Hillary not taking his name."

The business interests Clinton had alienated gave generously to White, and he used the money for a heavy media buy in the waning days of the campaign. His major spot, hammering away at Cubans and car tags, went unanswered. In retrospect, Clinton was clearly overconfident. The polls had him far ahead as late as mid-October, and no one—not even White—believed he would lose. But as the voters swung to Reagan in the final days, so they swung to White. Arkansas experienced the greatest shift from Carter in 1976 to Reagan in 1980 of any state.[13] In 1978 and 1980, voters all across the nation threw the liberal rascals out, and Clinton became yet another casualty.

The loss stung Clinton badly. But it taught him a fundamental lesson: that a reformer must find a way to do what his constituents want, not what he thinks they need. "If I had told the people I was going to repeal the car license, I wouldn't have been defeated," he said later. "The fact that I did it and the fact that I kept telling people, 'You gotta like it,' struck most people as an act of arrogance."[14] Clinton also learned—many would say too well—that he had to be more cautious, to pick his fights.

In the 1982 campaign, a rematch with White, Clinton made a point of communicating his newfound humility to the public. He apologized for trying to "lead without listening."[15] His wife quietly changed her name, to Hillary Clinton. Clinton also fired back whenever White went negative. (Another lesson of 1980, he told a group of Florida Democrats, was that "if your opponent picks up a hammer at you, you need to pick up a meat ax and cut off his arm.")[16] In a brutal campaign, with the economy again hurting the incumbent, Clinton won 55 percent of the vote.

The Education Reform Agenda

Clinton learned one other thing from his 1980 defeat: "I learned that if you do a lot of things, and you talk about a lot of different things while you're doing it, the perception may be that you haven't done anything. You have to be able to give a little clearer sense of direction. If you want to get broad, popular support for what you're doing, people have to be able to understand or explain it in a sentence or two. And I think to the folks out there a lot of what I did came across just as a lot of good government things that didn't have any unifying theme that people could really buy into." The second time around, Clinton built his administration around two themes: first, education reform; then, economic development.

Clinton's standardized tests had shown just how bad the schools were. On the first test, fourth graders scored in the 44th percentile, meaning that 56 percent of all students nationwide did better than the average Arkansas student. Eighth graders scored in the 38th percentile.[17] The longer they had been in school, the worse Arkansas students did—a devastating comment on Arkansas schools.

The lowest scores came in Arkansas's many small, rural school districts. With the fewest students of any Old South state, Arkansas had twice as many districts as its closest rival. Half of all districts had fewer than five hundred students—not in one school, but in the entire district. Ninety districts had fewer than three hundred students.[18]

With small schools and limited resources, rural districts could not afford to offer many classes. In 1982–1983, according to the *Arkansas Gazette*, 217 public high schools (roughly half of those in the state) offered no physics; 265 offered no advanced biology, 177 no foreign language, 126 no chemistry, and 164 no advanced math (beyond algebra II). Fifty-seven districts offered only one of these five subjects; 23 offered none.[19] "Typically, in a small, rural school, the boys would be getting two to three hours a day of agriculture, and the girls would be getting home economics," says State Rep. Gloria Cabe.

Consolidation of rural districts is a recurring theme in Arkansas politics. In 1983, it emerged again. Worried about the threat, the administrators of small school districts convinced a legislator to introduce a bill creating a citizens' committee to recommend new standards of accreditation. They saw this as a way to blunt the consolidation drive, and they were successful.

Knowing that he had only one year to pass legislation (with two-year terms, controversial issues are difficult to handle in the second year), Clinton appointed his wife to chair the committee. Hillary Clinton is no ordinary politician's wife. A lawyer, a veteran of the McGovern campaign and the Watergate impeachment committee staff, she is very much a partner in the governorship. She and Clinton met at Yale Law School, where, according to those who knew them, she was the better student. Slight, attractive, and all business, she has become, like her husband, an excellent speaker. And through her work on education, she has transformed herself from an extreme negative, in 1980, to a tremendous asset today. Many argue, quite seriously, that she is more popular than her husband.

The Clintons' goal was a fundamental reform bill, which would upgrade accreditation standards, raise teachers' salaries, lengthen the school day, and improve curricula. To build a constituency, Hillary Clinton took her committee on the road, holding hearings in all 75 of Arkansas's counties. By her estimate, ten thousand people showed up to voice their opinions. One issue came through loud and clear: raise teachers' salaries, yes, but first get rid of incompetent teachers.

It is difficult for an outsider to understand how large this problem looms in Arkansas. Hillary Clinton's committee was deluged with horror stories about poor teachers; some parents gave them letters teachers had sent home full of spelling and grammatical errors. Arkansas teachers are of course the product of Arkansas schools, which—in many of the poor, rural sections of the state—is the heart of the problem. Principals in these schools often ask applicants to write a paragraph about their educational philosophy, just to see if they can write. Failure rates on National Teacher Exams, taken by teaching applicants, were over 50 percent at some teaching colleges.[20]

This created intense pressure to weed out incompetent teachers by making existing teachers pass a competency test. Clinton decided to introduce a teacher-testing bill to go with the new education standards his wife's committee had recommended. He also introduced three tax increases to pay for more teachers and higher salaries: a one-cent hike in the sales tax, an increase in the severance tax on natural gas (the lowest in the nation), and an increase in the corporate income tax. Here he was stymied by the Arkansas constitution, which requires a three-fourths vote of the legislature to raise any tax other than the sales tax. Predictably, only the sales tax increase passed.

The final package mandated that 70 percent of the new sales tax revenue be used to raise teachers' salaries. It required that schools offer chemistry, physics, advanced math, computer science, foreign languages, "global studies" (a cross between geography and international affairs), special courses for "gifted and talented" children, fine arts, and instrumental music. It mandated smaller classes, a longer school day and year, tougher requirements for high school graduation, and kindergarten in all districts. It raised the legal dropout age from 15 to 16.

Rather than denying graduation to those who failed a test, as some states have done, Arkansas's package denied promotion to any eighth grader who failed the standardized exam—the first such law in the nation. The idea, according to Hillary Clinton, is to catch problems before students reach high school. If students fail two years in a row, they must be given some form of alternative education. For those who fail the standardized test at any grade level, third, sixth, or eighth, schools must set up remedial programs. Any school in which more than 15 percent of the students fail the tests must develop a plan to improve its performance. If its students fail to improve within two years, the state can force changes in school management—another national first.

"We've tried to prod the system, to build expectations, because these schools are going to be judged by how their kids do," says Mrs. Clinton. "What gets kids learning is not a test, but the expectations of their teachers and schools, and the efforts made by their teachers and schools."

The reform legislation also set up a committee to examine teacher education and evaluation. The results included new training programs for evaluators, new standards for teacher colleges, and a requirement that every school district evaluate its teachers three times a year. In addition, any college in which more than 20 percent of graduates fail the National Teacher Exam will be put on probation and threatened with the loss of state accreditation if improvements are not made within three years.

The Clintons pulled out all the stops to get the reform package through the legislature. They raised money from the business community for ads in the media. They gave out thousands of blue ribbons, asking people to wear them to broadcast their theme: "Our kids need a blue-ribbon education." And they drummed home the message that education meant jobs. "Do you believe that God meant for us to drag up the rear of the nation's economy forever?" the governor asked in his speeches.[21]

The teacher competency test overshadowed all other issues. The struggle for education reform became a battle between the governor and the state's largest union, the Arkansas Education Association—a battle that symbolized the growing conflict between the public interest and the most powerful Democratic interest groups.

"I think the teachers felt like they were being bit by their own dog," says Diane Blair, a friend of the Clintons and a professor of political science at the University of Arkansas. "The AEA is the group that had been fighting for years and years to try to upgrade education. They had been doing that long, slow, painful education process. And then, finally, they have a feeling we're getting some of these things, but it's out of our skin and off our backs. They felt exploited."

Many teachers believed the governor was using them as scapegoats. By forcing them to take a test, they felt, he was accusing every one of them of being ignorant and incompetent. When teacher jokes began circulating, along the lines of Polish jokes, it did not help.

AEA President Ed Bullington charged that Clinton used teacher testing "for political popularity, to secure his political base." He argued that the test could not effectively weed out incompetent teachers. In its place, the AEA supported a "very extensive evaluation program," by which administrators could pinpoint incompetent teachers and either force them to improve or fire them. "But just to characterize the whole teaching profession in Arkansas as being deficient or being suspect in those areas was wrong," Bullington said. "It has been very demoralizing. We're having good teachers leave the state out of frustration, we're having teachers quit, and we're discouraging students from becoming teachers by giving the profession a negative image."

The Clintons stressed repeatedly that the test was not to evaluate teachers, but simply to find those who could not spell, multiply, divide, and so on. They pointed to the new evaluation program as evidence of their commitment to broader efforts to weed out teachers who might be able to read and write but needed improvement in other areas.

The test itself was quite simple. It measured reading, grammar, basic math, and basic knowledge in each teacher's subject area. To pass, teachers needed to demonstrate only eighth-grade levels of competence. They could take the test repeatedly between March 1985 and June 1987, and the state offered a variety of programs, including classes on educational television, to help them improve. In addition, teachers could get credit for passing the subject area test simply by taking six units of college courses in their area. Some teachers felt the test should have been far tougher. I talked with many teachers who were bitter about the test, but not one felt that those who failed should be allowed to keep teaching.

Despite the eighth-grade level of the exam, 10 percent of those who took it when it was first administered failed. In every subsequent test, roughly 10 percent failed. Overall, 1,315 teachers—3.5 percent of the state's total—had to leave teaching because they could not pass the test.[22] By far the highest proportion of failures came in areas that were heavily black, fueling charges that the test would purge the system of black teachers. Clinton insisted that the test was colorblind; it was checked carefully for racial bias, he noted, by a committee that included 12 blacks. He argued that the black failure rate simply revealed the woeful education provided blacks in Arkansas, and promised that his reform package would change that. He also pointed to the state's efforts to help those teachers who failed, to upgrade their skills. "If we can pull this off politically," he said, "it will make a statement to the whole country about the potential for real equality of performance between blacks and whites."

To make his case, Clinton pointed to the experience of the University of Arkansas at Pine Bluff (UAPB), most of whose students are black. In 1980, when a certification exam was first given to college graduates who wanted to teach, only 42 percent of UAPB students taking the test passed. Chancellor Lloyd Hackley used the results to force through a total revision of the curriculum, which required all students to spend two years in a kind of preparatory program to bring them up to speed, called University College. In 1986, 85 percent of UAPB students taking the test passed. Nursing students went from a 20 percent pass rate to 100 percent on their licensing exam.[23] Hackley, who is black, argued passionately that discrimination was no longer the primary barrier holding black students back; instead, he blamed low standards, low expectations, and practices such as automatic promotion from grade to grade.

In 1983, the National Education Association publicly condemned Clinton and called on a wide array of Democratic party, labor, and civil rights leaders to lean on the governor. Two years later, in an effort to repeal the testing bill, the union brought thousands of teachers to the Statehouse to lobby their legislators—so many that on one lobbying day the Little Rock schools had to shut down. The union played on fears that the test would decimate black teachers and passed out bumper stickers that read No More Clintons in '86.

The AEA twisted enough arms to push repeal through the House. "One of the threats that the AEA can make good on is 'We'll find you an opponent,'" says Diane Blair. "You see, a lot of these guys ordinarily just don't even have any opposition, and the mere thought of having an opponent is enough to make them buckle. The AEA can't always beat 'em, but they can put them through the pain and suffering. And they did beat a couple of them."

When the House passed repeal, Clinton went over the politicians' heads. He put an ad on radio asking people to call their legislators. "It was a madhouse," remembers Mahony. "The telephone switchboard was on from dawn to midnight." The bill died in the Senate.

In the court of public opinion, Clinton's victory was even more decisive. Polls showed 60 to 65 percent of those surveyed favoring teacher testing, with only 25 percent opposed.[24] Other states have since implemented their own teacher competency tests, and both the National Education Association and the American Federation of Teachers have changed their positions to support everything *short* of a competency test—tests for teacher applicants, teacher evaluations, easier firing, and so on. At a time when the Mondale campaign was bringing the issue of interest-group captivity to the fore, Clinton's stand also tagged him as a Democrat who was not afraid to stand up to a powerful Democratic constituency.

The Early Returns

Once the teacher test had been given, attention finally began to shift to the rest of Clinton's education program. From 1983 through 1985, there was a tremendous surge in education spending, fed by the new sales tax. Average teacher salaries went up by $4,400, the fastest growth rate in the nation.[25] Arkansas moved up from 50th to 46th in teacher salaries and from 50th to 47th in per pupil expenditures, according to a state-by-state analysis published by the Carnegie Foundation.[26] "Arkansas jumps out at you as the state that has made the greatest gains over the last two years in the variable that matters the most related to teaching," said the report's author, Emily Feistritzer.

By 1985, Arkansas was actually above the national average in teacher pay as a percent of per capita income, according to data gathered by Diane Blair, whose book *Arkansas Politics and Government: Do the People Rule?* includes a chapter on the education reform effort. Per pupil expenditures as a percentage of per capita income rose to 91.2 percent of the national average.[27]

In addition to the new state money, Blair adds, 85 percent of Arkansas school districts increased their property tax rates to fund educational improvements—a move that requires a direct vote of the people. Roughly 65 districts consolidated with other districts between 1983 and 1987, bringing the total number of districts from about 385 to 329.[28] The rest scrambled to hire new teachers, construct new buildings, and offer new courses.

Perhaps the best way to understand the changes taking place is to look at a few of the rural school districts affected by the new standards. Lead Hill is a small town near the Missouri border, on the shores of Bull Shoals Lake. The entire school district has only 350 students, but community life in Lead Hill centers around its school. Its football and basketball games provide the area's major entertainment; its cafeteria is used for community suppers; its school buses do double duty transporting senior citizens. "Our folks did not want to lose the school," says school superintendent William Ernst. "They think a small school is the best method of delivering education to children, plus it's the center of activity for the entire community. So the bottom line was, we meet the standards or we consolidate."

By a 62 to 38 percent margin, Lead Hill voted virtually to double its property tax rates, to pay for everything needed to meet the standards. Even the retired population gave the increase a healthy majority.[29] "If it weren't for the standards, the taxes probably would not have passed," says Ernst.

Lead Hill has used the money to complete a new elementary facility and library, to add more classroom space, and to modernize other facilities. It has added classes in French, Spanish, art, and instrumental music; created new programs for the gifted and talented; and expanded programs for those with learning disabilities. The high school has hired a new science teacher so it can offer both physics and chemistry every year.

The process has not been without problems. "For six months, maybe even nine months, there was deep frustration over the teacher test," Ernst explains. "To what degree the classroom suffered from it, I don't know. But the quality of education does suffer when morale is low, and morale was low." There has also been frustration because "it is very difficult to do all the things that are necessary in the timeframe in which we have to meet them. But it's just like anything else—if you don't have a bottom line, chances are it probably won't happen."

Fordyce is a larger town, of about five thousand, in the pine belt of south central Arkansas. Dominated by the timber industry, it is small and dusty, its two-block-long downtown a symbol of better days. Thirty years ago, two of Fordyce's schools were white and two were black. Today they are fully integrated—two elementary schools, one junior high, and one high school.

With 1,480 students, Fordyce already offered most of the classes required under the new standards. Its biggest changes have been the new promotion and retention policies it adopted, which go even further than the state requirements. The school board started talking about stricter promotion policies back in 1981, two years before the statewide debate. But without the state effort, says superintendent Wanda Miles-Bell, it probably would not have gone forward. "We probably would have felt that no one would have stood behind us," she says. "And now we feel the state will stand behind us. Everybody's reading about education reform in the paper and hearing about it, and it's just a good opportunity for us to do what needs to be done."

Miles-Bell and her school board instituted mandatory tests at every grade level. Those who fail at the third, sixth, and eighth grades (after three chances at passing the test) are automatically held back, unless their teacher offers other evidence that they should be promoted. Those who fail at other grades are held back unless their parents insist that they be promoted. For all those who fail, teachers must prepare an individualized remedial program.

In 1986, the first year the new retention policy was put into effect, 27 out of 125 sixth graders failed the test. According to Miles-Bell, that came as a shock to the students. "They've discovered that we really mean business now—that they're not going to get to go on if they don't do the work, and that all that homework and those test assignments do in fact lead to something," she says.

The district held three weeks of summer school for third and sixth graders who failed their tests, the first time it had ever offered summer school. Both parents and students took the summer school seriously, and all but five of the sixth graders finally passed the test and were promoted.

"I cannot tell you how dramatic the change in our achievement scores has been," says Miles-Bell. Fourth graders went from the 42d and 36th national percentiles in reading and math in 1983–1984 to the 59th and 81st in 1985–1986, respectively. (This increase came in spite of a shift to a different standardized test, which was predicted to lower scores by seven percentile points.) Fifth graders went from the 32d and 31st to the 57th and 75th percentiles in reading and math, respectively. Sixth, seventh, and eighth graders made gains that were almost as dramatic.[30]

During the regular year, students are tested every week or so on basic skills. Teachers grumble about the paper work involved in giving and correcting tests. They also explain that they have to cut out more interesting material to make sure they have time to cover the basics. But they generally agree that the tests hold them accountable in a way that was not possible before.

Teachers also complain that the state has gone too far with some of its requirements. In DeQueen, Arkansas, for instance, the junior high school had to drop a speech class and a "how-to-study" class to make room for a "careers" course and additional physical education classes required by the state. In Little Rock the elementary schools had to let their social workers go, to hire the required counselors.

The biggest problem, however, has been financial. In 1985 and 1986, the Arkansas economy, like those of other farm states, went into recession. As a result, the state came up $25 to $30 million a year short in tax revenues budgeted for education. Just as the local districts geared up to meet the standards, their projected state funds were cut sharply. Teacher salary increases slowed, and by 1986 Arkansas was back in 48th place.[31] During the 1986 campaign, Clinton promised to come up with enough new revenues to make up for the shortfall, and in 1987 the legislature agreed to a tax-increase and spending-cut package that raised $50 to $60 million over two years.

It is easy to quibble with Clinton's program, whether on financial grounds or on questions of paper work and curriculum. What is hard to deny, however, is that it has had an enormous impact on how seriously Arkansans take education. Curtis Turner, Jr., the superintendent of schools in Delight, Arkansas, speaks for many when he says, "Education is a conversation piece at most dinner tables now. People all over are talking about it. They want their children to have the best education possible. I'm being asked to talk to civic groups, to be on panels to discuss the standards—how this movement is going to affect our school system, how it's going to affect the quality of education that the students are going to be able to receive."

Diane Blair, who has studied polling data on attitudes toward education, has found a remarkable turnaround. "In some respects," she says, "the major accomplishment of the Clinton education reforms is not in class hours per day and so on, but in the fact that he and his wife hit the road for the better part of a year, essentially preaching educational excellence, the inadequacies of our system, and what needed to be done. And public opinion changed. People decided, number one, that their schools were inadequate, and number two, that it was worth a commitment to do something about that." The 1986 election results support her thesis: Clinton, who sought to turn the election into a referendum on his education program, was the only gubernatorial candidate in either party who refused to consider some form of delay or weakening of the standards. He was reelected (over Frank White) with 64 percent of the vote.

The Winthrop Rockefeller Foundation has launched a three- to five-year study of the effects of the new standards, which will follow individual students in 15 school districts. Until its results are in, the only scorecard available is test scores—and they reflect more the climate of change than the actual reforms, because school districts did not have to meet the standards until the 1987–1988 school year. Between 1980 and 1985, average test scores in the fourth grade increased from the 44th percentile to the 61st. In the tenth grade, they went from the 43d percentile in 1982 to the 51st in 1985. In 1986, the state switched tests, which makes further comparisons difficult. But between 1986 and 1987, the upward movement continued.[32] In a separate reading test given to eleventh graders by the Southern Regional Education Board in 1986, Arkansas was the only southern state among five tested in which students scored above the national average. The same group, when tested in 1981 as sixth graders, had scored below the national average.[33]

These scores, of course, reveal a sobering truth: no matter how important they have been, Clinton's education reforms have done little more than bring Arkansas up to the level many other states reached long ago. They are a good beginning, but much more needs to be done—particularly in the state colleges and universities. "They are important because they are the first step, and the first step is often the most difficult to take," says Tom McRae of the Winthrop Rockefeller Foundation. "My concern is that they're creating a mentality of, 'Whew, now we've done educational reform, what do we do next?' What we have to do is keep it up. This sort of development is a 15-year process."

Adult and Vocational Education

Although Clinton has increased funding for higher education, he has not tackled the fundamental reform most observers agree is necessary. He has made significant efforts, however, in two other areas that have a direct impact on the state economy: adult illiteracy and vocational-technical education.

In 1983, estimates of functional illiteracy in Arkansas ran as high as 25 percent of the adult population.[34] Clinton more than tripled appropriations for adult education, from $1 million to $5.4 million a year, and enrollment in adult education rose from 12,800 to 30,000 in three years. By 1986, these programs were responsible for 15 percent of the high school degrees handed out in Arkansas.[35]

Clinton's goal of wiping out adult illiteracy may seem rudimentary, but it is terribly important. Two examples illustrate why. The first involves agriculture, where literacy would not seem to be critical. In 1976, the Winthrop Rockefeller Foundation awarded a grant to the Rosston Swine Cooperative, which ran an unprofitable hog co-op built ten years earlier with federal funds. "We assumed the major problem was poor management," says Tom McRae. "After two years of hard work, we solved the management problems in the co-op, but it continued to lose money, albeit at a much slower rate."[36]

Further research showed that the remaining problem was not management, but the farmers producing for the co-op: their pigs were inferior. The farmers were hardly incompetent; these were tough, wily operators. They had access to the latest publications of the Agriculture Extension Service on how to raise good hogs. The only problem, McRae discovered, was that they could not read them. "After a great deal of work, we developed systems that would tell the farmer in simple language and symbols what he needed to do each day," he says. "We were rewarded with a co-op that was profitable even in a declining industry."

The second example dates from 1986, when Governor Clinton ordered a study of where the Arkansas economy was heading in the 1990s. In the poorest area, the delta of eastern Arkansas, business people surveyed brought up the literacy problem constantly. Training programs are fine, they told study coordinator Craig Smith, "but you've got a whole base of people out there who can't be employed because of the literacy problem. Give us people who can read and write, and we'll train 'em."

The state system of vocational-technical schools posed a tougher problem than adult education, for bureaucratic reasons. In 1982, the Winthrop Rockefeller Foundation reported that the system was underfinanced, that its courses and equipment were obsolete, and that industry rarely used it. "Many vo-tech schools were created solely to advance the careers of individual legislators," the foundation said. "They provide job placements for some politicians' friends and associates. Little thought has been given to locating the schools with respect to population distribution, job opportunities, and industrial needs, or to their possible role in Arkansas's development."[37]

This situation was typical of many states. Reform required that politicians lay off instructors and close institutions—neither of which was easy to do. Yet in a period of rapidly changing technologies, outdated vo-tech schools not only waste taxpayers' money, they are a cruel hoax on those who attend them and are trained to perform jobs that no longer exist.

In 1981, Governor White reorganized the department in charge of vo-tech schools and brought in a new man, Dr. Barry Ballard, to run it. Between White and Clinton, funding for the vo-tech schools increased 78 percent over the next five years. By the end of 1986 Ballard had increased pay scales, upgraded equipment throughout the system, closed down 34 courses and created 40 new ones (out of a total of about 450). He had also put in place performance standards requiring that high school programs place 50 percent of their graduates in jobs within a year and adult programs place 70 percent—or be shut down. He was developing competency tests for graduates, to give instructors and administrators a way to judge how effective their courses were.

Two of Ballard's experiments are particularly innovative. The first provides vo-tech programs in the state prisons. According to Ballard, inmates who take both general (high school) equivalency degree (GED) courses and vo-tech courses have a five-year recidivism rate of only 7 percent, compared to 60 percent for those who do not participate. The second experiment involves an effort to take literacy courses, GED courses, and vo-tech courses right into the factories, tailoring them to individual industries. According to Ballard, the state performed this service for 150 companies in 1987.

New Economic Development Tools

If one had taken a snapshot of the Arkansas economy in the mid-1980s, one would have seen a picture of rapid transition. Every month seemed to bring a new plant closing. As the manufacturing, farm, and timber sectors sagged in 1985, unemployment bounced back up to the 9 percent range. For the first time in 50 years, land values dropped. Growth in per capita income, which had outpaced the national average for two decades, fell behind. Loan losses in Arkansas banks almost doubled, from about $75 million in 1984 to $136 million in 1986.[38]

Arkansas, in sum, was caught with a preponderance of industries that were losing out to foreign competition and a shortage of technology-based industries with potential for significant growth in world markets. Three key ingredients for these sunrise industries were lacking: a well-educated work force, a critical mass of research institutions, and sufficient risk capital to invest in new enterprises. While Clinton tackled the first problem with his education reform program, he crafted an economic package to deal with the last two.

In 1981, the legislature had created a task force to look at what the state should do in the area of science and technology. It had recommended a new Arkansas Science and Technology Authority (ASTA), whose mission was vaguely defined as helping to create a biotechnology corridor—perhaps by opening a research park—between the National Center for Toxicological Research and the handful of medical institutions in Little Rock, 30 miles to the north. Typically, however, the effort was hamstrung by the legislature's tightfistedness: it appropriated only $500,000 for the first two years.

The state hired John Ahlen, former science adviser to the Illinois legislative council, to run the new program. In early 1984, Ahlen called Belden Daniels. Daniels had briefly worked with Clinton's economic development chief, Robert Nash, when Nash was with the Winthrop Rockefeller Foundation. So Daniels, Nash, and Ahlen met at the airport one day. "It all clicked," says Ahlen, and from that meeting evolved the governor's economic development planning group. Working through the rest of 1984, the group—which expanded to include the banking commissioner, the head of AIDC, and the head of the Arkansas Housing Development Authority—crafted an economic package consisting of some 60 bills.

The group had neither the funds nor the inclination to create a research park. Indeed, Arkansas lacked the critical mass necessary to attract top research outfits to a park. Among the 50 states, it ranked 50th in per capita spending on research.[39] "On a list of the top 100 research *institutions* in the nation, the entire state of Arkansas—with all its research institutions lumped together—would rank 80th," says Ahlen.

To begin to attack the problem, Ahlen and his colleagues crafted legislation to give ASTA the power to make grants for both basic and applied research. The legislature appropriated $1.8 million for the first two years, and Clinton convinced them to add $3.4 million a year for projects related to economic development at universities and colleges—particularly projects that sought to transfer the technological expertise of academia into the business world.

Arkansas's shortage of capital is not as severe as its research deficit, but it is a problem. The working group decided the state needed to do three things: import more capital, keep more Arkansas capital at home, and make better use of the little capital it did have.

To import capital, they wrote legislation transforming the Arkansas Housing Development Authority into the Arkansas Development Finance Authority (ADFA) and giving it new powers to float bonds and make loans. Since most bonds are sold out of state, the result would be more capital flowing into Arkansas.

To keep more Arkansas capital at home, they wrote a bill that relaxed the traditional restraints on investments by public pension funds and encouraged them to invest at least 5 percent of their assets in Arkansas. By 1987, the pension funds had invested $150 million in SBA-guaranteed loans, certificates of deposit at banks that agreed to use the money for business loans, and below-market-rate loans to family farmers.

To put capital in Arkansas to better use, Daniels and his team wrote a series of bills allowing banks to invest in new areas. For instance, they allowed state-chartered banks to buy up to 25 percent of the stock in a business. Arkansas has a tight usury law, which prevents banks from charging interest rates high enough to justify many small-business loans. By allowing them to buy equity, the state has given them another incentive to loan to businesses—another way to get a return. To help family farmers, Clinton pushed through a bill allowing banks to hold farm land in foreclosure for up to ten years and to lease it back to farmers, with an option to repurchase the farm if their finances improved.

Clinton also created several new financial institutions, including a seed capital fund run by the Science and Technology Authority and a $1 million-a-year minority loan fund. He convinced AIDC to use $5 million a year of its federal community development block grant for loans to small and medium-sized businesses, in areas with high unemployment. His legislative package restructured a moribund business development corporation the state had helped create in the 1950s, the Arkansas Capital Corporation, and gave it access to low-interest loans from the state.

Finally, the economic development package authorized ASTA to fund small-business incubators. By 1988, ASTA had opened four university-based incubators and committed funds for four rural, community-based incubators.

Most legislators, who were accustomed to thinking of economic development as the process of luring manufacturing plants from the North, had trouble understanding the new package. But Clinton's only serious opposition came from Stephens, Inc., the largest investment bank outside Wall Street. Until the creation of ADFA, the agency that floats umbrella bonds for cities and counties, Stephens had a virtual monopoly on bond underwriting in the state. In a private meeting, Jack Stephens, one of the wealthiest men in America, told Clinton in plain language that he would not tolerate the creation of ADFA. Rather than intimidating Clinton, however, the confrontation lit a fire under him. "When we tried to get that legislation passed, they fought us tooth and nail," says one of his aides. "But we beat 'em. We beat 'em because people knew it was the right thing, and because we worked hard."

Clinton has taken a number of other initiatives in the economic arena. In 1983, he set up a Dislocated Worker Task Force, which brings together several government agencies, the AFL-CIO, and the private sector to respond to plant closings. He passed a law allowing workers to collect partial unemployment benefits under a "shared work" program, in which companies could put employees on half time to minimize layoffs. In 1987, he set up a Rural Development Action Team, made up of representatives from his major economic development institutions, to work with the ten most depressed rural counties in Arkansas. The state conducted studies of the local economy in each county, convinced local leaders to pull together an implementation committee, and using the studies as a base, helped the committees write community development plans. The Action Teams then promised to target state and federal resources on projects designed by the committees.

Perhaps the most important step Clinton has taken in rural development was not a government program, but support for a private-sector initiative launched by the Winthrop Rockefeller Foundation. The foundation has committed $5 million to a new development institution. Called the Southern Development Bancorporation, it is a holding company that will oversee a bank, a real estate development firm, a venture capital fund, a seed capital fund, and a staff of "enterprise agents" who will originate deals, train nascent entrepreneurs, and work with new companies.[40] The model is based loosely on the Shorebank Corporation in Chicago, whose officers have worked closely with the foundation to design and implement the strategy. (For a discussion of the Shorebank Corporation, see chapter 9.)

The Southern Development Bancorporation is perhaps the most radical experiment in rural economic development since the Tennessee Valley Authority. Its goal is to nurture home-grown businesses in rural and small-town Arkansas. It will even include one loan fund built on a model developed in Bangladesh, which makes small-business loans to low-income people, using a process that substitutes peer pressure for collateral.

The Clinton administration has helped the Southern Development Bancorporation raise $6 million from private investors, including $150,000 from the Arkansas Capital Corporation. Clinton's economic development chief has devoted a great deal of time to the project, and Clinton has promised that his finance agencies will act as coinvestors with the Bancorporation on individual projects. More important, Hillary Clinton is an active member of the Bancorporation's board.

Evaluating Clinton's Economic Development Record

Though it is too early to see many concrete results, Clinton's economic development program is moving in the right direction. There are problems: although Clinton has managed to gradually change the thinking of those running AIDC, the state still puts too many of its resources into smokestack chasing. The usury law, which limits interest on loans to five percentage points above the Federal Reserve Board's discount rate, continues to inhibit both long-term, fixed-rate loans and riskier, short-term loans. (Clinton's economic development team recommended that it be abolished, but the governor, fearing that his next opponent would label him as the governor who raised interest rates, chose not to take the risk.) Overall,

Clinton's programs are not yet of sufficient scale to deal with the huge challenges Arkansas faces. But taken as a whole, they are an impressive beginning.

"This is more a criticism directed at legislators than at the governor, but legislators tend to say, 'Well, look at all we've done,'" says Tom McRae. "And then you compare what a state like North Carolina has done just to create the research capacity at Triangle Park to go after bio- or medical technology. It's $80-, $90-, $100-million commitments on their end, and $1- or $2-million commitments on our end. So from that point of view there is a total lack of realism about what kind of investments have to be made if you're going to seriously compete in that area."

Given Arkansas's fiscal condition and the need to put money into education, one might wonder how Clinton could have spent more on economic development. There is one area in which he and the legislature have wasted large sums of money, however: tax breaks for business.

The governor has initiated or supported a job tax credit of $100 for every new job created, adoption of the generous accelerated cost recovery system (ACRS), which lets businesses depreciate many of their investments over three and five years, a capital gains tax cut, a research and development tax credit, enterprise zones, an investment tax credit, and a sales tax exemption for replacement machinery in existing plants.[41] In 1986, the last three alone cost the treasury about $10 million.[42]

In addition, Clinton has failed to veto a raft of even more dubious giveaways—particularly in 1985, when the practice got out of hand. In part, Clinton was horse-trading to get votes for his economic development package. But there were also failures of nerve. Combined with a slowdown in the state economy, this raid on the treasury broke the state. Beginning in July 1985, Clinton had to cut spending for six quarters in a row to keep budgets in balance.

When the raid began, Arkansas already had the lowest state and local taxes per capita of any state in the nation. Since state government in Arkansas is heavily dependent on the sales tax, further business tax breaks simply made the overall tax structure even more regressive than it already was. In terms of stimulating economic growth, they subsidized the wrong businesses. "If you look at the tax system as a whole, the exemptions, the exclusions, the benefits tend to favor the kind of industries that are our past, not our future—the large, out-of-state industrial employer," says McRae. "What we need to realize is that most new jobs are going to come from the small-business sector. They're going to be locally financed, and they're going to be relatively small employers. The tax system as a whole is skewed against those sorts of people."

By spending so much on tax incentives, Arkansas also makes it that much harder to come up with the money for quality education, for research, and for targeted economic development efforts such as ASTA. Indeed, Arkansas is a classic example of how tax incentives designed to stimulate economic development can actually retard it.

During the 1986 campaign, Clinton admitted that the state had gone too far with its tax loopholes and talked about tightening some of them up to raise more money for the schools. "In 1983 unemployment was 13 percent, and for three years I was desperate to do anything to keep manufacturing jobs," Clinton told me. "But I think I did overdo it."

In 1987, Clinton proposed that the state increase revenues by $60 million a year, in part by tightening up its tax incentives. In his first try, he got roughly half of what he wanted through the legislature. He then called the legislature back into session and raised another $21 million, over two years, for programs other than education. To create a political constituency broad enough to push more fundamental tax reform through the legislature, Clinton has appointed a tax reform commission made up of leaders from industry, labor, and other sectors.

When he speaks about economic growth in Arkansas, Clinton is careful to warn that there are no quick fixes. "We must be prepared to pay the price of time," he said in his 1985 inaugural. "The process of reforming our education system, retraining our work force, and restructuring our economic base cannot occur overnight. We will need a decade of dedication"—his favorite phrase—"to reap the full benefits of our efforts."

A decade is a long time for a politician, but the reality of Arkansas is more sobering than even Clinton would admit. All of the effort poured into education will only bring Arkansas up to parity with many northern states, and only in its elementary and secondary schools, at that. In economic development, even parity would be a blessing. With the weakest research base in the nation, with few technology companies from which to spin off new enterprises, and with relatively limited amounts of capital, Arkansas has few tools with which to work. It is so far behind its competitors—and so much of its economic base is in declining industries—that it must run hard just to stay in the same place. Between 1978 and 1985, it could not do that, and per capita income fell from 78 percent of the national average to 76.5 percent.[43] To reach Clinton's "ultimate goal"—the national average in per capita income—will take almost a miracle.

Clinton's final term, which ends in 1991, will be critical to the future of the state. He has started Arkansas on the right path. But will he now be able to follow through? Will he put the same kind of effort into higher education as he has into the elementary and secondary schools? Will he close the rest of the tax loopholes that are draining his treasury? Will he convince the public pension funds to invest in venture capital, as they have in Pennsylvania and Michigan? Will he plant the seeds necessary to make real the dream of a biotechnology corridor? The answers to these questions will determine a great deal about the future of Arkansas.

The Politics of the New Paradigm

Bill Clinton is a classic new-paradigm liberal. Stung by his 1980 defeat, he is no longer the crusading liberal reformer of his first term. He discovered, painfully, that such tactics did not work. (The two most liberal governors elected in the early 1980s, New Mexico's Toney Anaya and Wisconsin's Tony Earl, discovered the same thing. Earl was defeated in 1986; Anaya clearly would have been if he had been allowed by state law to run again.) Clinton is still willing to take on powerful constituencies when the issues at stake are central to his priorities; witness the teacher-testing battle or the struggle with Jack Stephens. But he often chooses to duck battles that might divert attention from those priorities and alienate powerful constituencies in the process, particularly battles over taxes. He was blindsided by the "car tag" tax in 1980, and like other politicians victimized by the late-1970s tax revolt, he remains gun-shy.

"Some people would say Frank White ruined Bill Clinton, by beating him," says John Ward. "Before, he didn't worry about the political heat, he just did what was right. *Ruined* is too strong a word, but he's more cautious. He weighs the political consequences more carefully."

Clinton argues that he has simply learned what it takes to be effective. "If you look at lasting change, I have effected far more lasting change in both of these last two terms than I did in my first term," he says. "We've picked our fights. You can't mobilize all those constituencies and all those fights at the same time. I think the acid test is, when you're through, have you made a difference?"

Nor is Clinton a classic liberal on spending. He has raised social spending in selective areas: a $4-million-a-year increase in welfare benefits (which are still extremely low, by national standards); a small investment in job-search activities for welfare recipients; a $3- to $4-million-a-year program to provide health care for poor pregnant women who are not eligible for medicaid; and a doubling in the number of personnel involved in efforts to stop illegal drug use. But he believes that most social spending increases must wait until the economic growth issue is solved.

Hillary Clinton calls her husband a "pragmatic progressive" (the same phrase Cuomo uses), and the description seems apt. For all his history as a McGovernite and activist, Clinton is today closer to business than to organized labor or community organizations. More important, by stressing education and economic development, he has gone beyond traditional Democratic or Republican dogma. In the process, he has clearly struck a chord within an electorate that believes the traditional approaches have failed. "We must understand that the established dogmas of both national political parties are inadequate to the needs of the present," Clinton said in his 1985 inaugural address. "The Democratic party has been too concerned with dividing the fruits of our labors when the real need is to increase them, too receptive to the demands of its individual interest groups when the real need is to go beyond them in the public interest. The Republican party has been too concerned with returning power to the states when some problems, like the farm crisis, require a national solution, too willing to leave people and places behind that are unprepared to compete in the world marketplace."

Clinton then summed up his own synthesis brilliantly. "We may want the government off our backs," he said, "but we need it by our sides."

More than perhaps any other governor of the 1980s, Clinton has demonstrated how to talk about issues such as education and economic development in ways that not only make sense to voters but move them. This is not easy, particularly with economic development. "Rockefeller used to talk about the road program for Arkansas, but that farmer didn't want to know about the road program, he wanted to know about that chuckhole in front of his place," explains John Ward. "Economic development is the same. When you go into Deshea County to talk about economic development, those people want to know if you're going to bring in another Sunbeam plant. You've got to be able to translate your vision into something that's in their frame of reference, something they can go out and touch."

Because he is such a gifted speaker, Clinton can do that. During the 1986 campaign, the *Memphis Commercial Appeal* noted that "Clinton's stump speeches in the area sound as much like seminars on the economy as pleas for votes, and most political analysts agree that the strategy is working."[44] The comment was apt, for Clinton's stump speech was indeed an attempt to give every Arkansan a vision of the economic future, a way to understand both the wrenching changes experienced in so much of the state and the path to a better future. Clinton made it work because, like Ronald Reagan, he painted that vision with particulars, with anecdotes that meant something to the average person.

Listen to him as he closes his stump speech, at the Washington County Democratic Rally. "The other day I was at the Arkansas Eastman plant, in rural Independence County," he says, the Arkansas twang deep in his voice. "It's a modern, high-tech plant. I went up to this plant and I toured around and looked at all the antipollution equipment, and the guy was tellin' me, 'All this is run by computers, and I want you to see the man who's runnin' the computers.'

Clinton describes 30 minutes of build-up about the computers. "At the end of the 30 minutes," he says, "I'll be honest with you—I didn't want to meet the guy running the computer, because I didn't think I'd have anything in common with him. You know, I thought he'd be some Einstein sitting up there like the Wizard of Oz in some mysterious room, making all of this go. And I really felt like I was going to meet the wizard.

"So we climbed up the steps, and we got to the door of the computer room, and we opened it, and I nearly got knocked down by the sound of country music. And there was the man running the computer, wearin' cowboy boots, Levi jeans, a western shirt, baseball cap, he had a big ol' championship rodeo belt buckle on—you know how big and silver they are, they look like those wedding plates you give people for wedding presents. And he was chewin' Red Man in his jaw. And the first thing he said to me was, 'Boy I'm glad to see you, my wife and I are going to vote for you, because we need more jobs like this.' I was never so glad to hear anything in my life.

"That's the case I have to make to the people of this state. That guy had cattle and horses and he was pure Arkansas, but he was smart enough to know that his future depended on what he knew, not what he could do with his back or his hands. The future of this state depends on what we know. And ultimately that is the fundamental question in this election. I need your help, because tomorrow is waiting for us, if we will seize it. Thank you all and God bless you."

4
ARIZONA: PROTECTING THE ENVIRONMENT, RETHINKING SOCIAL SERVICES

Life in Arizona is something few Americans raised east of the Mississippi would recognize. Two-thirds of all state residents were born elsewhere. Half arrived in the last fifteen years. Every fall a third of the students in the typical Phoenix school district are new. In 1986, 61 new shopping centers were completed or under way in the Phoenix metropolitan area.[1]

In the mid-1980s, Phoenix was the nation's fastest growing city; Arizona one of its fastest growing states. At the current pace, the Phoenix area will double its population of 1.9 million—nearly half the state total—within 15 years.[2] Every year this mushrooming metropolis—an endless expanse of one-story, suburban-style homes and shopping centers—gobbles up thousands of acres of desert in a race for the horizon. At 400 square miles, it now covers more ground than New York City.

This explosive growth has transformed a dusty, sparsely populated frontier state into a land of the modern, Sunbelt metropolis. Arizona was the last of the contiguous 48 states to join the union, in 1912. By 1940, it had only 500,000 people, spread out in small, desert towns and over vast Indian reservations. Phoenix had only 65,000 people. But World War II brought military bases and defense plants, and the postwar boom brought air conditioning and air travel. Suddenly Arizona's location and climate were advantages, rather than disadvantages. The defense contractors, aerospace companies, and electronics manufacturers poured in, bringing an army of young engineers and technicians with their wives and their children. This was the Eisenhower generation—raised during the depression, hardened by World War II, anxious for the security of a job, a home, and a future for their children. With their crew cuts and their conservatism, they transformed Arizona from a sleepy, almost southern Democratic state into a bastion of Sunbelt Republicanism.

Before the Republican takeover in the 1950s, the farmers, the mining companies, and the bankers had run the state. Copper, cotton, and cattle were king. "It used to be that there were five or six men who would sit around a luncheon table at the old Arizona Club and pretty much decide on how things were going to be," says Jack Pfister, general manager of the Salt River Project, the state's largest water and power utility. "Some legislators were said to wear a copper collar."

At first, the new suburban middle class did not change this arrangement a great deal. Real estate developers, the new millionaires on the block, joined the club. But even as the Republicans cemented their control in the 1960s, rural legislators held onto the reins of seniority—and thus power. State government was tiny, the governor a figurehead. And the new suburbanites embraced the frontier ethos in which the old Arizona had taken such pride. Ignoring the fact that without major government investments—in military bases, defense plants, and dams—Arizona would still be a rural backwater, they believed their newfound prosperity was the product of untrammeled free enterprise. Beginning in 1952, they voted Republican in every presidential election. They had little truck with Washington. In the 1950s, Arizona declined to participate in the federal Interstate Highway System; in the 1960s, it turned down medicaid. As local people still say with a hint of pride, Arizona is the last preserve of the lone gun slinger.

The combination of explosive growth and a frontier mentality created problems very different from those encountered by the other states profiled in this book. "In the East, you have old cities, old infrastructure, and a fight for economic survival," says Republican Senator Anne Lindemann. "Here, we're trying to control the growth as best we can."

This process was not without its lessons for the rest of the nation, however. Because Arizona is a desert, with a fragile ecosystem, its rapid growth threw into sharp relief the most serious environmental problems of the postindustrial era—particularly those involving water and toxic chemicals. And because the political climate makes public resources so scarce, the struggle to cope with the social problems created by a modern economy stimulated a degree of creativity rarely seen in a conservative state.

The task of dragging Arizona into the modern era fell to Bruce Babbitt, who by the time he left office in 1987 had changed the very nature of the governorship. A lanky, scholarly type whose habitual slouch and thoughtful manner hide an enormous drive, Babbitt looks like a cross between Donald Sutherland and Tom Poston. He has sandy hair, a lined face that has begun to sag with the wear of 14 years in politics, and large, pale eyes that bulge out from behind his eyebrows when he scowls. In a small group, when he is in his natural, analytic mode, Babbitt can be brilliant. On a dais, when he tries to sound like a politician, his body stiffens, his eyes bulge, and he does a good imitation of Don Knotts.

Despite his weakness as a public speaker, Babbitt captivated the Arizona electorate. He was elected in 1978 with 52 percent of the vote, reelected four years later, during a recession, with 62 percent. Summing up the Babbitt years, the *Arizona Republic,* a conservative newspaper, called him the "take-charge governor."[3] "He is without a doubt the smartest, quickest elected official I have ever met," an environmental activist told me, in a comment echoed by many others. "Babbitt plays it on the precipice," added a state senator. "He is constantly pushing this state forward, and he has an uncanny ability to pull it off."

In addition to his brains and his daring, Babbitt was not hurt by his name. For Americans who have read Sinclair Lewis, the name Babbitt evokes the sterility and petty materialism of middle-class life. But in Arizona, the name has a different ring—the ring of a Kennedy in Massachusetts, a Rockefeller in New York, a du Pont in Delaware. "It's well known here that the Babbitts own the northern part of Arizona, the DeConcinis own the southern part, and the rest of us live in the middle," says Anne Lindemann.

"The Babbitts came here in the 1800s," adds Alfredo Gutierrez, until 1987 the minority leader in the state Senate. "They were pioneers. They set up an Indian trading store. And they built an immense empire in northern Arizona. There are Babbitt car dealerships, Babbitt department stores, Babbitt trading posts, Babbitt property managers, Babbitt everything. And they own an enormous amount of land. The Babbitts are like the Goldwaters—saying the name Goldwater connotes something in history; saying the name Babbitt does too."

In the style of the West, the Babbitts were anything but baronial. A large Roman Catholic family, they were known for their commitment to the Flagstaff community. As a boy, Bruce was the "in-house genius," according to a childhood friend.[4] In 1956, he was valedictorian of Flagstaff High. He attended Notre Dame, where he studied geology—his link to the grandeur of northern Arizona—and served as student body president. From there he went to the University of Newcastle on a Marshall scholarship to study geophysics. But a summer project in Bolivia changed his life.

It was 1961, the first year of Camelot, and change was in the wind. Babbitt had gone to Bolivia on a research project with Gulf Oil. Ferried to and from a lavish base camp by company helicopter, he was struck by the contrast between the opulence of Gulf Oil and the poverty all around him. He decided he was more interested in people than rocks, more concerned with where the continent was going than where it had been.

He returned to the United States and checked into Harvard Law School—the kind of place politically oriented young up-and-comers attended in the early 1960s. Still under the Kennedy Peace Corps influence, he returned to South America during his summer vacations to work in a variety of social action projects. In 1965, he headed South for the civil rights march on Selma, then joined the War on Poverty as a field agent in the Office of Economic Opportunity (OEO).

Living out of a suitcase, the 27-year-old Harvard Law graduate traveled from one south Texas town to another. His job was to help set up community action agencies, through which federal resources were channeled to the poor. It was heady stuff, telling local politicians they had to share their power with blacks and Mexican-Americans. "There are times in government when you can walk into town—the New Deal was one of those times—and suddenly . . . you have the authority and the discretion that would only be available if you were an assistant secretary in normal times," Babbitt later told the *National Journal*. "It was that kind of environment."[5]

In 1967, Babbitt followed his boss, who had been named director of VISTA, to Washington. "There are believers who perhaps may be naive and others who are realistic," said one former VISTA official. Babbitt "was a believer who was realistic."[6]

The realist in Babbitt could see that the War on Poverty was to be short-lived. Spending on the Vietnam War had already forced cutbacks at OEO, and Congress was under intense pressure from local politicians to rein in the young idealists who were giving them so much trouble. More important, the program was not working. "The War on Poverty bore some good fruit, but what I learned was you can't force thoroughgoing social change from the top down," Babbitt told the *National Journal*. "The whole War on Poverty had a certain kind of arrogance. . . It could not be a lasting process of change when it depended upon GS-7s hired in Washington dispensing federal money with terms and conditions that they prescribed in local communities."[7]

After a decade of adventure, which had taken him from South Bend to South America to south Texas, Babbitt dusted off his law degree and returned to Phoenix. He joined a firm, served on the local legal services board, and did legal work for the Navajo tribe. He was one of a handful of liberal activists in Phoenix, a hardy band who stuck together because they were so outnumbered. In 1974, they drafted Babbitt to run for attorney general. He had the name, he had the money, and he had the right politics.

Babbitt understood the potential of the attorney general's office in an era of corruption and consumerism. Watergate dominated the national news, and land fraud and price fixing were hot at home. Babbitt filmed a TV commercial in a supermarket, in which he vowed to stop price fixing. "He was kind of a gangly, inarticulate fella, walking through the aisles of a supermarket, trying not to bump into things, talking to people about being ripped off," remembers Art Hamilton, Democratic leader in the Arizona House.

It seemed odd to some, but it worked. "A lot of us have always believed it was luck, or just dumb fool ability to bump into the right issue," says Hamilton. "But after 11 or 12 years, you begin to realize that isn't the case.

The man's bright. He sizes up issues quicker than anybody I've ever known, and he has a real sense of what drives folks, what motivates them beneath the surface."

This sense quickly showed in Babbitt's use of the attorney general's office. The laissez-faire, frontier mentality was so strong in Arizona that organized crime had moved in to take advantage of it—just as it did to the north in Nevada. Priscilla Robinson, a veteran environmentalist who has long been active in state politics, tells a story to explain just how deep the laissez-faire attitudes ran. "In the midfifties I had a woman friend who got married in Pinal County. It was a big wedding, lots of politicians, and a bunch of the bride's friends from the attorney general's office. On the way back a bunch of us stopped at a place in Apache Junction, the Apache Junction Inn. They had a big room full of gambling—roulette wheels and everything else—all wide open. Of course this was totally illegal. And half the politicians in the state, plus the governor, two or three guys from the attorney general's office, and the sheriff of Pinal County were wandering through. I mean, the notion that there was anything wrong with this wide open gambling never crossed anybody's mind. That was the atmosphere in which the Mafia came in—a certain amount of naiveté combined with a very relaxed attitude about enforcement of nuisance laws."

In Nevada, where gambling was legal, the mob bought casinos. In Arizona they put together phony land deals. By the early seventies, the state was becoming known as the land fraud capital of the world. The most memorable media story concerned the sale of fictitious Arizona lots to GIs in the Saigon Airport.

Babbitt convinced the legislature to pass a bill allowing him to appoint a statewide grand jury, then set it to work on land fraud—prosecuting over 100 cases and effectively ending the practice. He also attacked price fixing in the milk, bread, funeral home, and liquor industries. His name did not really hit the headlines, however, until he prosecuted the murderers of *Arizona Republic* reporter Don Bolles, in 1976. Like Babbitt, Bolles was investigating the role of organized crime in land fraud. On June 2, 1976, his car blew up. The case became a cause célèbre for the media, and when Babbitt's name turned up on the accused murderers' hit list—for his role in prosecuting organized crime—he became something of a hero.

Babbitt's game plan, at that point, was to run for reelection in 1978, then to challenge Barry Goldwater in 1980. That plan was derailed when he awoke one March morning in 1978 to discover that he was governor. Raul Castro, the governor, had resigned to be ambassador to Argentina. Lt. Gov. Wesley Bolin, who succeeded him, had died. The secretary of state was appointed, not elected; hence she could not assume the post. Bruce Babbitt was next in line. Two months short of his fortieth birthday, he became the youngest governor in Arizona history.

Traditionally, the governor's office in Arizona had been extremely weak. Arizona was perhaps the only state in the union in which a governor would consider the ambassadorship to Argentina a step up. State government was run by a small group of senior legislators and their staffs, who brought out the governor for ceremonial occasions. The notion that a governor might try to set an agenda for the state, or dare to veto a bill, never crossed most politicians' minds.

Babbitt immediately set out to change that. Six weeks into his term he vetoed two bills on the same day—then timed his veto message for the evening news, knocking the wind out of a planned override. The legislature reacted with shock. "Our idea of an activist governor was one who met with us once a month to seek our advice," said Alfredo Gutierrez. "This guy called us daily to tell us what he wanted to do."[8]

Babbitt vetoed 21 bills in 1979, 30 more over the next two years.[9] His total of 114 vetoes in nine years was more than double the record set by Arizona's first governor, who served for 13 years.[10] "My business friends used to complain that we had a weak governor," says Jack Pfister. "After Babbitt was in there about two or three years, you never heard anybody complain about that again. What he demonstrated was that it was more the individual than the structure of the office itself."

The Environment

In his second year as governor, Babbitt tackled the one issue that dwarfs all others in Arizona: water. In the postindustrial era, environmental protection is no longer an obstacle to growth; it is a central ingredient of growth. As a society, we need new institutions through which we can come together to design equitable solutions to difficult environmental issues. No state has provided a better model than Arizona—because no state is more threatened by the limits of its fragile environment.

Phoenix gets seven inches of rain a year. (Boston gets 44.)[11] Where the metropolis ends, the desert begins. Even in the midst of plenty, luxurious homes are meticulously landscaped—with rocks, dirt, and cactus.

Phoenix and Tucson were both settled because of water. The Spaniards built a walled presidio along the lush marsh lands of the Santa Cruz River, and Tucson was born. The U.S. cavalry harvested galleta hay that grew wild along the Salt River, then planted crops in the beds of ancient irrigation canals that combed the valley. Gradually Phoenix grew up.

Except in abnormally wet months, the Salt and Santa Cruz rivers are now dry, dusty scars in Phoenix and Tucson, memories of a time when water was not so precious. Residents of Tucson have pumped so much water out of the ground that the Santa Cruz River has simply dried up. In Phoenix, the Salt River Project built a dam 32 miles east of town and siphoned every drop of water into a 1,262-mile grid of aqueducts that serves the valley. Farmers literally call in their orders, whereupon engineers send the proper amount of water down from the storage dams to the diversion dam and through the canals, where it is guided by remote control into the right irrigation ditches.

But river water could not quench Phoenix's thirst. By 1980, Arizonans were pumping almost five million acre feet of water out of the ground every year, nearly twice the amount nature was putting back in.[12] (An acre foot is enough to cover one acre to a depth of one foot.) In central Arizona, where most of the people live, groundwater levels were dropping ten feet a year.[13] Huge fissures—up to nine miles long and four hundred feet wide—had begun to open up in the parched ground.

It was irrational. This was a desert state, in a nation whose farmers produced far more than they could sell. Yet farmers were consuming 89 percent of the water.[14] Since the 1930s, the state's political leaders had understood the severity of the problem. But repeated attempts to solve it had come to naught before the power of the farmers and their allies, the copper kings, whose mines consumed another 3 percent of the water.[15]

In 1976, the Arizona Supreme Court forced the politicians to act. The court ruled that a landowner could not transport water from one area to another if by doing so he injured another party—by lowering the water table, for instance. Had the decision been enforced, it would have shut down the copper mines and threatened the survival of the cities. The effect would have been so devastating that the agribusiness corporation which had sued—and won—chose not to seek an injunction to enforce the decision.[16]

The mining companies immediately went to the legislature and demanded action to clear up the problem. The Senate and House majority leaders brought representatives of the mines, the farmers, and the cities together. Meeting in private, with an agreement that the legislature would not be allowed to dot one "i" or cross one "t" in their bill, they wrote legislation which settled the immediate issue. To address the larger and tougher question of groundwater depletion, the bill called for a Groundwater Management Study Commission. It gave the commission unusual powers: if the legislature failed to pass a groundwater depletion bill by September 7, 1981, the commission's proposal would automatically become law.

The gravity of the issue was reflected in the meticulous care with which seats on the commission were distributed. Fourteen legislative seats called for in the act were carefully parceled out between allies of the mines, the farmers, and the cities. The act also gave the governor power to appoint eleven people: two representatives each from agriculture, mining, and the cities; one representative of the utilities; one representative of the Indian tribes; and three public citizens. Governor Castro filled these last three seats with a Hispanic, the state AFL-CIO chief, and a prominent Democratic party fund raiser. The commission began meeting in November 1977. Its cochairs set a goal of wrapping up by the end of 1978—a deadline they would miss by 18 months.

The rational solution was obviously to cut back on agricultural irrigation. The Arizona Water Commission (AWC), a public body created a decade earlier primarily as a planning agency, studied 12 different options and recommended that the state simply buy agricultural land and take it out of production. It concluded that "safe yield" (a balance between the amount of water pumped out of underground aquifers and the amount returned) could be reached by the year 2020 in the Phoenix and Tucson basins if 128,000 acres were retired—about 9 percent of all land irrigated in the state.[17] Though it may have been the simplest solution, the AWC proposal failed the basic test of politics. Representatives of the cities and mines had no interest in taxing the public to pay off the very interests they believed were responsible for the problem. "We're not going to buy farms so the farmers can move to La Jolla and raise martinis," the two mine representatives announced.[18]

Another simple solution would have been to allow all groundwater rights to be bought and sold, to let supply and demand drive up the price, and to let the market ration water. This approach also flunked the test of politics. "If you really pushed a market approach, you would end up with an Owens Valley-type situation, where all the water runs uphill to money," explains Priscilla Robinson. "Drying up the rural areas of the state is not in our long-term interest, regardless of how the economists pencil it out." (The Owens Valley, in California's Sierra Nevada Mountains, was pumped dry to satisfy the thirst of Los Angeles.)

To reflect political realities in Arizona, the solution would have to be some sort of trade-off between the three basic power blocs, the cities, the farmers, and the mines. But after two years of work, the commission remained deadlocked. Finally, in November 1979, its key players went to the governor and asked him to mediate.

Babbitt agreed to work with the rump group that had approached him. For six months they met in a Phoenix conference room, working six and seven days a week, often meeting into the night. Like the earlier group, they agreed that whatever compromise they reached would be final; no amendments would be allowed by the legislature. "Everyone realized that this was a last-ditch effort," says Kathleen Ferris, a young lawyer who directed the commission staff and later ran Babbitt's Department of Water Resources.

Babbitt took the easy issues first. He allowed every issue to be discussed at interminable length, until a consensus emerged. If none did, he deferred the issue or assigned it to a subcommittee. He took no votes. He made sure each of the three interests won their share of concessions. And he waited. "I don't think I've ever seen a politician so patient," says Ferris. "He was absolutely willing to outwait anyone."

Much of Babbitt's leverage resided in his mastery of the enormously complex issues at stake. According to participants, he quickly knew more about the intricate details of the plan than anyone else in the room. "The first thing you learn when you're negotiating is if you don't keep on top of the details, you lose your leverage to really make things happen," says Babbitt. "All I ever learned in a big law firm was, the power is in the hands of the draftsmen. . . . As the architects say, God resides in the details."[19]

If no consensus was possible, Babbitt imposed a solution. Occasionally tempers would flare and one group or another would stomp out. But Stan Turley, a state senator who cochaired the commission, would cajole them back to the table. "Babbitt had a good sense of when he was pushing one group too hard," says Jack Pfister. "He was willing to push all the groups; he didn't show any patent favoritism." As time wore on and the three power blocs each extracted significant victories, they slowly developed an investment in the project's success. When the toughest issues finally came to a head, Babbitt drew on this investment to impose solutions.

In March, the group came to agreement on general principles. They chose a system with strong state regulation, combined with a limited marketplace in which groundwater rights could be bought and sold. The central feature was a requirement that each of three urban "Active Management Areas"—the water basins in which most of the state's groundwater was consumed—adopt a series of increasingly stringent ten-year plans, culminating in safe yield by 2025. A new Department of Water Resources would monitor depletion rates in each basin and draw up the ten-year plans.[20]

Once this agreement was reached, Ferris and her staff drafted a 200-page bill. When the rump group met again to resolve several new issues raised by the task of codifying its agreements in precise language, one issue threatened to derail its consensus. The group had earlier voted to ban the construction of any new development in an Active Management Area unless it could demonstrate a one-hundred-year "assured water supply." Now the cities insisted that they should be exempt, because all new developments within cities should be assumed to have an assured water supply. If this was done, developable land inside city limits would be far more valuable than land outside city limits. The farmers, who owned most of the developable land outside the cities, naturally objected. The commission deadlocked. Day after day passed without resolution. Babbitt had called a special legislative session to pass the law. The first time a deadline for printing the bill approached, he announced a week's postponement. Seven days later the deadline loomed again. Babbitt refused to postpone the session a second time.

At 2:00 A.M. on June 2, 1980, with no resolution in sight, Babbitt brought the negotiations to a close. He announced to the press that he would not allow one issue to jeopardize the entire bill. He then huddled with representatives of the cities, who insisted that their bottom line was a 50-50 compromise, in which the assured water supply rule would not apply within city limits until 2005. Babbitt accepted the compromise, phoned the other members of the commission, and extracted their agreement. The legislature passed the bill without amendment.[21]

It was an enormous political coup for the young governor. All the participants agreed that without Babbitt, they would never have succeeded. Where others had tried and failed for 40 years, Bruce Babbitt had cut the Gordian knot.

Over the next six years, Babbitt had two opportunities to demonstrate that the Groundwater Management Act was no fluke. The first came when the Reagan administration announced a new policy encouraging states to share in the cost of federal reclamation projects. Without significant new money from the state, the Central Arizona Project (CAP), which would bring Colorado River water by aqueduct to Phoenix and Tucson, would be seriously delayed. Babbitt established and chaired a committee that spent ten months negotiating a cost-sharing deal in which the state wound up shouldering $371 million of the project's remaining $1 billion price tag. It was the first time a state had agreed to match federal reclamation money on this scale, and it ensured that CAP water would complete its 333-mile journey from the Colorado River to Tucson during the 1990s.[22]

CAP provided a new supply of surface water, and the Groundwater Management Act preserved Arizona's supplies of groundwater. But neither touched the issue of water quality. Throughout the 1980s, one toxic pollution scare had followed another. Drinking water wells had been closed in both the Tucson and Phoenix areas. With high-tech giants Motorola and Hughes Aircraft allowing toxic chemicals to seep into the groundwater, people began to worry that by the time the state reached safe yield, the water would no longer be safe to drink.

The legislature wrestled with the issue for two years, deadlocking over which state agency should be given regulatory power over this new problem: Industry favored the Arizona Water Control Council, which it dominated; environmentalists favored the state Department of Health Services.

What finally broke the logjam was a decision by several environmental organizations to put a water quality measure on the ballot. Industry leaders understood that it might pass. Their principal ally, Senate majority leader Burton Barr, wanted to run for governor—but not as the dirty water candidate. With both sides ready to compromise, Babbitt pulled together an Ad Hoc Water Quality Committee in January 1986. It included Republicans and Democrats, industry representatives and environmentalists, and representatives of the farmers, mining companies, and cities.

As a partisan of clean water, Babbitt took a more forceful position than he had in the groundwater management negotiations. When his subcommittees reported back on the difficult issues, he would listen carefully to the various arguments made by those around the table, then finally announce the position he would support. "He was really kind of the judge," says Priscilla Robinson, one of the environmental representatives. "He would say to us, 'You can't have that.'"

Babbitt relied on an implicit threat that he would veto any bill he was not satisfied with, and that the environmentalists' initiative would then appear on the ballot. "Industry people would make a case," says Robinson, "and he would smile at them in his congenial way and say, 'You've failed to convince me. Let's proceed. On to the next item.' And that was it. He controlled the process. Of course what he was saying was, 'I'd veto that.'"

The resulting bill has been widely described as the toughest water quality law in the country. It created a new Department of Environmental Quality (DEQ), prohibited all discharges of groundwater-threatening pollutants without a permit from DEQ, and strengthened the regulation of fertilizers, pesticides, and so on. It also made polluters liable for the cost of cleaning up tainted water and established a $5-million-a-year state superfund for use when the culprit could not be identified. The environmentalists' major victory, however, was a requirement that all groundwater be kept pure enough for drinking. Unless explicitly reclassified by the new department, every aquifer in the state must meet federal EPA standards for what will eventually be a list of 120 chemicals. For months the mining companies, which have polluted many aquifers, resisted this. But the environmentalists insisted. Finally, when the mining companies had won several other concessions, they gave in.[23]

With the new Environmental Quality Act in place, Arizona completed its transformation from the state with the least environmental regulation to the state with the most. Delegations from other states—and nations—now regularly visit Arizona to look at its water management system. The most important lessons Arizona teaches, however, are to be found in the realm of politics. Bruce Babbitt proved that with the right kind of leadership, even the most intractable environmental disputes can be resolved. What it takes is a leader willing to bring the right parties to the table and capable of bringing the right pressures to bear.

Babbitt received high marks from all concerned for his accomplishments. Perhaps the most glowing encomium came from Wesley Steiner, who ran the Arizona Water Commission, then was tapped by Babbitt to organize and run the new Department of Water Resources. Steiner, who served under five western governors, including Reagan, said, "Bruce Babbitt is undoubtedly the best governor I have ever worked for. It would be impossible for anyone to have a larger, more significant contribution to a state than to help manage its most important resource. He is head and shoulders above other state governors."[24]

Rethinking Social Services

If it seems surprising that the nation's most conservative state has its toughest environmental laws, it is doubly surprising that Arizona boasts some of the nation's most experimental social service delivery systems. In both cases, necessity was the mother of invention. Whereas a shortage of water forced stringent controls in a laissez-faire state, a shortage of money forced creativity in the social arena. When Arizonans elected a former War on Poverty activist as governor on the same day that they passed a constitutional amendment limiting state expenditures to 7 percent of personal income, creativity became an absolute necessity.

The basic innovation was to push social services out of government, into the community. During the early seventies, Arizona had consolidated seven social service departments into one, the Department of Economic Security. At the time, the state barely delivered any services beyond those mandated by the federal government. But as social spending began to grow under Babbitt, the state faced a choice: it could let DES grow huge and unwieldy, or it could push more and more service delivery into the community. The explosion of federal programs during the 1960s and 1970s had stimulated the growth of many community and nonprofit organizations. So when Babbitt began to give priority to social programs, a "third-sector" infrastructure was already in place.

The man who gave this evolving philosophy a formal stamp of approval was Douglas Patiño, who ran DES during Babbitt's final term, when Babbitt increased its budget by over 50 percent. Born to poor parents in Mexico, Patiño held three positions under Jerry Brown before coming to Arizona. A large man whose enthusiasm and warmth quickly made him one of the most popular figures in Arizona government, he is a rare combination of dreamer and administrator.

According to Patiño, Arizona provides roughly $280 million a year in contracts to community-based organizations. It contracts for the delivery of virtually all social services, with the exception of federally mandated programs such as AFDC, unemployment compensation, and food stamps. Rather than setting up a state bureaucracy to deliver meals on wheels, for instance, or to prevent child abuse, or to provide drug and alcohol abuse programs, it contracts with organizations such as Chicanos por la·Causa, the Urban League, and Catholic Social Services. "I believe this is the wave of the future," Patiño says. "Germany has a very similar system, except they use the churches more than we do in Arizona."

"Privatization" of government services—by turning them over to for-profit corporations—has been widespread during the 1980s. Arizona's strategy is fundamentally different: it relies primarily on nonprofit, community-based organizations. The idea is not only to get more bang for the buck, but to get more compassion and more commitment from those delivering the services. It is also to promote competition, to use small units capable of more flexibility and humanity than large bureaucracies, and to take advantage of the diversity of community organizations to serve populations that are often beyond the reach of a state bureaucracy. Finally, the use of community organizations allows government more flexibility in shifting resources to respond to changing needs and circumstances: it is far easier to terminate contracts than to lay off civil servants.

Arizona is ahead of the curve, but the use of community and nonprofit organizations to deliver social services is clearly a nationwide trend. It is very much a legacy of the postindustrial era. When the economy stagnated in the 1970s, tax revenues slowed and public needs expanded. To make matters worse, during the high-inflation years of the late seventies voters sought to hold prices down in the one area they could affect: government. In this new fiscal climate, state and local governments were driven to seek more cost-effective ways of delivering services. As they did so, they began to learn that in a rapidly changing society, the diversity and flexibility of community organizations gave them a tremendous advantage over large government bureaucracies.

One example of the new trend in Arizona is Chicanos por la Causa (CPLC), a community development corporation set up by the Ford Foundation in 1969 to empower the huge Hispanic population of South Phoenix. In its early days, CPLC was more a militant advocacy group than anything else. It still plays that role, but today it has 127 employees, a $4.2-million annual budget, a for-profit real estate subsidiary, a revolving loan fund, nonprofit housing development projects, and a key role in developing a $15-million Mercado—a traditional Mexican marketplace—in downtown Phoenix.[25] CPLC is larger and more successful than most CDCs. But what is most unusual about CPLC is that half of its budget comes from social service contracts with the city and state. CPLC provides job training, ·counseling services, day-care centers, meals in schools, training programs for unwed mothers, services for the elderly, a shelter for victims of domestic violence, and alcohol, mental health, and drug abuse programs.

"The advantages are that you bring services down to the local level, you

get the community involved in the project," says Pete Garcia, CPLC director. "Rather than the bureaucracy, it's the community saying we're going
to do what we think our community needs."

The Babbitt administration even pushed the *administration* of social
programs down to the community level, by contracting with certain community organizations—or, at times, local governments—to act as area administrators. These "administrative entities," as the umbrella groups are
known, award contracts to community organizations, monitor their performance, and administer their grants. According to Garcia and others, they
are far more responsive to the needs of local community organizations than
were the old state administrators. "We don't look at them as the state, we
look at them as community groups that want to help," Garcia explains.
"We've had to fight 'em, to make some changes, to make them aware of
problems in our community that weren't being met. When we came into
the elderly services system, we had to beat up on the Area Council on
Aging. They were unaware of the Hispanic elderly. Their staff was all
white. Their center charged money for meals and things, which our Hispanics just couldn't afford. We beat up on the lady who ran that council,
but she became a believer. If it had been the state, it would have been a lot
more difficult. You attack this administration [of Republican Governor
Evan Mecham], they'll cut your funds off, especially if you're perceived as
a Democratic group."

The umbrella system also makes it easier to cut off funds to groups that
are not performing, Garcia says. Under the old system, the state would
continue funding groups regardless of their performance, for fear of the
political protest if they cut them off. "These organizations get a little political clout, and the state won't touch 'em. And who suffers? The community
suffers."

One of the umbrella groups that oversees CPLC is known as
CODAMA, which stands for Community Organization for Drug Abuse,
Mental Health and Alcoholism Services, Inc. One of Arizona's more respected administrative entities, CODAMA was founded in 1969 by a group
of doctors and addicts, to combat drug addiction. In 1978, the organization
broadened to include alcoholism and mental health, and in 1984, it won a
three-year contract from the state to handle behavioral health services in
South Phoenix and adjacent areas. CODAMA contracts in turn with over
two dozen organizations, ranging from a small home for recovering alcoholics to a large county program for the chronically mentally ill. Its largest
contract is for $3 million a year, its smallest for $4,500.[26]

CODAMA's director is Alan Flory, a tall, slender young man with all
the energy of a true believer. Flory rattles off the advantages he sees in
using community organizations to administer social service programs. "It
takes the state three to six months to get a contract amendment through

the system," he says. "I can take care of a contract amendment in a day. The state uses civil servants. They went through cutbacks a few years ago and they ended up with all the people that had been there for years and years and years. They can't fire anybody. My people—I can push 'em, I can make 'em work hard.

"We can also respond a lot quicker. We don't have the restraints of state government. We've got four agencies right now that would be out of business if we weren't loaning them money. Another agency wrote us and said they're going to cancel the contract—they can't afford to do this service any more. So we said, okay, we're going to take this whole thing over. Only temporarily, because I think it's a conflict to do it permanently. But we're gonna run it ourselves. There are only three employees, and we said, 'We can't afford to hire all of you, but we're going to hire two of you.' The state couldn't possibly do that—there's no way.

"One of the agencies we fund is a county, another is a city program. It gives us an interesting perspective, because we see the differences between government and nongovernment. In October, I went over and met with the head of the county health department. As I was leaving, I said, 'Oh by the way, we have five months of your money that you haven't received yet, from last year's contract. Nobody from the county has even asked us why we aren't giving it to you. We've just been sitting on it because you were not complying back then for something.'

"We had half a million dollars, and of course his teeth just dropped out. He ranted and raved. It was kind of funny. I drove back to the office, and I said, 'Make sure their check's ready.' I told my assistant, 'I want you to tell me the moment you hear from anybody from the county about the money.' A typical agency—any other agency—before I had gotten back to the office, they would have called. It took the county ten days—finally somebody wrote us a letter."

During CODAMA's first year as an umbrella agency, Flory went and talked to the previous funding sources for each of his programs. One of his largest contracts was with Phoenix South Mental Health Center, which had been funded by both the state and the county. "We went over to the county and said, 'Tell us about the program. We'd like to get copies of your site visit reports, visits you've done, and your write-ups on the programs.' We discovered that they hadn't done any—ever."

The county informed him that Phoenix South's overhead was far too high. "I said, 'Okay, could I have some write-ups showing me some of the documentation of where you said that to them?'

" 'Oh, well, we never told them we thought their overhead was too high.' "

Then he went to the state, which told him the same thing. Had they done anything about it? No.

"Why not?" Flory asked.

" 'Well, they have a lot of political clout.' Everybody said, 'We don't want you to cut their overhead, because we know they're too politically powerful.' "

Flory cut their overhead by $150,000. "We said, 'You can keep the money, but you've got to put it into services.' Not a single politician called me. How could they? I didn't cut any money from 'em. I said spend it on clients." Overall, Flory says, CODAMA cut average overhead costs in its system from 21 percent to 17 percent in its first year as an administrative entity.

The second year Phoenix South applied for another contract to run a new residential treatment program. They lost out to another group. "They were real curious why," says Flory. "I said, 'The reason you didn't get funded was real clear: you were gonna do it for $300,000, they were gonna do it for $200,000; they were gonna hire 15 staff members, and you were gonna hire six!' I said, 'I'll be damned, that doesn't make any sense to me!' "

The biggest advantage Flory sees in the use of community organizations is the commitment they have to the job. "In our system, the average salary for bachelor-level counselors is $13,000. The lowest salary is $8,000, and that agency's *director* makes $14,000. They've all worked there for ten or 15 years, and they're just really committed people. They're people who were alcoholics and started this alcohol program for women. It's called Casa de Amigas. They own a house, 12 beds, and they do alcohol services. Women come in and live and get treatment, then go on somewhere else. We provide less than half the support for the program. They have a bingo operation, which their board members run for free. One of the board members is an accountant and does their financial work for free. They're just real grass-roots, real impressive. It's not the professional, Ph.D. kind of stuff, but that's not necessary."

Flory adds that the nonprofit organizations are not only more efficient than the state, they stretch the state dollars by matching them with funds they raise. "The state has an interesting philosophy—they basically don't give all the money. The contract says the state will give 50–75 percent of the money. So the nonprofits or whoever have to come up with the rest. It forces people to fund raise, it forces people to be tied to the local community, to have the community support."

Flory says few people understand the system of umbrella organizations. "We are real controversial. People that don't understand it or don't want to understand it will say that this is an extra layer of bureaucracy, that everything has to go through this administrative entity before it gets down to the local delivery. That's true, but that layer of bureaucracy has got to be there somewhere. And we're a cheaper layer than if anybody else did it."

In addition to pushing service delivery into the community, Patiño argues that government must begin to treat social services as an integral part of its effort to create a competitive economy. "I see human services as a support for the private sector, for our economy," he says. "What are the implications for the employer if there is drug addiction in the family, or a high drop-out rate, or a very low-income family that needs to give its kids postsecondary education? Not until very recently were economists willing to agree with me that family malfunctioning has an impact on productivity."

That reality means that we must redefine the roles of the public and private sectors, Patiño believes. "We have to share responsibility. What we've tried to do in Arizona is make government a support system, and see if we can get other institutions to begin to take the lead." To stimulate more day care, Patiño sponsored a conference of corporate CEOs to talk about why day care for employees was a good investment. In welfare, he allowed companies that hired welfare recipients to use their welfare checks as subsidies for six months. "That probably gave us the greatest amount of credibility with the Arizona Association of Industries," Patiño says. "For the first time they saw that we were willing to use the same dollars differently."

Another of Patiño's favorite subjects is children. He believes that the changing American family—the rise of divorce rates, the heightened mobility of American society, the increasing number of mothers who work—has created a crisis in the nurturing of children.

In 1984, Patiño raised this issue with Babbitt. "I can tell you in all honesty, these were new issues for him," he says. But Babbitt shocked him by devoting his entire 1985 State of the State address to children's issues. Babbitt's speech also took the press and public by surprise. In an editorial headlined "Babbitt's Dish of Quiche," the *Arizona Republic* complained that Babbitt was ignoring the "meat and potatoes" of state government—roads, prisons, and water—to talk about quiche. But the speech generated a tremendous amount of attention, and Babbitt eventually got the majority of what he wanted from the legislature. The new items included health coverage for all poor children under six; a new Governor's Office of Children; more money for the enforcement of child support payments; $7 million to expand Patiño's Child Protective Services program, which contracts with nonprofit organizations to help families in which child abuse is suspected; and several other items.

Babbitt's real priority was expanding day care. The state already had a modest day-care subsidy program for poor families, but statistics showed huge gaps in the availability of care. Over a third of all Arizona youngsters between the ages of six and 11, for instance, were left without adult supervision after school.[27] Babbitt sought a tax credit of about $200 per family for day care, but the legislature refused to pass it. Without public money to spend, Babbitt concentrated on getting businesses and nonprofit organizations to respond. He gave speeches about child care, sponsored the CEO conference on day care, appointed a task force and held a conference on latch-key children, and urged local YMCAs, churches, and school districts to open after-school facilities. Babbitt claims that over the next year more than one hundred new programs were launched, and most observers support his contentions.

Arizona's strategy of delivering social services through nongovernmental organizations is not without its problems. Patiño admits that the state never invested the money necessary to do a good job of monitoring and evaluating the hundreds of small organizations that receive state contracts. To some extent, umbrella agencies like CODAMA make up for the state's deficiencies. But not all of the umbrella agencies do as good a job as CODAMA. "In order to go into this mode a state really has to redefine its role," says Gloria Bacera, Patiño's former deputy. "When it gives up delivery, it has to concentrate on oversight and evaluation."

The model is often mistaken for simple privatization of government functions, such as contracting garbage collection out to a private firm. But it is fundamentally different. Although the state occasionally contracts with a for-profit firm, most of its contracts go to nonprofits or local governments. In 1987, for instance, CODAMA contracted with two for-profit firms, two local government agencies, and two dozen nonprofit organizations. "The for-profits and the government agencies have both been real problems for us," says Flory. "Their value systems are not the same as ours. The for-profit firms are in business to make money, and the public-sector agencies have little interest in saving money. Nonprofits are clearly the best."

Essentially, Arizona is doing in social services what Massachusetts and other states have done in economic development: using the public sector to define the problems, but relying on third-sector institutions to tackle them. The third sector does this better than the private sector precisely because its goal is to solve social problems, rather than to make money.

To his credit, Babbitt understood the distinction and was careful to stay clear of rhetoric about privatization. "I've had some bloody fights over the limits of privatization," he explained. "We have a legislature here that would contract out the governor's office if it could. And what we've learned is this: the contracting-out of definable tasks is easy and important and we've been relentless about it, we've gone much further than many states. But the notion that social services can be bid out to the profit-making sector needs a lot of care. I successfully resisted for nine years the notion that you can bid out the most difficult and dangerous social service job of all, which is running the prisons. I just don't believe in it." (Babbitt twice vetoed bills allowing private companies to build and operate prisons.)

The real lesson came in health care. "In the first version of our AHCCCS program (the Arizona Health Care Cost Containment System) the legislature said the medicaid program would be contracted out, there would just be a turnkey operation. My sole job was to accept bids and contract it all out. I opposed it but accepted it. We contracted it out to [a subsidiary of] the McDonnell-Douglas Aerospace Corporation, and they succeeded in discrediting and destroying the entire program within 12 months. It was an unbelievable mess, the reverberations of which are still going through the courts in this community. It was a very sobering lesson."

Health Care for the Poor

The AHCCCS program was indeed the perfect example of what can go wrong when a firm whose sole goal is profit is put in charge of a social program. Conversely, once the state took over, it became an example of what can go right when government makes creative use of the third sector. AHCCCS was the most radical experiment in medicaid history, and despite its disastrous beginning, Babbitt turned it into a success. It provides a model of health care for the poor that offers hope of taming the rampant inflation which has plagued medicaid and medicare.

When the federal government created medicaid in 1965, promising to underwrite at least half the cost of providing health care to the eligible poor, 49 of 50 states quickly signed up. The fiftieth was Arizona. "We felt medicaid would bankrupt us, like it bankrupted other states," says Senator Lindemann.

As in most other states in the premedicaid era, the county hospitals took care of the poor. By the 1970s, the task consumed 25 percent of county revenues, and the counties began pressuring the legislature to adopt medicaid so the federal government would pick up part of the tab. Then voters passed a ballot initiative limiting county tax revenues. By 1981, several counties, caught between rising health costs and limited revenues, faced bankruptcy.[28] Reluctantly, the legislature bailed them out and began serious consideration of a medicaid program.

Medicaid has traditionally reimbursed private physicians for the care they provide on a fee-for-service basis—meaning that the doctor charges a fee for each separate service, whether a flu shot or an appendectomy. The more the doctor does, the more he or she is paid. American medicine has traditionally operated on this principle. But by 1980, the fee-for-service system was under serious challenge from a wave of health maintenance organizations (HMOs). HMOs receive set monthly fees from their clients;

in return, they agree to provide all health care, no matter how sick the client gets. Thus an HMO maximizes profits by limiting its services, whereas a fee-for-service doctor or hospital maximizes profits by expanding services. Not surprisingly, HMOs have discouraged unnecessary surgery, cut down the time patients spend in hospitals, employed walk-in clinics rather than hospitals for minor surgery, and embraced other measures to control costs. (Some of these have involved trade-offs of quality for cost.) HMOs have also introduced price competition into the health care marketplace, since consumers can price-shop between HMOs in a way that is impossible between physicians who charge on a fee-for-service basis.

When Ronald Reagan was governor, California tried using HMOs for medicaid recipients in several parts of the state. But the experiment ended in what several experts described as "disaster, with rampant fraud and patient abuse."[29] In 1979 and 1980, Babbitt proposed that Arizona contract with existing HMOs to provide medical care for AFDC recipients in the Phoenix and Tucson areas. The legislature ignored his proposal, but when the crunch came in 1981, they decided to explore the concept.

Republican legislative leaders designed AHCCCS, with some input from their Democratic counterparts. Babbitt's only role was to veto their first bill, because it had not been approved by Washington and would therefore receive no federal funds. As ultimately passed, the system was to be run by a private firm on a contract with the state. That firm would solicit bids from existing HMOs, as well as hospitals, county health departments, and others who wanted to create HMOs or independent practice associations. (IPAs are groups of physicians in private practice who band together to offer prepaid care to consumers.)

Two groups of poor people were eligible for the program: those receiving AFDC and SSI (a social security program primarily for the blind and disabled); and other families with incomes at roughly 50 percent of the federal poverty line and below. Each HMO or IPA would receive a set monthly fee for every person it enrolled, regardless of its expenses. If it kept costs down, it would make money; if not, it would lose money. The system would be financed by the federal government, the state, and the counties, which had to contribute 45 percent of their previous annual health care budgets.

The legislature's first mistake was mandating that AHCCCS begin operations less than 11 months after the act was signed. As the first statewide, HMO-based medicaid program ever created, AHCCCS was an enormously complex undertaking. Yet the legislature wanted it up and running in time to campaign as saviors of the poor during the 1982 elections. "We needed another year, just to prepare for it," says Richard Trujillo, who handles AHCCCS eligibility determinations for Maricopa County (Phoenix and its suburbs). "We're still trying to recover. It was like trying to paint a moving train. Since then we've changed trains, and we're still patching and fixing. It was a fiasco, a real fiasco."

The second mistake was choosing a firm that had no experience with HMO-based health care systems: McAuto Systems Group, Inc. (MSGI), a subsidiary of McDonnell-Douglas. To take one example, MSGI's computer system was 15 years old. The counties had to put the names of those determined eligible for AHCCCS on a computer tape; McAuto would fly the tape back to St. Louis once a week to be read by its computer. Half the names would be rejected because the computer programs didn't quite match up, leaving thousands of people without health care. Community Legal Services of Phoenix finally had to sue to get the problem corrected.

The third mistake was picking a firm that operated more like a defense contractor than a health provider. After the program was under way, Arizona officials discovered that McAuto, under a previous name, had been part of a firm convicted of defrauding the federal government on a data-processing contract. "They were wheeler dealers out of New York City," says Lou Harper, who took a management position with McAuto but left after only three months. Harper and others believe that McAuto's managers realized the state contract was so poorly written that they could bid as low as they wanted and make it up later, in overcharges. They won the 40-month contract with an $8.2-million bid, but over the next two years they negotiated some 80 unwritten modifications and raised their fee to more than $30 million.[30]

McAuto made little attempt to monitor the performance of the health care plans with which it contracted. Several of them exploited the lack of oversight to deny care to many of their members, thus increasing their profits. At one point Community Legal Services called doctors belonging to two plans that had won bids to serve South Phoenix, a poor Hispanic community. It found that many of them did not even have offices in the area. One of the HMOs had two phone lines for 40,000 patients. It often failed to notify patients assigned to it that they were in the plan, or to assign them to a primary care physician. When they got sick it would take them hours to get through to McAuto to find out which plan they belonged to, because McAuto never had enough phone lines. Then it would take hours or days to get through to the plan.[31] "What person with the flu would go through all this?" asks John Dacey, then an attorney with Community Legal Services. "Some of the providers really did play what I think were deliberate shell games to avoid providing care to their patients."

Like McAuto, AHCCCS also failed to monitor performance. "AHCCCS was awarding contracts to provide health care for the poor the same way they would to build a road," says Dacey. "But if a road builder defaults, you've got a surety. If a health care provider defaults, you've got thousands of people with no health care."

Many of those involved with AHCCCS believe that organized crime even got into the picture, to skim profits out of AHCCCS. One IPA contracted with a private company to manage its plan. A senior manager of that company was later indicted in Chicago on mob-related charges. ("He even looked mob," says Lou Harper.) Just as an Arizona grand jury prepared to indict him for embezzling funds from the IPA, he announced that he had cancer. Within a week he was dead and cremated. Observers suspect that he turned federal witness in the Chicago case and was given a new identity; indeed, Arizona legal officials never dropped their indictment.

The owners of another HMO with a tainted reputation took more than $700,000 out of the firm for their personal use just before it went bankrupt. They were careless enough to talk about it on their car phones, which could of course be overheard by others. Someone recorded the conversation and gave it to the newspapers.

Both of these organizations went bankrupt. The first, which reported huge profits in its first year and went belly up in its second, recorded the largest bankruptcy in Arizona history.[32] Of 16 original health care providers under AHCCCS, three went bankrupt and two others were sold to their creditors for one dollar.[33] Part of the problem was corruption; part of it was poor design and execution by the state; and part of it was a decision by the state administrator (under pressure from the legislature) to force bids down as low as possible. By the program's third year, ten of the 14 providers had negative equity: more debts than assets. So many plans were close to bankruptcy that the state unilaterally raised its payments beyond the bid levels.[34]

By 1984, AHCCCS was a serious black eye for Babbitt and Republican legislative leaders, who of course blamed each other. All along, the Republican leadership had been making the political decisions that guided AHCCCS. Finally, in the spring of 1984, Babbitt went to them and offered to take over, if they gave him the money and the legislative changes he needed. They readily agreed. At the time, many were urging that the state simply call off the AHCCCS experiment. According to knowledgeable observers, the Republicans believed the program was such a mess that Babbitt could never set it right. They saw it as a political tar baby.

Soon thereafter the state refused to pay McAuto's latest overcharge and McAuto walked away—both parties charging breach of contract and filing suit. Babbitt fired the director of his health department and demoted his AHCCCS director. He hired Donald Schaller, a respected physician who had founded Arizona's first HMO, to run AHCCCS as a department of state government. Starting virtually from scratch, Schaller built an organization of three hundred and installed a new financial system and a new data system. He ordered the reorganization of two health plans that were in financial trouble, hired auditors to comb through the rest of the AHCCCS plans, and redesigned the program's basic operating procedures. AHCCCS had run up a $65-million deficit, and Babbitt spent close to double that to save it.[35]

There are still major problems, but even the program's critics now prefer it to the old county system. It is impossible to tell whether it is saving money, because there was no previous medicaid program with which to compare it. But based on several studies, the experts generally believe that the HMO system has kept costs lower than they would be under a conventional, fee-for-service medicaid program. A survey done by Louis Harris and Associates showed that those who were eligible for AHCCCS believed that it had improved both their access to medical care and the quality of that care.[36]

Most of the remaining problems stem from the fact that so many of the poor are *not* eligible for AHCCCS, which in turn reflects the legislature's habit of pinching pennies. To save money, the legislature set the eligibility level for those not on AFDC or SSI extremely low. A family of four must earn under $5,300 a year to qualify—roughly half the federal poverty line, and $1,700 less than one would earn at a full-time, minimum wage job. In Maricopa County alone, close to 120,000 people who live below the poverty line do not qualify for AHCCCS.[37] These people, known in the trade as the "notch group," are roughly synonymous with what we normally call the working poor.

The legislature also saved money by excluding most long-term care, such as care in most nursing homes. For those who need long-term care, as for the notch group, the counties remain the only resort. This dual system—with the state responsible for half the poor, the counties for the rest—is the worst of all worlds. It creates endless administrative headaches, but more important, it creates financial incentives for each side to dump patients on the other. The counties are still in charge of determining who is eligible for AHCCCS. They can save money by declaring people eligible who technically should not be, and the state can save money by creating so many hurdles that even legitimate applicants are denied. Not surprisingly, both have done just that.

Tragically, the system has actually *reduced* access to health care for the notch group, according to a careful study by two academic experts, Howard Freeman and Bradford Kirkman-Liff, based on the Harris survey mentioned above.[38] The county hospitals, which lost roughly half of their funding base to AHCCCS and now must compete with other HMOs for AHCCCS patients, have been forced to become more efficient. In response they have tightened up their eligibility requirements, worked harder to collect for services from the notch group, and minimized the amount of free care they dispense.

Babbitt's preferred solution was to make everyone up to the poverty line eligible for AHCCCS. (Indeed, he proposed during his presidential campaign that the federal government extend medicaid to this group.) In Arizona, this would roughly double the number of people eligible, and thus double the expense. Knowing that his legislature would never go along, Babbitt instead proposed that all children under the poverty line be covered. Faced with a mom-and-apple-pie issue, the legislature agreed. Typically, however, it covered only children under six in the first phase, then promptly postponed the second and third phases when a budget shortfall hit.

Arizona has shown that HMO systems for medicaid make sense, but it has also demonstrated the pitfalls other states should avoid. Other states are listening, with encouragement from the federal government. Roughly 30 states are trying some kind of HMO program for at least one group of people eligible for medicaid, in at least one county.[39] California is experimenting with a system in which hospitals bid to provide hospital care for medicaid patients at fixed daily rates. Pennsylvania is trying the HMO model in Philadelphia. And Wisconsin is gradually implementing a statewide program similar to Arizona's.[40]

"Wisconsin looked at Arizona, went home and did it right," says Kirkman-Liff, one of the reigning national experts on the subject. Wisconsin's approach actually bears a striking resemblance to Babbitt's original proposal. The state is starting in only two urban counties, serving only AFDC recipients, and using only preexisting HMOs. To provide an incentive for HMOs to participate, it is combining the medicaid population with state employees, a relatively healthy and profitable population. (Arizona originally intended to do this, but the headlines of the first two years made it politically impossible.) As the program proves itself, Wisconsin will gradually expand into other counties, bring in the SSI population, allow new HMOs to compete, and finally bring in the poor who are not on AFDC or SSI.

Kirkman-Liff believes the Wisconsin approach is the right one. He cautions, however, that states must still work hard to monitor HMO finances and quality of care—particularly if they want to use for-profit HMOs and thus mainstream the poor. Both California's and Arizona's experience showed that HMO systems create incentives to cut corners and invite severe fraud. The federal government, which has been experimenting with HMOs for medicare patients, is learning the same lesson.

In urban areas already served by HMOs, Kirkman-Liff believes, systems designed along the lines Wisconsin has chosen should work. In rural areas, there may not be enough HMOs or enough medicaid patients to stimulate competition between HMOs. Another open question is whether for-profit HMOs will ever be willing or able to handle long-term care, chronic mental illness, or substance abuse—all of which are more frequent among the poor. With these provisos, most experts believe Arizona has pioneered a model that will succeed in controlling medicaid costs. "You can't expect a miracle," says Kirkman-Liff. "You're not going to cut your costs 30 percent. But over time you may see some large savings."

Economic Development

In Arizona, the economic problem has been too much growth, not too little. Ever since Motorola built an R&D center for military electronics in Phoenix in 1948, high-tech manufacturers have flocked to the state. They have been lured—many of them from nearby California—by the cheap land, the cheap labor, and the desert climate, all of which make Arizona perfect for manufacturing precision electronics. As time passed, the only problems they experienced arose from the state's failure to keep up with their growth.

The most pressing problem, aside from water, was the higher education system. Arizona State University, the major school in the Phoenix area, was known for big-time sports and big-time parties. *Playboy* once named it the nation's number one party school. Its engineering and business schools were second rate. As the high-tech industries boomed, they began having trouble recruiting engineers—many of whom wanted to update their education every three to five years to remain on top of their fields—because of the poor reputation of ASU's engineering school. In 1978, industry leaders created an advisory committee to work with the school and took their case to the governor.

Babbitt stole their thunder. His friend Pat Haggerty, the founder and then chairman of Texas Instruments, had convinced him that sustained high-tech growth depended upon top-quality higher education and research institutions. He interrupted the committee presentation, told them about Haggerty, and instructed them to think big. "I'm not interested in being behind short-term or small-time budget increases," he said. "Come back to me with a sweeping multiyear program, and I'll support you."[41]

The advisory committee drew up a five-year plan calling for $32 million in new investments in the engineering school—from industry, from the federal government, and from the state. (As it worked out, industry raised $18.5 million, the federal government contributed about $8 million, and the state provided about $28 million.[42]) With both the governor and the business community pushing the package, the legislature embraced it. Between 1979 and 1984, the College of Engineering and Applied Science built a 120,000-square-foot Engineering Research Center, installed $15 million worth of new equipment, hired 65 new faculty, moved from $1 million a year in research to $9.4 million, and set up a continuing education program that included televised classes beamed right into local plants and offices.[43] In 1984, the National Academy of Sciences ranked ASU's Mechanical Engineering and Electrical Engineering departments second and third in the nation, respectively, in improvement over the previous five years.

In July 1985, the advisory committee and the engineering school adopted a second five-year plan. This one called for $62 million in new money, split among industry, the federal government, and the state. The goal was to move the school into the top ten in the nation.

ASU also launched a university research park. It decided to allow professors to own their own companies, to spend 20 percent of their time working in industry, and to keep a portion of the patent rights on their discoveries. The Babbitt administration played a role in both developments. Babbitt also pushed through a new Disease Control Research Commission, to fund medical research.

Throughout this period, Babbitt worked hard to convince the public that investment in its universities was critical. "In earlier, less complex times, universities were nice to have but not essential to economic growth," he said in a 1983 speech to a high-technology symposium he organized. "When Arizona's first great industry, copper, developed in the late nineteenth century, the main ingredient for success was a strong back and a lot of courage in the face of drought. Then came tourism; its principal ingredients were sunshine and hospitality.

"Now, in 1983, high technology is our growth industry, and the essential resource to sustain high technology cannot be mined from the hills or grown in our soil or derived from hospitality. The main ingredient of the new high-technology evolution is education, in the form of well-educated citizens with strong scientific and technical skills. . . . Universities and colleges are now an economic asset as important to our economic future as copper ore, farms, banks, factories, and airlines."

Another ingredient of growth in the 1980s is entrepreneurial initiative. Surprisingly, this too has been a weakness of Arizona's. Most of the state's manufacturing growth—on which much of its booming real estate, service, and retail economy rests—has come from large corporations headquartered elsewhere. By the mid-1980s, seven of every ten high-tech workers in Arizona were employed by 14 large firms—Motorola, IBM, ITT, Sperry, Honeywell, and others. Only one of the 14 was headquartered in Arizona.[44]

"We are very vulnerable, because many of our major employers are branch plants, not headquarters, and many of them are now moving offshore," says Ioanna Morfessis, executive director of the Phoenix Economic Growth Corporation. "Many of our employers are also part of companies that are moving toward automated facilities, and the trend has been to pull the automated facility back close to the home office. We have an opportunity to keep them, if we provide the environment they need—the skilled labor force, the type of educational programs, the universities, the research base, and the kind of talent they need. But clearly our number one goal is to create a self-generating economy. We do have some spinoffs from the university and the Motorolas, Honeywells, McDonnell-Douglasses."

Arizona's dependence on branch plants came home to roost in 1986, when a slump in the semiconductor industry forced cutbacks. Meanwhile significant production was moving across the border to Mexico, where labor cost $4.50 a day. After several decades in which rapid growth was taken for granted, Arizona's unemployment rate jumped above the national average for the first time in years.

Babbitt understood the necessity of building a more entrepreneurial economy. His economic policy chief, Larry Landry, met Bob Wise and Michael Barker at CSPA in 1978, then invited Barker, Michael Kieschnick, and Roger Vaughan out to Arizona to take a look at the economy and suggest a course of action. They sold him on David Birch's analysis, which he in turn sold to Babbitt. Landry produced a strategy document called *Arizona Horizons*, which recommended that the state focus on the creation and expansion of new and small firms, on the diversification of the high-tech industries, and on improving the quality of education.

Other than a few efforts aimed at rural areas, Babbitt eschewed the programmatic approach of some of his colleagues in other states. He preferred to focus on "the basics"—education, research, training, infrastructure, and water. Occasionally, he did try to change private-sector behavior. Arizona's banks have a reputation of being uninterested in lending to small or young manufacturers; as Arizona boomed, their gravy train was real estate lending. To change that Babbitt pushed through interstate banking, to inject more competition into the state. Six of Arizona's seven large banks were immediately purchased by out-of-state banks. (Whether that will improve the business lending climate or just re-create the branch plant mentality in banking, or both, only time will tell.) Babbitt also tried to liberalize the laws governing public pension fund investments, but failed.

One reason why Babbitt did not do more was that soon after he developed his overall strategy document, he began running for president. In 1985 and 1986, according to Beth Jarmin, Landry's successor as economic policy chief, Babbitt no longer paid much attention to economic development. Some of the state's high-tech entrepreneurs, who have formed their own Arizona Innovation Network to develop and lobby for economic initiatives, lament this fact. "What I dislike about Babbitt is that he really was running for the presidency by late 1984, and it interfered with his responsibilities for the state," says Reginald Owens, who set up ASU's research park and helped create the Innovation Network. "My God, the man was out of the state two-thirds of the time. He could have done a lot more on economic development by physically being present. Nobody is really taking the lead. We need a science and technology task force; we need a Thomas Edison program [Ohio's version of the Ben Franklin Partnership]; we need more venture capital; I'd like to see a major research institute at the research park. The greatest gap here is the commercialization of R&D. We have the R&D, we have the industrial base, but the gap between the two is serious."

Babbitt's Commerce Department did launch one small but intriguing effort in this area. Its two-man Office of New Business Development convinced the University of Arizona Foundation to create a for-profit corporation to act as a seed capitalist for ideas developed at the university. The new corporation started by sponsoring a competition for the best commercial proposals from professors. Out of 34 proposals, it picked two winners. The corporation and the Office of New Business Development then began searching for venture capital and for entrepreneurs who could start companies to commercialize the research. "The idea is to get a deal flow," says Bill Tompkin, director of the Office of New Business Development. "I'd like to see 12 deals in three years. I also see the role model effect. Once people begin to see these guys do what they're doing, we won't have to hold competitions." Tompkin has also created a mentor program through which he recruits successful business people to help entrepreneurs who have started their own companies. His success suggests that Babbitt's reluctance to create new government programs was a mistake.

Education Reform

The final soft spot undermining Arizona's economic health was its primary and secondary education system. With Babbitt doing much of the pushing, Arizona raised its high school curriculum and university admission standards; reformed its teachers' colleges; required new teachers to pass a competency test; partially equalized funding for poor and rich school districts; put extra money into enrichment programs for prekindergarten through third grade; provided free high school textbooks for the first time; created a loan forgiveness program for college students who became math or science teachers; and set up a small program with local industry under which teaching graduates could work in industry during the summer and teach the rest of the year.

Babbitt was an early advocate of merit pay for teachers. He initially proposed that the state dedicate certain revenues to teacher pay increases, but only in districts that linked their salary systems to performance. The teachers' union opposed Babbitt's proposal, and the legislature ignored it.

Instead, it funded pilot "career ladder" programs, which have been far more palatable to teachers, in ten school districts. These involve a series of three or four steps, beginning with some kind of apprenticeship and ending with "master teacher" status, in which outstanding teachers spend part of their time helping other teachers improve their performance. With each step up the ladder, a teacher is paid more—thus introducing some notion of merit into the salary structure.

Career ladders did not solve the basic problem of inadequate pay for teachers in Arizona, however. Raising teachers' salaries was Babbitt's top priority, and in 1985 he saw his chance. The Republicans and the business community had united behind a 20-year, multibillion-dollar highway building program. Because Arizona had stayed out of the federal Interstate Highway program, its needs were acute. With 1.5 million people, the Phoenix area had 17 miles of freeway. Republican leaders were determined to address the problem.

Six weeks before the end of the legislative session, Babbitt began hinting that unless the legislature increased teachers' salaries, he might veto its highway bill. In a special address to the legislature, he laid out his plan for a 10 percent increase in spending on teacher pay. Babbitt also suggested that the legislature put an initiative on the ballot allowing a 5 percent increase in the constitutional spending cap for education and exempting revenues from state-owned land, so that income from the State Land Trust could be dedicated to teacher salary increases.

The Republicans, who controlled the legislature, scoffed at Babbitt's suggestions. They accused him of grandstanding, noting that it was too late in the session to consider a major new initiative. But six weeks later, as the session reached a climax, Babbitt got their attention. He announced that he would veto the highway bill they so badly wanted unless they passed his education package, plus a welfare benefit increase and an assortment of other items. The Republicans screamed that the governor was holding highways hostage, which was precisely what he was doing. Babbitt held firm: no kids, no concrete.

The confrontation played as high drama on the evening news. "He got the public excited," said Gutierrez. "He's a poker player, that fella. Watching him has become a kind of spectator sport in this state." When the dust settled, Babbitt had pulled it off. He had to do a little negotiating—he traded away dedication of Land Trust revenues for a 10 percent spending increase on the ballot—but he got what he wanted. He also extracted a promise from business leaders to support the ballot initiative, which passed in 1986.

The showdown symbolized Babbitt's entire governorship. "If you look at what I've done over the last ten years," he says, "you will find that in any given year I have selected one or two or three issues and used everything at my disposal—initiative, referendum, the bully pulpit, the press, browbeating, trade-offs, threats, rewards—to get what I needed. My agenda is concentrated and aimed at overwhelming the opposition."

The Babbitt Record

A great governor of Arizona can accomplish less than half what a good governor of Massachusetts or New York can, if accomplishments are measured by new programs created. But if the yardstick is the significance of the problems tackled and the depth of the solutions provided, Babbitt's record is impressive. Despite his failures in a few areas, such as economic development, he did take on the big issues in Arizona: water, education, and social services. Just to address those issues, he had to transform Arizona politics. To solve them, he had to display enormous leadership.

Even the Republicans acknowledge that Babbitt changed the nature of government in Arizona. "I have to admit he forced us to take on some issues we probably would have preferred to ignore," says Rep. Jane Hull, a Republican who has no love for Babbitt. "I guess in some ways he did drag us kicking and screaming into the twentieth century."[45]

Leadership is the core of Babbitt's image with the Arizona public. Pat Cantelme, head of the Central Arizona Labor Council, offered a typical observation after Babbitt's legislative victory in 1985. "He uses his veto power like a scalpel," Cantelme told me. "The legislature lines up to beat him, he stays aloof, and then in a week's time at the end of the session, he gets everything he wants. He's made the governor's office what everybody thinks it should be. It's not a caretaker, and it's not somebody who looks for consensus. The office today is one of leadership."

Babbitt's decisiveness is associated in the public mind with his independence of political constituencies. The best example was a 1983 copper strike at the Phelps, Dodge Corporation. When the company hired strikebreakers to keep its mines and smelters running, frustrated strikers gathered at mine gates—throwing rocks, smashing windows, and threatening those who were taking their jobs. Someone shot at the home of an employee who had gone back to work; his three-year-old daughter was hit as she slept. On August 8, when a thousand strikers gathered at one Phelps, Dodge facility and threatened to storm the gates, the state police told the governor they could not handle the situation. Babbitt ordered the mine closed for 24 hours, then negotiated a ten-day cooling-off period, during which it stayed closed. Negotiations continued, but with no resolution. When the mine reopened, Babbitt ordered 350 Arizona National Guardsmen onto the property, to back up the state police.

The National Guard has been used throughout American history to break strikes. To labor, it was a red flag. The copper workers have never forgiven Governor Scabbitt, as he became known in copper country. Even many of Babbitt's strongest supporters felt that he should have put the Guard at a neutral site, rather than on Phelps, Dodge property. But the governor believed lives were at stake, and if the workers stormed the gates, National Guardsmen stationed elsewhere would have been useless. In the public mind, the governor had taken decisive action—and demonstrated his independence from an important liberal constituency.

The New Paradigm

Babbitt is a classic example of the new breed of Democrat elected in the post-Watergate era. "I think anybody who attempts to peg Bruce Babbitt on a traditional political spectrum will come up wanting, because he doesn't fit anywhere," says Art Hamilton. "He and a lot of the other governors just don't fit the traditional New Deal spectrum from liberal to conservative. They are a different kind of animal. They understand that the needs of those constituencies that made up the Democratic party have changed, and that the old solutions not only don't work any more, they aren't even desired any more. I think that's the difference between these folks and Walter Mondale. Theirs is a total break from the past—it's not merely a stepping back and taking a less-intense version of the old Democratic party. They just don't want to be part of the old Democratic party."

Consider Babbitt's fiscal record. In 1978, he supported the constitutional amendment limiting state spending to 7 percent of personal income; during the 1982–1983 recession he mandated successive across-the-board cuts of 5 and 10 percent in all state budgets. Both of these actions would qualify him as a conservative Republican, on the traditional New Deal spectrum. On the other hand, he pushed through large increases in spending on social services, health care for the poor, education, and environmental regulation. This part of his record would qualify him as a liberal Democrat.

Babbitt believes in decentralization and limited government, and he talks often about keeping government services at a level where they can be held accountable by voters. He supports the death penalty; he helped tighten the criminal code; and he forced the legislature to build new prisons. But at the same time he is prochoice on abortion, very liberal on environmental issues, and fiercely committed to civil rights and racial equality. It was Babbitt who opened up state government in Arizona to Hispanics and women.

The same absence of a traditional liberal or conservative pattern emerges on national issues. Babbitt has long called for a balanced budget; a national task force he cochaired in 1984 spelled out precisely how it should be done, and as a presidential candidate he did the same. But he has also been the nation's most outspoken advocate of cutting federal subsidies for the affluent, the middle class, and the wealthiest corporations. He first made a national name by campaigning for means testing of entitlement programs—specifically, full taxation of social security benefits and imposition of partial medicare payments for those who could afford them. Babbitt talks about all this in very populist terms: he wants to take from the rich so as to preserve programs for the poor.

"It's a very different thing," says Babbitt, referring to his politics and those of like-minded governors. "In the eyes of most people *conservative Democrat* means somebody who does not advocate environmental values, who is not in favor of civil rights enforcement, who is not in favor of expanded education and health care spending, all of which we stand for. We are not conservative Democrats, in the sense that that word is commonly used. We are, in a philosophical sense, conservative in two areas. One, we really do worry about what percentage of GNP you can fairly devote to government. And some of us, perhaps myself more than others, are conservative in the sense of caring very deeply about what level of government does what. A few of us really believe that these accountability issues are tremendously important."

Democratic governors have been so successful during the Reagan era, Babbitt believes, for two reasons. "First, we have manifested our concern for economic growth—we are absolutely perceived as being growth oriented. Second, on the fiscal side, we are seen as people who are really willing to wrestle with this issue of governmental limits, to try to lay out priorities and order our requests so that things balance out. I would say that those are the two things that distinguish us from national Democrats. In every other respect, we share the agenda. The voters know I'm a fairly fanatical environmentalist, but it's okay, because they don't perceive me as antigrowth. They perceive me as liberal on all the traditional social issues, but again, it's not important, even if they don't agree, because they are reassured by the sense of some fiscal limits. We have gone beyond a lot of the issues that used to give rise to these left-right characterizations."

Babbitt once called his politics "radical centrism."[46] The idea is that voters no longer want traditional liberal or conservative ideology, but they do want radical action that will cut to the heart of the nation's problems. In a sense, they want a leader like Franklin Roosevelt—nonideological, thoroughly experimental and pragmatic, but in the end radical because of the fundamental nature of his reforms.

The natural base for Babbitt's politics is the educated middle class. This is true for two reasons. First, those with education can best deal with a politics that eschews the simple party line, the politics of black and white, us and them. Second, the particular interests of the middle class more often approximate the "general interest" Babbitt is trying to defend than do those of, say, organized labor, the poor, or the wealthy. The critical question—for a Democrat—is whether these politics can transcend their natural base and appeal to blue-collar and minority constituencies.

Babbitt acknowledges the problem. "It's real," he told me in a 1985 interview. "There's so much process in all of this that people's eyes glaze over. It's not exactly the stuff of stump speeches. Ultimately your politics don't prevail until you can yoke the strands of populism to the substantive programs. That's why I'm such a fan of the early William Jennings Bryan. You go back and read some of the speeches, and you'll see a very profound understanding of how it was that you took the economic travails of the day and linked them conceptually and rhetorically in a way that would drive people to a frenzy."

Babbitt knows he will never accomplish that. "All I can tell you," he said, "is that what we are doing here that may get some people excited is this issue of talking about the next generation. What do I talk about when I go to talk to an audience of three hundred blacks? I talk about education and day care and all of those kinds of related areas. I try to say, 'Look at what we're doing for your kids.'"

Here Babbitt's greatest strength—his intellect—becomes his greatest weakness. He is a cerebral politician, instinctively uncomfortable appealing to the emotions. "If the governor has a weakness politically, I think it's that people admire him and respect his intelligence, but don't really feel they can touch him," says Hamilton, a man of immense warmth and speaking ability himself. "Babbitt's not a Huey Long populist, he's not somebody who's one of the good old boys. He's more like a Gary Hart. Very cool. At times chilly, for people who don't know him."

For many voters, Hamilton says, Babbitt's brains and leadership make up for his lack of warmth. "There's something about the Babbitt intellect— his style and his ability to cut through issues—that folks just can't let go." But among the poor and minorities, there is respect and admiration, "but not a lot of affection for him. I just don't think he really devotes a lot of time to reaching out and generating that affection."

A year after Hamilton uttered those words, Babbitt made perhaps his most concerted effort to win that affection. In 1986, he and Hamilton tried to push a bill through the legislature making Martin Luther King's birthday a state holiday. They lost by one vote. They talked it over, and at Hamilton's suggestion, Babbitt did it by proclamation. When his successor, Evan Mecham—an extreme conservative who won because two Democrats divided 60 percent of the vote—rescinded the order, it triggered a major political storm in Arizona.

In many ways, the incident captured Babbitt's strengths and weaknesses in a single frame. His proclamation demonstrated leadership; it framed the debate in a way that ensured that Babbitt could not lose; and it provided live political drama. The timing was also perfect: the uproar, which put Babbitt on national television, came just as he prepared to formally announce his presidential campaign. But when Martin Luther King Day finally arrived and Babbitt addressed 10,000 black marchers outside the state capital, his weaknesses were equally glaring.

It was an unusually chilly January morning, but the crowd was fired up. When a gospel group kicked off the festivities, the crowd clapped and swayed and sang along. When Babbitt was introduced, they gave him a rousing welcome, although it was clear that Hamilton was right: they admired Babbitt, but from a distance. They knew he was on their side, and for that they were grateful. But he was an ally from another world; he was not one of them.

Babbitt did his best not to let them down. He put his hand to his heart and shouted, "Welcome to *our* state capitol—let's take it back!"

Babbitt spoke the right words. He praised Art Hamilton, a crowd favorite. He lambasted Mecham. He talked about marching on Selma. He evoked the memory of Martin Luther King. He tried hard to catch at least a hint of the rhythm of a black preacher, and by the end of his speech he had a few in the crowd echoing his sentences, gospel style: "That's right! Amen!"

Babbitt even concluded with King's words: "Free at last, free at last, thank God Almighty, we're free at last!" But as he uttered these magic words, his body was stiff, his movements awkward, his brow knit with tension. It was as if Don Knotts had turned revivalist.

"He tries," one of the marchers said afterward, with a smile and a shake of the head. "He tries."

5
MICHIGAN: CREATING THE FACTORY OF THE FUTURE

Bob Bowman, Michigan's state treasurer, will never forget his first day on the job. At 27, Bowman was the youngest state treasurer in the country. He faced the worst budget crisis in the 50 states. A young investment banker from Goldman, Sachs, he had been hired at the recommendation of former assistant treasury secretary Roger C. Altman, his old boss in the Carter administration. "We decided to break new ground and get an investment banker," Gov. James Blanchard later explained. "We wanted someone who could put together a recovery plan and sell it to the investment community."[1]

With short hair and tortoise shell glasses, Bowman looked his age. The framed magazine profiles, the photo of him and the governor, and the membership in "Who's Who" were not yet on the wall. But Bowman was a young man in a hurry. His rapid-fire, wisecracking style—"Mr. Speaker! How the hell are ya? Yeah, we talked about that, and we agreed it was bullshit"—was tailor made for the log rolling and crisis juggling that awaited him.

It was already late January 1983 when he flew in and called his first staff meeting. The numbers were all negative. "We haven't had a positive cash flow day since 1981," his staff informed him. How did they meet the state's payroll? By borrowing from various state funds dedicated to specific purposes.

"So I asked, 'How much can we borrow from these dedicated funds?' " Bowman later recalled.

" 'Oh, between $500 and $600 million.'

" 'Well, why don't we take a look at February?'

" 'Well, February's not done.'

"I said, 'February's not done? Of course February's don`. Bring it in.' So they hustled around and within an hour, they brought in February. And there it was, on February 28, which is a payroll day, negative $614 million. I said, 'What do we do this day.'

"And they said, 'Well, we don't meet a payroll.' "

"We were cynics on Wall Street," Bowman recalls. "We were writing the epitaph for Michigan. But I had no idea the state was going to be *broke*."

Michigan already had the worst bond rating in the nation, even worse than Puerto Rico's. To keep its schools open, it had been forced to borrow from the Japanese, because Wall Street would not underwrite its bonds.[2] But this was not the only bad news the new administration faced. Unemployment was over 17 percent. The auto industry was on its knees. "There was a feeling," said one state official, "of the last one out turn off the lights."

The budget numbers were particularly frightening: if state government had shut down the day Blanchard took office, the books still could not have been balanced.[3] The state was $1.7 billion in the red, a deficit that amounted to *one-sixth* of total annual expenditures and *one-third* of operating expenses. Spending had already been cut to the bone: the state mental institutions were operating at 75 percent; the universities had been cut almost as severely; and state buildings were no longer being maintained.[4]

Like 49 other states, Michigan is required to balance its budgets. But Blanchard's auditors discovered that as the economy had crumbled, the Republican administration of William Milliken—waiting desperately for the recession to end—had juggled accounts and manipulated calendars to hide $800 million of the shortfall. Officials had gone so far as to tell the state liquor commission not to pay its bills for a few months, so the Treasury could take out the cash and call it income. "They would just accrue something, or treat something as cash—whatever was needed to say we had a balanced budget," remembers Bowman. "They'd do up the 'Hail Marys' and say, 'Isn't it wonderful, and by the way, the first day of the fiscal year we have a $200-million deficit.'"

Like his young state treasurer, Jim Blanchard was an unlikely person to face this crisis. Although he will turn 46 in 1988, Blanchard looks younger. On the short side, with an oddly cherubic face, he is gregarious and likable but hardly charismatic. A former fraternity leader and student body president at Michigan State, he once set a record for tree sitting. People still describe him as "very fraternity."

"Jim Blanchard would never captivate the state or the nation with a speech, and he'll never walk into a room and have everyone stand up," says state Senator William Faust, a popular former majority leader. Nevertheless, Blanchard has worked wonders with the Michigan legislature. "Once he makes up his mind, he goes after it with great energy. And to know him is to like him; when he was first elected he'd go across the street and have a beer with the reporters or legislators. He became an equal, whereas Milliken had always been patrician, removed."

In Congress, Blanchard was a typical member of the class of '74: elected from a Republican district, In the Detroit suburbs, his knee did not jerk on spending issues. In his first year he introduced what became the Sunset Act, which mandated a periodic review of federal legislation to eliminate wasteful spending. His claim to fame, however, was cosponsorship of the Chrysler loan package. The experience forced him to think through the problems of declining industries and international competition, and it made him a believer in government intervention to force business and labor cooperation, a favorite theme of industrial policy advocates. It also brought him together with Chrysler Chairman Lee Iacocca, forging an alliance he would later use to great effect.

When he announced for governor in 1982, Blanchard was a relative unknown. He won the nomination because big labor backed him; he won the election because the economy was in shambles and the Republicans nominated an extreme conservative, Richard Headlee. Although many traditional Democrats had given up on their party—70 percent of blue-collar workers went for Reagan in 1984—Blanchard's constant promises to deliver "jobs, jobs, jobs" earned him a 6 percent margin.

When he took office, Blanchard was widely seen as labor's boy. Business morale, already reeling from three years of what might accurately be called a depression, hit an all-time low. To business leaders' surprise, however, the new governor kept his distance from labor and launched the most aggressive program to help business the state had ever seen. He not only closed the deficit, he quickly demonstrated the two strengths close associates always point to: an uncanny sense of political strategy, and an ability to appoint top-notch people to key positions. The story of the Blanchard administration is less a story of the governor than of a handful of talented people he recruited for key positions. "I used to have a rule," says Faust. "If a person wasn't smarter than me, I wouldn't hire him. I think Blanchard's done something like that, too."

During his campaign, Blanchard said repeatedly, when pressed, that he would raise taxes only as a last resort. Now he faced a $1.7-billion shortfall. To cut spending, he trimmed $225 million from budgets his predecessor had slashed four times in two years. He slapped on a hiring freeze, set up an early retirement plan, deferred payments of $500 million to universities, school districts, and local governments, and announced plans to abolish 30 programs and boards.[5] Then he raised taxes.

"We decided not to do a temporary solution, a one-year tax just to get us through '83," explains Bowman. "Then we'd have to go back and do it again in 1984 and possibly in '85. Our thinking was, to the extent possible, let's get a permanent solution."

In other times, adds John Thodis, president of the Michigan Manufacturers Association, a Democrat would have raised business taxes. Blanchard instead raised Michigan's flat personal income tax—without making it any more progressive—from 4.6 percent to 6.35 percent. That left it lower than those of 28 other states, and allowed Blanchard to cut taxes slightly for small business. But as Thodis says, "He didn't get much credit for that."

Only one Republican in the state Senate voted for Blanchard's tax increase, but that vote put it over the top. "I was called everything under the sun," remembers Sen. Harry DeMaso. "I was almost ridden out of the party. I could have ducked, or voted no, but I'd done my own checking, and I knew the state was on the verge of disaster." DeMaso's Republican colleagues did not see it that way: they seized on the tax increase to launch recall drives against a dozen Democratic senators and Blanchard himself. Gleeful conservative activists set up hundreds of card tables at shopping centers, their signs blaring: "Are you mad about the 38 percent tax increase?"

In two suburban, working-class districts around Detroit, the recalls succeeded, and Blanchard lost his Democratic majority in the Senate. These were districts hit hard by auto industry layoffs, where people were struggling desperately to hold on—districts full of blue-collar Democrats who blamed Carter for ruining the economy and voted for Reagan in 1980. Now a Democrat was once again taking bread off their tables. Blanchard's approval ratings fell into the twenties, the lowest ever recorded for a Michigan governor. Feelings against him ran so high that the two senators under attack asked him not to campaign for them. "When you went door to door," one Blanchard aide recalls, "you had a feeling that you'd dropped into a set from *Village of the Damned*."

The medicine may have been painful, but it worked. In November 1985, Michigan began its first fiscal year in a decade with genuinely balanced books. It became only the third state to accomplish that feat under Generally Accepted Accounting Procedures.[6] The state's bond ratings are now among the best in the country. As state finances improved—thanks in part to the auto industry's recovery, which helped bring unemployment down to 8 percent by 1986—Blanchard gradually rolled back the tax increase. In March 1986, as his reelection campaign began, it fell to the original 4.6 percent.

Blanchard has increased spending, but slowly. From 1979 through 1982, Milliken cut spending by over $1 billion (in constant 1979 dollars), roughly 15 percent of all state expenditures. In his first month in office, Blanchard cut another $225 million. In his next four budgets, he gradually brought spending back to 1979 levels (again, in constant dollars). Most of the increase went for public education, prison construction, infrastructure, economic development, and environmental protection.[7] Meanwhile, Blanchard trimmed in ways not often associated with Democrats—using computers to ferret out welfare cheaters, instituting a new budget system, and paring the state payroll.

"I've served under five governors, and of all five, Jim Blanchard has been the biggest surprise to everybody," DeMaso said in a 1985 interview. "He came in with the label prolabor. He came in at a time when most individuals, if they knew the situation, would not have run for governor. He could have continued with business as usual, hoping that the economy would turn around, jockeying the books. But he didn't. He put his political future on the line. He did what had to be done. If Congress would bite the bullet in the same way—people don't like taxes, but if they can see an end result, they'll accept them. And in this state, they can see the results."

Jobs, Jobs, Jobs

Once the budget crisis was behind him, Blanchard turned to the task of fulfilling his campaign promises. Of the six states discussed in this book, Michigan has been hit hardest by the realities of the new global economy. Michigan is the nation's premier manufacturing state; one of the highest percentages of its work force in manufacturing of any state in the union.

The recession had devastated precisely those industries that form the backbone of the Michigan economy. Between 1978 and 1982, the auto industry eliminated 110,000 jobs; steel, 40,000. The manufacturing work force as a whole shrank by almost 25 percent.[8] For four years running, Michigan had the highest unemployment rates of any state. By 1985, there were still 59,000 fewer people working in the state than there had been in 1979.[9]

During the recession, Americans were routinely treated to televised images of Michigan families looking for work in Houston. Indeed, there was an exodus. Between 1980 and 1984, the population of Michigan shrank by 187,000.[10] Per capita income dropped from nearly 107 percent of the national average in 1979 to 96.7 percent three years later.[11]

As the recession began, an informal group of business and education leaders convened to discuss the economy. They believed that the state needed a new economic strategy, that it had to diversify its economy and stimulate technological innovation, particularly in manufacturing. They took their arguments to William Milliken, the moderate Republican who had served as governor since 1969.

In his State of the State address in January 1981, Milliken embraced their ideas. He created a Governor's High Technology Task Force, made up of leaders from government, academia, the financial industry, and the more technology-oriented sectors of the business community. They proposed a number of new programs: a new state development bank, two new research institutes, and a public venture-capital unit using 5 percent of the state's public pension funds. With bipartisan support, Milliken pushed these initiatives through the legislature.

Michigan turned out to be the perfect laboratory for innovation: times were so bad that no one—not business, not labor, not the public at large—could defend the status quo. Even the fiscal crisis had its advantages. "You can't get cooperation and coordination between departments if everybody has enough money," says Phil Power, a newspaper publisher who chaired two commissions for Blanchard, one on higher education, the other on job training. "Scarcity forces innovation. The private sector always operates with scarcity; the public sector doesn't."

Blanchard embraced Milliken's fledgling programs, simply turning up the volume. But with unemployment at 17 percent and a mandate to create jobs, he needed faster results than Milliken's initiatives would provide. To design a short-term agenda he set up two groups: one to develop a series of proposals, the other to ensure that they had heavyweight political backing. The first was a Cabinet Council on Economic Development, similar to Dukakis's Development Cabinet and Thornburgh's Economic Development Committee of the Cabinet. The second was a Commission on Jobs and Economic Development, chaired by Lee Iacocca and former United Auto Workers president Doug Fraser. It brought together the state's top corporate executives, its labor leaders, and the presidents of Michigan's three major universities.

For director of his Cabinet Council staff, Blanchard chose a bright young newspaper reporter who had joined the governor's staff and lobbied the financial rescue package through the legislature. "I didn't know much about economic development," says Pete Plastrik, who was then 32. "One day a transition person from the National Governors Association walked in my door and said if I signed a letter, the Mott Foundation would give me $50,000 to bring in Bob Friedman and his team." (Friedman's Corporation for Enterprise Development had received a grant from the Michigan-based Mott Foundation.) "I didn't know who Friedman or any of these guys were, but I figured that was all right. About two weeks later, Bill Schweke [from CfED], Barbara Dyer [from CSPA], Roger Vaughan, and Mike Kieschnick showed up to help us figure out what we were doing. And I can't imagine a better way to start."

The consulting team laid out the basic policy framework they had developed at CSPA and CfED, then fleshed it out with specific programs in areas such as entrepreneurial development, capital availability, and infrastructure. "They'd put this framework together in the late seventies, but they hadn't done all that well selling it yet," says Plastrik. "We became in part an incubator for their models."

Blanchard quickly announced a first wave of initiatives, designed in large part to help new and small businesses. He cut small-business taxes by roughly $18 million a year. He lowered unemployment taxes for new employees. He reformed the state's securities laws, making it easier for companies to issue stock in Michigan and triggering a burst of new public offerings.[12] He rewrote a law that had given Michigan a reputation as the toughest state in the country in which to sell a franchise, and within three years the number of franchises tripled.[13] He appointed a small-business ombudsman, to help small-business people cut red tape and fight the bureaucracy. He supported a bill to create five small-business incubators and provided funds to get them off the ground. He set up teams to weed out unnecessary bureaucracy, targeting eight hundred regulations and 17 percent of all state forms for elimination or overhaul.[14] He even established a Michigan Executive Corps, to draft business executives into temporary service with state government.

On more traditional fronts, the new governor created one of the nation's largest summer jobs programs, which employed 55,000 youths in its first three years; created a small Conservation Corps to employ five hundred young welfare recipients; and set up a fund to begin rebuilding the state's crumbling infrastructure.

Plastrik had staffed the Cabinet Council with people brought in from various departments related to economic development. As their proposals were enacted, Plastrik sent them back to their bureaucracies to implement the new programs. This gave Blanchard a core of managers devoted to his agenda, just as the council itself gave him a way to bring his key department heads together around a common agenda. Hence the Cabinet Council not only originated the governor's economic development agenda, but also became the means by which he forced his bureaucracy to implement it.

The Path to Prosperity

After the initial flurry of activity, Blanchard and his Cabinet Council decided they needed to know more about the state economy. They commissioned a careful study by a small group of economists and political scientists, a step too many states have neglected. "After the first year, we sat back and said, 'How the hell do all these things go together, and what the hell is it that we're really trying to accomplish?'" remembers Lou Glazer, then Plastrik's deputy at the Cabinet Council, now deputy director of the Commerce Department. "After learning a lot, we learned we didn't know a lot. And that's where *The Path to Prosperity* came from. The idea was to provide a thematic whole for state economic development."

To direct the study group Blanchard chose Doug Ross, a former state senator he had hired earlier to run his summer jobs program. Ross was typical of a generation that had been shaped by the 1960s but was now forced to come to grips with an entirely different set of problems: those of economic decline. He had worked for Bobby Kennedy in 1968 and led a grass-roots citizens organization in Michigan, then served as one of the most liberal members in the state Senate. It was his organizational ability—as well as his knack for finding and articulating the heart of an issue—that made *The Path to Prosperity* group work.

The study came to conclusions similar to those of Milliken's High Technology Task Force and Thornburgh's *Choices* report. It argued that Michigan's future rested upon technological innovation; that new and expanding businesses would be more important than plants recruited from out of state; and that the private sector was the engine of growth and innovation. The public-sector role, it said, was to encourage and channel private-sector investment by reducing the cost of doing business, encouraging entrepreneurship, filling capital gaps, and investing public dollars in areas such as infrastructure, education, research, technology transfer, and the quality of life. It also called for a "coordinated human investment strategy" to train those left behind, so they could benefit from the new jobs created by emerging industries.[15]

In one crucial aspect, *The Path to Prosperity* went beyond the *Choices* study. It carefully distinguished between Michigan's economic base—the sector of its economy that drives its growth by exporting products or services out of state, or by substituting for products or services that might otherwise come in from out of state—and its "local market economy" of retail firms, restaurants, and the like. Growth, it pointed out, comes from the economic base; the local market economy simply feeds off that base. If a manufacturing firm goes under, the state is that much poorer. But if a restaurant or dry cleaning shop disappears, demand simply shifts to other restaurants and dry cleaners and no wealth is lost. Hence a state should target its efforts to the economic base and let the local market economy take care of itself.

Because Michigan's economic base was so heavily dominated by durable goods manufacturing, *The Path to Prosperity* argued that its future lay in the development of advanced, automated manufacturing. As Ross and his colleagues saw it, a high-wage manufacturing state like Michigan had three options. It could "get poor," driving wages down so as to attract new industries. It could "get out," shifting from manufacturing to services and information industries. Or it could "get smart," using new technologies to position itself back at the manufacturing frontier. Though wages have come down sharply, the third option was obviously the most desirable, and it has defined Blanchard's entire program.

What is the manufacturing frontier? In a word, it is automation: robots, machine-vision systems, laser instruments, computerized machining centers, flexible manufacturing systems, and the like. Michigan already hosted over one-third of the nation's major robot users, and nine of the ten largest robot producers had operations in the state.[16] It also had a disproportionate share of the nation's machine-vision firms. With a boost from state government, *The Path to Prosperity* argued, Michigan could become the undisputed home of both the automated "factory of the future" and the hundreds of new companies producing technologies that went into it. With the right strategy, Michigan could become the place to go to make robots and laser systems and the rest, just as Detroit once became the place to go to make cars and the Silicon Valley became the place to go to produce semiconductors.

To achieve this goal, the report explained, the state's manufacturers would have to go through a technological transformation; its entrepreneurs would have to bring hundreds of new technologies to market; its research universities would have to excel in engineering and industrial technology; its industries would have to pioneer new labor-management relationships; and its government would have to minimize the disruption caused by the transition from brawn to brains. Blanchard has developed new initiatives—or supported Milliken's fledgling programs—in all five areas.

"We couldn't suddenly say, let's go into aerospace, or let's go into microcomputers," explains Ross, who moved on to direct Blanchard's Commerce Department. "You can't do that. You have to start with what you are, and then figure out how to adapt it and build it toward what you think is happening. The report gives us an economic sense of what the future looks like, which gives some hope, and begins to send signals as to what different institutions are supposed to do. Since ultimately you can compel almost no one to do anything, you need those kinds of cues."

During his election campaign, Blanchard had announced that he would target three industries for special state efforts: auto suppliers, forest services, and food processing. But the authors of *The Path to Prosperity* were skeptical of any attempts to pick winners, and Ross's Commerce Department has since backed off as well. The only significant targets are now advanced manufacturing and new and small businesses.

"We are trying to build on our strengths," explains Blanchard. "We want to help our major industries redevelop for the future and be globally competitive, we want to diversify our economy as quickly as possible, and we believe that targeting small business as a growth sector is a good idea. We want to once again be the center of complex manufacturing in this country—that's high-tech manufacturing, not low-skilled, low-paid manufacturing. That's not the future for Michigan, that's the future for China, for Singapore—and anybody who thinks otherwise is not going to work in my Commerce Department."

The Michigan Venture Capital Fund

Dwight Carlson is president of Perceptron: The Machine Vision Company. A high-tech entrepreneur in a state dominated by huge manufacturing corporations, Carlson launched his first start-up in 1969, when he was 24. With dark hair and crisp features, he is precisely what one would expect in an entrepreneur: a passionate advocate of new directions for Michigan. His company is precisely what the Michigan economy needs: a high-tech start-up with potential for rapid growth. Carlson has been deeply involved in both Milliken's and Blanchard's efforts to create a new infrastructure for the new economy, and he has been one of its many beneficiaries: Perceptron might not exist had it not received venture investments from the public pension fund.

Back in the late 1970s, the president of the Environmental Research Institute of Michigan (ERIM) approached Carlson with an idea. Formerly Willow Run Laboratories at the University of Michigan, ERIM was the state's premier advanced technology research institute. Most of its research contracts came from the Department of Defense, in remote sensing, radar, and surveillance. With some 50 high-tech firms spun off from research done in its labs, ERIM was already a successful example of the technology transfer process Milliken and Blanchard hoped to promote. Its president had an idea for yet another spinoff: to adapt the advanced "remote sensing" technologies ERIM had developed for military spy satellites to manufacturing. Carlson liked the idea, and today Perceptron produces machine-vision systems and measurement devices that help manufacturers check their products for quality as they move through the assembly line.

"The initial focus of Perceptron was to solve the fit problem, usually in sheet metal, now more in plastic," explains Carlson. "U.S. products have a quality problem, because they don't fit as well as a BMW or a Mercedes fit. That's true not only of automobiles, it's true of computers and appliances."

In most plants, checking parts for fit is laborious and time consuming. It is done by hand with mechanical gauges, after the parts have been manufactured. If a problem is discovered, an entire day's run must often be discarded or reworked—something a manager will normally do only if the problem is acute.

In contrast, Perceptron builds systems that allow parts to be checked as they are built. Imagine a swarm of sensors surrounding a spot on an assembly line, something like a scaffold cluttered with small black boxes. In each box is a laser, a video camera, and a microprocessor. The laser projects a beam on a spot; the cameras record the reflection; and the microprocessor converts that information into dimensional data, revealing fit, contour, and the exact position of holes or studs.

The data are integrated by a computer and presented on a screen, where technicians can see if the assembly line is functioning properly. The minute a problem appears, they shut down the line and repair it. Some systems come with as many as 120 sensors and perform two hundred measurements in 22 seconds.

By the end of 1985, Perceptron had sold some one hundred systems, for prices ranging from $60,000 to $1 million. It was among the industry leaders in sales, and it was the first machine-vision firm to have turned a profit. It hit hard times in 1986 and 1987, when problems with automation at General Motors and other firms triggered a sudden slowdown in sales. But Carlson has unveiled a second product, a robot guidance system, and Perceptron has captured 60 to 70 percent of the market for machine-vision systems for assembly and stamping plants. Although that market is stagnant, and several machine-vision firms have gone under, Perceptron appears well positioned to survive the slump.

The Perceptron story is a prime example of both the rebirth of entrepreneurship in Michigan and the emergence of the factory of the future. But it is also an example of the role state government is playing in that rebirth. Without the Michigan Venture Capital Fund—the Treasury Department's name for the 5 percent of state pension funds it is authorized to invest in venture capital and related investments—Perceptron might never have made it into production. One of the fund's first venture investments was in Perceptron; in fact, it participated in both the second and third rounds of financing, along with half a dozen private firms.

But by 1984, explains Carlson, "The capital markets were tight—extremely tight. All of the high-tech, West Coast darlings of venture capital—the personal computer, the software companies—were having real difficulties. And as a result, the whole venture capital community was getting very nervous." Carlson searched for money for the better part of a year, while Perceptron's future hung in the balance. Finally Bob Bowman, who oversees the pension fund, decided to push the company over the hump. He put in another $2.5 million, and "at that point everyone else got gutsy, and we got the round done," says Carlson. "Just the fact that the round was so difficult slowed us up, though, and this is a fast-moving business. When the state came in with some very strong support, that's what we needed, because everyone else came in right behind them."

With 5 percent of the state pension funds, or $800 million, to invest, Michigan now runs what may be the world's largest venture capital fund. It has had an enormous impact on the state. "In 1978, Michigan had about $6 million of resident venture capital," Ian Bund, one of the pioneers of venture capital in Michigan, told me in 1986. "By the beginning of this year, it had in excess of $300 million actually invested and at work. Back in 1980, when I formed the Venture Capital Forum, which is a monthly gathering of venture capital professionals to work together on deals, we were able to pull together four people. Tomorrow we'll have our regular monthly meeting, and we'll have in excess of 40. Statistically, the industry has gone from virtually nothing to what [*Venture Capital Journal* publisher] Stan Pratt, who is the leading commentator on our industry, describes as the fastest growth rate in the country."

Bund and other venture capitalists agree that the major catalyst for this explosion has been the state pension fund. "Would it have happened anyway?" asks David Brophy, a professor of finance at the University of Michigan's business school and the state's leading academic authority on venture capital. "I don't think so. In previous years, a lot of the venture capitalists in the country would fly over Michigan, would never think of looking here for deals. Public Act 55 [which created the state fund] was like bringing a sledgehammer down on a gong. It made a big noise, and a lot of people paid attention to it."

Among those who paid attention were prominent venture capitalists on both coasts. When they came to Michigan to solicit investments by the pension fund, Treasury officials showed them promising deals in the state. The result was an increased flow of private venture capital into Michigan. "You get the titans of the industry, the Schwartzes and the Adlers of the world, and they come to Michigan and we show them the projects we're looking at, and they get a little more interested in Michigan," says Bowman. "It's such a small community that word gets around."

Bob Williams of Regional Financial Enterprises (RFE), a large venture firm in Connecticut, agrees with Bowman's analysis. "That's accurate," he says. "They're great coinvestors, because they have deep pockets. They show us deals and we show them deals. They are a major force out there; they're very astute." One of the reasons RFE opened an office in Michigan last year, in fact, was its work with the state fund.

"Venture capitalists are like everybody else in the world," explains Brophy. "They smell the cheese, and they're comin'. When I came to Michigan, I was told by everybody that if there were good deals here, money would find them—'Money's liquid, money flows, and Michigan's got lots of money.' And I said, 'I couldn't agree with you more, Michigan has tons of money. It's not money that's really lacking, it's the professional financial manager, the person who can size up an opportunity, structure a deal and make it go.' If we had those people around here in abundance, I don't think you'd need a Public Act 55. We saw to it that we'd never have those people by our reaction to the problems of the early thirties, because we just ripped the guts out of the financial community here in Michigan. We greatly restricted the banking system, put out of business the only large insurance company we had. So we were left with a financial system that would have done credit to the state of Mississippi, trying to run the sixth-largest state in the country. That's what we were missing.

"How did Act 55 bring those people here? By hitting the gong with that hammer, saying there's money here devoted to this purpose. It's being professionally managed and professionally doled out, and if you can step up here and pass muster, you can have some of it. That has put some money in the hands of some pretty skilled venture capitalists. And it has caused the state of Michigan to become a somewhat attractive place to be."

By October 1987, the state had invested $296 million, roughly two-thirds of it in 24 private venture capital funds, the other third directly in 34 start-up businesses, most of them in Michigan.[17] Bowman hoped to earn a 35 percent annual return on his investments: "Three out of ten will go bankrupt, three out of ten will be all right, three out of ten will be good, and one, if it goes well, will be an absolute barn burner. We've already turned down several opportunities to sell out to another investor, one at a 700 percent profit."

Michigan is not alone in putting pension money into private venture firms; at least a dozen other states now do the same. But Michigan was the first state to invest directly in business start-ups, and it has moved more aggressively than the one or two other states that do likewise. This is the key to its strategy: by sharing deals with the largest private funds in the country, it is able to showcase Michigan's start-ups from coast to coast.

The coinvestment strategy also minimizes the potential of political considerations affecting its decisions. "You wouldn't get anybody to coinvest with you if that was the case," says Williams. "We wouldn't stay around for two minutes if we saw any of that." Perceptron is a good example. Dwight Carlson sat on the task force that first recommended that Michigan invest pension money in venture capital. If the state were investing alone, its investment in Perceptron might lead to accusations of cronyism. But it can easily defend its decision by pointing to major private-sector investors who have also judged Perceptron to be a good risk.

Skeptics might argue that private venture capitalists would have eventually discovered Michigan on their own. They may be right, but Treasury Secretary Bowman argues that by speeding up the process, state government played a critical role. "I would argue that it's similar to justice—justice delayed is justice denied, and financing delayed, in an internationally competitive market, is a loss for the state of Michigan," Bowman says. "You take a state like California—it's a national economy. Somehow it all fits together. But in states that are predominantly manufacturing, as we were and still are, you occasionally have to push a little here, nudge a little there, to try to shave two years off. Maybe that's all we shaved off this whole race for the automated factory, but that 24 months could prove to be the difference between winning the race and coming in third—which is all the difference in the world."

Brophy adds his own bottom line. "The net result of all this," he says, "is that we're learning how to finance new and growing businesses—high tech, low tech, no tech, it doesn't matter. That's a residue that's going to stay with us. Even the banks now—I'm getting all kinds of calls from my banker friends: 'How do you do venture capital? I want to talk to you about this stuff.' And that's healthy. If you've got an environment where new companies can form and new ideas can be pursued, your chances of surviving economic change are a hell of a lot better than if you're locked into a kind of company-town philosophy and nobody's doing anything out on the edge. You'd better be able to finance new companies and help them grow if you want representation in the industry of tomorrow, whatever that may be. That's going to be the ultimate public benefit for Michigan."

The Michigan Strategic Fund

Venture capital will meet the needs of only a tiny sliver of Michigan's economy, the few start-up firms with technologies that are advanced enough to show promise of dramatic profits. Yet as Brophy points out, Michigan's banks are relatively conservative in their lending practices. Since the auto industry reached maturity, Michigan has been among the least entrepreneurial states in the union—in part because of the culture engendered by the big three auto producers, in part because of the financial markets. Thus once the venture capital gap was closed, there remained a significant gap between venture capital and the banks.

To fill that gap, Blanchard created the Michigan Strategic Fund. Although it includes several retailing operations, the heart of the effort is a set of new wholesaling programs, designed to change private-sector investment patterns. In June of 1985, Blanchard asked Pete Plastrik, who had lobbied the Strategic Fund through the legislature, to serve as its president.

Like Bowman and Ross, Plastrik is one of the unusual young talents Blanchard has tapped. The son of a well-known American Trotskyist, he grew up on New York's Upper West Side, watching his parents put together *Dissent*, the radical intellectual journal, around the kitchen table. He attended Columbia University during the late sixties, caught hepatitis in India after graduation, and while convalescing decided to go into journalism, in a moment of inspiration brought on by the Watergate hearings. The University of Michigan's graduate program brought him to Ann Arbor, and after graduation he landed a job with the *Kalamazoo Gazette*, then quickly won a slot in the coveted state capitol bureau. During the 1982 gubernatorial campaign, Blanchard tried to hire him, but Plastrik declined. After the election Blanchard asked again, and this time Plastrik decided to come on board.

During the 1982 campaign, Blanchard had promised a major new development bank to create jobs and stimulate growth. Once in office, he found himself with no money, an old industrial development bond agency, Milliken's new loan fund, called the Michigan Economic Development Authority (MEDA), and a Republican Senate opposed to any large new financing mechanisms. His solution was to fold the two existing institutions into a new Michigan Strategic Fund and assign Plastrik and his staff to add a series of other programs. After a long battle in the state Senate, Blanchard convinced the legislature to transfer MEDA's funding base—$20 million a year from oil and gas leases on state land—to the Strategic Fund.

To design new programs, Plastrik again turned to his consultants, particularly Bill Schweke of CfED and Pete Hansen, Jerry Brown's former aide. The result was a new generation in sophistication, built around the concept of wholesaling. If Massachusetts wrote the book on state development banks, Michigan has published a new edition.

"We want to use what money we have to help make possible bankable private deals that aren't getting made," Plastrik explains. "We want to influence the behavior of private financial institutions, without increasing their risk. We believe there are gaps in the private marketplace—for instance, entrepreneurial capital below the venture capital level. Venture capitalists want a 35 percent annual return on their money within four or five years, usually when the company goes public. Not every company can do that, but those that can't are often still too risky to get bank loans. Other firms have real growth potential, but lack the zippy technology venture capitalists are fond of. Small businesses also have trouble getting capital, because it's too much trouble for the banks. So we want to help the private sector create new lending vehicles for small business."

"There's a real sense in all of this that the state has limits, that the private sector is what drives the economy," adds Lou Glazer, who also helped shape the program. "When push comes to shove, they've got the money, and we don't. On the other hand, at the margins, by sharing the risk, the state can act as a catalyst. Wholesaling also injects social goals into the marketplace without asking government bureaucrats, who generally don't have much investment expertise, to act as bankers and venture capitalists."

Perhaps the most elegant of the Strategic Fund programs, called the Capital Access Program, simply offers banks a carrot to make riskier loans. If a bank will establish a "loan loss reserve fund" to cover a special portfolio of riskier loans, the state will contribute to it. In theory, the existence of an insurance fund will allow banks to make more loans to new businesses, small businesses, and other firms that would not qualify for a conventional bank loan. Pete Hansen pioneered this model in California, but Proposition 13 wiped out the funds necessary to implement it.

The reserve fund, which ranges from 6 to 14 percent of the value of the special portfolio, allows the bank to absorb loss ratios far higher than those on their normal business loans (which are typically under one percent). If the fund runs out, however, the bank absorbs the rest of the loss. Unlike 80 or 90 percent loan guarantees from the SBA, this program forces the bank to evaluate the loan with some degree of prudence. Since the bank makes the underwriting judgment on its own, no government bureaucracy is necessary. The government is simply providing a small insurance fund to share the risk, so the bank can stretch its lending net to encompass more firms.

During the program's first year of operation, the 48 banks that signed up made 50 loans. They went to precisely the kinds of firms the program was designed to serve: 12 went to start-up companies (which can rarely secure bank loans); 44 went to firms with annual sales of under $500,000; and a significant number went to firms that had insufficient collateral or were too highly leveraged to get a normal bank loan.[18]

A second Strategic Fund program copies a Pennsylvania effort: state money to catalyze the formation of seed capital funds. "We want to invest widely in business development, in people who can help businesses at the risky end get over the hurdles," says Plastrik. "Venture capitalists have become more risk averse than in earlier days, because they hit a period when they could make a 35 percent return without much risk. Now we have to rebuild the early venture capital role—the venture capitalists need a farm system that grows prospects for them. With that you need money, but you also need management expertise, help on the development plan, and so on."

Whereas Pennsylvania demanded $3 in private money for every $1 in public contributions, Michigan required only $1 in private money for each $2 in state money. The Strategic Fund chose four private seed funds, all of which will operate statewide, and loaned each one $2 million. The loans do not have to be repaid until the fund is dissolved, and the interest rate is 9 percent.

For small businesses that cannot attract seed or venture capital, the Strategic Fund has helped capitalize Business and Industrial Development Corporations (BIDCOs), on the California model. The idea is to create an entirely new financial industry designed to fill the gap between venture capital and bank loans, with perhaps 20 or 25 BIDCOs operating around the state. Plastrik and his staff envision the BIDCOs as smaller versions of the Massachusetts Capital Resource Company. Their primary role will be in mezzanine financing—making subordinated loans in tandem with banks, for instance, often with the option to purchase stock if the firm is successful. They can also make SBA-insured loans, and if they desire, they can create SBA-licensed Small Business Investment Companies, as subsidiaries, to make equity investments.

In California, where the state provided no start-up capital and the

BIDCOs were thinly capitalized, they have been relatively cautious, primarily making SBA-insured loans. To ensure that Michigan's BIDCOs have enough capital to be more aggressive, the Strategic Fund is investing up to $2 million of equity in each one. It requires that the BIDCOs' private investors come up with at least twice that much. One BIDCO, which has already received a $4-million investment from Chrysler, will specialize in factory automation products. Another may specialize in turning around failing firms.

The Strategic Fund's role is simply to act as a catalyst; as each BIDCO becomes successful, the Strategic Fund will sell its stock and back out. In addition, the state pension fund will invest in BIDCOs that meet its criteria, purely for the market return. Plastrik hopes to use the pension fund example to convince private insurance companies to follow suit.

The Strategic Fund has two other new programs, both of them retailing operations. (Plastrik and his board phased out MEDA, which was a more conventional loan fund.) One is a Product Development Fund, similar to those in Massachusetts and Connecticut. It provides venture capital for new products and processes developed by established firms, taking its return in the form of royalties. The other is a Minority Business Loan Fund, which is somewhat akin to the Community Development Finance Corporation in Massachusetts. By 1987, it had made roughly $1.5 million in investments. Every company it invests in is assigned a free consultant of the Strategic Fund's choosing. In addition, the Strategic Fund has solicited investors for a minority-owned BIDCO. Unlike the other BIDCOs, this one had to raise only $500,000 in private money to get $1.75 million in public funds, and the Strategic Fund will convert the money to a grant if the BIDCO meets certain performance targets.

Even the Michigan Chamber of Commerce, which is normally allied with the Republican party, has applauded the Strategic Fund's move to wholesaling. "We think that's a much more positive approach than having the state making the determinations on who should receive loans," its president, Jim Barrett, said in 1985. "Those who have the expertise—in this case the financial institutions—will have much more of an incentive than they had in the past [to fill the state's capital gaps]. And it should help deal with this problem that is commonly voiced by small-business people, regarding capital availability."

The Research Strategy

With its Strategic Fund and its public pension fund, Michigan has taken a significant step toward closing its capital gaps. But the transformation of the Michigan economy will take more than new forms of capital. It will also take new ideas, new companies bent on commercializing those ideas, and new approaches by existing companies. To create seed beds for those ideas and companies, Governor Milliken's Task Force on High Technology recommended that the state finance new research institutes in industrial technology and in biotechnology.

In similar situations, many states have poured money into existing academic departments, or created applied research consortia at universities, jointly funded by industry and government. But Milliken's task force decided that if Michigan's new programs were to be of real value to industry, they would have to be independent of academia, driven by industry's needs rather than those of academic researchers (who advance in their professions by excelling in basic research). Reaching this goal has been far more difficult than the task force anticipated.

The institutes' funding has come primarily from state government and from Michigan foundations. The Industrial Technology Institute (ITI) received over $50 million from foundations, plus $17.5 million from the state for the first five years. The Michigan Biotechnology Institute (MBI) received roughly $23 million from foundations, plus $6 million from the state for the first five years.[19]

Located in Ann Arbor, the Industrial Technology Institute is a critical link in the state strategy to target automated manufacturing. Automation Alley, as the stretch between Ann Arbor and Detroit is becoming known, already boasts the largest concentration of machine-vision and robotics firms in the nation. ITI is designed to help the area reach critical mass—to make it, in former director Jerome Smith's words, a "Silicon Valley in southeast Michigan for durable goods equipment suppliers." It is also designed to help Michigan's manufacturers adopt these new technologies and thus remain competitive. These two goals—the *development* of new technologies and the *deployment* of new technologies—have proven difficult to reconcile.

Very few research institutes around the country focus on the process of manufacturing, rather than on specific product technologies, such as robotics or software. But ITI's creators believed that the state needed a bridge between basic research on the application of microelectronics to manufacturing, which took place mainly in universities, and the applied research done by industry. Their convictions were based more on intuition than on market research or a careful look at models in other countries. But the experience of ITI has proven their intuitions correct.

If ITI's founders were clear about the niche they wanted to fill, they were not so clear about how ITI could fill it. They decided to construct a new building, complete with a fully automated model manufacturing facility; to hire a staff of 250 by 1992; and to set a goal of over $20 million a year in research contracts by 1992, a level that would make the institute self-supporting.[20] Their "technology development" role was fairly easy to visualize. ITI would do advanced research on new manufacturing technologies, on contract with individual firms, consortia of industrial firms, or government laboratories. The "technology deployment" role was a bit more difficult. ITI's founders believed that the staff could consult with firms to analyze their production problems and to help them adopt automated equipment; that it could help managers analyze the costs, benefits, and effects of adopting automated systems; that it could analyze new product designs for industry to assess their manufacturability; and that it could teach managers how to adopt new approaches—particularly to labor relations—required by the new technologies.[21]

ITI's first president, Dr. Jerome Smith, proceeded to hire a first-class research staff, whose instincts have pushed the institution toward academic research. ITI has done some important research work, and in some cases it has also played the technology deployment role. A good example of both is provided by the General Motors manufacturing automation protocol (MAP), which is designed to facilitate communications between all computerized machines used in the factory. MAP is essentially a shared operating system and language, akin to the IBM operating system that allows every manufacturer to produce personal computers which can operate programs designed for IBM PCs. Wearing its technology development hat, ITI has done contract research on MAP. Wearing its technology deployment hat, it has been recognized by GM and the National Bureau of Standards as an authorized testing center, where companies can test their equipment to see it if is fully compatible with the MAP system.

For the most part, however, ITI has not succeeded in fulfilling its founders' vision of a technology deployment role. Most of its efforts have gone into contract research. Even here, the institute has had trouble proving its value to industry. In 1986, with only $3.2 million of contract research (and only about half of that from industry), it fell far short of its goals. Virtually none of its research was for small or medium-sized firms, because they could not afford its rates. Disappointed with these results, the board began searching for a new president who would be better able to sell ITI's services to Michigan manufacturers. It also began to push the idea of forming research consortia involving a number of firms—something ITI had done only to a limited extent—rather than simply pursuing research contracts. Many laboratories can fulfill research contracts, but few institutions can foster joint research within an industry, a role ITI is perfectly positioned to play.

The Michigan Strategic Fund, which controls the state money earmarked for ITI and MBI, began a simultaneous effort to move ITI toward technology deployment. When ITI applied for a second five-year grant from the Strategic Fund, Plastrik and his board agreed to provide $4 million, but only for specific technology deployment projects, with specific performance benchmarks and review processes built in. One project will develop a software program that can help a consultant diagnose a firm's needs for new production technologies, much as a medical diagnostic program can help a physician decipher a complex set of symptoms. A second will examine why durable goods manufacturers have had such trouble implementing machine-vision and other sensing technologies, such as those developed by Perceptron. A third will create a training program for factory managers in computer-integrated manufacturing, using the ITI model manufacturing facility.[22] To encourage ITI to work with small firms, the Strategic Fund gave it another $3 million to do work on contract with the Michigan Modernization Service, to which I will turn in a moment.

The Michigan Biotechnology Institute has experienced similar problems. It was created on the assumption that it could provide research that would benefit the state forestry, wood products, agriculture, and food-processing industries. Dr. Gregory Zelkus, its first director, has put the institute on the road to its desired status as a world-class biotechnology research institution. But defining an economic development role—a market for its products—has proven extremely difficult. Working with the Institute's board, the Strategic Fund has convinced MBI to create a for-profit subsidiary to commercialize its research breakthroughs—by licensing them to existing firms, by joint venturing with existing firms, or by creating new firms to take them to market.

It will not be clear for some time whether the revamped research institutes can successfully fulfill their missions. One clear lesson has already emerged from their experiences, however: technology development and technology deployment are very different functions, which may often belong in different institutions. Once a top-flight research staff is in place, an institution almost inevitably becomes driven by a research—rather than a development—agenda. In Japan, which vigorously pursues the kind of work done by ITI and MBI, responsibilities for technology development and deployment are generally kept separate. Michigan would probably be better off if Milliken's task force had looked at Japanese models and done the same. As it is, MBI has decided that it needs a separate corporation to take its technology into the marketplace, and the Strategic Fund has earmarked roughly half of its second grant to ITI for work on contract with a separate state institution, whose primary mission is technology deployment.

When the legislature funded MBI and ITI, representatives from Detroit pushed hard for a third institution, in their city. As a result, the legislature also appropriated $1.5 million for a Metropolitan Center for High Technology (MCHT), an advanced technology research and incubator center in the Detroit ghetto. Whereas the other centers had clear technology focuses, MCHT simply had a huge, unrenovated building and a vague idea that jobs could be generated in the inner city. Predictably, it has not fared as well as the other two institutions. It has failed to attract the "anchor tenant" it wanted—a large research firm or project—to give it credibility, and its list of other tenants is still short.

The Michigan Modernization Service

In the shadows of Michigan's large durable goods manufacturers lie some 15,000 manufacturing firms with five hundred or fewer employees. Nearly two-thirds of them have 20 or fewer employees. These smaller companies employ more than half a million people, with an annual payroll of $11 billion. Close to 50 percent of those jobs are in industries linked to automobile production, such as plastics, primary and fabricated metals, and machinery. These "foundation firms," as Blanchard administration officials call them, form a supply chain that makes it possible for industrial giants such as GM, Ford, and Chrysler to function in Michigan.[23]

Many of these foundation firms are small machine tool operations, which contract to provide components for larger manufacturers. Studies of the state's machine tool industry during the difficult years of the early 1980s revealed both great turbulence and significant vitality. Between 1978 and 1984, the industry lost 2,900 jobs. Yet 53 percent of the firms that survived grew in size, adding nearly ten thousand new jobs. In addition, four hundred new machine tool companies were born, creating another five thousand jobs.[24]

Another study looked at the characteristics of growing machine tool firms. It found that the fastest growing companies were those which had begun using computer numerically controlled (CNC) machines, the most advanced of all machine tools. By and large, these successful firms were younger and smaller than the industry average.[25] Thus a wave of innovation was sweeping through the industry, pushed forward by new firms that embraced the latest technologies.

With the auto makers pushing to cut costs and moving toward computer-integrated manufacturing and just-in-time delivery systems, suppliers who are also using computerized production processes have a great advantage. Yet it is far more difficult for the small firm to automate than for the large firm. The process is expensive and time consuming. It requires careful planning, and it requires that the work force be retrained to use the new machines. Few of those running small firms have the time or capital necessary to accomplish this transformation; hence the tendency for new technologies to be exploited more often by start-ups than by existing small firms.

Based on *The Path to Prosperity*, the Blanchard administration decided the public sector could play a critical role in helping foundation firms adjust to the world of automated manufacturing. It began by creating a new Technology Deployment Service (TDS)—a small group of consultants, most of them from the private sector, who work closely with foundation firms that are considering installing computer-based production technologies. These agents carefully assess the client firm, draw up a 50 to 60 page report recommending a plan of action, and refer the firm to private-sector consultants if necessary. TDS also contracts with "training associates" at community colleges, who draw up detailed training plans for the firms and help them apply to a small training fund set up by the administration for this purpose. In the program's first year TDS representatives delivered 45 reports and training plans and secured training for 2,400 employees. TDS also developed a pool of 75 private-sector "manufacturing technology consultants," to which it refers clients with more complex problems.[26]

In the same division of the Commerce Department as TDS, Blanchard created an Office for New Enterprise Services (ONES) to work with entrepreneurs who were trying to start their own technology-oriented companies. ONES helps them write business plans, formulate marketing strategies, and find potential sources of financing, both public and private. For firms with strong business plans, it acts as an advocate with state funding sources. In its first year, roughly half of its clients were related to manufacturing.[27]

TDS and ONES were successful enough, as demonstration projects, that in 1987 Blanchard decided to build a comprehensive industrial extension service, which could offer an array of services to foundation firms. He calls the new entity the Michigan Modernization Service (MMS). In addition to TDS and ONES, it includes a Market Development Service, to help with marketing and exports;[28] a Research and Analysis Program, which among other projects is conducting a detailed census of Michigan manufacturers; an Educational Services Program, to provide workshops for managers, union leaders, and entrepreneurs; and a Workforce Development Service, to provide retraining and to help foundation firms adopt more cooperative labor-management relations.

Using the basic TDS model, Workforce Development Service consultants will do assessments of a firm's labor-management relations, then recommend strategies to improve them. MMS will then pay for up to ten days of consulting to implement the new system; after that the firm is on its own. In addition, the MMS program will sponsor an annual Governor's Conference on Labor-Management Relations, training programs for union leaders and corporate managers on the cooperative model, and research on labor-management relations. It will work closely with the Department of Labor, which has a staff of labor mediators and a small grant program for area labor-management committees, and with the Governor's Office of Job Training, which has a small program to help groups of workers interested in employee ownership.

Finally, MMS has established a partnership with ITI. The Strategic Fund has provided $3 million to ITI for work on contract with MMS, and half of the MMS staff has moved to the ITI building in Ann Arbor. By contracting with ITI for particular services, such as trouble-shooting on the installation of a complex computer-integrated manufacturing system, MMS will bring ITI's expertise to the world of foundation firms.

The result of all this is an institution that can help small manufacturers upgrade their production technologies, retrain their workers, revamp their labor-management systems, find new markets, even launch new companies. With an annual budget of almost $5 million, access to another $2.5 million in training funds, a full-time staff of 27 civil servants and another 30 to 40 field representatives, the Michigan Modernization Service is one of the nation's most comprehensive and sophisticated industrial extension systems.[29]

Recruitment Strategies

Blanchard has not only developed new economic programs built around the themes of technological innovation, the factory of the future, and wholesaling, he has built an industrial recruitment effort that is consistent with these themes. Blanchard asked a team at the University of Michigan's Institute for Labor and Industrial Relations to develop an input-output model of the state economy, through which the state could estimate the effects of any new plant on total earnings, jobs, and state and local tax revenues—and thus the appropriate level of financial incentives.[30]

In 1984, Blanchard used this model to fashion a package of $80 million in local property tax reductions, $20 million in state job-training subsidies, and $20 million in state loans to convince Mazda to build a new plant in Flat Rock. The model indicated that Mazda's long-term contribution to the state economy would outweigh the financial subsidies. In addition, Blanchard saw the Mazda plant as a psychological turning point for the state. "Mazda was important because it got coverage," he argues. "People here were used to believing the propaganda, that Michigan was somehow a bad place, that we were dying, that nothing would work. There was a sense of helplessness. But Mazda was a major transformation, because we were able to get the most modern auto plant in the world, in competition with South Carolina, a right-to-work state. That shook everybody up. Then we were able to come in with all these examples of things that were happening that were good for Michigan in terms of economic development, and they're now being covered by the press. If you look back, that was the event which turned things."

In contrast to the Mazda deal, Blanchard later withdrew from the bidding for a Mitsubishi plant when his input-output model showed that the long-term benefits would not outweigh the subsidies Mitsubishi wanted.[31] The real breakthrough for Michigan came when GM put its Saturn plant up for bid in 1985, however. In their efforts to land Saturn—the most sought-after plant of the decade—Blanchard and his staff put together perhaps the most unusual state offer ever made to lure an industrial plant.

GM launched Saturn to build an entirely new car in an entirely new way—to rethink the entire process of automobile manufacturing. Saturn executives brought the same "clean sheet" approach to their labor bargaining with the UAW: there would be no layoffs at the plant, hierarchical distinctions would be minimized, time clocks would be done away with, work rules would be minimized, 20 percent of all pay would come in the form of performance bonuses, and participatory decision making would be the rule.[32]

If Saturn and the UAW were creating a new kind of partnership on the assembly line, Blanchard reasoned, why not offer a new partnership outside the plant as well? "We were trying to say to Saturn: 'You've rethought so much of your way of doing business that it only makes sense that you do the same with state government, that you begin a long-term partnership that has the flexibility to change your way of doing business,'" says Plastrik, who with MMS founder Jack Russell developed the proposal. The partnership would be embodied in a new public authority called a "Manufacturing Innovation Partnership (MIP)," made up of Saturn, the UAW, the local community, and the state.[33]

For a plant that would have 5 percent of its work force in retraining at any one time, the state offered to invest $100 million in training over ten years, most of it to build and operate a new "Saturn Institute" on the plant grounds. Jointly designed and run by Saturn, the UAW, Saturn's suppliers, and the state, the institute would provide not only training and education but also child care, recreation, counseling, retiree programs, even health and fitness programs.

Nearby the MIP would construct a "Saturn Industrial Park" for suppliers, built to Saturn's specifications to facilitate just-in-time deliveries to the plant. The state would put $50 million into a fund to support research and development in industrial technology, particularly joint ventures between Saturn, its suppliers, and state research institutions like ITI. The fund would also provide development capital and technical consultations for small manufacturers who needed to upgrade their technology to sell to Saturn.

For the local community, the MIP would have a $5-million development fund, for projects such as small-business incubators, housing, neighborhood development, or recreation facilities. Finally, the state would put up $100 million over ten years for a "Clean Sheet Development Fund," to be used for any unanticipated investments the partners felt were necessary.

On the regulatory side, the proposal was equally radical. Since the company pledged no layoffs, the state offered to rebate all of its unemployment taxes. Since Michigan's workmen's compensation taxes were high, the state would allow Saturn and the UAW to opt out and negotiate their own system. On environmental matters, Michigan would minimize interference by operating far more than usual on trust. It would reduce monitoring, give the company "maximum discretion" in applying the best available technology to control pollution, and jointly finance advanced pollution control research. Finally, to ensure a minimum of red tape all around, Blanchard promised to appoint a "Saturn Regulatory Ombudsman."

Overall, counting $200 million in property tax abatements offered, the package would have cost the state at least $500 million over ten years. Aside from the property tax abatement, "all of our investments were intended to be ways of building the asset base in Michigan, rather than just subsidizing GM," says Plastrik. "With the training, we would be building a manufacturing elite in Michigan. With the R&D money, we would be creating engineering expertise here, which is the key to being a leader in advanced manufacturing."

As it turned out, Michigan lost the plant to Tennessee, primarily because Tennessee had a location more central to the Saturn market and suppliers. But Michigan's proposal did succeed in catapulting a high-wage, high-cost state into the final three. Roger Smith, chief executive officer of GM, called it the most innovative proposal he received. And Michigan won a consolation prize: the Saturn headquarters and technology center. Even though this facility will not create as many jobs as the actual plant, it will have other advantages for the state. It will be far more likely to become the source of innovative spinoff companies than an assembly plant would, for instance.

The Blanchard administration has not abandoned the model it developed for Saturn. It has pursued the auto companies ever since to create a similar partnership, but they have been slow to change their traditional view of state government as little more than a tax collector. It launched an "Auto-in-Michigan" research project, which brings industry, labor, state, and academic people together under MMS auspices to analyze the auto industry and pinpoint potential weaknesses. And in addition to its labor-management cooperation programs, it is creating a statewide advisory council on labor-management cooperation, made up of leaders from business, labor, government, and academia.

Even before the Saturn proposal, Blanchard had indulged his taste for business-labor-government partnerships on an ad hoc basis. In 1983, for instance, the White Pine copper mine in the Upper Peninsula closed because world copper prices had plunged and the workers had refused to take a deep enough pay cut to offset the drop. One thousand people lost their jobs. "We got the union and management together, we found a buyer for the company, and we forged a cooperative agreement in which it was bought out," says Blanchard. (The state also gave the company a hefty loan.) "There was profit sharing, an employee stock ownership plan, and the union gave concessions in the contract. They resolved the whole thing, and the mine reopened." By late 1987, the price of copper had risen sharply and the firm was doing so well that it was considering going public with a stock offering.

Perhaps Commerce Secretary Doug Ross best articulates the philosophy behind these efforts. "When 95 percent of the American economy was domestic, we were able to afford this polarity in the marketplace between labor and management," he says. "And the politics of a state like Michigan reflected that polarity: we were the party of labor, the Republicans were the party of business. Clearly, and we see this more dramatically here than anyplace, we cannot tolerate that warfare and be competitive. And so a kind of synthesis is coming out of that labor-management dialectic, which we are trying to embody. We are an administration, and we hope increasingly a party, that is supportive of economic growth based on labor-management cooperation. The key is, we have to establish ourselves as honest brokers for the community when it comes to issues of economic development. That's the position Blanchard has tried to establish; that's the place on the floor we want to shoot from."

The Blanchard Record

In contrast to Governors Dukakis, Thornburgh, Babbitt, and Clinton, Jim Blanchard has been in office only since 1983. Though he accomplished a great deal during his first term, it is still a bit early to evaluate his economic development efforts. Governor Milliken's decision to use public pension funds for venture capital investments has clearly sparked a venture capital boom in Michigan, but it is not yet clear how successfully the state's entrepreneurs will be able to capitalize on the new financing. Milliken's research institutes have both experienced problems, but the Blanchard administration is working to correct them. Blanchard's own key initiatives—the Michigan Strategic Fund and the Michigan Modernization Service—were not put into place until 1986 and 1987. Both are extremely sophisticated on theoretical grounds, perhaps the most sophisticated in the nation. Because most of the programs involved are barely off the ground, however, it is too early to tell whether they will fulfill their promise. One fact *is* clear: Michigan has put so much effort into modernizing its manufacturing base that national government and industry groups have begun to recognize the state as the center of industrial revival. In 1987, the Blanchard administration won two big prizes. The National Center for Manufacturing Sciences, an industry-funded research consortium, decided to locate in Ann Arbor. And the National Science Foundation picked Michigan as the site of its new communications network to link all research and development facilities.

A number of other observations about Blanchard's efforts are possible. First, the theoretical work done to guide Blanchard's economic development strategy has been first rate. *The Path to Prosperity* is one of the best economy strategy documents produced by any state, and its conclusions have been followed closely by the administration. As in Pennsylvania, giving authority over the Commerce Department to the person who oversaw the study has proven to be very important.

What makes *The Path to Prosperity* unique is its recommendation that the state target many of its economic development efforts on advanced manufacturing. Given Michigan's history and domination by durable goods manufacturing, this targeted strategy appears to make sense. If the auto industry and other durable goods manufacturers cannot remain vital, neither can the Michigan economy.

Blanchard also appears to have had an impact on the overall business climate in Michigan. With his tax cut for small business, his workmen compensation reforms, his reform of the state securities and franchise laws, and similar measures, he has successfully changed the image many Michigan business people have of government. Blanchard has also financed an extensive promotion campaign that paints Michigan as a state on the manufacturing frontier, a state in which rapid innovation is creating new technologies and state-of-the-art manufacturing capability. Whether this campaign has had any impact on attracting new investment to Michigan, it appears to have had some psychological impact on those in the state. Blanchard has given both the state's leaders and its people a positive vision of the future, a reason to have faith in Michigan. In economic development, that is half the battle.

On the negative side, Blanchard has done little to stimulate interaction between university researchers and Michigan businesses; when he appropriated $25 million a year to fund research, the universities won a legislative battle over control of the funds and divided them up for traditional academic purposes. He has created regional development organizations, called Community Growth Alliances, but they pale in comparison to Thornburgh's efforts. Hence, even though Michigan has created model development finance programs, its other efforts to stimulate an entrepreneurial climate have lagged behind Pennsylvania's.

Nor did Blanchard tackle the state education and training systems during his first term. (He did create a small Governor's Office of Job Training and a novel Michigan Education Trust. If the IRS rules payments to the latter program tax-deductible, it will guarantee children four years of tuition at any state college or university if their parents put $3,000 to $4,000, in installments, into an Education Trust.) Finally, Blanchard has not made significant efforts to bring the poor into the development process, a critical omission in a state in which one of every eight residents is on some form of public assistance.[34] After *The Path to Prosperity* came out, he created a group to prepare a similar report on the poor, informally known as the "Path to Opportunity" group. It did not function as well as its predecessor, and when its report revealed just how severe the problems were in Michigan, Blanchard chose to bury it rather than release it during an election year.

In fairness, these issues are at the top of Blanchard's second-term agenda. In his 1987 State of the State address, he announced that his second administration would be built around "a strategy to invest in the knowledge and the skills of our people." To manage the process, he created a Cabinet Council on Human Investment, similar to his Cabinet Council on Economic Development. Its major projects include a review of the state job-training system and the development, with the Iacocca-Fraser commission, of a set of basic employability standards for the entry-level jobs of the future. The idea is to develop a basic skills test that will give students, schools, and training programs a benchmark against which to measure their work, while giving employers a way to measure the readiness of job applicants. Welfare reform is also on Blanchard's agenda, and in early 1988 he proposed an $85-million-a-year urban strategy.

The Politics of Jim Blanchard

Blanchard is not a traditional liberal Democrat. He has done a few things for Michigan's poor: funded his summer jobs program, created a Conservation Corps, launched a small grant program for community groups involved in housing rehabilitation. Until his 1988 proposal, he paid little attention to the massive problems of Detroit. For most of his first term the money was not there—and when it began to appear, he preferred to cut income taxes back to their 1982 levels.

"We constructed the tax program in such a way as to take care of the problem, but not to do any more," says Conrad Mallett, Jr., who was Blanchard's legal aide during his first two years as governor. "Frankly, what the governor did was to say, 'Listen, I want to solve the problem, but I am not here as a New Deal governor, I am here as a manager for the eighties.'"

One result has been that traditional Democratic constituencies such as organized labor and urban blacks have been restive, and traditional Republican constituencies such as business have been pleased. "Everyone just figured that [former state AFL-CIO chief] Sam Fishman and [UAW president] Owen Bieber would pull the strings on him," says John Thodis, who runs the Michigan Manufacturers Association. "But he has persuaded the business community that he is not a tool of organized labor. I don't think there's been a governor in the last 25 years who's been as understanding of the problems of how to create and retain jobs in this state."

Blanchard has tried to stake out a position as a leader who will do what is right, regardless of ideology or political popularity. Buoyed by the economic recovery, he won reelection in 1986 with 68 percent of the vote. In a state in which more people identified themselves as independents than as Democrats, this was a remarkable level of support. But there is no telling how much of it will melt away during the next recession, which will inevitably hit Michigan hard. A Democrat can never take business support for granted, and a Democrat who angers labor may find himself without support from either side.

"There is a soft underside to Jim Blanchard," says Mallett. "I think what we're all looking for in our leaders is a bit of passion about one or two issues, something that they absolutely firmly believe in. From that perception, you and I can predict their behavior. In the absence of that, everyone gets a little uncomfortable—where is this guy coming from? What people are looking for is this Coleman Young, Ronald Reagan kind of thing—shoot from the hip, this is what I believe, damn the torpedoes and full speed ahead."

Blanchard has sought to give voters that sense—while transcending the traditional liberal and conservative categories—by creating a new category. He has portrayed himself as a governor who is passionately committed to leading Michigan into the new age of global competition and technological innovation. In his 1987 State of the State address, he laid out four goals that defined his task:

"The people of Michigan will be the best educated, most skilled in the world at whatever they choose to do—and they will be able to learn new skills and acquire new knowledge as needed.

"The companies in Michigan will be the best equipped, most advanced, most cooperative, and most competitive in the world.

"The products made in Michigan will be quality products.

"And the economy of Michigan will invite and invigorate a spirit of entrepreneurship and innovation that will keep Michigan on the cutting edge of change—and on the front line of America's economic future."

Perhaps Doug Ross best sums up Blanchard's role. Ross likens Michigan's journey to the Kubler-Ross stages of mourning. "We have been mourning the last phase of the industrial revolution, the mass-production phase, which we were losing because the world was changing," he ex-

plains. "Our anger stage involved a lot of antitax, antigovernment stuff—
'We're mad as hell,' but we're not quite sure who to be mad at. Then we
went through our depression stage. We've gone through denial, anger,
and depression, and then you have to come to acceptance. I think this
administration was dealt the task of bringing the state out of depression, to
acceptance."

6

MASSACHUSETTS: REDISTRIBUTING
ECONOMIC GROWTH

Michael Dukakis's loss to Ed King in 1978 came as a terrible shock. It was "horrendous," his wife later said, a kind of "public death."[1] The rejection was so traumatic, according to those who know him well, that it came to overshadow every other event in his life. Dukakis spent the next three years teaching at Harvard's John F. Kennedy School of Government, analyzing his failure, and plotting his comeback. One by one, he mended the fences that had cost him the governorship. He made promises to organized labor; he settled his differences with welfare rights activists; he courted other liberal constituencies he had offended. Throughout this time, he talked publicly about what he had learned from defeat. In particular, he promised that he would be a less-rigid governor the second time around, a governor who had learned the value of compromise and consensus.

Like Dukakis, Ed King had stumbled in office. Faced with a liberal press in an essentially liberal state, he had remained largely on the defensive. Worse, his administration had been damaged by scandals. And where Dukakis had been victimized by the inflation-induced tax revolt, King was hurt by the recession. He began the 1982 campaign far behind Dukakis in the polls.

Once again, however, Dukakis had trouble lighting a fire under the electorate. Like the cross-country runner he was in high school, Dukakis is earnest, disciplined, and plodding. He is competent but cool, cerebral but uninspiring. Slight (5'8") and slope-shouldered, with dark hair, craggy eyebrows, and eyes that narrow thoughtfully at the edges, he is even-tempered to a fault. ("I fight—he discusses," says his wife.)[2] When he shakes a voter's hand, he or she is more likely to hear his analysis of a problem than bask in his warmth. George Keverian, speaker of the Massachusetts House, once joked that if Dukakis wanted to depress the central highway running through Boston (a recurrent issue in local politics), all he had to do was talk about it.

After four rocky years with King, however, Massachusetts voters chose competence over charisma. They ushered out the populist, rhetorical King, who inspired working-class conservatives but aroused loathing among the liberal elite, and brought back the competent Dukakis, chastened by his four years in the wilderness.

As promised, Dukakis was a very different governor his second time around, one more in tune with the new political climate of the 1980s. Defeat had given him a new appreciation for economic growth, transformed his attitude toward business, and made him extremely sensitive to taxpayers. It had also forced a deliberate change in his style. During his first term, he had typically staked out the position he believed was right and refused to budge—in the process alienating the legislature and the business community and earning himself an image of arrogance and self-righteousness. Now he sought to reach out to business and the legislature, and when confronted with difficult issues, he repeatedly strove to bring the warring parties together to work out compromise solutions. He changed so much, in fact, that one can argue that he learned his lessons too well—a subject to which I shall return.

Dukakis's top priority remained the same: the revitalization of poor communities in Massachusetts. But this time both the context and the style were different. For most of his second term, Massachusetts enjoyed an unemployment rate between 3 and 4 percent, the lowest of any industrial state. Blessed with sudden prosperity, the public found Dukakis's desire to reshape patterns of growth far more palatable than it had in the 1970s. When growth is no longer the fundamental issue, the location of growth can be.

The rapid growth had begun in 1976 and 1977—before Dukakis's new economic programs were in existence and before the property tax cuts mandated by Proposition 2½, to which conservatives often attribute the boom. The engine behind this growth was technological innovation: between 1975 and 1981, high-tech firms generated 81 percent of the manufacturing jobs created in Massachusetts, and computer-related services grew even faster than high-tech manufacturing.[3] The roots of this phenomenon go back to World War II, when the Defense Department funded the creation of one of the world's first computers—appropriately named Whirlwind—at MIT. A generation of graduate students worked on Whirlwind, then left academia to found the hardware and software companies that made Route 128 famous. MIT's role can hardly be exaggerated: when MIT professor John Donovan studied 216 high-tech companies in the greater Boston area, he found that 156 of them had been born in MIT departments or laboratories.[4] Another continuing influence was defense spending: when it fell after the Vietnam War, Massachusetts suffered the worst recession of any industrial state; when it doubled under Reagan, the economy shifted into overdrive.[5] (It is worth noting that high taxes, which prevailed before Proposition 2½, did not prevent the boom.)

Although the economy took off, the population did not. Between 1975 and 1983, while the U.S. population grew by 8.6 percent, the Massachusetts population remained steady.[6] As word of the state's new prosperity spread in the mid-1980s, immigration, particularly from Ireland, began to rise. Still, the combination of rapid economic growth and slow population growth drove unemployment below 3 percent in 1987. Over the previous seven years, per capita income increased a phenomenal 75 percent.[7]

Dukakis administration officials admit that they have had little impact on the growth rate; they claim primarily to have effected the *distribution* of growth. "Have we fundamentally influenced the size of the Massachusetts economy? The state's role is measurable but marginal," Alden Raine, Dukakis's economic development chief, told me in 1985. "A lot of the roots are in the fifties and sixties, in terms of high-tech industries. The academic base is a lot of it. There is obviously something in the water we drink here that makes this an entrepreneurial state."

Dukakis answered the question in similar fashion. "I think our unique contribution," he added, "is that we've been able to consciously bring a great deal of this growth to communities and regions which in the absence of our efforts would not experience it. In the policy areas that the Great Society was trying to address, we're moving very aggressively. But we're doing it in ways that are cost effective."

This goal defined the Dukakis administration's second term. More than any other governor, Dukakis made a concerted effort to bring poor communities and poor people into the growth process. He focused his economic development apparatus on poor regions. He continued to build the community development network he had launched in 1978. He created new programs to revitalize mature industries, whose decline was responsible for the decline of many Massachusetts communities. He launched a comprehensive program to get people off welfare and into jobs. And he created new programs to stimulate the development of low- and moderate-income housing. As I will argue in the pages below, these efforts were not always well designed or successful; there were failures along with successes. But taken as a whole, they offered important lessons about the process of bringing the poor into the mainstream economy.

Targets of Opportunity

During his first term, Dukakis had focused on declining urban areas. But by the 1980s, cities such as Boston and Lowell were already on the rebound. Hence Dukakis shifted his sights to declining *regions* in Massachusetts—what he called its "targets of opportunity." Rather than creating a formalized program, he followed the ad hoc pattern set in his first term, trying to bend every aspect of state government to favor his targeted regions.

Alden Raine, Frank Keefe's deputy during the first term, became chairman of Dukakis's Development Cabinet and director of the Governor's Office of Economic Development—the equivalent of Keefe's old Office of State Planning, which King had abolished. Raine put a staff member in each of five regions of the state, who worked with local political and business leaders to create new regional organizations to stimulate development. The state continued work on the seven new heritage parks Dukakis had planned back in 1978, on the Lowell model. Once again Dukakis poured infrastructure investments—in roads, sewers, even community colleges and universities—into his targeted areas. In a new wrinkle, he led groups of Massachusetts CEOs on tours through his targets of opportunity, working to convince them to channel their expansion into those areas. And when anyone bit, Raine's staff pulled out all the stops to provide what they needed: tax-exempt financing; investment by the state's quasi-public capital funds; worker training; and so on.

"The states are perfect for this kind of thing," Dukakis argued. "We can't set Federal Reserve policy, we don't deal with trade policy, but this kind of targeted development in distressed areas is something that the states are particularly suited to do."

One of the toughest areas, because it was farthest from the booming Boston region, was the northern Berkshires. Adams and North Adams, the largest towns in the area, were old textile and paper manufacturing centers. As those industries moved South, the area had gradually declined. Surrounded by the picturesque Berkshire Hills, it was by the 1980s one of the poorest areas in Massachusetts, with an unemployment rate of over 10 percent. It provides a useful snapshot of the Dukakis strategy.

In 1983, Dukakis created a Governor's Task Force on Northern Berkshire County, made up of local business, academic, and political leaders. He also funded a heritage park in North Adams. In February 1985, he brought his economic development staff and 30 businessmen to the area. For two days, they toured the region—listening to local business executives extol its virtues, visiting a new industrial park, touring a small-business incubator, and hearing a pep talk from Al Raine about what the state could do to help them invest in the area. "There is just about nothing that you can think of in terms of public financing and training funds that we can't do for you," Raine told the executives.

On the trip Dukakis announced that he would ask the legislature for funding to turn Mount Greylock, the highest peak in the state, into a world-class cross-country ski resort. By 1987, Dukakis had convinced the

legislature to appropriate $12 million to buy the land. The state then nego-
tiated with a private developer who agreed to invest $260 million in restor-
ing an old golf course, a lake, and ski facilities, while building an inn, 1,275
condominiums, shops, and other facilities, all on a New England village
theme.[8]

In 1986, Sprague Electric, one of the largest employers in the area,
decided to leave North Adams. Dukakis assigned one of his quasi-public
agencies, the Government Land Bank, the job of keeping Sprague in the
area. The Land Bank put together $8 to $10 million in public money, negotiated with the unions involved, and found a site in the local industrial
park, whereupon Sprague hired a private developer to put up the buildings. "We saved the 475 jobs we wanted to save," says Timothy Bassett,
executive director of the Land Bank. "I think what we basically did was we
bought time and showed it could be done."

The Sprague experience demonstrated the need for a local development
authority that could handle such deals, so Dukakis created a Northern
Berkshire Regional Industrial Development Authority and gave it $150,000
a year. It is now working with the Land Bank to develop a new industrial
park in the area.

The state also convinced Sprague to donate its old complex—28 buildings in the center of town—to Williams College for a huge art museum,
convention center, and shopping and office complex. Williams secured the
long-term loan of one of the finest collections of modern art in the world.
At this writing, the project awaits only passage of state legislation authorizing up to $35 million in convention center funds. If it proceeds, it will
clearly have a major impact on the North Adams economy. By the spring of
1987—before construction at Greylock Glen began—unemployment in the
area had fallen to 6.2 percent.[9]

Similar stories can be told about other regions. Before his second term
was two weeks old, Dukakis convened a group of elected officials, business people, labor leaders, and educators from southeastern Massachusetts to talk about economic development. He later set up a $1-million job-
training pool for firms expanding or moving into the area. He put $100,000
into a Southeastern Massachusetts Partnership, a consortium of the state,
five cities, and area businesses to pursue economic development. Raine's
office put together financing packages and job training for a series of companies expanding or locating in the region.

In 1983, when the state legislature was debating where to put a new
Microelectronics Center, Dukakis fought hard for the southeastern Massachusetts city of Taunton, where he had donated state land for an industrial
park during his first term. Though he lost, the front-page attention given
Taunton helped the city fill the new park and bring its unemployment rate

down from 13.9 to 4.5 percent in three years.[10] Taunton Mayor Richard Johnson, who supported King in 1978 and 1982, now lavishes praise on Dukakis.

The governor has even targeted his research and development effort, the Centers of Excellence program, on the state's distressed regions. Although it also involves funding for several new academic facilities and a statewide Microelectronics Center (initiated by King), the core of the effort is a small matching grant program to fund joint business and academic research projects at the state universities. This effort so far involves three "centers without walls": biotechnology, in Worcester; marine science, in southeastern Massachusetts; and polymer science, primarily at the University of Massachusetts campuses in Amherst and Lowell. A forthcoming center in applied technology will focus, not on R&D, but on helping small and medium-sized businesses modernize their production facilities and adopt new technologies. Still in its infancy, the Centers of Excellence program is insignificant compared to similar efforts in Pennsylvania, Ohio, New Jersey, and elsewhere. But it has potential.

The Community Development Network

Dukakis's geographic targeting relies heavily on the quasi-public institutions and the support network for community development corporations he created at the end of his first administration. When it was created, this network was probably the most ambitious effort ever launched by a state to stimulate development in poor communities. The Massachusetts experience with it has been an object lesson in the difficulty of the task.

Perhaps the central institution in this network is the Community Development Finance Corporation (CDFC). The Wednesday Morning Breakfast Group had conceived of CDFC as a development bank that would invest in businesses owned or sponsored by community development corporations (CDCs). CDCs were an outgrowth of the activism of the 1960s, particularly in minority communities. The first CDCs were created, with foundation funding, to empower poor communities—to give them the tools to build from within, by creating businesses, rehabilitating housing units, and investing in their people. They were run by boards made up of community members, which hired professional staffs. A few years into the War on Poverty, the federal Office of Economic Opportunity adopted CDCs and began pouring significant funding into them. In the late 1970s, several cities and states launched modest programs to subsidize them, and by the time the Reagan administration cut off federal funding in 1981, most CDCs had become adept at securing federal, state, local, and foundation grants, particularly for low-income housing development. Estimates of their number by the mid-1980s varied from two thousand to five thousand.[11]

When CDFC was funded in 1977, only a handful of CDCs existed in Massachusetts. The Wednesday Morning Breakfast Group correctly foresaw that CDFC would trigger a rush of new CDCs, so it lobbied two other programs through the legislature to provide the fledgling institutions with technical assistance and small operating grants. Today, with roughly 60 CDCs, Massachusetts has one of the strongest networks in the nation.

The managers of CDFC set out with the idealistic vision of investing in firms launched directly by CDCs. Such businesses would not only create jobs, they reasoned, but also generate income for the CDCs. This vision quickly ran headlong into reality. All five such ventures—including an energy audit and retrofit business, a supermarket, and an employee-owned press—rapidly failed.[12] In response, the CDFC board and staff shifted their aim: they would finance businesses referred to them by CDCs, as long as the owner had the CDC stamp of approval and gave it a seat on his board. This strategy fared only slightly better. By 1986, CDFC's loss rates for its first four years were 84 percent, 42 percent, 40 percent, and 85 percent. Out of the first $6 million it invested, it had lost almost $4 million.[13]

The problems were manifold. The CDCs "took every disadvantage you could have and combined it into one—marginal businesses, poor work forces, everything you could imagine," says Carl Sussman, director of the technical assistance program and an early member of the Wednesday Morning Breakfast Group. Few CDCs had the expertise to evaluate business plans or provide technical or managerial assistance to businesses, much less the ability to recruit solid entrepreneurial talent capable of launching new firms. And small-business people generally disliked the idea of having someone from a community organization sitting on their board and looking at their books. Sussman eventually came to the conclusion that, despite the Wednesday morning group's dreams, most CDCs were not well suited to the task of developing businesses.

Another problem was the inexperience of the CDFC staff. It failed to establish clear standards to guide its investment decisions. It never tried to establish relationships with banks that might also lend to its businesses, and thus brought very little private money into poor communities. It also failed to work closely with businesses after it invested, to help them survive.[14]

The CDFC experience quickly showed that entrepreneurs in poor communities needed much more than capital, yet neither CDFC nor the Community Economic Development Assistance Corporation (CEDAC)—the technical assistance program for CDCs—had the capacity to provide adequate management assistance, nor the resources to hire first-rate consultants to do the job. Ironically, an evaluation done by Belden Daniels's firm in 1982 concluded that even though the presence of CDFC had stimulated the formation of many CDCs, it had pulled them away from their real area of strength, housing development, to a field in which they generally failed, business development.[15]

After receiving Daniels's report, the board fired the CDFC president. In the interim, with an acting president from the King administration, it made a $1,325,000 loan that demonstrated one of the key pitfalls facing public or quasi-public development funds: the temptation to make investments because of political pressure to save jobs. This problem is common enough that it is worth exploring the case in question.

The company was Arnold Print Works, a firm that printed high-quality fabrics and upholstery. Located in an old brick mill complex in the center of Adams, Arnold Print Works had been one of the town's largest employers for 120 years. In the 1970s, it had failed to invest rapidly enough in the new rotary screen printing technology with which others in the industry, particularly the Japanese, were shifting from long, standardized runs to flexible, short-run printing. By 1981, its work force had shrunk to 450.[16]

Early in 1981, Arnold's CEO contacted CDFC for a loan. CDFC turned him down because he lacked an adequate business plan for reorganization and revitalization. It referred him to the technical assistance program, which hired a management consulting firm to analyze the company and develop a plan. Arnold's CEO ignored most of the consulting firm's suggestions, and a few months later he filed for bankruptcy, to protect the Print Works from creditors while it reorganized.

By April of 1982, it appeared that Arnold Print Works was going to close its doors. That possibility set off alarm bells within the King administration, which faced a tough reelection campaign against Dukakis. If Arnold closed, its major customer, Waverly Fabrics, would leave town, and Adams would lose 550 jobs—plus hundreds more as the loss rippled outward. King assigned Richard Demers, an undersecretary of economic affairs who had shepherded the CDFC and CEDAC bills to passage when he was in the legislature, to head a crisis intervention team. Demers had been mayor of Chicopee, another western Massachusetts town. "I knew North Adams," he said later. "If you lose 550 jobs you might as well take a shade and pull it down—that end of the state is shut down."[17]

Feelings in Adams were equally bleak. "I think there was this overwhelming feeling that if the business failed, then so would the town," said Deborah McFadden, the director of the Adams Community Development Corporation and a participant in the rescue attempt. "The Print Works has a very special meaning to this community. Everybody that was in that deal, including I think every director on my board, either worked there, had a spouse that worked there, or a parent that worked there."[18]

It was obvious that a plant closing would hurt King's reelection campaign. Demers and his team wasted little time: in July, CDFC proposed to buy Arnold Print Works. It extended credit to cover operating losses, proposed an investment of about $1.3 million, and began to recruit other investors.

Demers and his colleagues had no experience in the rescue business. They were essentially flying blind, learning as they went. The one weapon they did have was political clout. They convinced a group of local banks to lend $650,000, brought in the Massachusetts Capital Resource Company for $200,000, and approached the Bank of Boston for another $550,000. After significant arm-twisting by Demers, the bank agreed—on condition that CDFC find a new CEO for the company and secure a 90 percent loan guarantee from the SBA.

Rather than using a headhunting firm or advertising for a new CEO, the rescue team made a deal with an industry executive who had been recruited by Waverly Fabrics. Here they hit a critical snag. The SBA insisted that the prospective CEO put $200,000 of his own money into the firm—$150,000 of it unsecured and at risk—so he would hurt if his company failed. The CEO refused, and the SBA turned down the loan guarantee. Time was running short: Arnold's owners had cut the work force back to 210, then temporarily shut down. Demers and his group brought every pressure they could muster to bear on the SBA. They used Senators Kennedy and Tsongas, but their principal ally was Rep. Silvio Conte, who represented western Massachusetts and served on the House committee that oversaw SBA appropriations. The prospective CEO adamantly refused to put more than $12,500 of his own money at risk. But finally, after months of pressure, the SBA capitulated. On January 3, 1983, CDFC bought Arnold Print Works.

The new owner was actually Adams Print Works, Inc., a new corporation whose largest stockholder was CDFC. The total investment, by all parties, was $3.3 million. CDFC made the other loans possible by agreeing to take a back seat to all other creditors if the company failed. It was a deal that could never have passed a market test—as all its participants acknowledged.

The new CEO of Adams Print Works quickly laid off more workers and secured a 10 percent pay cut from those who remained. He invested heavily in new machinery, gradually converting to the new rotary screen process. But problems developed anyway. The most disturbing development concerned Waverly Fabrics. During the rescue operation Waverly's owners had insisted that they could not stay in Adams unless the Print Works survived. They had recruited the new CEO and promised to continue buying from him. Once he took over, he had gradually shifted Waverly's patterns to rotary screens. When the process was complete, he handed Waverly the patterns "for safekeeping," ostensibly because his workers were threatening to strike. At that point, Waverly did the unthinkable: it took its patterns and its business elsewhere. Suddenly Adams Print Works had lost half its market. Its new CEO threw in the towel, and the Print Works closed for good. Shortly afterward, Waverly left town as well.

Some observers suspected collusion between Waverly and its hand-picked CEO for Adams Print Works, to keep the plant alive just long enough to transfer Waverly's patterns to rotary screens—whereupon Waverly could move South and buy from cheaper firms. Whatever the reality, the state investment of $1,325,000 had kept the plant operating for only 18 months. CDFC may recoup $250,000 from an insurance settlement. (Several months after it closed, Adams Print Works went up in flames.) But most of the state money is gone.

Although the King administration was clearly desperate to avoid a major plant closing during a reelection campaign, those personally involved in the rescue were genuinely committed to saving jobs in Adams, regardless of politics. The real problem was not their motivation, but their inexperience. The Arnold Print Works story captured all of the weaknesses of CDFC in one frame: its lack of business expertise; its poor relationships with private bankers; its lack of investment standards; and its failure to work closely with the managers of firms in which it invested.

In early 1983, the CDFC board hired a new president. In Charles Grigsby, a respected black venture capitalist, it found someone with the experience necessary to turn CDFC around. As a young man, Grigsby had served as the only black lending officer at a major Boston bank. In 1970, he had asked the bank president for $10 million to lend to inner-city businesses in Boston. When the president declined, Grigsby had resigned and founded Massachusetts's first Minority Enterprise Small Business Investment Company (MESBIC), a small venture capital firm, licensed and partially capitalized by the SBA, to invest in minority-owned firms.

During the nine years he ran a MESBIC, Grigsby earned a solid reputation in a difficult field. He invested in a variety of businesses, including the first black-owned bank in New England. By the time he took over at CDFC, at age 44, he was a seasoned venture capitalist. Affable, articulate, and low key, he had learned how to work with entrepreneurs—how to encourage them and how to turn the screws when they began losing money.

Grigsby immediately established CDFC's independence from political pressure, in the process demonstrating the strength of the quasi-public model. During his first months Dukakis asked him to invest $1 million in a large furniture company that was on the edge of bankruptcy. "Dukakis said to me, 'You've got to make that loan, you've got to save that company,'" Grigsby remembers. "I devoted one whole board meeting to why I wasn't going to make the deal. The board listened, and that was the last time I got any pressure." A few weeks later, the company filed for bankruptcy.

Grigsby made a series of other changes. He minimized the role of CDCs in business development, but shifted 50 percent of CDFC investments to low- and moderate-income housing, an area in which CDCs play central roles. He set up investment guidelines, and he began riding herd on firms in which CDFC invested, as a private venture capitalist would.

For instance, the First Bank of Commerce, the minority-owned bank Grigsby had helped get off the ground, was losing a great deal of money. CDFC had invested $800,000 in the bank. Grigsby used CDFC stock to force out the president and bring in a new one, and he invested another $100,000 in equity to keep the bank alive. He had to withstand a lawsuit, and the Dukakis administration had to sit through an internecine battle in the black community, started by one of its quasi-public agencies. But in Grigsby's view, "That's the kind of role this place has to play. When things are going wrong, you don't just sit there." Today the bank is not only profitable, Grigsby says, "it is the only bank that is marketing aggressively in what I call the southwest quadrant of the city."[19]

Grigsby did the same thing with a minority-owned supermarket —the largest employer in Boston's black ghetto—in which CDFC had invested. With smaller companies, he brought in experienced business advisers, sent the owners to entrepreneurial training courses, and forced them to develop and meet weekly business plans detailing how much would be produced, how much would be spent, and how much would be brought in.

"Companies consider that torture," Grigsby says, "but I consider it technical assistance. To me it's the only way to make a small company work out—it's the only thing that's worked in three years here and nine years in venture capital. It's like Alcoholics Anonymous: you've got to go in there and confess. I tell them, 'You're going to write these six checks this week—you sign one more and I'm going to cut you off.'" If he were white, Grigsby adds, he often couldn't do this.

Grigsby established working relationships with the banking community, bringing banks in on every deal he could. He also launched a loan guarantee program, through which CDFC guarantees 50 percent of the shortfall on bank loans of $50,000 or less, thereby making it easier for companies to secure those loans.

Other plans have been postponed by the legislature's failure to appropriate more money for CDFC. These include a program to provide surety bonds to minority and women contractors, who often cannot get bonding from private surety companies; efforts to expand the use of "godfathers" (experienced business people who agree to help a start-up firm); and a program to "regrow" small businesses that close because the owner dies or retires, by finding new owners and bringing in godfathers to help them.

Since Grigsby took over, CDFC has been profitable. By 1987, the portfolio from his first full year, 1984, had experienced a 6 percent loss rate—although Grigsby expected it to get to 10 to 12 percent eventually. (Profits on other deals would more than compensate for such losses.) These figures are appropriate for an institution designed to take greater risks than private banks; were its loss rate lower, one might argue that it was not taking enough risks.

The CDFC turnaround under Grigsby demonstrates the importance of finding experienced investment people to run public or quasi-public development agencies. More important, it shows how critical hands-on assistance is if small businesses are to succeed. Even if it continues to improve, however, CDFC is too small, and its geographic target is too large, to have a significant impact. It has invested $16 to $17 million since 1978, and its current portfolio is about $7 million.

Given its limited resources, CDFC's most important function today is probably as an intermediary between the commercial banks and poor communities. "The banks now come to us with deals that they can't otherwise do, but they think ought to be done," Grigsby explains. These are primarily deals that appear sound to the banks, but fall outside the relatively conservative standards they must use to evaluate loans—because they are not fully secured by collateral, for instance. By subordinating its debt or handling the nonsecured portion of the loan, CDFC makes it possible for the banks to take part of the loan. Thus it stretches the boundaries of what the private financial community can do in poor communities.

The other major player in the Massachusetts community development system is the Government Land Bank, which is essentially a real estate development bank for distressed areas. The Land Bank was dreamed up in 1974, before Dukakis became governor, to redevelop the military installations closed down by the Nixon administration. In this role, for instance, it bought the 140-acre South Boston Naval Annex from the federal government for $4.7 million, sold it to the city of Boston's Economic Development and Industrial Corporation on a long-term mortgage, and provided resources to help transform it into a Marine Industrial Park, which employed almost 1,500 people by 1985.[20]

In 1980, the legislature broadened the Land Bank's mandate to deal with blighted or substandard properties throughout the state. Dukakis has convinced it to invest primarily in his targets of opportunity. Although the Land Bank has more resources than CDFC (by the end of 1986 it had spent $32 million and had close to $20 million in funds still available), real estate development requires more capital than small-business investment.[21]

With its limited resources, the Land Bank has tried to develop a wholesaling strategy by creating pilot programs that can then be duplicated by others. In the early 1980s, for instance, it initiated a program to rehabilitate abandoned housing, an effort later picked up by the Boston Housing Partnership (a partnership between Boston's major banks, the city, several foundations, CDFC, and Boston's CDCs). More recently it launched a program to develop low- and moderate-income cooperative housing, to demonstrate the viability of housing co-ops to others active in the marketplace. It has also rehabilitated commercial buildings in distressed urban centers, provided mortgages for industrial facilities, and financed a small-business incubator in Fall River. A legislative commission on small-business incubators has proposed that it run a statewide incubator program.

The Land Bank makes all of its investments in partnership with the private sector, normally sharing a first mortgage with a bank. It shares the risk on deals a bank would not normally accept, and it provides the expertise needed to evaluate the deals—"pulling down the learning curve" for the bank, in Director Timothy Bassett's words. By 1987, it had participated in 35 deals. Only one had gone bad, but the Land Bank recouped its loss when the property was sold.

Like CDFC after its reorganization in 1983, the Land Bank has been successful, but its success has been mitigated by its small size and large target area. Between them, the two institutions have invested close to $50 million, spread over about 75 firms and projects. Other programs, particularly state housing programs that use CDCs as developers, have also invested significantly in the CDC network and in poor communities.

Despite the early failures of CDFC, the bulk of this money has been used wisely, and the state is better off for the investment. Carl Sussman estimates that CDCs and related community organizations have developed seven thousand units of housing since 1975, with perhaps two thousand more in the pipeline.[22] But even as the success of Massachusetts tells us something about the possibilities of development institutions in poor communities, the limits of its strategy tell us that Massachusetts has not yet found the best models.

The basic problem is that the state's investments are spread too thinly across dozens of poor communities. Moreover, the system is not really doing what its creators intended: building the capacity for entrepreneurial development in poor communities. CDFC builds capacity in a few small businesses, and the entire network builds the capacity of CDCs to develop housing. But there is no institution or program that systematically builds the capacity to create or grow businesses.

Hindsight and experience elsewhere suggest that the state might have been wiser to use the $60 million it put into CDFC and the Land Bank to finance a comprehensive development institution in each of its targets of opportunity. Such an institution might make conventional bank loans, business loans, venture investments, and real estate investments, while also providing job training, creating incubators, providing hands-on assistance to local entrepreneurs, and so on. (For a thorough discussion of such a model, see chapter 9.) It is impossible to say whether such an effort would work until a state tries it. But Chuck Grigsby, for one, agrees that it would be preferable to the current model. Massachusetts is in many ways the perfect state to try it: it has the resources, the personnel, and the experience necessary to guide the experiment.

Revitalizing Mature Industries

Dukakis has been criticized by some for focusing his efforts primarily on declining communities, rather than declining industries. His strategy has led him to recruit new high-tech companies to places like southeastern Massachusetts, while doing little for mature industries that are already there. One by-product of such a strategy is that it helps regions more than people, because high-tech firms tend to import educated workers for their better-paid jobs, rather than hiring local people who once labored in mature industries but who lack the necessary education and training for more skilled jobs.

In 1984, Dukakis responded by launching a series of programs designed to help mature industries. They came out of a commission he set up to negotiate a compromise solution to the nettlesome issue of plant closings. Again, the results have been mixed.

To win labor's backing in the 1982 election, Dukakis had pledged to back a measure requiring advance notification of plant closings.[23] Rather than trying to push through a bill to which the business community was uniformly hostile, he created a 38-member commission, made up of leaders from business, labor, government, and academia, to negotiate a compromise. He sought to broaden the issue by also asking the commission to develop a comprehensive strategy to strengthen the state's mature industries.

At the time, only 15 percent of the Massachusetts work force was employed in "mature" industries—machine tools, needle trades, fabricated metals, and the like.[24] Most of these industries were located in Dukakis's targets of opportunity; indeed, these regions were distressed precisely because their industries were in decline. In four western counties, 17 percent of the manufacturing job base disappeared between 1980 and 1985.[25]

Because business and labor locked horns on the plant closing issue, the commission spent most of its time working out a compromise. After months of stalemate over the issue of mandatory notification, a handful of the principal members met behind closed doors and worked out a deal. Essentially, labor gave up its demand for mandatory notification of plant closings in return for increased benefits for laid-off workers. Business agreed to formulate a voluntary "social compact" that defined standards of appropriate corporate behavior in plant closings—including 90 days' advance notice, 90 days of continued health coverage, reemployment assistance for displaced workers, and severance pay. The business members promised to convince corporations to sign the compact, and the state pledged to deny financing from MIFA or the other quasi-public agencies to companies that refused to sign. The state also agreed to set up a reemployment assistance program offering counseling, placement, and retraining services to laid-off workers. In certain circumstances—if a company went bankrupt, for instance—the state would underwrite health and severance benefits. If a company failed to give 90 days' notice, the state would pay for extra unemployment benefits.[26]

Politically, the compromise was an important coup for the Dukakis administration. Labor was pleased, business was relieved to avoid mandatory notice, and with rapid economic growth filling state coffers, few complained that the public was subsidizing the deal. Since then, however, neither the business community nor the administration has moved aggressively to market the social compact, and many corporations have not signed it. Nor has the state enacted any sanctions for firms that sign the compact, take money from MIFA or another state agency, and later fail to give notice.

Perhaps the major weakness of the act was its failure to create a financial incentive for businesses to give advance notification. Indeed, it did just the opposite. Workers whose companies do not provide 90 days' notice are eligible for supplemental unemployment benefits from the state. Knowing this, firms concerned about their employees often choose *not* to give formal notice. Even though this helps their workers get supplemental benefits, the absence of notice (unless given surreptitiously, as is sometimes the case) hurts the state's ability to respond with early counseling, training, and placement services. The state Division of Employment Security reports that the percentage of employers who gave no notice *increased* from 1985 to 1986; as a result, funds for supplemental unemployment benefits were exhausted halfway through the 1986–1987 fiscal year.[27] If businesses had to pay for supplemental benefits themselves, they would have a financial incentive to provide early notice, as several commission members pointed out in their comments on the commission report.[28]

Once it had reached a compromise on the plant closing issue, the administration lost interest in the broader mandate to help mature industries. When the Dukakis administration chose to leave the commission's recommendations out of its legislation, Rep. Timothy Bassett, then chairman of the House Committee on Commerce and Labor, put them back in. "I had hoped we would be able to build the skeleton of some kind of reasonable industrial policy," Bassett explains. "We had the trauma of plant closings, but the long-term way to buffer and change the economy was to create some different kinds of institutions that could respond over time."

The new institutions included:

•an Economic Stabilization Trust (EST) to provide loans to mature firms that are struggling to turn themselves around;

•a Massachusetts Product Development Corporation (MPDC), to provide venture capital for mature firms developing new products or processes;

•an Industrial Services Program (ISP), to help dislocated workers and to work with troubled firms seeking to upgrade their production technologies, management, and the like;

•a monitoring group to analyze economic trends within industries and regions, in order to provide the information necessary for intelligent intervention; and

•an Industrial Advisory Board, with members from business, labor, and government, to oversee the programs and advise the governor and legislature.

The administration failed to create the quality economic monitoring function called for, and it took two years to organize the Massachusetts Product Development Corporation. But the Industrial Services Program has performed well. It has set up more than 45 worker assistance centers in areas where there have been substantial layoffs—hiring laid-off workers as counselors or outreach specialists, to make it easier for dislocated workers to use the program.[29] ISP claims this has given the program the "highest participation rates in the country." It boasts a placement rate of 78 percent, at 85 percent of previous wages or more.[30]

The most innovative piece of the ISP package is the Economic Stabilization Trust, which together with the Business and Financial Services staff of ISP forms a fledgling industrial extension service and turnaround bank. Between June 1985 and August 1987, EST made 19 loans for roughly $4.4 million. More important than the money, however, was the business services staff, which worked with 180 companies over the same period.[31] "The money is the bait that gets people to come to you," explains William Currier, EST's first director. "But then having the opportunity to give advice is much more valuable."

Currier is a businessman who specializes in turnarounds. Over the 13 years before he came to EST, he had bought, turned around, and sold three companies. (After leaving EST in 1987, he bought a fourth.) Adamant that BFS use only experienced business people, he hired people with backgrounds in management, corporate finance, and marketing. By late 1986, they were getting close to an inquiry a day, many from firms that were already insolvent or filing for bankruptcy. The calls came from corporate owners, from managers, from consultants, even from union members. In response, a BFS staff member tried to get to the plant within 24 hours, to begin analyzing the company's problems. After a thorough diagnosis, the staff suggested a variety of remedies, from new management to new marketing strategies to new products. "We take the attitude that there is nothing that can't be done, until the heart stops beating," Currier explained. "You've got to be creative and innovative, and you can't take no from anybody."

The experience of Savage Arms, a manufacturer of rifles and shotguns near Springfield, demonstrates what happens when the program works. In 1985, Savage Arms found itself in the same position Arnold Print Works had been in three years before. Its doors were all but closed, and its major bank, Fleet National, was about to call its loan. Two other local arms manufacturers had already filed for bankruptcy, making other banks extremely reluctant to lend.

The business services staff worked closely with Savage Arms for a year—analyzing its problems, trying to convince bankers to make loans, talking with potential investors. At one point, Currier and a state senator from Springfield visited Fleet National Bank, which is in Rhode Island, and read the riot act. "They told them if they didn't hang on long enough for somebody to buy the thing, and some two hundred jobs went down the drain, they were never going to come into the state of Massachusetts again," says Gen. Robert Friedman, then the Savage Arms chairman and CEO.

Eventually Friedman and his partner found new investors. Over a five-month period Currier, Fleet National Bank, and the new investors worked out a deal. Currier insisted on a series of conditions, including new management for Savage Arms. When they were met, the Economic Stabilization Trust made a loan.

"We were within a millionth of an inch of filing for bankruptcy several times," says Friedman. "People were saying to us, 'You're crazy to hang on.' But [the new investors] seemed to us so damn real, and with the support we were getting from the state, we just sort of bit our tongue and hoped like hell the company would stay whole." A year after the buy-out Savage Industries, as it was renamed, employed four hundred people and was aiming for sales of $25 million a year. "The company is profitable, the jobs are secure, and the volume is up," Currier reported.

"Without Bill's office, the thing would have been totally undoable," says Friedman. "If anything, they were better than most of the private-sector consultants I've seen, because they had been in the same kind of spot themselves, and they had gained experience in other companies that were in dire straits. They were also very close to government, which had an interest in preserving the jobs. A private consultant couldn't have come in and done that job."

EST's purpose—to save companies on the verge of collapse—takes it further out on a limb than any other quasi-public agency in Massachusetts. Even though its board expects some of their loans to go bad, they analyze how much the firm in question would contribute in wages, tax revenues, and income to other area businesses if it survived for an extra six to 12 months. If that figure is greater than the amount of the loan, they lend the funds. "Obviously," one EST report explains, "this is a risky and difficult business."[32]

The Mature Industries Commission made one crucial mistake in creating EST: it failed to insulate the program from political pressures. The five-member EST board, which makes all lending decisions, is appointed entirely by the governor; it includes both the secretary of economic affairs and the director of the Executive Office of Labor. To make matters worse, EST is dependent for its funding on annual appropriations from the legislature. This gives legislators enormous leverage when they want a loan for a company in their district.

In its second year, the board bowed to political pressures and loaned $1.5 million—one-third of its entire portfolio—to a company it had originally turned down. Nine months later, the company announced it was closing anyway. This was the mirror image of the Savage Arms story, a classic case of what can go wrong when public investment funds are not well enough insulated from politics.

When the EST board first turned down the Morse Cutting Tool Company, a local union official immediately went to the governor's office. A state representative from New Bedford had already introduced legislation for a special appropriation of $1.5 million. With the union mounting an effective lobbying campaign, the legislature voted the special appropriation and the board reversed its decision—against Currier's recommendation. When the owner refused to implement one of Currier's principal conditions for the loan—that he hire an experienced turnaround specialist to manage the firm—the board again relented.[33]

Unlike the Adams Print Works loan at CDFC, however, all EST loans are personally guaranteed by the company's owner. This guarantee gave EST enough leverage to force the owner to look for a buyer for the company, rather than simply selling off the plant and equipment. When he received bids from two companies, the Dukakis administration urged the bankruptcy judge to choose the firm that planned to keep the plant open, even though it had offered at least $100,000 less than another bidder. The judge agreed, and EST rolled over its loan to the new owner. At this writing, then, EST has once again saved 375 jobs in New Bedford. The entire experience, oddly enough, has demonstrated both the pitfalls of quasi-public agencies that are susceptible to political pressure and the strength of a public role in this kind of situation.

Morse Tool's new owners may yet prove the loan a wise investment. Even if they do, however, simply by making the loan EST has set itself up for pressure from every legislator in the state. A few months before leaving

EST, Currier described the pressure he was under to lend to one firm. "There are four people in the company making $100,000 a year," he said. "They used to make $150,000, and get a bonus besides. One of them doesn't even work in the company, and another one takes three months of the year off. And they're looking for state money to come in and finance their losses."

Eventually, political pressure can kill a program like EST. If the Morse Tool loan had gone bad—or if it does so in the future the legislature (or a new governor) might be tempted to take a second look. Precisely that happened to a much larger program in Alaska, the Alaska Renewable Resources Corporation. Dependent on biannual appropriations from the legislature, it invested more to prop up failing firms than to seed new industries, its ostensible purpose. When the losses piled up, it was shut down.

EST is too valuable an experiment to suffer the same fate. It offers a vivid example of the wrong way to structure a public capital fund. State governments should provide enough capital for the fund to operate for five to ten years, then get out of the way. They should also make sure appointments to the board are spread out between the governor, the business community, and labor.

Evaluating Massachusetts' Economic Development Efforts

The Commission on the Future of Mature Industries stimulated a number of valuable experiments. But in many ways, it was a missed opportunity for Massachusetts. Its initiatives were important, but they do not add up to a coherent state strategy to deal with mature industries. In similar fashion, the Dukakis administration has done a great deal for the regions that have suffered through the decline of mature industries, but it has not created comprehensive, long-term development strategies or institutions such as Pennsylvania's Advanced Technology Centers and Local Development Districts. Though it has helped form several regional development coalitions, most of its energy has been spent in ad hoc efforts to solve problems or to recruit businesses that might move into its targeted regions.

This may work for regions close enough to Boston to capture its overflow, such as Lowell and southeastern Massachusetts. But the recruitment efforts have not paid off in the rest of the state. More important, an ad hoc strategy only works if the particular projects initiated pay off. Lawrence, an old mill town not far from Lowell, provides a good example. The Dukakis administration pulled out all stops to bring a semiconductor plant and a private college to Lawrence. Both efforts fell through at the last minute. Unlike Lowell or Taunton, Lawrence was left empty-handed. Had

Dukakis helped set up viable development institutions in Lawrence, it would be able to move on to other opportunities.

Dukakis's shortcomings stem in part from his failure to commission in-depth studies of the regional economies of his targets of opportunity—or of the Massachusetts economy as a whole. A report funded by his Executive Office of Communities and Development demonstrates the potential value of such studies. Called *The Northern Tier Economy: A Strategic Analysis*, it was prepared by Mt. Auburn Associates, an economic development consulting firm. The report dissects the local economy, then provides a series of recommendations aimed at stimulating new business formation and reinvigorating the region's mature industries: incubators, programs to link local university experts with local industry, industry councils, a community investment board, and a new source of risk capital. Were the administration so inclined, the report could form the basis of an intelligent regional development strategy for the Northern Tier. State Senator John Olver, who requested the report, has secured money for a one-man staff to see what can be done. But without support, it is an uphill struggle.

Dukakis's response to the Northern Tier project is typical of his reactive posture. The administration organized a CEO tour of the region, provided $20,000 to print a brochure to promote tourism, and considered the project's technology transfer proposals as potential components of its applied technology centers. "But nobody in the administration has ever said, 'Okay, let's take a look at what additional things can go on out there, what kind of money we can pump in to make some of this happen faster,'" says project director Michael Kane. "There's not much of a policy set in the administration that could take a long-term look and say, 'Here's a model we could use in other parts of the state, or as the basis for our regional strategies.'"

Other governors could, of course, be faulted for the same thing. But other governors have not made development in poor regions their top priority. The roots of Dukakis's surprisingly reactive mode are probably to be found in his 1978 defeat. Stung by business opposition in 1978, Dukakis shaped his second-term economic development apparatus to make it extremely responsive to business. His Governor's Office of Economic Development, which took the place of Keefe's old Office of State Planning, exists not to develop policy or programs, but to bring all possible state resources to bear when crises or opportunities arise. Al Raine, who runs it, calls himself a fireman, and his office does an excellent job of both putting out fires and capitalizing on opportunities. In the process, it earns the respect and gratitude of local politicians and business people—cementing Dukakis's political base. But it does not ride herd on overall economic development policy.

A small program launched by the Executive Office of Labor (EOL) also illustrates what happens when there is no long-term regional strategy. Called the Cooperative Regional Industrial Laboratories (CRIL) program, it was designed to involve dislocated workers in economic development efforts to revive their communities. "The basic idea was that nobody pays any attention to what the workers know in these situations," explains Michael Schippani, the former Dukakis staffer who initiated the effort. "We thought they ought to be at the table. I want the workers involved in decisions about where their industry is going."

In the Greenfield area of western Massachusetts, where there had been a series of layoffs in the machine tool industry, the project funded a joint effort by a group of dislocated workers and the Franklin County CDC. Calling themselves the Machine Trades Action Project (MTAP), they surveyed the skills of the local work force and found that a third of the workers expressed interest in starting their own businesses. As a result, they tried to get funding for a small-business incubator and helped launch an entrepreneurial training course offered by ISP's local Workers Assistance Center. They also brought in engineering professors from the University of Massachusetts at Amherst to help local machine shops upgrade their technology and hired a local businessman to market their products.

In Fall River, a similar Needle Trades Action Project initiated a new training program, hired an engineer to work with local companies to upgrade their technology, put together marketing campaigns, brought new contracts to Fall River, and functioned as an informal early warning system to alert state and local officials when firms were in trouble.

Both of these were creative efforts, with significant potential. But the rest of the Dukakis administration virtually ignored them. Because they were not part of a larger administration strategy, they had little access to significant resources or state programs. When the Machine Trades Action Project decided the Greenfield area needed an incubator, there was no state incubator program to which it could turn. When it wanted to bring engineering professors in to work with area firms, there was no state program to fund such efforts. Secretary of Economic Affairs Joseph Alviani, who took over in 1986, has taken several steps to fill these gaps. He has created a Center of Excellence in Applied Technology and Productivity, which will fund consultants for industry. He has launched the first of several efforts to bring management and labor in an industrial sector together, called the Massachusetts Metalworking Partnership. Though he has a long way to go, Alviani has shown signs of offering the policy leadership Massachusetts needs in economic development.

How much impact has Dukakis had on growth rates in his targets of opportunity, where unemployment averaged just 4.8 percent in 1986?[34]

Clearly, much of it would have occurred regardless of what the state did. New industry is moving into southeastern Massachusetts, but a few miles away in Rhode Island, where the Dukakis programs are unavailable, a nascent boom is also under way. Lowell has enjoyed a low unemployment rate for several years, but 30 miles away another once-depressed mill town, Manchester, New Hampshire, has boasted the lowest unemployment rate of any American city.[35] Logic suggests that all of this growth is part of the same regional boom, which has gradually radiated out from its hub in Boston.

Within this regional economy, Dukakis has no doubt brought investments into communities that would otherwise have been avoided by the private sector. Despite the limitations of his strategy, he has had a visible impact on cities like Lowell and Taunton. But travel further than an hour away from Route 128 and the success stories fade, suggesting that much of the credit must go to the private marketplace. Dukakis has certainly helped areas like the northern Berkshires. But he could have had a greater long-term impact had he taken a more systematic approach.

After a decade of ad hoc experimentation, Massachusetts has the rudiments of a first-rate economic development system. The task now is to reevaluate, redesign, and reconstruct. In a way, Massachusetts suffers from having been first. When Dukakis and his staff hammered out their basic approach, there were few models in other states from which to learn. Ten years later, many of their programs have been in effect long enough to reveal conspicuously both their strengths and weaknesses.

This maturity creates enormous opportunities. Massachusetts has so many tools in place and so much experience with economic development in poor communities and declining regions that it is perfectly positioned for a major step forward. By reexamining its system and then carefully reconstructing it, it could take the effort to create growth in poor communities to a level never before achieved in this country. I will explore some of the possibilities in chapter 9.

Reinventing Welfare

Ruby Sampson is a 40-year-old mother of three with dark skin, luminous eyes, and a smile that won't quit. The eldest of 13 children born to a Georgia sharecropper, she can barely remember a time when she was not working in the cotton fields. Her father died when she was nine; she dropped out of school to work full time after the seventh grade. She has been married and divorced twice. Like many other southern blacks, she came North looking for work. And like many others, she wound up on welfare—for 14 years.

In 1984, at age 37, Sampson received a brochure from a Boston health center about a training program for operating room technicians. At the time, she says, she was "a mess—weighed 180 pounds, laid around the house all day watching soap operas, feeling depressed, and taking an aspirin every hour."[36] But she had always wanted to work in medicine. So after putting the brochure aside for a time, she finally mustered the courage to knock on a friend's door—she could not afford her own phone—and call the number listed.

The training program was funded by the state welfare department. Ruby signed up and plunged into classes on anatomy, physiology, and surgical procedures. She had to be there by 7 A.M. every day, for 44 weeks. The welfare department paid for the three buses she had to ride to get there, as well as for child care. Her counselors made her find three backup babysitters, in case anything went wrong. They also helped her draw up a daily schedule—"even telling me when to take a bath." Before exams, Ruby studied until the small hours of the morning. She passed with a 97 average. After an internship at Massachusetts General Hospital, her counselors found her a job at Brigham and Women's Hospital, a large teaching hospital affiliated with Harvard.

On welfare, Ruby Sampson had never received more than $7,000 a year. After a year and a half as an operating room technician, she made $8 an hour—over $16,000 a year. The job changed her life. "The old Ruby is dead," she says. "Being able to work, support yourself—there's nothing like it. I'll probably work forever."[37]

Would she have found a job without help from the welfare department? "Oh God, no. I'd still be on welfare, without that program."

Ruby Sampson is a living example of Governor Dukakis's greatest second-term success: a welfare program called Employment and Training Choices. The administration has often exaggerated the achievements of E.T. Choices—or E.T., as it was inevitably nicknamed. But there is no question that the program has been a major advance. By demonstrating that many people on welfare want to work—and can do so with the proper support—it has had a dramatic impact on the national debate about welfare.

The evolution of welfare policy in Massachusetts is yet another story of ideological transition. As in so many other areas, the result is a new synthesis of traditionally liberal and conservative attitudes. But this time the starting point was on the right. During his first term, Dukakis's attitude toward welfare outraged many liberals. To balance the budget during the fiscal crisis, he eliminated General Relief, the state-funded welfare program for poor people who did not qualify for Aid to Families with Dependent Children (AFDC). Later he introduced a mandatory workfare program for unemployed fathers on AFDC. According to his current welfare commissioner, Charles Atkins, it failed miserably: two-thirds of those placed left their jobs within 30 days. During his three years at the Kennedy School, while the legislature experimented with a new approach to moving people off the rolls, Dukakis reexamined his welfare philosophy.

Supported Work

In 1981, the Massachusetts legislature appropriated $6 million for "supported work"—a new concept based on an experiment funded by the Ford Foundation. The idea originated with Ford staff members who traveled to Sweden during the 1960s to study a "sheltered work" program, under which the government subsidized businesses that employed the handicapped, ex-offenders, and others who had trouble competing in the labor market. Ford initially convinced the Vera Institute, in New York City, to develop a similar program for ex-addicts and ex-convicts. Based on its initial success, Ford created the Manpower Demonstration Research Corporation (MDRC) to run a pilot program for ex-convicts, ex-addicts, high school dropouts, and long-term AFDC recipients in over a dozen sites around the country. The project used foundation and government funds—including the monthly welfare checks of participants—to subsidize supported-work corporations.

Each corporation employed anywhere from 100 to 300 people at a time, mostly in businesses it created or in public agencies that contracted with the corporation for services. Employees were closely supervised and counseled, to help them overcome the difficulty of adjusting to work, and many belonged to peer support groups at their work place. As the year progressed, they were expected to handle more work, deal with more complex tasks, and function more independently. Some received job training on the side. At the end of the year, the supported-work corporation helped them find a job in the "real world."

Between 1975 and 1980, more than ten thousand people participated. The MDRC study, which followed an experimental group of five thousand and a control group of five thousand, was the largest control group experiment ever done on an urban program. It showed that the model was effective with long-term welfare recipients and, to a lesser extent, with ex-addicts. On high school dropouts and ex-offenders, it had no impact.[38]

The most successful of the projects was Transitional Employment Enterprises (TEE), in Boston. TEE had stumbled on a different model from those of other groups. Rather than creating jobs in sheltered environments, it had begun placing people immediately in private-sector jobs, but continuing the support mechanisms for up to six months. The seeds of this experiment had been planted when TEE convinced the state Public Welfare Department that its workers could outperform Kelly Girls. The department had hired a group of them to do clerical work, and they had performed well. The department then convinced Blue Cross/Blue Shield, with which it had a medicaid contract, to hire TEE workers. The TEE crew was so successful that the company began hiring them for permanent jobs.

That experience gave TEE the opening it needed. It developed a marketing campaign to convince other private corporations to hire its people, and in essence, it became a placement service for large Boston corporations. Its success allowed it to survive when funding for the National Supported Work Demonstration ended, unlike all but one or two of the other projects.

In 1980, the legislature voted to fund a statewide supported-work effort. The state eventually contracted with 21 different organizations to provide supported work, about half of which have survived. In 1987, TEE ran into serious financial problems—due in part to bookkeeping lapses—that left its future uncertain. But until then, it had consistently placed about four hundred welfare recipients in jobs every year. (The Bank of Boston had hired more than five hundred alone.)[39] According to TEE, 90 percent of those hired had remained with the same company for at least a year, 83 percent for at least two years—retention rates that are almost unheard of in other programs. By 1987, the minimum starting wage was about $6 an hour, or $11,300 a year, and a third of those placed were receiving promotions within the first year.

To get Boston corporations to hire its people, TEE actually put staff people in offices at major corporations to work with personnel offices and to help the companies train and supervise TEE people. TEE staffers also helped those placed in jobs with their personal problems—when their heat was turned off, for instance, or when problems developed with child care.

During their first four to six months on the job, participants remained on the TEE payroll. They were eligible for a series of raises and bonuses, depending upon their performance. After that time, if their work was satisfactory, the company hired them. Until then, they stayed on welfare, so they did not lose benefits if the job did not work out. Their welfare payments went directly to TEE, which used them to subsidize their wages.

Part of the genius of the model is that it assures a company of reliable employees, because those who cannot perform—almost a third of those who begin the process—wash out *before* the company is asked to hire them. This was TEE's pitch to the business world. "We're selling a service," explained Peter Cove, former president of TEE. "If the person doesn't do well, we'll have a new person in the next day. In a sense, like a temp agency, we're not selling the worker, we're selling a service. But unlike a temp agency, ultimately we are selling the worker."

As the icing on the cake, corporations are eligible for the federal targeted job tax credit, which saves them 40 percent of the person's first-year wages (to a maximum of $6,000 per person per year). Placements through

TEE cost the state about $4,700 each (plus child-care and extended health care benefits), a sum it usually earned back in welfare savings within the first year the person was on the job.

In 1984, Cove set up a for-profit company, America Works, to take the model nationwide. By 1987, it had subsidiaries in Hartford and Buffalo, and it was negotiating with welfare agencies in other states. America Works is completely based on performance: it only gets paid by a state or county welfare agency after it has placed a client. With 85 percent retention rates after one year, the welfare department is virtually guaranteed a return on its investment, which ranges from $3,500 to $5,500, depending on the city.

Because it is a for-profit corporation, America Works benefits from the federal targeted job tax credit while people are on its payroll. Cove has used this advantage to attract private investment. For every $1 million in wages America Works pays each year, its owners can take $400,000 in tax credits, thus wiping out $400,000 in taxes due on income from their other businesses. Hence the federal government is offering a hefty subsidy to the program.

The principal limitation of the model is the number of people placed: each America Works subsidiary has placed only one hundred to 150 people a year. Cove argues that there are two main barriers to larger numbers. First, most state legislatures must vote special line items to pay for supported work, whereas welfare expenditures—as entitlements—go up or down based on demand. Hence even though supported work saves money, it requires legislators to go on record in favor of spending. Second, welfare departments have historically been organized to write checks, not to find people jobs. Even in Massachusetts, the welfare department did not refer people to TEE; it had to advertise to attract clients. If welfare departments routinely referred people, placement levels might rise.

Though TEE is nonprofit and America Works is a for-profit firm, both are classic third-sector organizations. Unlike the public sector, they are driven by the bottom line to invest in people with the potential to succeed in the marketplace; if they fail to do so, they will lose money and jeopardize their own existence. (When TEE lost track of its bottom line, it suffered the consequences—something that rarely happens to a normal government bureaucracy.) Unlike the private sector, TEE and America Works use public subsidies to serve a portion of the market that traditional for-profit firms ignore. Hence they combine the creativity and discipline of the private sector with the social goals of the public sector.

Employment and Training Choices

When Dukakis was reelected in 1982, Governor King had just launched a workfare program. It required many welfare recipients to look for work through the state employment service and take any job offered at the minimum wage or above, if it did not lower their income. Those who refused to participate were sanctioned—taken off the rolls or given reduced grants. Those who looked but could not find work were given the option of training, supported work, workfare, or continuing to look for jobs on their own. Predictably, those forced to take jobs rarely stayed with them. The department claimed only a 69 percent retention rate after 30 days; an independent investigation reported only a 37 percent rate.[40]

Meanwhile supported work, which was up to a thousand placements a year, had demonstrated that a voluntary program which made serious efforts to prepare people for private-sector jobs could work. Dukakis and his welfare staff decided to opt for a voluntary program, but to adopt the principle of providing a range of options to participants. The result was E.T. Choices.

Those who elected to participate in E.T. Choices first met with an E.T. worker to discuss their background and needs. If they felt they needed it, they were referred to a career counselor to explore job options. They could then choose remedial education, vocational or higher education (the state would pay for two community college courses), training, supported work, or direct job search through the employment service. When they finished one component, they could move into another.

While they were in one of these components, the state provided day care and subsidized their transportation. In a major step beyond even the best previous programs, the state also subsidized child care and transportation during their first year on the job. The federal government provided four months of medicaid after they found a job, and for a small group of the most needy, E.T. Choices extended this to 15 months. These measures were extremely important; by subsidizing some of the costs of working, they began to make work more attractive than welfare. In the absence of such subsidies, a low-wage job often translates into worse poverty than a welfare grant.

Another important innovation was the use of performance-based contracts with training programs, supported-work agencies like TEE, and the state employment service. The welfare department required that these contractors achieve certain rates of job placements before paying them, and awarded bonuses for jobs paying higher wages. The department also set monthly placement goals for each local welfare office.

The welfare department worked hard to change the attitudes toward welfare recipients of its own case workers, of the employment service staff, and of those who ran training programs funded by the federal Job Training Partnership Act (JTPA). "It used to be under WIN [the federal job placement program] that these other agencies didn't want to hear about welfare people, because they brought down their placement rates, and they used to get their federal money partly based on their performance in placement," says Alan Werner, director of research for the welfare department during E.T.'s early years. "They had the prevailing prejudice that welfare people didn't want to work, or you just couldn't get them a job no matter what. And they didn't want to see them. The whole notion that E.T. gets voluntary people, that E.T. has such a high profile under Dukakis, and that it had some early successes, has really changed the culture of employment and training in the state. The welfare business is now the glamour business."

At any point in time over the past few years, about 85,000 families were on AFDC in Massachusetts. Close to half of those left the rolls within any year, and new families took their place.[41] According to the Public Welfare Department, somewhere in the neighborhood of 200,000 families moved through the AFDC system during E.T.'s first five years. During that time, perhaps 40,000 people found jobs on their own and left welfare.[42] Against this backdrop, Welfare Commissioner Charles Atkins set a goal of ten thousand job placements a year for five years—almost one-third of the remaining caseload. During its first three years, E.T. Choices met that goal, boasting 30,000 placements.

Though Atkins and the administration broadcast the 30,000 figure widely, they rarely explained the fine print. Only two-thirds of the 30,000 jobs were full time. (Even that figure defined full time as 30, not 40, hours a week.) Only about 60 percent paid enough to get families completely off welfare. Of the 60 percent who got off welfare, some fraction actually found jobs on their own, after simply being assessed by an E.T. worker.[43] Adding it all up, E.T. Choices probably placed about 15,000 people in jobs that got them off welfare over its first three years.

Numbers of placements are not the critical measure by which to judge a program, however. The key is how many people keep their jobs for any length of time. Many welfare programs shuffle people into jobs they do not want, at wages so poor that they cannot afford to work. As a result, most of those placed wind up back on welfare within six months—a process that may do more harm than good, by convincing people that it is not worth trying to work.

It is here that E.T. Choices shone. Welfare department surveys showed that 86 percent of those placed in jobs that paid enough to get them off welfare remained off a year later.[44] Like the figure of 30,000 placements, the welfare department broadcast this number far and wide. Again, this exaggerated the program's achievements, because it excluded the 40 percent of E.T. participants placed in jobs that did not pay enough to get them off welfare. When the department surveyed all those placed in *full-time* jobs, it found that 67 percent were still off welfare a year later.[45] The difference between 86 and 67 percent was simply the difference between a livable wage and an unlivable wage. At $5.00 an hour (roughly $10,000 a year) or more, one-year retention rates were 80 percent. At $4.50 to $5.00, they dropped to 67 percent. At $3.50 to $4.00, they dropped to 57 percent.[46]

Past programs have had far lower retention rates. A General Accounting Office evaluation of the federal WIN program found that only 38 percent of those counted as placements were off welfare six to 18 months later. Of those who earned enough to get off welfare initially, 62 percent were still working six to 18 months later.[47] The comparable figures for E.T. Choices are 67 percent and 86 percent, respectively.

When the welfare department looked at the results of E.T.'s first three years, several things were clear. First, higher wages led to higher retention rates. Second, training programs and supported work resulted in higher wages and higher retention rates than did direct job placement.[48] In other words, the more Massachusetts invested in each welfare recipient, the more likely that person would be to get permanently off welfare. Finally, the department's survey showed that only 55 percent of those still working had medical coverage, and that of those no longer working, 36 percent cited problems with child care as their primary reason.[49]

In response, the department did several things. To raise wage rates for those it placed, it set wage floors for its contractors. Starting in July 1986, E.T. quit reimbursing contractors for part-time placements and for placements in jobs that paid less than $5.47 an hour in the greater Boston area, $4.65 in lower-wage areas. It began reimbursing contractors only after someone had stayed with a job for 30 days. It quit counting as E.T. placements people who merely met with an E.T. worker and then found a job on their own. It expanded medical care by making those placed in jobs eligible for a year of membership in a neighborhood health plan and it continued to expand the number of day-care vouchers it offered, to 7,500 by early 1987.

Under the new rules, E.T. placed ten thousand people in full-time jobs between July 1986 and July 1987. The average wage rose to about $6.50 an hour by July 1987, and more than 77 percent of those placed earned enough to get off welfare.[50] To expand its efforts in 1987–1988, the department secured almost a 50 percent increase in its budget for job placement, education, training, supported work, and related services.

What impact has E.T. Choices had on the welfare caseload in Massachusetts? That is a difficult question to answer, because so many other factors have been at work since it began—particularly an overheated economy.

Movements on and off welfare always hold their share of mystery. During Dukakis's first term, for instance, unemployment fell from 12 to 6 percent, yet the welfare caseload grew by 15 percent. The statistics for

Dukakis's second term are equally contradictory. On the one hand, the welfare caseload dropped by only about 5 percent during the first 3.5 years of E.T. Choices, despite the hot economy. On the other, the average length of stay on AFDC dropped from 34 to 27 months, and the number of people on AFDC for five years or longer fell by 25 percent.[51] Why? Without being able to compare the experience of E.T. participants with a control group that was not eligible for E.T., all one can do is guess.

There are several plausible explanations for the failure of the caseload to shrink by more than 5 percent. One is that both Massachusetts and the U.S. Congress liberalized eligibility criteria for AFDC during Dukakis's second term. Another is that Massachusetts increased welfare benefits by 47 percent between 1982 and 1988—making welfare more attractive than many low-paying jobs.[52] In neighboring Connecticut, which had an equally robust economy but only raised benefits 11.5 percent between 1982 and 1987, the caseload declined by 9 percent.[53]

Another factor may be what Thomas Glynn, deputy commissioner of the welfare department, calls the "family distress index," the rising number of single-parent families, particularly among the poor. According to former research director Alan Werner, this group—which stays on welfare the longest—has increased dramatically as a percentage of the caseload over the past ten years. Overall, in Massachusetts, the number of female-headed families has grown from 225,000 in 1980 to 275,000 in 1986. Nearly 70 percent of the state's poor families are now headed by women, a figure that is far above the national average. Rapid growth in this group explains why the percentage of Massachusetts families living in poverty *rose* from 7.6 percent in 1979 to 8.2 percent in 1986 (still far below the national average of 11.4 percent).[54] Even in Boston, with its booming economy, the percentage of families (not individuals) living in poverty rose during the 1980s, reaching almost 20 percent. If these trends had intensified while the state did nothing to help poor, single mothers get jobs, the welfare caseload would probably have risen, as it did during Dukakis's first term.

These statistics underscore just how difficult it is to reduce welfare dependency. Many welfare officials in other states worry that by exaggerating E.T.'s accomplishments, the Dukakis administration has made it sound far easier to get welfare recipients into permanent jobs than it actually is. In truth, those who stay on welfare for long periods of time, particularly unwed mothers, become so trapped in dependency that even when "help wanted" signs are everywhere, it is difficult to get them into full-time jobs.

Others have criticized E.T. Choices for "creaming"—placing those who are the most job-ready and ignoring the rest. Some of this is inevitable in a voluntary program: by definition, the program includes only those who want to work. To deal with this reality, the department has tried to target its services toward the harder-to-place. It has created new programs for teenage parents and Hispanics, for instance, and it has limited supported work to those who have been on welfare for at least two years or who live in public housing.

But there are two sides to the creaming issue. No state can afford to train and place its entire caseload, particularly in the first years of any program. Bob Friedman, president of the Corporation for Enterprise Development, points out that "the coerced trainee makes no sense." He argues that by starting with those who were the most motivated, Massachusetts ensured an early success. It was then able to advertise that success, thus offering hope to welfare recipients and convincing businesses that it would not hurt to hire people off welfare.

Dukakis claims that after subtracting the cost of E.T. Choices, the program saved the state and federal governments $120 million in fiscal 1987. Though solid in other respects, this figure ignores the fact that some of those placed by E.T. would have found jobs on their own. Without a control group, it is impossible to say how large this group would be, or what its wage rates and retention rates would be. A careful study by the Massachusetts Taxpayers Foundation pegged the savings at 40 percent of the administration's claims—still an impressive figure.[55] This study was quite conservative: it did not count increased tax revenues; it ignored savings from reduced grants when people found jobs but remained on welfare; and it assumed that those placed in jobs would have left AFDC on their own after one more year. Even the administration estimate ignores the social benefits of a better-trained work force, less welfare dependency, better health care, and lower crime rates. Whatever the most accurate figure, E.T. Choices is clearly a wise investment.

After all the debates, and despite all the exaggerations, the bottom line is simple: E.T. Choices has placed a significant number of welfare recipients in jobs paying enough to ensure that they can afford to keep them. In the process, it has proven three important points. It has shown that many people on welfare want to work—even those with young children. (In 1986, 41 percent of E.T. participants were women with children under the age of six.)[56] It has demonstrated that different welfare recipients have very different needs, and that with help they can choose the appropriate path to self-sufficiency. And third, it has proven that the more money government invests in educating, training, and providing supported-work environments for welfare recipients, the greater the payoff will be.

Most important, the Dukakis administration has, by virtue of its public relations effort, altered the national debate about welfare reform. In the early 1980s the debate centered around workfare: Should government force people to work for their welfare checks? In large part because of E.T. Choices, the debate now centers around the best method of helping welfare recipients get training and find jobs. At rare moments, events come together in ways that crystallize new perceptions of reality. Michael

Harrington's book, *The Other America*, had that effect in the early 1960s, suddenly thrusting the issue of poverty onto the national agenda. Dukakis's E.T. Choices program has had a similar impact. Massachusetts was not the first state to develop a decent program to get welfare recipients into jobs—indeed, most of E.T.'s components were not new. But it was the first state to market the approach successfully.

"The way you develop political and financial support for these things is you market success," says Friedman. "When Dukakis gets up and says we've found a way out of poverty, or when you turn on the television and you see a welfare recipient saying, 'I was on welfare and then I heard about this E.T. Choices program, and now I'm earning my way,' that sells."

Other Programs

Welfare reform and economic development are hardly the only areas in which Massachusetts has innovated. Explosive inflation in housing prices has made the greater Boston area one of the nation's most expensive markets, and in response, Dukakis and the legislature committed over half a billion new dollars to housing in 1983 and 1985. Dukakis created a new Massachusetts Housing Partnership, through which the state helped create more than 50 partnerships between local governments, private developers, local bankers, and community organizations to build subsidized housing. The entire effort has made Massachusetts a national leader in housing.

A training program launched by Governor King has also emerged as a national model. Called the Bay State Skills Corporation, it acts as a venture capitalist in the training arena, providing matching grants as a way to get corporations and educational institutions to set up new training programs. By offering start-up capital (grants are often for 100 percent of the first year's costs, 50 percent of the second, and a small portion of the third), BSSC acts as a catalyst, bringing business and academic institutions together to create new programs that respond to genuine demands in the marketplace.

BSSC is a demand-driven program—that is, it funds only those training programs the business community is willing to help pay for, and therefore genuinely needs. As a result, it is extremely efficient. Even when BSSC programs to train welfare recipients, dislocated homemakers, the mentally retarded, and other disadvantaged populations are included, 87 percent of its trainees find jobs during their first year out of training.[57]

Demand-driven programs tend to skim those who are most job-ready, because businesses prefer to invest in those who are easiest to train. Bay State Skills deals with this tendency by creating distinct training programs for the disadvantaged, for which it requires smaller matching grants by participating businesses. By all accounts, the model works for even the least job-ready populations. Its success is attested to not only by its extremely high placement rate, but also by the fact that four other states have already copied it.

Dukakis's tax amnesty program has also received national attention. It offers a perfect illustration of the governor's 1980s fiscal posture, which sought to avoid the dramatic clashes that brought him down during the 1970s.

Thanks in part to tax cuts passed under King, Dukakis inherited a $300-million deficit in 1983. For the second time, he faced the specter of raising taxes in his first year. "The Senate president, everyone in the legislature, they all said, 'Increase taxes now and get the four years of free ride off it,'" remembers Frank Keefe, who became Dukakis's budget chief. "But he was absolutely adamant this time—we did not want to increase taxes, we wanted to manage our way out of it."

The solution was twofold. "First," says Keefe, "we put clamps on everything, and we had the highest level of savings from appropriations in the history of the commonwealth, for the final six months of fiscal year '83 [January–June 1983]." Second, Dukakis cracked down on tax evasion and announced a 90-day amnesty during which people could pay their back taxes without penalty.

The legislature proposed the amnesty, and Dukakis's commissioner of revenue, Ira Jackson, designed the crackdown. Called the Revenue Enforcement and Protection (REAP) program, it turned misdemeanors into felonies, increased audits, and gave the state new powers to use private collection agencies and to revoke licenses and public contracts with tax scofflaws. The amnesty brought in $84 million (some of which would no doubt have come in anyway, through prosecution).[58] But armed with REAP, Jackson followed the amnesty with a series of highly visible seizures of property from people who owed taxes. State tax collectors shut down popular restaurants, swept down the seashore seizing yachts, and padlocked businesses. Voluntary compliance shot up, and the state increased its permanent revenue base by roughly 5 percent.[59] By 1986, 17 states had copied the Massachusetts program.[60] "Why somebody in Washington doesn't pick up on this as a part of deficit reduction continues to baffle me," the governor said.

Coming on top of an economic boom, REAP gave Dukakis the ultimate luxury: room to increase spending rapidly and cut taxes at the same time. Tax revenues jumped 13 percent in both fiscal 1984 and 1985, 16.7 percent in 1986.[61] Dukakis used this largesse to increase spending by almost 50 percent during his second term (three times the rate of inflation). In 1985, when the High Technology Council pushed for repeal of the 7.5 percent surcharge on state income taxes he had imposed in 1975, he agreed. In

1986, when the authors of Proposition 2½ (which had cut property taxes) put another initiative on the ballot—to cap the growth rate of state tax revenues at the growth rate of wages and salaries—Dukakis did not campaign vigorously against it. Thus he carefully avoided getting on the wrong side of public opinion on taxes.

The Politics of Michael Dukakis

Dukakis likes to call himself an activist governor, and the title is apt. He has created what, for its size, is perhaps the most active state government in the country. To his credit, it is relatively efficient and well run. Dukakis's strengths, in the eyes of the public, are his competence and his integrity. He is even seen that way by his peers; in a 1986 *Newsweek* poll, the 50 governors rated him the most effective in the nation.[62]

This was quite a turnaround for a governor who could not get reelected after his first term. Though much of his success is related to the economy, his new style also helped. His consensus style is criticized by partisans on both sides of many issues: liberal activists consider him too timid, and many business leaders, though more positive than during his first term, still consider him too wedded to the notion that government can solve all problems. "You hear a lot of flute music about public-private partnerships," says Howard Foley, executive director of the High Tech Council. "But when you participate in one of those commissions or whatnot, you're just drowned by all the public partners. We feel government should be there to fill in the gaps, not to steer the ship." Other critics argue that by compromising on so many issues, Dukakis has been a follower, not a leader. "All you have to do is threaten to make trouble and you know he'll back down," says Barbara Anderson, who as head of Citizens for Limited Taxation (CLT) sponsored both Proposition 2½ and the 1986 tax cap. "That's not what I'm looking for in a leader."[63]

But Dukakis's new style has allowed him to resolve a number of difficult issues and move a great deal of his agenda through the legislature. "You can't judge Dukakis's consensus style by saying, 'My God, the Duke has gone halfway,'" says Ralph Whitehead, a political analyst and professor at the University of Massachusetts at Amherst. "He has also brought his adversaries halfway. We have a far more enlightened corporate establishment than we did five years ago. And the legislature has basically moved the governor's program."[64]

The real problem with consensus politics is not that it compromises principles, but that it compromises the quality of solutions. Politicians who want to include every interest group often fail to look at the big picture, to design long-range programs that go beyond interest-group needs to address the heart of a problem. And by their nature, committees tend to create lowest-common-denominator solutions. This tendency has plagued most of Dukakis's major initiatives: his economic development strategy, an education reform bill he pushed through in 1985, and his plant closing initiative.

"The way they've done most of these things is with participatory initiatives," explains Doug Baird, who runs a day-care business that serves six hundred low-income children in Boston. Baird served on Dukakis's 50-member Governor's Day Care Partnership Project, where he encountered the problem firsthand. "If you ask any really tough questions, you create divisiveness, and if you create divisiveness, you create lack of motion. So there is an awful lot of finessing that goes on, and things get watered down. What you get is a solution for today or a year from today, but you're not allowed to ask the long-term questions, because if you do, you begin to get people arguing about philosophical approaches and you slow the process down too much. This is very big-D Democratic, in the oldest coalition-building sense of the term. But it suffers from being shortsighted."

This quality leads to a "yes, but" feeling about Dukakis among many supporters: yes, he is a good governor, but he could be better. In 1986, he was reelected with 69 percent of the vote. But his opposition was almost nonexistent: the Republicans had to draft a last-minute candidate after their first two were tainted by scandals. The vote indicated broad-based approval, rather than passion or deep allegiance. On several ballot initiatives, including the CLT tax cap plan and a measure to repeal a mandatory seat belt law Dukakis had pushed through, the public voted overwhelmingly against the governor.

This inability to move the electorate has always been a Dukakis trademark. To a degree, it is inherent in any politics that favors technical solutions over ideological vision. At heart, Dukakis is a technocrat. His natural base has always been the educated middle class, and his instinct has always been to embrace the rational solution, regardless of the passions of business, labor, or other interest groups.

Through bitter experience, Dukakis has learned to reach out to the traditional constituencies on both right and left. Whereas he once scorned business demands for tax cuts and ignored liberals' complaints about his social spending cuts, he now—thanks to the booming economy—backs moderate tax reduction and pushes record increases in social spending. He is at once a social liberal and a fiscal moderate, proenvironment and progrowth, an advocate for the poor and a friend of business. All of this reaching out has blurred his image. "People are confused as to whether he's liberal, moderate, or conservative," says Edward Reilly, a political consultant who has conducted polls monitoring Dukakis since 1982.[65]

In truth, Dukakis is neither liberal, moderate, nor conservative, in traditional terms. He has gradually evolved, over the past 15 years, into a new-paradigm liberal. His favorite themes in recent years have been economic growth and "opportunity for all." From time to time he has evoked the theme of community, or the goal of bringing down the barriers that keep people in poverty, but just as often he has glorified technological innovation or spoken in lofty terms about "creating the future." He has defended government as a force for good, but at the same time he has stressed the value of public-private partnerships and advocated "entrepreneurial approaches" rather than "bureaucratic programs."

Were Dukakis better at communicating these themes, he might be able to turn them into a powerful new message about the changing role of government. But Dukakis has always been a master of the prose of government, not the poetry. He is the opposite of Ronald Reagan. "If Mike Dukakis were an automobile," says Ralph Whitehead, "he'd be a Honda Civic. Compact, efficient, reliable—short on style but long on utility."[66]

As a politician, this is Dukakis's great weakness. When the economy is healthy, voters are satisfied to have a competent, pragmatic helmsman. But when the economy slumps, no constituency remains steadfast, because there is no shared vision and no ideological fire. It takes a sense of vision to weather the storms, and vision is not Michael Dukakis's strong suit.

NEW YORK: HOUSING THE POOR

On January 1, 1983, Mario Cuomo delivered his inaugural address in Albany, New York. "Like all of us in this room today—and all of us in New York State except for our Native American brothers and sisters—I am the offspring of immigrants," Cuomo told the crowd.

"When my mother arrived at Ellis Island, she was alone and afraid. She carried little more than a suitcase and a piece of paper with the address of her laborer husband, who had preceded her here in search of work.

"Like millions of others, my mother and father . . . asked only for the opportunity to work and to be protected in those moments when they would not be able to protect themselves.

"That they were able to build a family and live in dignity and see one of their children go from behind their little grocery store in South Jamaica where he was born to occupy the highest seat in the greatest state of the greatest nation in the only world we know—is an ineffably beautiful tribute to the magnificence of this American democracy."

The new governor then turned to his central theme, the core of his philosophy: "Those who made our history taught us above all things the idea of family. Mutuality. The sharing of benefits and burdens—fairly—for the good of all.

"We must be the family of New York—feeling one another's pain, sharing one another's blessings, reasonably, equitably, honestly, fairly—without respect to geography or race or political affiliation."

When he was finished, the new governor paused and looked up from his text. "And Pop," he added, "wherever you are—and I think I know—for all the ceremony and the big house and the pomp and circumstance, please don't let me forget."

Tears came to the eyes of hardened politicians. The band struck up Aaron Copeland's "Fanfare for the Common Man." And a star was born. Twenty months later, Cuomo would repeat the performance at the Democratic party's national convention in San Francisco. It would have the same effect, this time on a national audience—and Mario Cuomo would suddenly become the bright new hope of the Democratic party's liberal wing.

In the glare of national publicity, Cuomo's image—already the product more of his silver tongue than of his deeds as governor—has flattened into that of the traditional liberal. Too often, however, the glare has functioned more to hide reality than to illuminate it.

To understand Cuomo, one must understand the context in which he works. Under Nelson Rockefeller, a Republican, New York built up the largest government, the biggest budgets, and the highest taxes (as a percentage of personal income) of any state. Under Hugh Carey, a Democrat, it endured perhaps the most painful period of belt tightening. Carey was a typical class of '74 Democrat, a transitional figure who recast the mold of Democratic politics. Mario Cuomo is the only governor profiled in this book who came after the transition. Though his instincts are liberal, he has never had any choice but to accept the new realities of the 1980s. Like Michael Dukakis, he has struggled to address the concerns of the 1960s— poverty, housing, and urban development—with the methodology of the 1980s. Along with Dukakis, Cuomo has opened a second front in the policy revolution sweeping America's statehouses.

From Rockefeller to Carey

The story begins with Nelson Rockefeller, the man who led New York to the brink of bankruptcy. A domineering force for 15 years, Rockefeller ran state government the way he ran his life: money was there to be spent, and there would always be more where the last dollar came from. When Rockefeller was elected, in 1958, he inherited a state budget of $2 billion. Fifteen years later, it stood at $8.7 billion—an increase, after accounting for inflation, of almost 300 percent.[1] Per capita state taxes had risen *700 percent*—so far, in fact, that they were fully two-and-a-half times those of the median state.[2]

Rockefeller did colossal things with the money. He built highways faster than any New York governor ever had—highways that "would stretch all the way to Hawaii, and back," as his campaign commercials put it.[3] He built 90,000 housing units, three model communities, 23 mental health facilities, 55 state parks, close to 40 state office buildings, and two hundred waste treatment plants. When he took office the state university system had 38,000 students on 28 campuses; when he left it had 246,000 students on 71 campuses, making it the largest public university system under one control in the world.[4]

Rockefeller's "edifice complex," as it became known, was brought to a majestic climax with his Gov. Nelson A. Rockefeller Empire State Plaza, which dwarfs downtown Albany the way the pyramids dwarf the desert. Sitting majestically atop a hill in the center of town, this mammoth structure, whose surface could hold 15 football fields, supports ten marble and glass office buildings and a cultural center shaped like a giant egg. Because it was built on a spot that would not support its weight, it sits atop a vast platform, whose concrete bowels hold a fallout shelter, a 3,300-car garage, a pedestrian concourse, and a four-lane highway.[5] The entire structure took 13 years to complete and cost $1.7 billion.[6] "Mean structures," said Rockefeller, "breed small vision."[7]

Rockefeller was a Republican, but if spending is the criteria, he was the greatest Great Society liberal of them all. The payments for his spending spree came due soon after he left office. The first crisis erupted in his Urban Development Corporation, which defaulted on its bonds. The legislature bailed it out with $178 million of taxpayers' money, but by the end of the year four more state agencies were near bankruptcy. As a national recession took hold, New York City teetered on the brink of default, and the state—its bonds no longer salable on the national market—slid dangerously close to insolvency itself.[8]

To this day, Hugh Carey is remembered largely as the man who saved New York City and State from default. He did so by turning city government and finances over to appointed boards, by temporarily raising state taxes, and by reining in the state's forty public authorities, which had long acted almost as independent governments.

In Congress, Carey had been a liberal Democrat. His Republican opponent in 1974, Rockefeller's long-time lieutenant governor, Malcolm Wilson, attacked him as a profligate liberal who would bankrupt the state—one of the finer ironies of American politics.[9] As with Dukakis in Massachusetts, however, the crisis Carey inherited, and the trials he endured to overcome it, changed him profoundly. Over eight years, he pared the state work force by nearly 20,000 and cut the maximum earned income tax rate from over 17 to 10 percent.[10] During his first term he kept overall spending steady (in real dollars) and allowed inflation to eat part of the bureaucracy.[11] Like Dukakis, Carey was relatively unpopular after four years of austerity; unlike Dukakis, he read the public mood and won reelection by focusing the campaign on his tax cuts. During his second term he fought so viciously to control spending by the legislature that budget deadlines went unmet and the machinery of state government at times ground to a halt.

Besides converting to fiscal conservatism, Carey was forced, like other governors, to put economic growth at the top of his agenda. The fiscal crisis in New York was so severe not only because of the unbridled spending by Rockefeller but also because of the state's economic slump. Between 1969 and 1976, New York lost over 600,000 jobs.[12] Most of the losses came in manufacturing; between 1967 and 1982, the number of factory jobs in the state declined by nearly 30 percent.[13] By 1975, New Yorkers were running dead last in average growth of personal income.[14]

To solve the economic crisis, Carey brought business and labor leaders together. "That was the start of a dialogue," says Raymond Schuler, who served as commissioner of transportation under Rockefeller and now runs the state's principal business lobby, the Business Council. "It put people at a table, talking, and let us build off that to discuss a lot of issues. The turning point in our state came with the economic crisis in the seventies."

The first impulse, as in most states in the mid-1970s, was to cut taxes. Most New York policy makers believed Rockefeller's high personal income taxes had driven investment from New York. At most, this was only partially true; neighboring Connecticut, which had no income tax, had experienced similar economic problems. But the belief was so widely shared that the AFL-CIO and the business community teamed up in 1977 to lobby for a personal income tax cut and an investment tax credit, both of which Carey supported and the legislature passed.

Carey continued to cut taxes during his second term, but he also began to develop a more sophisticated economic strategy. Hugh O'Neill, his chief economic policy aide, was one of those reading the new publications from CSPA. One day he called Roger Vaughan to ask if Vaughan knew anyone he might hire as assistant director. They had a long conversation, and "four hours later he called back and offered me the job," Vaughan recalls.

An economist, Vaughan identified with the neo-Austrian school of economics—little known in this country—which traces its roots back to Joseph Schumpeter. In contrast to the Keynesians, who were preoccupied with macroeconomic questions of demand stimulation and the like, Schumpeter focused on microeconomic issues such as the entrepreneurial process and the birth and death of individual firms.

With this perspective, Vaughan concentrated on changing tax and regulatory policy to make the market function more efficiently, particularly for new and small firms. He and O'Neill drew up legislation to eliminate the state's chief tax abatement program, which offered lavish subsidies to large corporations; to abolish the capital gains tax for investments in new enterprises held for more than five years; to make the investment tax credit refundable to new businesses; and to allow small-business owners to file personal (subchapter S) rather than business tax returns. They pushed for reforms in the regulations governing banks and insurance companies, efforts that came to fruition under Cuomo. They were successful in creating an international free-trade zone for banking in New York City, to exempt those involved in international banking from some of the regulations designed for the domestic market. And they convinced Carey to provide $30 million in no-interest loans to build a new Center for Industrial Innovation at Rensselaer Polytechnic Institute.

The other major players in the evolution of New York's economic development strategy were Stanley Fink, speaker of the Assembly from 1979 through 1986, and his principal aide, Frank Mauro. A liberal Democrat from Brooklyn, Fink had ascended to command of the Assembly in ten short years, with virtually no opposition. A brilliant, forceful man, he was known for both his blunt tongue and his analytical mind. Like Carey, Fink was profoundly affected by the state's fiscal crisis and economic decline, which forced him to shift his priorities from social problems to economic development, from issues of distribution to issues of growth.

When Fink became speaker in 1979, he set up an Office of Program Development, to initiate policy proposals. Its first director was Frank Mauro, an extraordinarily creative, intense young man who had left graduate school for government in the early seventies. Mauro had written a dissertation on government's response to new technologies, and after joining Fink, he fathered most of New York's technology programs.

Mauro and Fink also shepherded major infrastructure bills through the legislature. Their other concern was new and small business; like their counterparts in other states, they had read David Birch. In 1980 Mauro synthesized these emerging perspectives in a report, "Toward a Blueprint for Economic Survival." Very much in the spirit of what was going on at CSPA, in California, and in Pennsylvania, it focused on technological innovation, new and small business, regulatory reform, tax reform, capital formation, and infrastructure. "Ideas emerge in a lot of places at the same time," Mauro told me. "We started talking about this stuff in 1980, and we began to hear about it from others in 1981."

Out of this process came a stream of new legislation. Among those bills that passed were several efforts to streamline the regulatory process for business; tax cuts for small business and tax incentives to spur investments in new and small business; a five-year capital renewal plan for mass transit; and a bill that allowed the state public pension funds to invest 5 percent of their money in projects that would "benefit the overall economic health" of New York, including venture capital.[15]

The major successes, however, came in the area of technology. In 1979, Fink reactivated the state Science and Technology Foundation (STF), which had been shut down during the fiscal crisis. Over the next six years, he and Mauro built it into a $20-million-a-year economic development agency.[16] Today it funds virtually the entire menu of state technology programs created in the 1980s, including a seed capital fund; seven industry-university research consortia called Centers for Advanced Technology; a handful of Regional Technology Development Organizations, which act as local economic development agencies for technology firms; an industrial extension service; a supercomputer at Cornell University; and a small-business incubator for technology-based companies in the Buffalo area.

The Science and Technology Foundation (STF) also launched the first program in the country to match federal Small Business Innovation Research (SBIR) grants. Under the SBIR program, the largest federal agencies set aside one percent of their procurement budgets for developments by small businesses. They award $40,000 to $50,000 "phase one" grants for design work, then larger "phase two" grants for those products they want developed. When Mauro and his staff heard that New York companies had a poor track record in securing these funds, they investigated. They learned that the six- to nine-month delay between submitting the phase one design work and receiving a phase two grant created problems for many financially strapped small businesses. So they simply wrote a bill allowing the foundation to provide a matching grant at the end of phase one, to fund continued work during the waiting period. With this money as a carrot, the number of companies applying for federal SBIR grants from New York increased dramatically. "At the moment this is the only way we can be helpful in providing true seed capital to an entrepreneur," says Foundation Director Graham Jones. "This is money where we don't ask for a demonstrable prototype and we don't ask for equity. If you want to develop something, here's some money for it. We get involved in some very interesting things through that work—from single individuals to one hundred-employee companies."

New York is probably spending too much on bricks and mortar for its Centers for Advanced Technology, and the Science and Technology Foundation suffers from its vertical organization, in which each separate program is run out of the Albany office. The Ben Franklin model, in which programs are horizontally integrated at the regional level, is clearly superior. But New York has more tools available than most states, and when the new extension service hits its stride, the rudiments of an effective program should be in place.

The Emergence of Mario Cuomo

Responding to the demands of an electorate squeezed by high inflation and high unemployment, Hugh Carey and Stanley Fink underwent transitions similar to those made by Democrats all across the nation. Feuding more often than they cooperated, they nonetheless cut taxes, controlled spending, and created an economic development strategy centered on new and small business, technological innovation, and regulatory reform.

Carey's successor appeared to be cut from a different cloth. Mario Cuomo ran for governor in 1982 as a traditional Democrat, heir to the tradition of Roosevelt, Truman, and Kennedy. His campaign theme was "jobs and justice."

In reality, Cuomo was not nearly so rooted in traditional liberalism as the national Democrats with whom he is often identified. Cuomo entered politics at the age of 42, after two decades as a Brooklyn lawyer—a lawyer who often represented community groups *against* government. His views were forged neither in enthusiasm for the New Deal and the Great Society, as were those of most traditional liberals, nor in reaction to their shortcomings, as were those of the new-paradigm liberals. Mario Cuomo's world was more parochial. Two factors above all others shaped his political style and philosophy: the gritty realities of Brooklyn and Queens, where he lived and worked, and the missionary Catholicism of St. John's Preparatory School, College, and Law School, where he spent 26 years as a student and law professor.

In an interview, I asked Cuomo what his reaction had been to Johnson's Great Society. "I wasn't active politically, so it's difficult to describe my reactions in terms that would mean anything to you," he responded. "I always believed that government wasted, that government had more ineptitude than it needed to have. I spent the years of growing familiarity with government suing government. The politicians I dealt with were not superior beings. You know, I looked it up once: I never lost a lawsuit against government. We beat the attorney general's office something like 20 times in a row. It wasn't because we were good. We worked very hard, and we weren't bad. But they were awful. So my whole attitude about government was that it was inferior. I was scandalously harsh on politicians, I really was. [I thought] Johnson, government generally in the sixties, were con artists."

Cuomo never became active against the Vietnam War, or enthusiastic about antiwar candidate George McGovern. "I was in a bar with Jimmy Breslin, I'll never forget it," he told me. "I think it was a Saturday afternoon; I had come back from the office. There was a story on television about McGovern's welfare program: $1,000 apiece for a family of fourteen. I said, 'This is your guy, Breslin? You've got to be kidding, this guy's finished!' And Jimmy says, 'Why're you talking like that?' He's rumpling his hair"—Cuomo imitated his friend, feigning anxiety. "So we called over the bartender and said, 'Did you hear this thing about McGovern?' The guy says, 'This clown wants to give everybody $1,000? Get rid of him!' Breslin says, 'I think you're right,' and from there on in he went through the whole campaign saying McGovern's finished.

"I remember saying to Jimmy, 'Look, it's not because it's a bad idea, Jimmy. You know, it's probably a pretty smart idea.' But it was like Mondale's tax increase—you can't do it, this guy doesn't know who he's talking to, he doesn't understand. You can't tell my mother and father, who killed themselves working, that what we have to do is ask no questions, just give everybody money. You've got to be kidding, you tell my mother and father that! My father who bled from the bottom of his feet, you're going to tell him, here's the solution, give them money, for nothing?

"I didn't know McGovern personally," Cuomo explained. "But he was unrealistic. Probably the best word to describe me in those years was very, very realistic. I was unaffected by politics. I was the guy on the street, and what I did know about politics was almost all negative."

Cuomo finally came to politics by way of his lawsuits. For most of the 1960s he represented the homeowners of Corona, a working-class, Italian neighborhood in Queens, who were about to lose their homes to make way for a new school. When Cuomo drew up a settlement that saved most of the homes but still made room for the school, he earned the respect of an aide to Mayor Lindsay. In 1972, when a bitter dispute erupted over a city plan to put a large, low-income housing project in the middle-class, Jewish neighborhood of Forest Hills, Lindsay asked Cuomo to mediate. The controversy was front-page news, and the compromise Cuomo fashioned was so successful that he considered running for mayor the following year.

By this time, Cuomo had attracted the backing of some of New York's heavier weights. Breslin immortalized Hugh Carey's early admiration for Cuomo in his introduction to *Forest Hills Diary*, Cuomo's book about the dispute. "I got a genius nobody knows about," Breslin quoted Carey as telling him. "He's a law professor at St. John's. Brilliant sonofabitch. Mario Cuomo. I begged him to run with me. Nobody knows him. The first time they ever hear of him, they'll be right there in his hands. But I just couldn't talk him into running."

In 1974, Cuomo made the leap, taking an unsuccessful shot at the Democratic nomination for lieutenant governor. One speech he gave that year, to the liberal New Democratic Coalition, is particularly revealing. It shows both his reaction to the liberalism of the late 1960s and the scars from his recent encounter with the angry middle class of Forest Hills. The "glorious opportunity and heavy burden of our party," Cuomo said, was to serve the poor, "those without power or property." But while doing so, the party must not forget the middle class: "The worker, blue collar or white collar, of whatever skin color, who labors hard, lives modestly, asks little and gets less in return. The individual not poor enough for welfare but not rich enough to be worry-free. . . . He was and is the backbone of our work force, the stabilizing influence in our society. The hope of the future. And he was the strength of our party.

"Then we lost him.

"For some reason he felt alienated by a new Democratic Party which he thought neither understood nor related to him. He was made to feel voiceless, powerless and frustrated. So he became a Republican or a Conservative.

"We must bring him back to our party. . . . This is the real challenge for our party. To find a way to harmonize the competing interests. To serve the poor without crushing the middle class."[17]

Though Cuomo lost the 1974 race, Governor-elect Carey appointed him secretary of state. Three years later Carey pushed him into running for mayor of New York, a race for which he clearly was not ready. Cuomo ran as the neighborhood, populist candidate, even creating a line on the ballot called the Neighborhood Preservation party. But Ed Koch bloodied him. "Koch was dangling out capital punishment as symbolic of everything—he could solve the problems of the world because he was in favor of capital punishment," says Cuomo's long-time friend and aide Fabian Palomino. "He'd go to a senior citizen center and say, 'Everybody in favor of capital punishment raise your hands!' And poor Mario"—who opposed capital punishment—"would go to the same place and they'd be ready to spit on him."

In 1978, after two losses, Cuomo was rewarded by Carey with the nomination for lieutenant governor. During four years spent largely as an observer, watching and learning, he plotted his own run at the top. But once again his nemesis Ed Koch stepped in to spoil his plans. Even more than in 1977, Cuomo entered the 1982 primary a hopeless underdog. A liberal in the Reagan era, a two-time loser in his previous races, he was taking on a man who had just been reelected mayor with 75 percent of the vote and the nomination of both major parties. Cuomo would have had little chance had not Koch made his famous remarks disparaging upstate New York in a *Playboy* interview published just before the campaign. The suburbs were "sterile," Koch laughed, rural life "a joke."[18] Cuomo won by two-to-one and three-to-one upstate, but pulled in only 53 percent of the vote overall.[19]

In the general election, Cuomo squeaked by. The real story was Republican Lew Lehrman, a political novice who spent $8 million of his own money on a brilliant television campaign, the centerpiece of which was his pledge to cut state income taxes by 40 percent over eight years. Despite the Democrats' 900,000 edge in registered voters, the recession, and a heavy turnout of blacks and working people, Cuomo won by only 180,000 votes.[20] An unlikely winner in the primary, a narrow victor over a radical conservative in the general election, a man who was clearly to the left of the electorate, Cuomo needed all of his political and oratorical skills to transform his dubious mandate into the mantle of leadership.

Within Cuomo's first months in office, three events gave him that opportunity. The first was a fiscal crisis. During his campaign, Cuomo had promised not to raise income, sales, or corporate taxes. Yet the state faced a $1.8 billion deficit, out of a full budget that would exceed $31.5 billion. Cuomo's campaign had been built on volunteers from labor, many of them from the public employee unions. Now he faced the prospect of cutting budgets and laying off public employees.

Cuomo chose to "share the pain." He proposed $900 million in spending cuts and $900 million in increased alcohol, cigarette, phone, and other "nuisance" taxes. The state payroll would be slashed by 14,000 people, 8,400 of them through layoffs.[21] The new governor talked publicly about the symbolic importance of asking his labor supporters to sacrifice along with everyone else.

After negotiations with the legislature, Cuomo got most of what he wanted, including a budget agreement before the legal deadline. The tax package was changed slightly and increased to almost $1 billion, and the work force was cut by only 8,600, mostly through an early retirement plan.[22] After Carey's years of budget warfare and missed deadlines, Cuomo's performance received plaudits from the press. It earned him a reputation as a responsible fiscal moderate who could work with the legislature—an enormous plus for a new governor. He preserved that reputation in succeeding years by cutting personal income taxes, submitting the first budget balanced under Generally Accepted Accounting Procedures (GAAP), reducing the state debt, and advocating a mild form of spending cap.

In reality, Cuomo's fiscal moderation is often exaggerated. He had no choice but to produce a GAAP budget; a law requiring it had passed during Carey's last years.[23] His first tax cut, which reduced the maximum rate from 10 to 9 percent over three years, lowered state taxes by about $1.5 billion a year. Taking his first year's increase into account, Cuomo reduced taxes during his first term by only $500 million a year—just over one percent of the 1986 budget. Meanwhile, with state revenues skyrocketing, he increased spending by over 40 percent—almost triple the four-year inflation rate of 15 percent.[24] During his second term, when a huge surplus began to accumulate, Cuomo belatedly supported a legislative tax reform bill, patterned loosely on the new federal law, that will cut the maximum rate to 7 percent by 1991.

Politically, New York's overflowing coffers offered Cuomo the same luxury Dukakis enjoyed in Massachusetts: the ability to spend liberally while his aides told the world he was a fiscal conservative. When pressed, Cuomo admits that this label is misleading. "I'm not boasting of cutting," he told me. "Nobody's heard me boast that I came into government to reduce government. I didn't. I came into government to do it more intelligently, to do it better than we have. I don't see any wisdom in seeking to be a bigger spender or a lesser spender, or even a constant spender. Ask me what I spent on, how I spent it, did I waste, was it productive, what did the judgment imply?"

After eight years of austerity and two years of federal budget cuts, Cuomo argues, New York's needs were pressing. The best examples are the two other crises thrust upon him in the early months, prisons and infrastructure. When Cuomo was elected, the prisons were operating at

120 percent of capacity.[25] On his eighth day in office, the problems erupted. Prisoners at Ossining Correctional Facility—Sing Sing, to the world—took 19 guards hostage. Camping in his World Trade Center office for 53 hours on end, Cuomo settled the uprising with no violence. Again he shone in contrast to a former governor; when Nelson Rockefeller ordered his state troopers into Attica, a decade earlier, 43 guards and inmates had been killed. Having proven his leadership in a crisis, Cuomo proceeded to pour money into the prisons and the rest of the criminal justice system—so rapidly that spending shot up by 72 percent in his first three years.[26] By 1989, he planned 23,000 new prison cells, which would more than double the system's 1982 capacity.[27]

The infrastructure problem was equally severe. Many of New York's highways and bridges were in desperate need of repair. The problem was dramatized during Cuomo's sixth month, when a major bridge on Highway 95, a few exits from the New York border, fell into Connecticut's Mianus River. That autumn Cuomo led a successful campaign to pass a $1.25-billion "Rebuild New York" bond issue. Since three of the previous five bond issues had failed, even Cuomo's critics gave him credit for this feat.

Housing the Homeless

Cuomo had little alternative but to deal with the fiscal, prison, and infrastructure problems. The other priorities he chose early in his term—housing and the homeless—are more revealing of his own impulses and more consistent with his image and rhetoric. It is in these areas that Cuomo has made his mark—and pioneered new methods of attacking old problems.

Under Rockefeller, New York had been a national leader in housing redevelopment. But when the Urban Development Corporation defaulted in 1975, the state essentially pulled out of housing. With the economic boom of the 1980s, a shortage of affordable housing emerged as perhaps the foremost problem in much of the state, particularly the New York City metropolitan area. Cuomo set up programs to create low-income housing, moderate-income housing, and housing for the homeless. But he used a new model, one with significance for the entire nation.

Rather than providing subsidies for private developers or building apartments itself—the typical options in the past—the state has contracted with community-based groups to develop housing. In this way, it has used housing programs to build the capacities of community development organizations. To make sure it gets the most bang for its buck, it has made applicants compete for grants and required that they find much of their financing elsewhere. It has also shifted from a strategy of redevelopment, in which whole neighborhoods are torn down to make way for large new

complexes, to an "in-fill" strategy, in which abandoned buildings are rehabilitated and small blocks of townhouses are built to fill vacant areas. These
trends are evident throughout the country, but New York is clearly among
the leaders.[28]

One place the new model first emerged was New York City, which
during the 1970s found itself inheriting thousands of decaying apartment
buildings from owners who failed to pay their taxes. Traditionally the city
had simply auctioned off the buildings after 90 days, but in the late seventies city officials discovered that the same landlords who had defaulted
were changing their corporate names and buying more slum buildings at
auction. In 1978, the Koch administration decided to keep the buildings,
rehab them, and use them for low-income housing. A year later Bill
Eimicke, a young assistant finance director, was named deputy commissioner of the Department of Housing Preservation and Development and
put in charge of the program. Only five years out of graduate school,
Eimicke suddenly found himself with ten thousand buildings, four thousand of which were occupied by over 40,000 families.[29]

"In that first year it was kind of a disaster," Eimicke remembers. "Leaving aside public housing, the city of New York became the largest landlord
in the city overnight, and we were overwhelmed. Over time, through a lot
of people's innovative ideas, we changed our strategy. We said, 'Instead of
running it ourselves, let's get nonprofits, let's get the private sector, let's
try to find ways of spinning the buildings off. Let's fix them up, get them
stabilized, and if we can let's turn them over to community organizations
and tenant groups.' And now I think it's second to public housing as our
best experiment with low-income housing. They sell the units for $250
apiece to tenant cooperatives, and there's thousands of buildings all over
New York which were previously run by slum landlords that are now
rehabilitated tenant cooperatives."

Eimicke is an extremely energetic, hard-working young man whose
enthusiasm fairly bubbles when he talks housing. He first met Cuomo in
Albany in 1975, when Cuomo was secretary of state and Eimicke worked
for the Senate Finance Committee. "In retrospect these things always
sound like baloney, but I thought the guy could be president then,"
Eimicke says. He began sending Cuomo memos on housing and finance
ideas, and Cuomo began calling to ask his opinion about this or that question. On the Saturday after his election as governor, Cuomo called Eimicke
in and asked him to join the administration. Two years later—just 12 years
after he had received his Ph.D. in public administration—Eimicke was
New York's first housing "czar," with authority over all state housing
agencies.

On that Saturday in 1982, Cuomo had the homeless on his mind. "The
first thing the governor said to me was, 'This homeless thing has got me,'"

Eimicke remembers. "'I can't believe that in 1982 there are all these people living the way they are.' So he created a task force right after he was elected and put me in as head of it."

The task force held hearings all over the state. It heard, according to Eimicke, "that homelessness is not what it used to be, it's not drunks, drug addicts, and old white men—Skid Row, if you will." Instead, over 50 percent of the homeless were now families: "The typical homeless person is a minority woman, less than 25, with three kids, the oldest one no older than eight." Those people, the task force concluded, needed housing, social services, education, and training.

Despite the fiscal crisis, Cuomo proposed and the legislature passed a four-year, $50-million appropriation to build housing for the homeless. (They have since added another $40 million.) Cuomo, who also chaired an NGA task force on the homeless, gave the issue high visibility. He took great pleasure in pointing out that New York was spending more on the homeless than was the federal government.

Traditionally in New York City, where 85 percent of the state's homeless live, they were sheltered in run-down hotels and large shelters (armories and gymnasiums, principally). Because so few hotels would take the homeless, Eimicke explained, those that would—"sleazebag hotels" full of "squalor and roaches"—got away with charging $100 a night for a room. By 1986, the average stay was 11 months, which added up to $33,500 per family. In the shelters, which consisted of little more than cots on a state-owned gym floor, the city spent as much as *$70,000* a year per family. ("They've never been able to explain why it costs $70,000," said Eimicke. "I don't know what the answer is.") With four thousand New York City families homeless on any given night in the mid-1980s, the cost—simply to maintain people in homelessness—was astronomical.

Eimicke's task force decided the answer was new housing for the homeless, both permanent and transitional, with social services on the premises. In part because of his experience in New York City, Eimicke turned primarily to community-based organizations—church groups, social service agencies, and housing organizations—to develop and staff the new units. (Local governments may also bid for funds.) The nonprofits own and manage the buildings, meet the mortgage payments, and make sure services are provided: counseling, day care, training, drug treatment, and so on. The state provides up-front capital grants to write down the cost of construction or renovation, and the nonprofits come up with the rest of the financing, usually from a mixture of city, foundation, and private money.

"Most people who are in the business of housing come in with a jaundiced eye, always believing that the only people who can really do housing are the private sector," Eimicke says. "And historically, there's a great deal of foundation for that—the bad experience that many of us had in the

sixties with the stuff that didn't work out of Washington. But my experience in New York City was exactly the reverse. As a matter of fact, many of
the nonprofits were much more effective than the for-profits, because they
had community support. And in the city, without community support, it
doesn't matter how good you are—you don't get anything done."

The old model relied on public subsidies for private developers. "The
idea of Section 8 [the primary federal housing program, until it was largely
phased out by Reagan] was a good one," says Eimicke. "That is, housing
isn't affordable to poor people; let's close the gap. The problem is it had a
negative incentive. It said to developers, 'The more you spend on this
project, the more you're going to make, so throw every doodad into it.'
And then it said, 'It doesn't matter, whatever the difference between 30
percent of tenants' income and what it costs to run the program, we'll pick
up.' So there was no incentive to make it efficient."

By 1982, the average unit of low-income housing built under Section 8
cost $300,000 over the projected life of the mortgage.[30] One reason was
interest rates. When rates are high, subsidies over the life of a mortgage
become enormous. The alternative is to reduce the debt that must be financed by providing an up-front capital grant—the strategy chosen by
New York. "That way your money goes further, and you don't build in
negative incentives to be wasteful in the future," says Eimicke.

Advocates for the homeless generally praised the design of the new
Homeless Housing Assistance Program (HHAP). When the state put out a
request for proposals, requests flowed in for $300 million, six times the
amount available. But problems soon developed. Eimicke and Cuomo
placed the program in the Department of Social Services (DSS), which had
no experience building housing. They did so, in theory, because they
wanted to make sure services were an integral part of the package; in
reality, there were also political calculations involved. In any event, DSS
had to hire new people and learn an entirely new process.

In addition, community organizations already experienced in housing
shied away from the program, because their members were not eager to
bring more homeless people into what were already troubled neighborhoods. Hence church groups and social service agencies, which had little
experience developing housing, received most of the grants. Yet DSS offered them little technical assistance, particularly in the first years. The
delays and snags were endless, and eventually DSS had to take back some
of the contracts it signed when nonprofits failed to perform. To make
matters worse, the corruption scandal that unfolded in New York City in
1986 brought forth a blizzard of red tape and further delays, as the city
government slapped checks and reviews on all public construction
projects.

Four years into the program, HHAP had contracts for units containing 7,000 beds, but only 3,162 were finished and 873 were under construction.[31] In contrast, a second initiative undertaken by the city and state, the Emergency Assistance Rehousing Program, housed 4,680 *families* within its first four years.[32] It simply paid landlords the hotel rate of $100 a night for eight months (or, if they were public agencies, four months) if they would agree to rent to a homeless family at the maximum rate covered by welfare for an additional two years.

In fairness, HHAP is doing more than housing the homeless; it is also expanding the supply of low-cost housing. New construction, or substantial renovation, takes time. And there is obvious value in having nonprofit groups involved. Robert Hayes, a young lawyer who founded the Coalition for the Homeless, expresses the ambivalence typical of advocates for the homeless. "Generally, we think it's better to have smaller groups, community groups do the work," he says. "But our argument was, given the survival needs of so many people, and given the great expense and waste of public shelter programs, this was not an instance to go about things with business as usual." Hayes argued early on for a model in which commercial developers would be paid to build and renovate the housing, then would turn the keys over to the not-for-profits.

Sister Maureen Carey, who supervised the renovation of four buildings by Catholic Charities of Brooklyn, made a forceful counterargument as she showed me around one of her projects in 1986. The building was an old Catholic School, with high ceilings and wide hallways. Sister Maureen pointed with pride to the noninstitutional touches, which, she believed, would make living there in a single room a far better experience than if the state had done the work. The best example was the old chapel, which was being turned into a lounge. Had a private developer renovated it on contract with the state, she argued, he would have immediately thrown out the stained glass windows, painted over the murals that graced one wall and a ceiling, and put institutional linoleum over the wood floors. Catholic Charities had done none of that (it had even put the stained glass windows on hinges, so they would open), and the result was a stunning room. Nor would a private developer have listened to the community group that urged 24-hour security at the front door, she added, or to the applicants who suggested refrigerators in each room and a cafeteria in the basement (the original plan called simply for three kitchenettes for 88 units). Finally, the state would have met far more resistance than the Catholic church if it had tried to put a building for the homeless in the neighborhood.

Only time will tell if the program works as planned, complete with adequate social services. When the nonprofits have kept up the buildings and services for five or ten years, without further subsidy, they can claim success. At this early date, however, the model appears flawed only because the program was placed in DSS and insufficient provision was made for technical assistance.

In December 1985, Bill Eimicke ran across an article in the *New York Daily News* about Leonard Stern, the Hartz, Inc., chairman who had recently bought the *Village Voice*. According to the article, Stern had taken to dressing up in old clothes and visiting shelters for the homeless, pretending to be homeless himself. Outraged by what he found, he had given $1 million to legal aid organizations to help families who were turned out of the shelters. The wheels started turning in Eimicke's head. "I thought, it sounds like this guy is a combination of a nut and a guy who makes something happen," he recalls. "Maybe we can somehow tie him into this. I called the governor and said 'What do you think?' and he said 'Go meet with him, see what he has to say.'"

Eimicke called Stern and was invited to breakfast in his Fifth Avenue home, which once housed the Italian Embassy. ("It's like walking into a set from "Citizen Kane," says Eimicke. "It's unreal.") "So we had breakfast, and I said, 'You know, Leonard, this is great, legal assistance and all, but it doesn't really change where these people go—you win and you get 'em back into a sleazebag hotel. We've got to think of something better.' He said, 'Well, why don't we go into business for ourselves, why don't we compete with them?' He was going to his press conference for the legal aid thing, so in the interim I called the governor, and he said, 'Yeah, let's see what we can do—call Andrew [Cuomo's son and most trusted adviser]. You guys come up with something.' So before you know it, we were in the *New York Times* announcing something, and we didn't know even what we were announcing."

Over the next few months, Eimicke and Andrew Cuomo came up with a model to compete with the welfare hotels. "In essence," says Eimicke, "what we're doing is building a 200-unit motel [each unit has two rooms, a bathroom, and a kitchenette], like a Holiday Inn, in East Brooklyn, New York, on city-owned land." Tishman Speyer, a private development firm, built the motel for nothing. Martin Raines, one of the largest apartment managers in New York City, is managing it at cost. And the Red Cross is running it and providing social services and day care. "And the best thing," says Eimicke, "is that even including the debt service, the day care, the social services, recreational space, the furniture—everything, a model facility—it's going to cost about $20,000 per family per year. The cheapest hotel they're using now is about $30,000."

Eimicke dubbed the program HELP—the Homeless Emergency Leverage Program. A perfect example of public-private partnership, it is run by a not-for-profit corporation, with Andrew Cuomo serving as president and Stern as treasurer. The state has floated bonds to provide the financing; it contracts with the corporation, just as it does with welfare hotels. The East Brooklyn facility was scheduled to open in December 1987, and two more deals were in the works—250 units in Westchester County, and 25 in Albany.

Housing the Poor

The acuteness of the homeless problem in New York City is in part a symptom of the city's shortage of low-cost housing. Over the past decade rents have skyrocketed and the housing stock in poor communities has deteriorated badly, leaving low- and moderate-income people in a squeeze. Meanwhile the state has lost more than $1.5 billion a year in federal housing subsidies during the 1980s—a devastating blow, according to housing experts.[33]

Several studies have identified the shortage of affordable housing as the one real cloud on New York City's economic horizon. Private and state government studies done in the mid-1980s generally concurred that the city needed somewhere in the neighborhood of 200,000 new or substantially rehabilitated housing units to reach the 5 percent vacancy rate considered necessary to ease the shortage. In addition, 400,000 units were estimated to be in need of moderate rehabilitation.[34] (These numbers compare to the city's total of 2.8 million units.)[35]

Given its fiscal constraints, New York State cannot hope to make up for the loss of $1.5 billion a year in federal money. In 1985, Cuomo promised $1 billion in new money over ten years. So far he has delivered at roughly double that pace, and he has designed his programs to leverage a great deal more in private-sector and foundation money.[36]

Cuomo secured half of the new money by skimming the profits from another state project that has turned into a gold mine. Under Rockefeller, the state floated $200 million in bonds to create a 92-acre landfill across from the World Trade Center, near the southern tip of Manhattan. The area, called Battery Park City, was originally to be a "New Town," with a mix of high- and low-income housing. But the fiscal crisis intervened, and in 1979 the project was reorganized as an office tower and luxury housing complex. With the economic boom of New York's financial district in the 1980s, long-term leases on entire buildings have been snapped up by the likes of American Express, Dow Jones, and Shearson Lehman. Cuomo's appointee as president of Battery Park City, Meyer (Sandy) Frucher, dreamed up an innovative way to tap the profits for low-income housing, by floating $400 million in bonds against future revenues from leases already signed. "Nobody has ever done this," Frucher says. "Nobody has ever floated a bond against existing underlying real estate values."

In early 1988, Frucher announced that the program would be increased to $1 billion, either from bonds or directly from Battery Park City's abundant profits. The state has kicked in another $100 million it was offered by the Port Authority of New York and New Jersey to move out of its offices in the World Trade Center, to make way for more lucrative commercial customers. The entire $1.1 billion will be channeled into the city's existing housing programs for low- to middle-income people, particularly the renovation of buildings taken over in tax-default cases. The first $200 million in bonds, sold in 1987, will pay for the rehabilitation of 1,800 city-owned units in Harlem and the Bronx, which will then be turned over to community organizations.[37]

Most low-income housing advocates greeted the plan with acclaim. "I think conceptually it is excellent," says Kathryn Wylde, president of the Housing Partnership Development Corporation, an offspring of the New York City Partnership, a civic organization for business chaired by David Rockefeller. "It takes a little bit of the cream that flows from a major public investment over the last 15 years in the redevelopment of an area that's now going to generate tremendous profits, and it redeploys some of those profits into a dedicated stream of revenues for low-income housing for areas of the city that can't generate their own windfalls."

In 1984, a year before it swung the Battery Park City deal, the Cuomo administration had tried to dedicate revenues from a mortgage recording tax to a housing trust fund. (Housing trust funds, which have been proposed by low-income housing advocates for at least a decade, have sprung up in places as diverse as Maine, San Francisco, Phoenix, Pittsburgh, and Dade County, Florida.[38] Their advantage is that unlike normal appropriations, they will continue to provide money even when the legislature gets tightfisted.) When the Republican-controlled Senate refused, Cuomo settled for $50 million a year in appropriated funds. He and the Democratic-controlled Assembly wanted the money for low-income housing; the Senate Republicans wanted to subsidize moderate-income home ownership. So they split the difference, dividing the money between a Low-Income Housing Trust Fund and an Affordable Home Ownership Development Program, the latter aimed at households with incomes between $25,000 and $48,000 a year.

The programs are targeted, particularly in New York City, at renovating abandoned buildings and filling in vacant areas with new homes—generally small blocks of townhouses or duplexes. The loss of existing buildings has been a large part of the city's problem. According to the Citizens Housing and Planning Council, the city has been losing 18,750 units a year—enough in just 11 years to account for the entire 200,000 units it needs for a 5 percent vacancy rate.[39]

With the new programs, the state has adopted the same basic model it used for HHAP: competitive bidding for up-front grants by nonprofit groups and local governments. The grants top out at $40,000 per unit for low-income projects and $15,000 per unit for Affordable Home Ownership projects. (To ensure that buildings remain low income over the long haul, most of the low-income grants are actually long-term loans that will be forgiven if the buildings continue to house low-income people.) The nonprofits involved are not the church groups and service agencies that applied for the HHAP funds, but CDCs and other community organizations with experience in housing development. Though loath to bring the homeless into their neighborhoods, they have leapt at the chance to renovate vacant buildings, which are so often magnets for drug dealers and arsonists, and to fill in vacant areas with new homes.

Most of these community organizations emerged in the 1960s and 1970s, many of them out of War on Poverty programs. Bent on improving the housing situation in their neighborhoods, they often worked with private developers who were building federally subsidized housing; they managed buildings, or recruited community members for jobs, or acted as marketing agents for the buildings. Gradually they learned enough to begin buying small buildings on their own, often with federal grants. When federal subsidies dried up in the 1980s, cities, state, and foundations began turning to the community groups to act as developers.

The strategy of using community organizations rather than private developers has several advantages. It is less wasteful, as Eimicke points out. It allows the state to focus on small-scale construction and rehabilitation projects rather than the large new apartment complexes commercial developers prefer to build. It leverages more money from the private sector and the foundation world. But most important, it empowers local communities. By nurturing the growth of community organizations, the state is creating entrepreneurial entities that will continue to push the development process forward. For poor communities, which lack many of the private entrepreneurial forces we take for granted elsewhere, that process is critical.

By using community organizations, the state also improves the chances that its low-income housing will remain viable over the long haul. Under the old approach, once a building had been fully depreciated for tax purposes, "a developer-owner from outside the community didn't have any economic interest in the project," explains Kathryn Wylde. Small properties in low-income neighborhoods simply do not generate enough in rent to pay for maintenance and leave anything for profits. "In the absence of not-for-profit community-based organizations, the real estate doesn't make sense as an economic venture. So using community organizations is not just desirable, it's essential."

It is too early to say whether the program will be successful. Daniel

Conviser, former staff director of the Assembly Housing Committee and one of the authors of the Low Income Housing Trust Fund bill, puts the challenge into perspective: "What we are attempting to do is take some of the worst buildings in the state, rehabilitate them, and make them low income for a long, long period of time, without providing continual year-by-year subsidies. We're pushing at the margins of what we can accomplish without spending the incredible amounts of money that were spent through the [federal] Section 8 program. The real test will come five to ten years from now, when [the nonprofits] are faced with managing a low-income project without annual subsidies from the state."

In scale, the programs are relatively small: the low-income program has contracted for 650 units a year, the moderate-income program for roughly 3,500 a year.[40] But in the long run, their significance will be more in their effect on community development organizations than in the number of units they build or rehabilitate.

Nurturing Community Development

Perhaps the best way to understand the strategy of using community organizations to develop housing is to look at one in detail. In the mid-1970s, the leaders of St. Nicholas Parish, in the East Williamsburg section of North Brooklyn, were worried about their neighborhood. A drab, working-class district across the river from mid-Manhattan, East Williamsburg was in rapid decline. Most of those who could afford to do so had moved to the suburbs. (During the 1970s the population declined by 12,000.) Landlords were abandoning buildings, the city's economy had turned sour, and the fiscal crisis had forced a rapid withdrawal of city services. Investments in East Williamsburg—public or private—were few and far between.

Physically, East Williamsburg typifies the decaying, dreary landscapes of Brooklyn and the Bronx. Its streets offer little to please the eye: the buildings are mostly wood frame, covered with asbestos shingles or aluminum siding. Some five hundred light industrial enterprises still dot the neighborhood—garment factories, small food-processing plants, electrical plating operations. There are few brownstones and little charm; hence the young professionals who have gentrified other parts of Brooklyn have largely ignored the neighborhood. Long an Italian enclave, by 1980 it was 28 percent Hispanic and 4 percent black.[41] A few of the larger apartment buildings had been abandoned, and there were drug and unemployment problems. But East Williamsburg had never experienced the abandonment felt by the South Bronx, or the social pathology of New York's worst ghettos.

In the fall of 1974, the owners of one of the largest buildings in the neighborhood announced that they planned to close the building and leave it vacant. Soon afterward, a fire down the street from St. Nicholas, the local Catholic church, burned out eight families and killed several children. Stung by the events, a group of parishioners and business people began meeting at the church to search for ways to stem the neighborhood's decline. They decided to set up shop in the rectory basement and target the area's deteriorating stock of housing. Twelve years later, when I visited, the St. Nicholas Neighborhood Preservation Corporation had five hundred employees and an annual budget of $10 million. It managed six hundred units of housing, ran an industrial park, owned a residence for the elderly and a small shopping plaza, ran a home attendant program for the elderly, did tenant organizing, operated a fuel-buying cooperative, and published a community newspaper. It had rehabilitated some 20 buildings, and it was at work on others.[42]

The man who oversaw all this, St. Nicholas's executive director, was Gary Sam Hattem—a breezy young man who, but for his darker hair, could stand in for Art Garfunkel. Hattem is slender and tall, with blue eyes, a large nose, a wispy moustache, and a slight stoop. In his midthirties, he has the casual, flip confidence of a typical, if unusually relaxed, New Yorker.

Hattem took me on a tour of the neighborhood. Our first stop was a block of five apartment buildings on Metropolitan Avenue, one of Williamsburg's main thoroughfares. When St. Nicholas began work, two of the buildings were vacant, the other three were only marginally occupied, and the storefront shops on the street had all closed up. Hattem and his staff convinced the tenants to consolidate into two buildings, then secured $4.1 million of federal money to renovate the other three. When I saw them they held 65 units of senior citizen housing, complete with hallway cameras, 24-hour security, and new elevators. The other two units were slated for renovation as tenant cooperatives. In the immediate vicinity a fruit store, a hardware store, a repair shop, and a pharmacy had opened.

The next stop was a new retail plaza on Grand Street, the major shopping strip in the neighborhood. The previous buildings had been destroyed by fire in the early 1970s, and no private investors had stepped in to rebuild them. St. Nicholas went to Chemical Bank with construction plans for a new building, but the bank demanded commitments from tenants before it would agree to a mortgage. It was Catch-22: without a building, Hattem could not find firm tenants; without tenants, he could not construct the building. So he peddled the project to every government agency, corporation, and foundation he could find. He wound up with an $800,000 package of grants and loans from the state, the city, the federal government, Brooklyn Union Gas Company, and a foundation. Today St.

Nicholas owns a handsome red brick building, the city owns the land, and the neighborhood has a new pharmacy and a new children's clothing store.

Eight years ago, according to Hattem, the Grand Street shopping district was a disaster. It was unsafe, businesses were closing up shop, and no one was investing. Today the shops are filled and property values are on their way up. The new building has helped, but even before its completion St. Nicholas had organized the merchants to spruce up the area. With a small grant from the city's Public Development Corporation, St. Nicholas got the merchants to invest in new storefronts, brick paving, traditional street lamps, and large symbols—a huge hammer hanging in front of a hardware store, a basketball shoe over a sporting goods store—to call attention to what they dubbed the Grand Metro Shopping District. Then, in 1985, St. Nicholas got the city to designate the area a Business Improvement District (BID). An innovative effort launched under Governor Carey, the BID program allows business people to assess themselves additional property taxes to pay for improvements—if a majority of the property owners in the district and the city's legislative body approve the plan.[43] In theory, with the initiative in the hands of the merchants and the taxes coming out of their own pockets, the money will be used carefully and wisely. Grand Street, the fifth BID in the city, was the first created for a neighborhood commercial strip.

The third stop was Hattem's pride and joy, Jennings Hall—the building whose abandonment had triggered St. Nicholas's formation. "Jennings Hall was very special," Hattem told me. "It was the first big project to happen in the neighborhood in a godawful long time. And it happened in a pocket of the neighborhood that was really having trouble." Working with the Pratt Development Corporation and the National Council of Senior Citizens, St. Nicholas landed a $7.2-million mortgage from the federal government, constructed a brand new wing, and turned the building into a 150-unit complex for the low-income elderly. It opened in 1981 and has been managed ever since by St. Nicholas.

The day I visited the building sparkled inside and out. In a neighborhood with many elderly people, it served not only as low-income housing but as an important social center for senior citizens. Many of those who lived there also had 40-hour-a-week home attendants, to do their cooking and cleaning—again, thanks to St. Nicholas. The Preservation Corporation employed some four hundred home attendants on a $6-million-a-year contract with the city.

As we drove through the bleak side streets of the neighborhood, we passed a few of the light industrial plants that belong to the North Brooklyn In-Place Industrial Park, which is managed by St. Nicholas. Several years ago Hattem and his staff worked with business owners in the area to form the East Williamsburg Industrial Development Corporation, which in turn set up the industrial park. The corporation runs training programs and an employment service for area businesses, and it recruits new enterprises to the neighborhood. The industrial park is not limited to one physical area; it is simply an organization to provide services to businesses all over the district. St. Nicholas runs a small security force, keeps the street lights fixed and the vacant lots clear of rubble, and prods the police into providing adequate patrols in the area.

Finally, we swung by Greenpoint Hospital, which was closed by the city in 1982 and later turned into a temporary shelter for homeless men. Hattem had great dreams for the five-acre complex: "We want to do all sorts of things with it. A nursing home, a medical building, housing for the elderly"—plus four buildings for the homeless under the HHAP program, one transitional and three permanent. "We estimate about four hundred permanent jobs will be created, and we think it will have a real impact on the entire North Brooklyn area." St. Nicholas had fashioned a coalition of local organizations to pressure the city, which did not want to cut back the size of its transitional shelter to make room for the other elements of the coalition's plan. When I checked back with Hattem a few months later, HUD had approved his proposal for a $2.5-million rehabilitation of the largest building, but the city had not backed down.

On an afternoon tour one could hardly see all of the activities in which St. Nicholas was involved. It helped tenants organize against landlords who failed to maintain their buildings, managed buildings for tenant co-ops or landlords, helped homeowners get loans for rehabilitation and weatherization, ran a fuel cooperative that offered a discount on heating oil to members, and ran a project to combat arson in the neighborhood. And of course when Cuomo's new housing money became available, St. Nicholas immediately jumped in. In the first round it received a $792,000 low-income grant to renovate an abandoned, city-owned building with 24 apartments. With the state money in hand, Hattem and his staff secured another $500,000 in the form of a blended mortgage—half from a private institution at market interest rates, half from New York City at one percent. A final $200,000 would come from those who bought apartments in the cooperative—families with earnings in the $15,000 to $30,000 range. Nearby St. Nicholas planned to renovate 20 apartments for homeless families, with a grant from New York City. And across the street, on a vacant lot, Hattem hoped to build two-family houses under the Affordable Home Ownership Development Program.

The impact of all this on the neighborhood was clearly visible. A neighborhood in decline had been stabilized. The housing stock had improved, and seizures by the city for nonpayment of taxes had dropped from 50 to 100 a year down to 25. Applications for mortgages and home improvement loans were on the rise. Property values had tripled over the past four or five years, and rents had doubled in two or three years.[44] Perhaps the best indication was the commercial revival: between 1981 and 1985, 35 stores had opened and the vacancy rate for merchants in Central Williamsburg had dropped 40 percent.[45] "We're carried by what's happening in New York City as a whole, so it's hard to isolate the neighborhood," Hattem acknowledged. "But certainly Bushwick and East New York are neighborhoods that aren't experiencing that same sort of interest. We could have been left out of that resurgence in the city economy."

St. Nicholas is one of the more successful community organizations in New York, but it is far from the only one. A few miles to the south, the Bedford Stuyvesant Restoration Corporation, which faces far more intractable problems, has become one of the best-known and most successful community development corporations in the country. In the South Bronx, organizations such as SEBCO Development, Inc., the Banana Kelly Community Improvement Association, and the Mid Bronx Desperadoes Community Housing Corporation have renovated and built dozens of apartment buildings. A walk through the neighborhoods in which they work shows a remarkable rebound from the 1970s.

These organizations owe at least part of their success to the financial support they have received from the state Neighborhood Preservation Program. Begun in 1977, it was the first state program to provide funding for what are, in essence, community development corporations. The grants are not large: the maximum is $100,000 a year, and most groups get about half that amount. But unlike most other grants, they can be used to pay administrative staff rather than to fund specific projects. Kathryn Wylde, who began her career with a community group in Brooklyn, explains why that is important: "For several years, this is the only continuous source of money you have. Almost your entire budget is based on grants, which may or may not come, and which you never know if you're getting, so anything that is somewhat of a stable, predictable source of financing is just critical. This money allows them to attract decent professional staff. There's nothing more precious than administrative funding, and that's why this is such a critically important program."

By the mid-1980s, New York spent $12.6 million a year subsidizing 216 Neighborhood Preservation Companies, plus about $5 million a year for 84 Rural Preservation Companies.[46] (In addition, it granted these organizations millions of dollars through housing and other programs, as did the city of New York. In 1986 the Cuomo administration claimed that Preservation Companies built or rehabilitated 17,000 units of housing.)[47] Theoretically, the NPC and RPC programs are structured to gradually wean the community organizations from the subsidy. The maximum grant is $100,000 a year until they have received a total of $300,000, when it drops to $65,000 a year. When they reach a total of $650,000, they are cut off entirely.

Many observers believe the idea of ever cutting off the subsidy is folly. "The assignment to these NPCs is to carry out activities that don't support private-sector involvement or entrepreneurial involvement—the part of the market that isn't financially self-sustaining," says Wylde. "So by definition the NPCs end up with uneconomic propositions, whether they are buildings or people that cannot support themselves. If your chartered assignment is an uneconomic one, you can never be self-sufficient."

A similar problem besets the Low Income Housing Trust Fund. Participants complain that the program requires them to stitch together financing packages from a variety of sources, to deal with local housing bureaucracies and permitting processes, and to manage a complex development process—yet it provides no funding for administrative overhead. The problem is exacerbated, many participants argue, by the fact that the legislation was overwritten, leaving too little flexibility to the developers.

Eimicke has responded by dedicating roughly $500,000 of the first $50 million to technical assistance, to help community groups hire architects, lawyers, and others. He has also pushed the legislature to loosen the regulations and to increase the maximum grant from $40,000 per unit to $70,000, so community organizations do not have to go elsewhere for money.

Some housing advocates have suggested the creation of an intermediary organization, for both the Housing Trust Fund and the HHAP program. This would be a citywide or statewide organization, funded by both the public and private sectors, to provide technical assistance, to help centralize the fund raising for individual projects, and to provide financial assistance. Such institutions have been created in other cities, where they have succeeded in raising private funds for low-income housing—thus adding a wholesaling dimension to public programs.[48]

Welfare Reform

Housing is not the only area in which Cuomo has sought to help the poor. In 1987, he pushed a bill through the legislature dropping the age at which children start public school to four in poor areas. He has also experimented with several programs aimed at disadvantaged teenagers. One, called the School-to-Employment Program (STEP), offers poor teenagers who are judged to be at risk of dropping out of high school part-time jobs if they stay in school. It also finds jobs for dropouts if they continue some form of education. As of this writing, however, STEP is still in the pilot stage, with many bugs to be worked out. It is run only in selected communities, it finds jobs for fewer than two thousand teenagers a year, and it costs only $5 million a year.[49]

New York has made more progress in welfare reform. Republican leaders like to argue that the state welfare system is out of control. In 1985, 8.2 percent of New York's population was on some form of public aid, ranking it fourth behind Mississippi, Michigan, and California.[50] New York has more people on welfare—1.4 million in 1986—than 13 states have people. It costs more than $2.5 billion annually.[51] And because the system is administered and partially funded by the counties, the state cannot impose new programs without major legislation—one reason the system has grown so fat. "The Massachusetts commissioner of public welfare can go to a local office and say to the staff, 'I'm going to move you today,'" says Michael Dowling, who runs New York's welfare system. "I don't have that power. I've got to cajole and persuade. I've got 58 local commissioners who are semiautonomous."

A large, bearded Irishman with a heavy brogue, Dowling left Ireland at the age of 14 to look for work. He came to this country at 17, worked his way through night school as a longshoreman and construction worker, and ended up teaching social work at Fordham University, where he developed a reputation as a knowledgeable advocate in the field of welfare reform. "I got very involved in human welfare stuff basically because of my family background," he says. "I grew up in a house that didn't have electricity or heat or running water. My parents were on assistance for a while. My father was on disability for most of his life. So I can identify somewhat with a lot of these programs, because I've been through some of them myself."

Dowling believes there are several keys to getting people off welfare and into jobs. "Number one, you have to tailor services to the individual needs of the clients," he says. "Two, you have to focus on people who are on welfare for a long period of time. What has been happening over the years is that about 80 percent of the people who generally run through a welfare system are people who lack basic skills, and the system ignores them. As a result, they end up eating up most of your resources.

"Three, we can no longer afford to exempt women with young children [from work requirements]. We've got to deal with that group if we're ever going to try to get at independence, reducing dependence. Unless you get an 18-year-old mother and do something with her, and not wait until she becomes 24, I don't think you'll ever be able to get at it.

"Four, we have to reorient the welfare system to become just as cognizant of the need to deal with the training and education needs of people as it is about the maintenance needs of people. The welfare system should not be a place you just go and they say, 'We're going to provide you a grant.'

The welfare system should be something that, as you walk in the door, says, 'We're going to be very aggressive in our efforts to help you get off.'

"The final thing that is crucial is that we have to make the obligations and responsibilities of the individuals very, very clear. This gets into the mandatory versus the voluntary notion. I believe that people who are employable on public assistance have an obligation to do something to help themselves. And that should be strict. If a person says, 'I'm not going to participate,' we should say to them, 'Too bad, then you're going to be penalized.' This probably comes to the fore more with single youth, 17-, 18-, 19-year-old youth, who can be getting a welfare check, who are not involved in school, and who basically don't see themselves having any responsibility to try to help themselves."

Dowling does not, however, believe that most workfare programs, which require that welfare recipients do public service work to earn their grants, succeed in moving people off the rolls into long-term jobs. "I think that for many people workfare can be very valuable, but as one of our evaluations showed, it's only valuable if it is directed as part of a total program to help the client. If it is limited in duration, and there is good supervision, and the person is provided with the supports, putting them on a work site and training them in a skill is helpful. But dumping people in make-work jobs—I've never seen any evidence that that helps."

In 1986, Dowling fashioned a statewide employment and training program built around these principles, which Cuomo called "Work, Not Welfare." After months of negotiations, the legislature failed to pass it. Still, New York has been able to accomplish a fair amount by creating financial incentives for the county welfare departments to set up employment and training programs, and by experimenting with pilot programs. It has also provided child-care subsidies for those in training programs, plus nine months of additional child-care subsidies (up to $160 a month) and up to 15 months of medicaid for everyone who leaves the rolls for a job.

In New York City, where two-thirds of the state welfare recipients live, Dowling and the city's Human Resources Administration have worked out a program along the lines of Cuomo's 1986 proposal. Called the Employment Opportunities Pilot, it is quite similar to E.T. Choices: a case worker assesses each participant's needs, then steers the person to a range of education, training, and job placement services. Vocational counseling, child care, transportation subsidies, and other support services are also available. The program differs from E.T. Choices in that participation is mandatory for all AFDC recipients whose children are six or older. If they refuse to participate in education, training, or placement, they are referred to the city's workfare program. Theoretically, they must take a workfare job or face sanctions. In practice, however, the city does not yet have enough workfare positions (with public agencies and nonprofit institutions) to meet the demand.

A separate pilot program offers voluntary education, training, and placement services to several thousand women with children under six, in about 15 localities around the state. Again, it is similar in concept to E.T. Choices—with two interesting wrinkles. First, the 15 participating agencies were chosen in competitive bidding; winners included county welfare agencies, community organizations, job-training agencies, and adult education programs. Each was allowed to design its own "one-stop shopping" model to offer a comprehensive array of services. Second, each participating agency is paid according to how well it performs—its job placement rates, the wages paid to those it places, how many of them stay on the job for a significant length of time, and so on. Dowling and his staff have been quite pleased with the results. They hope to serve close to 10,000 people in 1989, the pilot's third year.

New York also signs performance-based contracts for training and placement with private corporations, nonprofit organizations, and even other government agencies. One example is RCA Services Corporation, which trains 400 people a year for secretarial, word-processing, and clerical jobs. To make a profit on its contract, it must place 66 percent of its trainees in jobs paying at least 20 percent above the minimum wage, and they must stay on the job for at least 30 days.

Another pilot program creates full-time jobs, at prevailing wages, for employable people who have been on Home Relief (New York's welfare program for those not eligible for AFDC) for at least three years. The idea, in Dowling's words, is that "at some point, welfare ends" and able-bodied recipients must work. The state will act as employer of last resort, paying the going wage for jobs in the public and nonprofit sector.

In 1986, one of the biggest obstacles to passage of Cuomo's "Work, Not Welfare" package was organized labor's opposition to workfare. The state already had workfare programs for both AFDC and Home Relief, in which certain recipients had to work off their grants at the minimum wage. But Dowling had proposed to scale them down and turn them into genuine on-the-job training experiences. The unions, which opposed workfare in any form, fought the bill until it was too late for passage. In 1987, Dowling and his staff spent five months negotiating with them on legislation for the public jobs pilot. They then set up task forces of representatives from labor, local governments, and nonprofit institutions to oversee each of the 14 local pilots. The idea is to start small, with only 800 jobs in the first year, but to set a precedent upon which the state can build.

Another of New York's pioneering experiments goes back to the Carey administration. Called the Temporary Employment Assistance Program (TEAP), it allows the state to use a person's welfare grant as a subsidy to an employer who agrees to train the person. Hugh O'Neill, Carey's second-term economic development aide, came up with the idea. He pointed out to the Department of Social Services that through workfare, it was subsidizing public and nonprofit institutions with free labor. Why not do the same, he asked, with the private sector?

No state had ever tried to use welfare grants as employment or training subsidies, according to O'Neill. In fact, New York had to get special permission from the federal government to do so with AFDC recipients. (Later it led a successful lobbying campaign to change the federal law in question, and several states have since followed its lead.)

Under TEAP, the subsidy can last up to six months, though the average training period is three to four months. Employers are required to pay the recipient the prevailing wage; as a subsidy they get his or her welfare grant. They are not required to keep the employee on the payroll after the training period, though that is obviously the goal. When the state formally evaluated the program in 1984, it found that over half of those who had completed their training programs were kept on, and many others had moved into other jobs. Fewer TEAP participants went back on the welfare rolls after holding jobs than did non-TEAP participants.[52]

TEAP remains a small program, in large part because it requires county welfare departments to aggressively sell the virtues of welfare recipients to private employers (as TEE and America Works do). In 1987, it served only 3,200 people. (Dowling's eventual goal is ten thousand a year.) But more important than the numbers is the principle: like TEE, TEAP has demonstrated that welfare checks can be used to get people off the rolls, rather than simply to maintain them in dependence.

In 1988, New York plans to take this principle a step further. Through yet another pilot, it will give six months of welfare checks, perhaps in one lump sum, to recipients who start small businesses, such as day-care operations out of their homes or repair shops. Called the "Self-Employment Demonstration," the project was developed by the Washington-based Corporation for Enterprise Development, which plans similar efforts in five other states.

Finally, New York has begun to link the training and hiring of welfare recipients to its economic development efforts. Like most other states, New York offers loans and other aid to dozens of corporations each year. Through its Job Creation Equity Program, it is asking for something in return. The economic development agencies routinely send information on every company they help to Dowling's office, which passes it on to the appropriate local welfare office. That office is then expected to contact the company and convince them (there is no requirement) to hire welfare recipients who have been through training programs.

Conceptually, this is an extremely important breakthrough. It inte-

grates the two state economic agendas, bringing the poor into the development process. Should the Cuomo administration succeed in its efforts to
institutionalize the practice, it will have taken a very important step in the
evolution of state development policy.

Economic Development

While Eimicke and Dowling press ahead with the second agenda, the
Cuomo administration has made less progress on the first. Despite a few
intelligent initiatives, economic development was not the governor's
strong suit during his first term. His administration put out enormous
sums of money, particularly in the form of grants and loans for large
projects, such as convention centers and new plants. But it failed to develop a well-thought-out strategy. Its focus was almost entirely on retailing, too much of which still involved smokestack chasing.

The problem was essentially one of personnel. Cuomo appointed people he knew and trusted to run his economic development programs,
rather than those with expertise in the area. To run the Urban Development Corporation (UDC), which evolved into his principal economic development agency, he appointed his former campaign finance chairman,
William Stern, whose two-year stint was far from successful. In 1984,
Cuomo decided that he needed an economic development "czar" to coordinate all the agencies involved, but his first choice was forced to resign
after a few months because he had falsified his résumé. Well into his third
year in office, Cuomo finally turned to Vincent Tese, his new UDC chairman. Cuomo's goal in appointing an economic czar had been to rationalize
and coordinate the state's chaotic economic development system, under
which some 20 different agencies play a role. But because Tese also ran
UDC, the move only made matters worse.

As Cuomo's second term began, the administration finally began to
make some headway. Tese pushed through a partial reorganization, which
will include the creation of regional economic development offices, and
finally hired a policy chief with expertise in economic development. He
also lobbied an "Industrial Effectiveness Program" through the legislature.
Somewhat like the Michigan Modernization Service, at least in its goals,
the program will provide technical assistance to manufacturing firms, financing to help them restructure and install new production technologies,
and grants to help them retrain their workers.

Cuomo's Industrial Cooperation Council (ICC)—a committee of labor,
business, and academic representatives—also came up with a number of
promising programs. One is a Center for Employee Ownership and Participation, which helps workers perform prefeasibility studies of potential
buy-outs, provides technical assistance, and helps secure financing for

worker buy outs from the state's Job Development Authority. The most comprehensive state program to support employee ownership in the country, the center is also trying to catalyze the formation of Local Ownership Development Corporations, which would do similar work in their own regions.

The ICC also worked out a plant closing compact similar to that in Massachusetts. Finally, it launched a Special Project on Trade and Competitiveness, which is conducting in-depth studies of five New York industries: financial services, telecommunications, food processing, steel, and the garment and textile industry. It will then create demonstration projects, which will bring labor and management from dozens of firms together to revitalize their sector of the industry—by improving marketing techniques, production technologies, work force skills, and other sector-wide weaknesses.

Perhaps the most innovative economic development effort in New York during the 1980s was created, not by the Cuomo administration, but by the Port Authority of New York and New Jersey, an agency largely independent of both state governments. Known as XPORT, it was the nation's first publicly sponsored export trading company. Unlike Japan, the United States does not have a tradition of large export trading companies, which handle exports for other businesses. There are small export companies here and there, but most businesses go it alone. For small and medium-sized businesses with little or no export experience, that can be difficult. XPORT was set up to help those firms get over the initial hurdles and develop enough experience to go out on their own. This focus on small, new-to-market exporters allows the Port Authority to expand the universe of exports from New York and New Jersey without taking existing business away from private export trading companies.

By 1986, XPORT was working with 70 companies. It had a staff of more than 20—some overseas, some in New York. After identifying a company that might benefit from their services and suggesting product modifications the company needed to make for export markets, the XPORT industry representative would sign a three-year contract with the company. For a small fee, normally about 10 percent of sales, XPORT would handle all aspects of the export business: it would make sales or find distributors for products overseas, take care of the substantial documentation and paper work necessary, provide the export license, and secure insurance. In addition, XPORT's New York clients had access to below-market-rate loans from the state Job Development Authority to finance exports.

Because individual companies only paid fees to XPORT if they made sales, there was little risk involved. Not all succeeded in breaking into new markets, but in a brief survey of XPORT clients I found almost unanimous praise for the professionalism and dedication of the XPORT staff.

As with many businesses, it will be a few years before we know whether XPORT can turn a profit. In 1986, its third year of operation, it made $12 million in sales, but earned only $600,000 in fees, against $1.6 million in total expenses. Projected fees were up to roughly $800,000 in 1987, but the XPORT director, Herb Ouida, is not sure the program will ever turn a profit. He argues that it is worth an $800,000-a-year subsidy, because it increases the volume of traffic through the ports, it results in more jobs and higher tax revenues, and it gives the Port Authority a way to monitor the fortunes of small and medium-sized manufacturers in the region. Other states appear to agree; at least four have passed legislation to emulate the program.[53]

The Cuomo Record

Cuomo's economic development record was in many ways symptomatic of the weaknesses he showed during his first term. His staff was "more notable for its loyalty than its brilliance," in *Newsweek*'s words.[54] And Cuomo was more notable for his communication skills than his administrative skills. Hence in some areas his administration was long on rhetoric but short on follow-through.

In his first months in office, Cuomo was widely criticized by legislators for appointing mediocre people. The problem stemmed from Cuomo's personal style, which was so shaped by the realities of urban, ethnic New York. Mario Cuomo is a man who relies only on those he trusts. With his national reputation, he could easily have lured the best and brightest in the nation to New York. Instead, he hired mainly from New York, mainly people he knew or who came recommended by those he knew. Cuomo also expected tremendous loyalty from his inner circle, and gave that loyalty in return. When his appointees performed poorly—even when he had clearly lost confidence in them—he refused to fire them.

When a brilliant orator has a not-so-brilliant staff, a gap between rhetoric and reality is almost inevitable. The issue of youth employment offers a good example. "We have the capacity to guarantee every high school graduate a job," Cuomo told the journal *New Perspectives* in 1985. "That's going to be our objective in next year's State of the State. I won't be able to do it my first year, but that will be our objective. We'll work with the private sector. Now, if you can make the young people in our high schools in the Bronx and Queens believe that they are going to have a good shot at a job, they'll stay in school. The dropout rate will come down 50 percent. I guarantee it. If you can get them connected, during their second year in high school, say, to a high-tech firm where they can learn some computer skills, by the time they graduate they'll be a junior computer operator. They'll stay. We can do it."[55] A year and a half later, Cuomo's School-to-

Employment Program was still riddled with administrative problems, funded at only $5 million dollars a year, and serving fewer than two thousand teenagers in the state. Most of its participants were working at fast-food outlets like McDonald's and Burger King, not at high-tech firms.[56]

During his second term, Cuomo has upgraded his cabinet, recruiting several highly regarded people from other states. In areas such as economic development, he has begun to make great progress. This is not unusual; when it comes to new programs, most governors do not make a real mark until their second term. And to be fair, precisely because Cuomo expresses his goals with such eloquence, he is held by many critics to very high standards. "I think Mario Cuomo's problem comes when you hold him up to his own standards," Robert Hayes of the Coalition for the Homeless told me, at the end of Cuomo's first term. "But I think that's fair. I love his political leadership; I admire it tremendously. He has to an extent raised the level of discussion on poverty and homelessness. In my heart of hearts, I don't see much better coming down the state or national pike. But he does need better managers. In this case, I think that's the difference between a good governor and a great governor."

Cuomo the Politician

These weaknesses are counterbalanced, of course, by Cuomo's awesome skills as a communicator—his ability to evoke symbols, to crystallize issues in terms people understand, to speak to people's emotions. In these areas, which are critical components of leadership in a media age, Cuomo has few rivals.

Like Reagan, Cuomo is so effective a speaker in part because voters find him appealing as a man. He has the magnetism, the larger-than-life persona we expect from a leader. And again like Reagan, Cuomo understands the importance of using his personality and his oratorical skills to evoke certain fundamental values, certain beliefs about government and society, that resonate among voters. "I believe in symbolism," he told Ken Auletta, author of a long profile in *The New Yorker*. Change "doesn't come in the form of great new ideas, it comes in the form of great new people—Jesus, Hamilton, Gandhi, Lincoln, Martin Luther King." Cuomo believes that great leaders "move the public more by their character, their example, their words than by the laws they pass," Auletta observed.[57]

How does Cuomo move the public? What are his themes? Though he campaigned in 1982 under the traditional liberal theme of "jobs and justice," that phrase soon faded from his repertoire. In its place he turned to the theme of society as family—with all that implies about cooperation, about helping one another, about taking care of those who cannot take care of themselves. He also talked often about the necessity of government "doing more with less," of blending "compassion and common sense," of "helping our people help themselves" without "stifling" them. "We should have all the government we need," he said over and over, "but only the government we need." In his second-term inaugural address Cuomo labeled this "the New York idea." "We have proved—together— that the New York idea works," he declared. "That government can have both a heart and a head, that it can have both common sense and compassion."[58]

In speech after speech, Cuomo has also evoked the traditional values of his parents: hard work, education, frugality, honesty, loyalty. Though he opposes the death penalty, supports women's and gay rights, and supports women's rights to an abortion under the constitution (despite his personal opposition to abortion, he says), Cuomo is no new-age liberal. Because his traditional values are so obviously genuine, Cuomo projects the image of an old-school Democrat on social issues.

What kind of liberal does this make Mario Cuomo? Is he a "big spending" liberal, like the presidential candidate he embraced in 1984, Walter Mondale? Or is he a fiscal conservative, like the man he rallied to as state campaign chair against the Kennedy challenge in 1980, Jimmy Carter? Is he a New Deal Democrat, or a new-paradigm Democrat?

The answers are not simple. Cuomo scoffs at the Great Society and at George McGovern, but equally at those who talk incessantly about "new ideas." He concedes the importance of new programs and new approaches, but stresses the value of the party's old principles. He accepts the fiscal limits of the era, but he is no fiscal conservative. He is probusiness, but also prolabor. "What you have here," says Business Council chief Raymond Schuler, "is a governor who has an image, because of the speeches he makes for the Democratic party, of being a New Deal liberal, but who is also advancing a program that is embracing some of the key issues that we see as important in the state."

At bottom, three qualities define Mario Cuomo. First, he has spent most of his life in New York City's outer boroughs, which are in many ways throwbacks to the cities of 50 years ago—the cities that provided a base for New Deal liberalism. Brooklyn and Queens are gritty, ethnic, and largely working class, and they have provided Cuomo with a set of experiences far different from those of most politicians of his generation. These experiences have left him fiercely committed to improving the lot of the poor and the working man and woman. "No matter how genially you put it, no matter how elegantly you put it," he insists, "I do not agree with this notion that 'Hey look, there's just a limit on how much you can help people, and if they don't make it they don't make it.' I reject that."

Second, Cuomo is a devout Roman Catholic who spent 26 years affiliated with St. John's University. His Catholicism shapes his response to every issue. Whereas other Democratic governors turn to economists such as Robert Reich and Lester Thurow, the most significant influence on Cuomo's economic thinking has been the Bishops' Pastoral Letter on Economic Justice.

Third, Cuomo is a pragmatist, not an ideologue. When I asked him how he had evolved since entering politics, how his thinking had changed, he said simply, "It hasn't. I'm looking for an analogy. You're going through a jungle, and nobody has ever seen the jungle before. Osborne says, 'Well, I know how to make it through, I'll take a jeep.' And Schlesinger says, 'I'll take a canoe.' [Steve Schlesinger, Cuomo's foreign policy aide, arranged the interview and sat in.] You're counting on all dirt roads, and he's counting on all water. And Cuomo says, 'I don't know about jeeps, I don't know about canoes, I'm going to take it one step at a time. I'm going to feel my way. When I have to swim I'll build a raft. When I have to go on foot, I'll find a donkey. But I'm not going to commit myself to your jeep or your canoe, because you're liable to run into water, and then what the hell are you going to do? You're a liberal, he's a conservative, you're in a jeep, he's in a canoe, and I'm whacking my way through it, and I'm gonna get there for sure. And that's what's happened. I am pragmatic, with a strong, fundamental foundation that has two or three big ideas about government: government is community, government is family, government has to recognize that we're all connected, and government has an obligation to help those who cannot help themselves."

Cuomo's label for his politics, "pragmatic progressivism," is quite accurate. He is clearly to the left of most Democratic governors, but he is not a traditional liberal. In part because of his commitment to the poor and the working class, in part because he has been blessed with rapid economic growth during his term, he has focused more on distributional issues and less on growth issues than his colleagues. But in doing so, he has forged new approaches consistent with the realities of the 1980s.

On the other hand, Cuomo is less a new-paradigm figure than the other governors portrayed in this book. He accommodates the new reality, but he comes out of a different world—urban, ethnic, working-class New York. He is a bridge figure between New Deal liberalism, which was built on that world, and the emerging paradigm. In this sense he is reminiscent of Al Smith, who was a bridge figure between Tammany Hall and the Progressive movement.

Because he bridges the old and the new, Cuomo has kept his party in touch with its traditional constituencies, at least in New York. Many of the new-paradigm Democrats have had trouble attracting blue-collar workers and minorities, or kindling any flames of passion within a restless electorate. Mario Cuomo has done both.

In this sense, Cuomo is much like Ronald Reagan. Reagan took a conservative message built around budget balancing and anticommunism—a message that in the hands of others could rarely generate the excitement or convince the majority needed to carry its bearers to power—and gave it a new dimension. "Ronald Reagan transcended right-wing Republicanism because he took those values and made them national," says Steve Schlesinger, "and he did it because he has such a marvelous presence and speaking ability. Mario Cuomo is always going to get the rap that he is a New Deal liberal, and he's going to have to prove to people that he's something more than that. And one of the ways he's going to be able to do that is his wonderful speaking ability, his ability to create images that grab people, that take his values and give them a national resonance."

Whether a liberal from New York City can have such resonance in the South and West is a matter of great speculation, of course—speculation reminiscent of that concerning an ex-actor from Hollywood. For now, however, the important thing is that Cuomo has shown his party how to reach out to its traditional constituencies, both in word and in deed. By embracing new methods to help the poor, the homeless, and those of moderate income, he has demonstrated how government can keep alive its commitments to the have-nots of American society within the economic and fiscal constraints of the postindustrial era.

PART II

THE LESSONS

THE FIRST AGENDA: CREATING ECONOMIC GROWTH

Economic development, to most people, means the creation of more jobs, more plants, and more buildings. We can see and feel jobs and plants and buildings; they are real to us in a way that concepts like innovation and investment can never be. When we discuss economic development, we carry these images with us. We instinctively assume that if government can simply marshal its forces and build things, it can create economic growth.

In reality, of course, any government can give the appearance of creating jobs, plants, and buildings, simply by spending taxpayers' money (which would otherwise have been spent on other things, creating other jobs, plants, and buildings). Many governments have done just that. They have recruited industrial plants with lavish subsidies. They have launched public-sector jobs programs. They have built infrastructure projects, as huge and as ambitious as the Tennessee Valley Authority. And growth has stubbornly refused to follow.

Economic growth is an elusive goal. It is not a thing but a process—capricious and unpredictable. It is a chain reaction in which one investment leads to another, one innovation triggers the next. This chain reaction requires certain ingredients, and government has a critical role to play in providing them: top-flight universities, quality education systems, funding for research, training, and other elements the private sector cannot provide on its own. Government obviously sets the rules by which the marketplace functions, and manages the macroeconomic fundamentals so important to a predictable investment climate. Recent state experience has demonstrated that government also has an important role to play—as a catalyst, broker, and partner with the private sector—in ensuring that the ingredients of growth come together in the right mix. But government cannot *control* the process of growth; it cannot be made to happen in a step-by-step manner.

The chain reaction ignites in unpredictable ways. A car dealer's son bruises his knee in a high school wrestling match. The kneepads he uses are clumsy and ineffective, and his father begins dreaming of a better kneepad. He contacts local professors with expertise in shock-absorbent polymers and biomechanical engineering. They get a government research grant to test various formulas and designs, and they come up with a superior kneepad. The father sets up a business. Soon he is making a line of shock-absorbent sports equipment: shoe inserts, shoes themselves, headgear inserts. He raises venture capital and branches into industrial products: shock-absorbent gloves, vibration dampeners for industrial machines. Before he knows it, he has 100 employees. This is the story of Bill Peoples, who with help from the Ben Franklin Partnership founded Polymer Dynamics, Inc., because he believed he could build a better kneepad.

Consider also the New England story. In 1944, the Servomechanisms Laboratory at MIT signed a defense contract to develop a flight simulator. The Navy wanted to train pilots without taking them off the ground. To accomplish this feat, it needed a machine that could make hundreds of instantaneous calculations—in essence, an electronic computer. After a year or so of work, Jay Forrester, the project director, realized the implications of what he was trying to do: if he could create this new machine, it would have far wider uses than training pilots.[1]

Whirlwind I, as Forrester and his team named their creation, became operational about 1950. For the next decade a stream of MIT professors and graduate students cut their teeth on the machine and its successors. The military, and soon the space program, created enormous demand for those who could build and program computers, and soon MIT's young veterans were leaving to form their own companies. The most famous was Ken Olsen, who founded the Digital Equipment Corporation.

Massachusetts banks were not interested in lending to start-up companies with no assets save their founders' knowledge and experience. But luckily for Olsen and the others, a Harvard Business School professor, Gen. Georges Doriot, and a future senator from Vermont, Ralph Flanders, had put together the nation's first venture capital firm. American Research and Development, as they called it, was designed to do what merchant banks had done before the depression, but could no longer do because of the Glass-Steagall Act: buy equity in businesses. Doriot and Flanders bankrolled Olsen and a series of others, working closely with them to help them survive the risky first years.

MIT continued to incubate new companies. Unlike most university administrators, those at MIT actively encouraged their faculty and graduate students to create their own businesses. The area's 64 other institutions of higher education were less encouraging and produced fewer entrepreneurs, but they did give the technology firms a large pool of educated workers on which to draw. With 2.6 percent of the nation's people (in the 1950s and 1960s), Massachusetts produced 11.6 percent of its Ph.D.'s in electrical engineering.⁷ The region's supply of skilled machinists and job shops, left over from the earlier industrial era, also helped.

With the cold war and the space race providing a healthy market, the young technology firms thrived. Soon they were producing spinoffs of their own; former employees of one electronics firm alone created 39 separate companies.[3]

As this process continued, venture capital firms multiplied and informal networks began to grow up—networks that made it easier for people with good ideas to find the capital and management assistance they needed to create new businesses. Consulting firms sprang up to provide technical and managerial expertise. Led by the Bank of Boston, the region's bankers evolved new patterns to deal with the growing technology sector; eventually, they learned to lend on entrepreneurial talent as well as collateral.[4] With an assist from state government, even the insurance industry came around.

Jane Jacobs's 1969 book, *The Economy of Cities*, still offers the best description of this process of economic growth. Jacobs defines development as "a process of continually improvising in a context that makes injecting improvisations into everyday life feasible."[5] In other words, economic development is the process of innovation, in a context that makes it possible to apply the innovations to the everyday creation of products and services. It is not enough to fund basic research and stimulate dramatic breakthroughs in the research lab. Innovation must take place throughout the economy: a new alloy here, an adapted software program there; a new method of financing small businesses here, a new labor-management structure there.

The microelectronic revolution and the global marketplace it helped create have rapidly intensified the pace of innovation—and increased the penalties for industries that fail to innovate. These penalties have always existed. Candle makers lost markets as light bulbs became common. Whaling died out after petroleum was discovered. And regional economies paid the price: New Bedford shrank when whaling died; Scranton/Wilkes-Barre has been contracting ever since its anthracite coal mines lost out to western Pennsylvania's bituminous coal. But the entire process was far more leisurely, and the dislocation less frequent, than it is today. Today we see regional industries cut virtually in half within five years: steel production in Pennsylvania, auto production in Michigan, copper production in Arizona.

Why the difference? During the industrial era, the pace of technological change was far more leisurely, and we had far less competition from abroad. Once Detroit established itself as the place to make autos, it faced little competition; hence it experienced 50 years of growth. The same was true of Pittsburgh and steel, until the 1960s. Even when American firms developed the computer in the 1950s and semiconductors in the 1960s, they faced little foreign competition.

Today all that has changed. Businesses that fail to innovate do not last long; regional economies in which innovation does not flourish quickly stagnate. Even service economies are vulnerable, for the microelectronic revolution makes it possible to move key punch operations to the Caribbean and computer programming to India.[6]

Robert Reich has done the best job of drawing out the implications of this change, in *The Next American Frontier* and *Tales of a New America*. The central lesson, he argues, is that we can no longer rely on the big breakthrough to guarantee our growth: the development of the open-hearth furnace to make steel, the assembly line to make automobiles, the transistor and semiconductor to make computers. "In a world where routine production is footloose and billions of potential workers are ready to underbid American labor," Reich writes, "competitive advantage lies not in one time breakthroughs but in continual improvements. Stable technologies get away. Keeping a technology requires elaborating upon it continuously, developing variations and small improvements in it that better meet particular needs. . . . Instead of a handful of lone entrepreneurs producing a few industry-making Big Ideas, innovation must be more continuous and collective."[7] Reich labels this process "collective entrepreneurialism."

False Choices

If continual innovation is the key to our economic growth, where does that innovation most often occur? No question has engendered more confusion in our thinking about economic development. Do small firms hold the key, or large ones? New firms or old? Manufacturing or services? Sunrise industries or sunset industries?

Although these questions are still hotly debated, state experience suggests that they are false dichotomies. Let us start with the questions of size and age. David Birch's 1979 study, "The Job Generation Process," set economic developers on a stampede to help small and young businesses. As Birch's research revealed, such firms now play a critical role in our economy. They provide a central mechanism through which our economy innovates—which partially explains why they have proliferated and larger firms have stagnated. (The other reasons have to do with the tendency of large firms to move many of their jobs overseas, and the decentralization made possible in some industries by microelectronic technologies.)

Ten years before Birch drew attention to the proliferation of small and new firms, Jane Jacobs provided the conceptual framework necessary to understand it. Indeed, Birch's study often reads like an effort to prove

Jacobs's arguments through empirical research. One might assume, Jacobs wrote, that large corporations would be better at creating new products and services than small organizations." In reality, the opposite is true. Were a large firm to continue innovating in many directions at once, each expanding division "would be growing at its own rate, bearing no relation to any other department's scale of production or needs. Space allocations in the organization, personnel distribution, budgeting, sales arrangements—all would become a wild, incoherent scramble. The organization would be a disorganization, a fantastic bundle of contradictions and cross purposes, related to one another only by the anachronistic bonds of a vanished community of purpose."

Large corporations deal with this problem, Jacobs argued, by spinning off new firms. "The breakaway . . . is a means of releasing captive divisions of labor to build up, for themselves, new, autonomous organizations. . . . In a small organization that is adding new work to its original work, the reproductive cells, so to speak, are almost the whole animal. . . . The period when an organization is most fertile at adding new work is while it is still small; its principal growth thereafter is apt to be growth in volume of the work already added."[8]

Birch's work is not the only empirical evidence to support Jacobs's argument. A study of innovations introduced on the American market between 1953 and 1979 showed that a research dollar invested in a small business was 24 times more likely to produce commercial innovation than a research dollar invested in a large business.[9]

All of this has led many people to conclude that small businesses are far more important to our economic health than large businesses. This is the false dichotomy. Most small firms would not exist without large firms. Reich explains: "My research suggests that the presence of a large technology company—an IBM or a Wang or a DEC—generates all kinds of demands for smaller high-tech companies that provide components or services or software. That may be the most important regional development for a state—the development of those large and medium-sized technology companies. That may tell a state to encourage and facilitate its large technology companies. It might even suggest giving some credits to a large technology company to seed small companies around it"—to encourage the spinoff process.

In addition, most small businesses are irrelevant to the process of innovation and growth. Only a fraction (Birch estimates between 10 and 15 percent) are potential growth companies.[10] The rest—the copy shops, the pizza parlors—will putter along for years with the same handful of employees. They provide services to larger businesses, or to the employees of larger businesses, and their growth is driven by those larger firms.

Finally, not all large corporations fail to innovate—particularly under the competitive pressures they face today. Even Jacobs noted the exceptions, such as IBM.[11]

Far more important than size is age; far more important than small firms are new firms. As Jacobs, Reich, and Birch all stress, the process by which new firms are spun out of large organizations (business or academic) is a critical component of innovation. New firms with growth potential are extremely important, and we should do everything possible to encourage their formation and survival. But large firms are intimately involved in that process, because they so often operate as seedbeds for spinoffs. Hence large firms cannot be ignored.

The real target should be innovation, in businesses of all sizes and ages—as even Birch argues. "I never said small business was the key," Birch explains. "From my point of view there is a very close tie between large and small business. You can't say that one is more important than the other—it's the system that is important. The system seems to be working better by fragmenting a little more, institutionally, but I hate to think what would happen if you dried up the large businesses.

"I found myself, in a very frustrating way in many cases, being touted as an advocate of small business. And in fact one of the things I pointed out was that most small businesses create no jobs, that only 10 percent of small businesses create 90 percent of the jobs and don't stay small for long. That wasn't very popular. Then when I pointed out that 80 percent of all new jobs in high technology were created by large businesses, not by small businesses, that was a surprise to the small-business constituency. One of the things that happens in a field like computers is that the small firms become big ones and just keep on going. But they're large companies that were very small a very short time ago. If you slice it by age rather than by size, you find it's all very young, unlike Exxon or Mobil."

A second common dichotomy is manufacturing versus services. The rapid expansion of service industries and the equally rapid decline of employment in manufacturing—from 24 percent of all U.S. employment in 1970 to 18 percent in 1985—has led some to conclude that services are the new backbone of the American economy.[12] Advocates of manufacturing respond that even though manufacturing *employment* has fallen, manufacturing *production* increased 65 percent between 1970 and 1985.[13] Meanwhile manufacturing as a percentage of our gross national product has remained relatively steady, at more than 20 percent.[14]

In reality, the "decline" of manufacturing and the "rise" of services are part and parcel of the same process: the microelectronic revolution. By applying the new microelectronic technologies to the assembly line, industry can produce far more with fewer workers. Using the same technologies, "service" industries such as communications, data processing, and computer programming can do things undreamed of thirty years ago.

Hence, while manufacturers produce ever more with ever fewer production workers, they rely on a growing array of new services to further heighten their productivity. (Federal Express is the perfect example: it offers a service that could not have existed before the computer age, and it primarily serves other businesses.)

Additional armies of workers provide services to those who buy high-tech manufacturing products—computers, Xerox machines, CAT scanners, and on down a long list. As manufacturers produce more sophisti cated products with higher components of "thoughtware," providing services to customers becomes an integral part of selling manufactured goods.[15]

Finally, economic development enthusiasts have vigorously debated the merits of "sunrise" industries versus "sunset" industries, high-technology versus basic industry. Skeptics of high technology, for instance, point out that high-tech industries provide only 6.4 percent of American jobs.[16] What these skeptics fail to appreciate is the extreme importance of those 6.4 percent, and how many other jobs they support. The same industries account for 43 percent of the total value of U.S. manufactured exports.[17] Between 1974 and 1984, according to one study, "advanced technology companies grew nine times faster in employment, three times faster in output and two times faster in productivity than the rest of the nation's manufacturing sector."[18]

But like manufacturing and services, high-tech and basic industries are not separate categories we can choose between. In competition with low-wage labor in other nations, our basic industries can remain competitive only if they move systematically up the quality ladder into sophisticated products that cannot be produced in the Third World. The primary way to do that is by integrating new technologies: replacing steel with carbon fibers, mechanical devices with computer chips, manual labor with robots. Reich lists three categories of manufacturing that cannot be shipped to Third World countries and performed by low-wage labor: technologies that are rapidly changing, and thus require a high degree of innovation; products that must be custom-made for particular customers ("flexible manufacturing"); and products that require precision engineering, complex testing, and sophisticated maintenance.[19] The first category *is* high technology; the second and third require the use of advanced technologies.

Other false choices are more obvious. For years we have debated the appropriate level of taxation: conservatives have argued that low taxes encourage investment and make our businesses more competitive; liberals retort that California, Massachusetts, and New York were all high-tax states when their economies began to boom in the 1970s, while Arkansas, South Dakota, and Mississippi were low-tax states. The truth is that tax levels are far less important than most of us assume. Extremely high tax rates obviously scare some investors away, and extremely low taxes just as obviously inhibit government's ability to pay for quality schools, highways, and the like. But between these extremes, the important questions do not concern the level of taxation. They concern the *kind* of taxes a government levies: Do they encourage investment or consumption? Speculation or productive investment? They concern the stability of tax rates over time: Can businesses plan their investments with some assurance that their taxes will not rise dramatically? And they concern the investments government chooses to make with its tax revenues.

Consider California's history. During World War II, its defense boom created huge budget surpluses. Despite pressure to cut taxes, Republican Governor Earl Warren insisted after the war that the surplus be put in a reserve for investment in infrastructure projects. He and Democratic Governor Pat Brown invested heavily in water systems, highways, and education. Perhaps their most important investment, given the realities of the postindustrial economy, was in creating the nation's finest public university system. Their strategy paid off handsomely.[20]

Or consider Minnesota, a state whose public investments in education, infrastructure, and social welfare recall those of the Scandinavian countries, from which so many Minnesotans immigrated. Between 1969 and 1979, Minnesota had the highest government-controlled costs in the Great Lakes region, yet its manufacturing job base grew by 15 percent. Indiana, with the lowest government-controlled costs in the region, lost 2.8 percent of its manufacturing jobs.[21]

"Research shows that land, labor, money, energy, transportation, and taxes cost more, not less, in thriving cities," Birch explains. "It's a whole new ball game. A city no longer needs a natural harbor, a surplus of labor, and lots of sunshine in order to prosper—it needs quality universities, quality workers, quality airports and telephone systems, and, yes, even quality government."[22]

A similar dichotomy confuses our thinking about wage rates and economic growth. Do low wages help American corporations compete? Yes, in the short run. But in the long run, if a product can be manufactured or a service performed in the Third World, a low-wage competitor will eventually emerge. What do we do at that point? Cut our wages to $1 an hour? That might keep us competitive, but it would be the opposite of economic development.

The solution is not *high* wages; it is a more educated, productive, flexible, and innovative work force, from management down to the lowest rung on the ladder. Such work forces are obviously not low-wage work forces, but again, the critical question is not the level of wages but the capacities of our workers.

How can we recruit industry unless we offer low wages? We cannot—

unless we recruit the type of industry that needs skilled, educated workers, top research universities, and an attractive quality of life. And in reality, such firms rarely migrate. They grow up in an area with a quality intellectual infrastructure, and when they become large enough to set up manufacturing plants with hundreds of workers, they consider locating them in low-wage areas. (Increasingly, they set up automated factories, in which case they often choose to keep them near corporate headquarters, where the brain power is.)

Recruiting those branch plants that remain labor-intensive makes some sense, if the goal is to redistribute jobs. Smokestack chasing can be defended on redistributive grounds: it is wise to shift jobs from booming Stamford, Connecticut, to the New Haven ghetto, or from Route 128 to Mississippi. But this is not economic development. Branch plants do not bring the process of innovation and growth with them. They do not spin off new products or companies; they simply continue to manufacture what corporate headquarters tells them to manufacture.

If enough plants are recruited, they may create temporary growth and raise a region's per capita income. But particularly in today's economy, that is not the same as creating a lasting process of economic growth. Oakland, California, was built on branch plants, and its economy has remained stagnant ever since.[23] The South used smokestack chasing to increase its per capita income to 86 percent of the national average, but in 1974 the progress halted.[24] As one part of a comprehensive economic development strategy, which focuses all the elements on growth, recruitment at times makes sense. But as anything more, it is a mirage.

The two dichotomies that are of value in economic policy are generally the least discussed: the dichotomy between a region's economic base and its local market economy, and the dichotomy between urban and rural development. As explained in chapter 5, a region's economic base (also known as its "traded sector") is made up of firms that export products or services out of the region, or produce goods or services that might otherwise come in from elsewhere. The "local market economy" consists of retail firms, restaurants, real estate developers, even small construction firms—none of which can be replaced by imports. The economic base drives regional growth; the local market economy simply feeds off that growth.

When they target manufacturing, state economic development programs automatically limit themselves to the economic base. But with their increased emphasis on small firms, they have often strayed into the local market economy. Tax breaks, incubators, and business assistance centers are often indiscriminate; they go to the 85 to 90 percent of small firms that are in the local market economy, as well as the 10 to 15 percent in the economic base. If the goal is helping women or minority entrepreneurs, or simply encouraging entrepreneurship in a stagnant region, these efforts make sense. But otherwise, the time to help a local market firm is when it begins to develop new products or services that move it into the economic base.

The dichotomy between urban and rural development is rarely discussed, perhaps because it is risky to do so, if one is a politician. The hard truth is that economic development happens primarily in urban areas, because the elements of innovation—the risk capital, the entrepreneurs, the skilled labor, the intellectual infrastructure, and the technology transfer networks—normally come together only in urban areas. As Jane Jacobs has persuasively argued, our economy is made up of a series of regional economies, which radiate out from cities. Rural regions supply those economies with food, raw materials, and, to a degree, standardized products from transplanted manufacturing plants. Rural areas rarely produce their own innovations. They develop by importing innovations from the cities: mechanized farm equipment, new strains of corn, new fertilizers, and of course manufacturing facilities. Thus, rural areas and their small towns are dependent regions. Their fates are linked to—and their economies are shaped by—the metropolitan regions they supply around the globe.[25]

This reality means that rural development is very different from—and much more difficult than—general economic development. In the short run, government can help rural areas by improving the markets for the goods they produce, such as food, oil, and coal. But in the long run, no government can control international markets. Government can also build bridges between rural areas and urban economies: highways, marketing strategies, tourism, and recruitment efforts. But paradoxically, the best thing government can do for most rural areas is to stimulate urban economic development within them. In some areas, small cities can cultivate enough of the elements of innovation to stimulate self-generated growth, particularly if they have universities or research centers. Even without universities, some small cities can become growth centers by innovating in traditional industries. A city with a base in the furniture industry, for instance, can use new production technologies to become a center of high-quality, custom-made furniture.

The Methodology of Economic Development

When we seek to separate what works in economic development from what fails, we tend to ask about specific programs: do incubators work, or are research parks better? Are small-business loans more effective than venture capital funds? But the most important lessons that emerge from the states we have considered concern *how* government should proceed, not *what* it should do. The specific programs chosen are far less important than the way in which each program is carried out: how it fits into an overall strategy, what principles underlie that strategy, and how the different pieces fit together. Most enterprise zones are ineffective, for instance, but if they are designed as part of intelligent local development systems, they can work. Some incubators work better than others, because they are part of comprehensive development systems that also provide capital, business assistance, and other aid.

No formal methodology of economic development exists; practitioners of the grow-your-own school have had to learn by doing.[26] But by looking carefully at the early results of state efforts, and by applying a little common sense, one can identify a series of principles that seem to spell the difference between success and failure for any government-sponsored development program.

Governments are most successful when they take time to analyze the economy before acting. When one compares the experience of Michigan and Pennsylvania with that of Massachusetts and New York, this principle leaps forth. By studying their economies—performing "strategic audits," as those in the development business like to say—Pennsylvania and Michigan focused in on their economic bases, identified their strengths and weaknesses, and developed initiatives that exploited those strengths and remedied those weaknesses. Massachusetts and New York skipped this step, and their development systems suffer for it.

By performing strategic audits, states can find their most productive niches within the new economy. Obviously, not all areas can become Silicon Valleys or Route 128s—or even Automation Alleys. But most regions have some strategic advantage they can exploit. Tulsa, Oklahoma, has become a center of hotel and airline reservation systems. Memphis, Tennessee, the home of Federal Express, has become a distribution center for the nation.

Wholesaling—changing the way the market works—has far more impact than retailing. In a $5-trillion economy, even the largest government capital funds and training programs are dwarfed by private capital markets and training expenditures. If government can use wholesaling strategies to change private-sector investment patterns, it will have a far greater impact than if it simply sets up public programs.

The most important way in which government can do this is by changing the rules of the marketplace, the complex web of laws and regulations that govern our markets and create incentives or disincentives for various investments. Almost as important is changing the climate of opinion. Governors like Clinton and Blanchard may accomplish more by creating a consensus about the necessity of improving public education or moving industry to the manufacturing frontier than by all of their specific policies and programs combined.

To flesh out its messages, government can encourage changes in private-sector behavior in many specific ways:

- It can *catalyze* the creation of new institutions or programs, as when Pennsylvania and Michigan initiated the creation of private seed funds and BIDCOs.
- It can *broker* private-sector actions by bringing different parties together, as Pennsylvania's Ben Franklin Partnership and Massachusetts' Bay State Skills Corporation do when they offer matching grants to bring business and academia together.
- It can *leverage* private-sector action with small public investments, as Michigan's Capital Access Program and Modernization Service do.
- It can *extract quid pro quos* from private corporations when it grants loans, tax cuts, or regulatory changes, as Massachusetts did when it traded a tax cut for creation of the Massachusetts Capital Resource Company.
- It can *create public-private partnerships.* When the NGA surveyed state economic development activities in 1985, it found that 26 states had created new public-private entities in the previous two years.[27]

When the private sector will not enter an area, government has no choice but to retail. But even where retailing is justified, government can use public-private partnerships to leverage private investment and teach private investors how to invest in an area. This is the strategy employed by the Community Development Finance Corporation and Government Land Bank in Massachusetts.

Economic and social problems are two sides of the same coin. Better social organization is a fundamental ingredient of innovation and growth. Yet our social programs have almost no link to our economic development systems. Training programs sometimes bridge the gap, helping specific firms while also aiding the hard-core unemployed. But this principle can be applied universally. Welfare checks can be used to subsidize firms that hire and train welfare recipients, as in New York and Massachusetts. Loans, grants, and tax breaks can be traded for commitments to hire and train targeted groups, as in New York. Industrial extension services can encourage manufacturers to adopt cooperative labor-management systems, as in Michigan.

Intelligent development strategies invest, rather than spend. Too many economic and social programs simply spend public money—to support people in poverty, to create public-sector jobs, to pay for housing. Too few *invest* in developing the capacities of people and communities—to learn new skills, to become self-sufficient, to develop housing. We have long understood this principle when it comes to physical infrastructure; we invest in highways and dams and water treatment systems so that we can sustain a growing economy. Increasingly, we understand the importance of investing in quality education. But we have rarely applied this principle to our training needs, our welfare programs, our housing programs. To use an ancient parallel, development is the process of teaching people to fish, not the process of feeding them.

Effective development efforts build the capacity of local institutions and actors. Economic development is a *local* phenomenon, generated by local actors: businesses, banks, universities, governments, labor unions. Often, the most important role government can play is to get these local actors interacting in new ways. This is the strategy Pennsylvania adopted with its Ben Franklin Partnership, its Regional Enterprise Development Program, and its other programs.

As Pennsylvania demonstrated, the best way to mobilize local leaders is often to bring them together to create a new program. The process of creation kicks off many sparks. It fosters new ideas. It creates new relationships—between workers and managers, between financiers and manufacturers, between academics and business people. It creates a climate in which people begin to see that change is possible, and that government is willing to support change. And it puts ownership of the program in local hands.

Development systems work best when they are comprehensive but decentralized. Development is local, yet most development programs operate statewide. Development is multidimensional, yet most state programs offer only one service. If a company needs a loan, it must visit one office. If it wants incubator space, it must visit another. If it needs training funds, it must deal with yet another. Typically, none of these departments knows what the others are doing, and all are located in the state capitol.

The notion of a comprehensive but decentralized system may seem like a contradiction in terms. But consider the Ben Franklin Partnership. Its four Advanced Technology Centers offer a comprehensive array of services, at the local level. They operate as the core of a local network, bringing together many of the elements necessary to nurture innovation: risk capital, incubators, entrepreneurial assistance, the intellectual infrastructure, even training programs. Because they are local, they have the capacity to make decisions quickly, the flexibility to respond to a wide variety of problems, and the credibility that can only be earned through daily contact with local people. Because they are comprehensive, each element reinforces the others, and the whole is greater than the sum of the parts.

Jane Jacobs describes economic development as a process of "improvisational drift." Governments, she says, should seek to nurture "an esthetics of drift," by "fostering creativity in whatever forms it happens to appear in a given city at a given time. It is impossible to know in advance what may turn up, except that—especially if it is to prove important—it is apt to be unexpected."[28] Comprehensive, decentralized organizations like Pennsylvania's offer the best means by which government can nurture such an aesthetics of drift.

Economic development programs need to be constructed on an appropriate scale. Too often, programs are so far below the scale needed to address a problem that they might as well not have been created. This is the case with many development programs aimed at poor communities. At other times, government uses a cannon where a shotgun would do—as in many traditional urban redevelopment projects.

The best economic development systems operate with long-term perspectives. Politics tends to drive the development process in the wrong direction. Most politicians win elections by focusing on short-term results: recruiting plants, cutting ribbons, and handing out checks. They do not win elections by conducting studies, changing the way bankers think, or building local capacity. The seeds that will bear fruit in a year or two, of course, are rarely the important ones. It takes far longer to change the lending behavior of banks than to create a public capital fund. It takes far longer to develop the capacities of local institutions than to build a road or recruit a plant.

To remain effective, development programs need market feedback mechanisms. The marketplace never stands still. Too often, government programs do. During the 1960s, programs to construct low-income housing kept building even as suburban flight created an oversupply of urban housing and triggered massive abandonment of underused buildings. Today, vocational education systems continue training people for jobs that no longer exist, on equipment that is no longer used by industry.

Change occurs so rapidly in today's market that any government institution designed to help nurture economic growth must be extremely responsive to the market. The solution is to build in feedback mechanisms that force programs to change when the market for their services changes. Both Arkansas and Florida did this, for instance, when they began closing down vocational education programs that placed fewer than a set percentage of their graduates in jobs.

Another method to heighten feedback is simply to let the private sector run programs. Two of the quasi-public agencies in Massachusetts are run almost exclusively by the private sector; both have shown great sensitivity to the market, because they are run by people who have had to develop that sensitivity throughout their careers. The Technology Development Corporation was created to address a shortage of venture capital; when that shortage disappeared, its board targeted start-ups whose market niches or time horizons made them unattractive to private venture capitalists. The Capital Resource Company was created to address a shortage of long-term debt for growing technology firms. When banks and insurance companies began to fill that gap, the Capital Resource Company shifted half of its investments into mature industries.

Market feedback is not a simple matter. In most government programs, pure market feedback is not enough, because the programs have goals the market does not measure. For instance, training programs that use feedback on placement rates and wage rates create incentives to avoid those who need training the most, because they produce low placement rates. In this situation, feedback must also be generated on the work experience and social background of those trained. Hence feedback mechanisms must reflect *all* the goals of a program—not just those measured by marketplace results.

These methodological principles provide guidelines by which government can most effectively work with the private sector to stimulate growth. Given these principles, what kind of programs make sense, and what kind do not? It is impossible to quantify the results of specific programs; too many variables are at work to link cause and effect with scientific rigor. But by looking closely at enough programs and listening to those who have learned from experience, one can begin to sort the wheat from the chaff.

Although one could organize state programs into any number of categories, I will group them according to the elements of innovation outlined in the introduction to this book: the intellectual infrastructure, industrial modernization, human capital, the entrepreneurial climate, risk capital, marketing, the culture of industry, and social organization. (I will omit the quality of life, simply because government efforts in this area need little explanation.)

The Intellectual Infrastructure

Just as physical infrastructure is more than roads and bridges, intellectual infrastructure is more than universities. It is not simply the advancement of science that holds the key to economic growth; the rate at which these advances are spread throughout the economy is also critical. A vibrant intellectual infrastructure is a network of interaction, in which research advances lead not only to academic papers but also to new knowledge-intensive companies, products, and processes.

The states have attempted to improve their intellectual infrastructures in two principal ways: they have invested in upgrading their universities,

and they have created programs to stimulate the development and commercialization of new technologies, in the hopes of creating high-tech
growth clusters like those around Boston and in the Silicon Valley.

Most of the technology development programs seek to build bridges
between universities and local firms, so as to encourage the rapid commercialization of research. This is precisely the right focus, for the commercialization of research is a critical weak link in our economy. The United States
excels at basic research, the kind that produces major breakthroughs and
Nobel Prizes. Japan excels at taking those breakthroughs and turning them
into manufactured products. Stories about products invented in the United
States but commercialized only by the Japanese—video cassette recorders,
compact laser disks, video cameras for consumer use—have become common. But the problem goes deeper. Applied research—the kind state governments often fund—focuses more often on small improvements in existing technologies than on new products. It is precisely this process of
continual refinement that keeps an industry competitive. The more time
our academic and industrial scientists spend developing these incremental
improvements, the greater will be our capacity to hold onto our manufacturing base.

The states have developed four basic models in this category: research
parks, joint business-academic research consortia, matching research
grants, and what I will call the comprehensive model, which is best exem-
plified by the Ben Franklin Partnership. One can evaluate these programs,
like all others, by testing them against the methodological principles laid
out above.

Most research parks are ineffective, for example, because they are not
comprehensive and they do not change private-sector behavior. On their
own, they create none of the elements necessary for the growth of a technology cluster: the strong research universities, the risk capital, the incubation institutions, the role models, the management advice, and the skilled
work force. Unless integrated in a more comprehensive system—one that
encourages interaction to transfer technologies from academia to business—they are little more than attractive plots of land for corporate research facilities. As a result, most fail. In 1980, when the Battelle Columbus
Laboratories analyzed the results of the first 27 university research parks, it
found 6 "clear winners," 16 "losers," and 5 with mixed records.[29] Reginald
Owens of the Association of University Related Research Parks predicts
that this ratio will hold for the 150 or so other parks created since 1980.[30]

Even the nation's most celebrated park—North Carolina's Research
Triangle Park—has generated virtually no spinoffs since its inception 30
years ago.[31] It has been enormously successful at attracting the research
facilities of major corporations, and it has begun to attract advanced manufacturing operations. But despite the high density of brain power created

by the research park and the area's three universities, no entrepreneurial explosion has occurred, because too many other elements are missing. In contrast, an unattractive, square-mile industrial corridor near MIT—an area that offered none of the grooming of the typical research park—has created more new jobs in the 1980s than each of 13 states, according to David Birch.[32]

Almost as popular as research parks are research consortia, often called "centers of excellence." Typically, these are applied research institutes at major universities, focused on a particular technology and jointly funded by business, government, and the university. Here the key questions are again wholesaling and comprehensiveness. Few research consortia are part of broader economic development systems that work together to maximize their impact. And most are dominated by research professors rather than by participating businesses. As a result, the state money gets soaked up by new buildings, new laboratories, and a stream of academic papers. Driven by academic researchers, the consortia tend to ignore the process of commercializing their work.[33] Businesses too often end up funding them more as charities than as investments, and keeping their top research projects in house.

Applied research institutes can be of real value, if they are structured correctly. For one thing, they can help move universities in the directions required by the new economy: toward cross-disciplinary work that has its roots in the real world of economic need. (Even fairly young academic disciplines grew up during the industrial era. As technological advance reshuffles the deck—bringing computer programming together with industrial engineering in the development of automated manufacturing equipment, for instance—academia has been slow to respond.)

In addition, joint research consortia that are created to tackle a specific set of problems crucial to an industry can be of enormous value. In this case, industry defines the problems and academia follows its lead. But such consortia are rare at the state level. Most industry-driven consortia involve major firms in at least several states; hence states do not initiate them, because they cannot capture enough of the resulting growth. As I will argue later, the federal government is the logical partner in such cases.

At the state level, technology programs that provide matching grants on a project-by-project basis, such as California's MICRO, Pennsylvania's Ben Franklin Partnership, Indiana's Corporation for Science and Technology, Ohio's Thomas Edison Program, and New Jersey's Innovation Partnership, do a better job of wholesaling. They provide a better guarantee that the research will be of commercial value, because a participating business is paying for a particular research project aimed at solving a specific problem. They keep academics out of the driver's seat, because academic researchers can get grants only for projects specifically funded by businesses. Unlike most research consortia, they also encourage small companies to participate. Small firms generally ignore research consortia, because they do not have the resources to finance general research. But when funding is focused on specific, limited projects, they can reap tremendous benefits.

The one model that meets all the criteria is the Ben Franklin Partnership. Each of its Advanced Technology Centers is built on knowledge of the local economy. The entire focus of the program is changing private-sector behavior, particularly the interaction between business and academia. The program attacks social as well as economic bottlenecks by funding education and training in technology fields. It invests, rather than spends. It builds local capacity. It is comprehensive but decentralized. It is significant enough in scale to have an impact. Its focus is on long-term change. And its funding process is driven by market feedback.

The Japanese, not surprisingly, have launched a major national program that bears an eerie similarity to the Ben Franklin Partnership—no doubt because both seek to emulate the process of innovation seen in the Silicon Valley and around Boston. Called the Technopolis Concept, it is an effort to create 20 new technology cities.[34] MITI laid down criteria for Technopolis cities and forced local business-government partnerships to compete for designation, based on the quality of their plans. Each region had to prepare its own study of the regional economy—its strategic audit—and build a plan based on what it found.

Although the quality of the plans is uneven, most call for new investments in local universities and research laboratories, joint R&D institutes, incubator-type institutions, industrial parks, research parks, an array of venture capital and loan funds, venture capital associations and forums, research grant programs, technical assistance—virtually the entire panoply of institutions developed in recent years by our state governments. They even plan "techno-centers" and "technopolis foundations," which appear quite similar in concept to the Ben Franklin Advanced Technology Centers and their boards. The national government will provide tax incentives, loans, technical assistance, technology deployment institutions, retraining programs, and financing for research institutes and joint industry-university research projects.

Luckily for the United States, the program has had enormous problems overcoming the centralization of Japan's intellectual infrastructure in the Tokyo region. And because economic development planning has always been dominated by the national government, the regional governments have not shown the creativity evident in America's states. But the Japanese have the advantage of a national business-government partnership capable of putting enormous prestige, power, and resources behind an agreed-upon strategy. If they make a collective decision to do what is necessary, including the decentralization of Japan's intellectual infrastructure, the Technopolis program may yet work.

Industrial Modernization

The *deployment* of new manufacturing technologies is as important as the *development* of new technologies, yet state governments have paid far less attention to this task than to the more glamorous attempt to recreate the Silicon Valley and Route 128. As President Reagan's Commission on Industrial Competitiveness said, "Perhaps the most glaring deficiency in America's technological capability has been our failure to devote enough attention to manufacturing or 'process' technology. It does us little good to design state-of-the-art products if, within a short time, our foreign competitors can manufacture them more cheaply."[35] According to the commission, if one ranked nations according to how thoroughly their manufacturers had implemented new production technologies, the United States would not even be in the top ten.

American industry *is* automating. According to Dataquest Inc., U.S. corporations bought $18.1 billion worth of factory automation systems in the first half of the 1980s, a figure that appears to be doubling every five years.[36] But we are not automating as fast as our major competitors. To provide one example, industrial robots were first developed in the United States, but Japan, with half the number of people we have, now boasts three times as many robots.[37]

Small manufacturing businesses have a particularly difficult time automating. A study conducted by Jacques Koppel, former director of the Technology Management Center in Philadelphia, sheds light on the problem.[38] TMC works with small manufacturers to help them adopt new production technologies (at times on contract with the Ben Franklin Partnership). Over a period of 18 months, Koppel and his staff interviewed the managers of 90 small and medium-sized companies in the machine tool, electronic component, and medical device industries. They found that only 10 percent had any plans to introduce computers or other advanced technologies into their production processes.

"The problem is not one of availability," Koppel explained. "It's that the new manufacturing technologies intimidate and confuse most managers, who thus resist adopting them. . . . These technologies are computer-based, and managers and engineers schooled in another era often find them baffling. They have difficulty identifying the type of system that could most benefit their operations. And even if a firm can match a particular technology with a particular application, they often cannot distinguish between the dozens of available products—both hardware and software—that would best suit their needs."

"When companies make investments in new tools—whether modest or relatively large-scale—without an overall strategy for their use, the well-documented result is 'islands of automation.' Sophisticated technologies acquired at random sit scattered on shop floors, contributing only a fraction of their potential worth toward manufacturing a better product. In one company we visited, a $90,000-robot sat idle for most of two years because the equipment it was supposed to load was 25 years old and kept breaking down."

Those who have purchased personal computers know how difficult and time consuming it can be to sort through all the available information, choose the appropriate hardware and software, and teach themselves to use it—especially when time and finances are short. The process of installing computerized technology in a machine shop or manufacturing plant—then training workers to use it—multiplies those difficulties a thousand-fold.

State governments have developed a number of different strategies to help with this process. The best models are generally the industrial extension services, such as the Michigan Modernization Service. These services provide consultants who analyze firms' needs, help them decide what new technologies to install, and, in Michigan's case, help them retrain their work forces. (The Ben Franklin Partnership does much the same thing by providing matching grants to engineering laboratories such as Lehigh's CIM Lab and consulting firms such as TMC.)

Research institutes such as Michigan's Industrial Technology Institute have the expertise needed to work on complex projects at large firms, but they tend to be driven more by the academic interests of their staffs than by the practical needs of industry. They also charge too much for small and medium-sized firms.

Massachusetts' Economic Stabilization Trust adds another important dimension: financing to help mature manufacturing firms restructure. But its target—companies on the verge of collapse—is too narrow.

The recent initiatives by New York and Massachusetts to bring labor and management from entire industrial sectors together to formulate modernization strategies are simply too new to evaluate. They are important experiments, however. Many sectorwide modernization initiatives will have to be undertaken by the federal government, because many industries transcend state lines. But experience in Europe suggests that in particular regional clusters, state governments can play vital roles. The state experiments will also yield valuable lessons for federal action.

Human Capital

Perhaps the only thing more important than technology is the people who use it. One has only to look at Japan, which has few resources other than its human capital, to understand the point. The primary reason we no longer lead the world in manufacturing is our use of human capital. Our education systems have produced too many people who can barely read; our inadequate training and vocational education systems have prevented us from making the most productive use of our labor force; and the hierarchical, adversarial culture of many American corporations has robbed us of the flexibility and cooperation necessary to take full advantage of our technological prowess. A recent survey of 2,300 businesses and five hundred university and government officials, conducted by the Conference Board, ranked human resource policies as the most important element of competitiveness for U.S. firms.[39]

No ingredient of economic growth is more fundamental than education. Fortunately, no problem has been attacked with more resolve by state governments in the 1980s. Many states have even begun to attack the problem of adult illiteracy.

Whereas Americans have always taken education seriously, we have never given the same attention to job training. Yet according to economist Pat Choate, 85 percent of those who will be in our work force in the year 2001 were already working by the mid-1980s.[40] This is simple demographics: the baby boom was fully integrated into the work force by 1985, and the cohort behind it is relatively small. By the time we began to improve our schools, in other words, virtually all of those who would make up our work force for the next 15 years were out of school. We have been busy rescuing the *Titanic* when 85 percent of its passengers have already jumped ship.

Training is critical for several other reasons. The pace of technological innovation today means that jobs are rapidly becoming obsolete: machinists are being replaced by computer-controlled machining centers; welders are being replaced by robots; typesetters are being replaced by computers. Many workers will have to change careers at least once—and perhaps several times—during their work lives. According to Choate, every year two million Americans lose jobs that will never return. Many who have spent their lives doing manual labor will have to learn to work with new technologies—to repair computers, to service robots—if they are to keep jobs paying anything close to their former wages. Even those who remain in manufacturing will need new skills. "The plant of the past required individuals . . . to perform a task within very specific parameters, very routine," explains David Merchant, vice-president for personnel at Mazda's new facility in Michigan. "The plants of . . . today require people to do a lot more than that."[41]

The new economy has also created a widening gap between the poor and the job market. Although estimates vary widely, one of the most respected indicates that 20 percent of American adults are functionally illiterate: they cannot read a job notice or make change correctly. Half of all

Hispanic adults and 40 percent of black adults fit this description.[42] Most of these people are poor, and many are unemployed. (A 1980 study by the Department of Labor found that between 50 and 75 percent of the unemployed were functionally illiterate.)[43] In the cities, where many of them live, it was once possible to find manufacturing jobs that required little more than a strong back. Today the booming urban job markets are in insurance and banking and other "information" industries. Clerical workers are in demand—clerical workers who can read and write.

Building a training system that educates and trains the poor, retrains the dislocated, and helps the average person learn to work with new technologies throughout his or her career will not, by itself, create jobs. But training will make our work force more productive, and it will help us eliminate labor shortages in growth sectors by retraining those who have lost jobs in declining sectors. More important, it will lubricate our economy. If workers know that retraining and relocation assistance are available, they will be less likely to fear the introduction of new technologies and more likely to help their companies innovate.

Our current training system is hopelessly inadequate. It is a hodgepodge of tiny programs, most of them federally funded, few of them coordinated. The Job Training Partnership Act (JTPA), passed five years ago, offers promise, but it is seriously underfunded. (In New Haven, Connecticut, a typical city, it trains and places about six hundred people a year out of an estimated 14,000 to 15,000 who are unemployed or underemployed.)[44] With so little money, it tends to "cream" the market, serving primarily those who are the most job-ready. Most of our vocational education systems are outdated, and our community college systems are uneven. Our Employment Service, created in 1933 to match the unemployed with job openings, is barely functional in most states.

The task of reforming these programs and rationalizing the entire system will be immense. Unable to summon the requisite political will, most governors have opted for an end run around the problem. They have set up new, more intelligent programs: the Bay State Skills Corporation and its imitators; the Employment Training Panel, in California; the "customized" job-training programs now run by many states. But most of these programs serve only a few thousand people a year.

Many states have also tackled the problem of plant closings, by creating emergency teams and worker assistance centers. These efforts provide training to those laid off, help in finding new jobs, supplemental unemployment benefits, even financial assistance in moving to another area. Some of these programs are extremely effective. But again, most are limited in scope: they ignore dislocated workers who lose their jobs one by one, rather than in massive layoffs. (California's Employment Training Panel is an exception.) State governments have responded to highly visible emergencies, but few have created the comprehensive, ongoing retraining and reemployment systems we need.

Training should be the centerpiece of our entire social welfare system. As a nation we have taken bold steps before; witness the GI bill, which enabled an entire generation of veterans to attend college and gave us the highest percentage of college graduates in the world. In today's economy, we need equally bold vision. Our competitors understand this. In Japan, West Germany, France, and Sweden, one to two percent of all workers are in training at any given time. In the United States, the figure is one-tenth of one percent.[45]

The ideal training system would be constructed on the same principles as the rest of our economic development apparatus. It would be built on a careful study of the needs of each regional economy, not copied from abroad or applied uniformly across the country. It would be designed to wholesale whenever possible. Most training is done by the private sector, yet economists agree that businesses underinvest in training, for the same reason they underinvest in basic research: the odds are too high that their competitors will capture the benefits of their investment, in this case when their employees leave to work for another company. As with basic research, the public role is to create incentives for private firms to invest in education and training, and to fill the remaining gaps by investing public resources in training. Those gaps will primarily involve those who are the least attractive to private employers, because they are the toughest to train for existing jobs: the poor, the uneducated, and the dislocated.

The ideal training system would also be linked to a state's economic development system. It would invest in people, rather than simply spending money on them. (CETA spent a great deal of money, for instance—$13 billion in its highest year—but much of it went for make-work jobs rather than investments in people's capacities to read and write, to master a particular skill, or even to function in a private-sector job.) And it would be both comprehensive and decentralized. JTPA, which is run by state boards and local Private Industry Councils, is decentralized, but it is not comprehensive. We need to consolidate our dozens of individual training programs into one coherent system. This does not mean that all *programs* would be combined into one, but that they would be part of one *system*, with one entry point. People who wanted training could visit one local office, have an interview with one person who thoroughly assessed their needs, and be steered to the appropriate program.

Finally, the ideal training system would be of an appropriate scale—large enough to respond to the population's needs. It would take a long-term perspective, offering a training infrastructure that people could use throughout their work lives. And it would build in feedback mechanisms, to guarantee that its programs were training people for jobs that were still in demand. One study of dislocated steelworkers in Youngstown, Ohio, found that those who participated in publicly supported training programs actually had worse luck finding new jobs than those who did not, because the training programs were built on obsolete information about what was happening in the labor market.[46]

Individual state programs have demonstrated many techniques consistent with these principles. California's Employment Training Panel has shifted resources from the spending column to the investment column by, in effect, dedicating part of the state unemployment tax receipts to retraining for dislocated workers (and those likely to be dislocated). The Minnesota Employment and Economic Development (MEED) program has catalyzed private-sector training by offering wage subsidies to companies that hire the long-term unemployed and give them on-the-job training. MEED offers up to $5 an hour in subsidies, normally for six months; if the company does not keep the worker on afterward, it must repay 70 percent of the subsidy. If it lets the person go within 18 months, it must repay a lesser portion.[47]

In Illinois, the Prairie State 2000 Authority has experimented with a voucher system, in which employers receive tax credits for contributing to an insurance fund that workers can draw on for training vouchers.[48] Roger Vaughan has argued for this kind of approach, which gives the training dollar directly to individuals rather than to institutions, for years. He calls it a "GI bill for training."

As the results of these and other experiments become clear, those that work could be built in as pieces of a comprehensive training system. That system might be constructed by expanding the JTPA program and gradually bringing other training programs under its wing. State boards could administer the system, but local Private Industry Councils (PICs) would be free to choose the appropriate mix of strategies: training contracts, wage subsidies, matching grants, public service jobs. Ideally, each PIC would be tied into a regional economic development organization.

If such a system seems utopian, consider the Swedish labor market system. Its basic unit is a regional board, made up of representatives from labor, management, and government. All employers are required to register their job openings with the board. Using funds allocated by the national system, each local board finances a broad range of activities suited to local needs, including training programs, wage subsidies, public service jobs, early retirement programs, and relocation subsidies. During recessions, the boards subsidize early retirement, create public-sector jobs, award grants to local firms that offer training sabbaticals rather than layoffs, and provide wage subsidies to new companies for on-the-job training. In good times, they train people for jobs in which labor shortages have begun to appear, they help people from depressed regions move to growth areas and train for available jobs, and they encourage firms to locate in depressed communities by making wage subsidies available. The system works to cushion unemployment during hard times, to avoid labor shortages during good times, to upgrade the skills of the entire work force, and to assure workers that technological innovation will improve, not destroy, their jobs.[49]

The Entrepreneurial Climate

Since the publication of David Birch's study, economic developers have embraced entrepreneurship. The new emphasis has created some balance in economic development systems that were previously focused almost exclusively on large manufacturers. But as so often happens when a new truth sweeps away an old one, the pendulum may have swung too far. Few state programs address the entrepreneurial process in large and medium-sized firms. The notions of "intrapreneurship" and collective entrepreneurialism have not penetrated the world of state economic development policy.

The other conceptual problem that plagues most state efforts is their heavy focus on financial capital. Time and time again those involved in programs to help small businesses have realized that their client's real problem was not a shortage of cash but a shortage of human skills: poor management, destructive labor-management relations, or an organization that discouraged cooperation and innovation. When those problems were addressed, cash flow began to improve, markets grew, and access to capital opened up. Hence many practitioners have begun to focus more heavily on comprehensive, hands-on assistance, through business assistance centers, incubators, and entrepreneurial training programs.

Overall, the lesson that emerges from state experience with such programs is that they work, but that their vision has been too limited. The most common business assistance organizations, for instance, are Small Business Development Centers, jointly funded by the SBA, state and local governments, and universities. They work with hundreds or thousands of businesses each year, their counseling is usually brief, and business students do much of it. Far more successful have been organizations that use larger professional staffs with business backgrounds and that offer intensive help over a longer time span.[50]

Pittsburgh's Enterprise Corporation, profiled in chapter 2, is a perfect example. Another model, described in chapter 4, is under development at the University of Arizona: a corporation to help form new companies designed to commercialize the work of research professors. The Institute for Ventures in New Technology (INVENT), at Texas A&M, takes a similar tack. Created in 1983 with $1 million of state money, it screens inventors carefully, picks the most promising, uses university laboratories to conduct further research, develops business plans, and finds private investors. In return, INVENT receives up to a 45 percent equity share in the venture.[51]

Such efforts need not compete with private management consultants. Often the public institution takes the early, low-profit niche, passing its clients on to private consultants once they can afford such services. The publicly financed New Enterprise Institute in Maine actually founded a professional association of management consultants, to encourage the growth of private-sector firms.[52]

Similar lessons emerge from state incubator programs, of which there were 14 by 1988.[53] By and large, incubators have been successful: according to the National Business Incubation Association, start-ups in incubators have an 80 percent survival rate after five years.[54] By comparison, survival rates for other start-ups appear to be about 35 percent after four years (though estimates range widely).[55] But incubators work best when they function, not simply as inexpensive offices with shared services, but as hands-on business assistance organizations, tied into larger economic development networks that can provide seed capital, research grants, and access to local banks and venture capitalists.

Randall Whaley served for 15 years as president of the nation's first successful incubator, the University City Science Center in Philadelphia. Asked what makes incubators work, he says, "There must be a set of resources to be tapped, role models to interact with, sensitive advisers or consultants to talk to, and some means to bounce ideas concerning the market off of knowledgeable people. I feel the best location is attached loosely to a going organization that can offer many kinds of help by people immersed in the day-to-day practical realities of running a business."[56]

A related area states have barely touched is training for entrepreneurs. We often think of entrepreneurship as a trait with which someone is born—or at least raised. That may be true of the temperament that leads people to start businesses, but it is certainly not true of the skills necessary to make a business succeed. Venture capitalists often work extremely closely with business people in whom they invest, providing what is in essence on-the-job management training. Experiments in the United States and around the world have begun to show that training for other entrepreneurs is equally important.

In 1980, France launched a program to create local *Boutiques de Gestion*, or "management shops," to provide training and assistance to people who wanted to start their own businesses. As of 1984, those who had participated in training were experiencing a bankruptcy rate half that of the average French start-up.[57] In Britain, the Manpower Services Commission has developed three separate programs to train entrepreneurs, one of which even provides trainees with a weekly allowance and a project budget for the business they want to start.[58]

Perhaps the most extraordinary example of entrepreneurial training comes from the Basque region of Spain, where the Mondragon Cooperatives Movement trains people to start worker-owned businesses. Begun in the late 1940s by a Basque priest, the Mondragon Movement had by 1985 created more than one hundred industrial cooperatives, which employed more than 20,000 worker-owners. It had also created 43 cooperative schools, 14 housing co-ops, and a consumer-worker cooperative with over 40 stores. In 25 years, only three cooperatives had failed.[59]

Risk Capital

Because politicans have decades of experience pushing money out the door, one of their first responses to the economic troubles of the 1970s was to make capital available to businesses. These efforts have been riddled with conceptual problems. Most state capital programs do too little wholesaling, and their retailing operations are often relatively unsophisticated. Government also tends to focus on bringing down the *cost* of capital, when it should focus on increasing the *availability* of capital.

The most common state capital programs are industrial development bond (IDB) programs, which lower the cost of capital by exempting interest from federal taxation. When interest rates hit 15 or 20 percent, subsidized capital at low interest rates can make a real difference to many businesses. But in normal circumstances, capital costs are such a small part of the overall expenses of a business that a few percentage points less on a loan will not make or break a project. Many companies could proceed with a bank loan, but prefer the subsidized public loan because it saves them a bit of money. Unfortunately, it is extremely difficult to tell the difference between firms that truly need lower interest rates to justify an investment and those that do not. Hence below-market rate lending programs, by their nature, waste money.

Much more valuable—and less expensive—are efforts to make market-rate capital available to businesses that cannot otherwise get it. Empirical studies have documented that private capital markets fail to invest in small firms and young firms to the degree that their risk and potential reward would justify.[60] (More than half of all small-business loans, for instance, are due within a year.)[61] Other firms that appear to have more trouble than their risk-reward ratio would justify include those owned by minorities and women, those located in depressed communities, and those with non-traditional structures, such as worker ownership. By helping new players enter the game—rather than subsidizing those who already play—government can affect the number of potential growth firms in the economy.

Wholesaling, as argued earlier, not only affects far more money than retailing but also minimizes the temptation to make investments for political reasons and keeps those with the expertise making the decisions. But in some cases, the private sector will simply not be lured into an area. This is particularly true in poor communities and with minority entrepreneurs. In poor communities, there is often a social return that far exceeds the private return any investor can get—a social return measured in lower crime rates, less welfare dependency, more productive members of society, and higher tax receipts. Hence government is justified in investing where the private sector would not. There is also a moral dimension: as a society, we decided two decades ago that we had an obligation to redress the effects of slavery and discrimination on our black citizens. Part of the response has been relatively unsuccessful attempts to nurture black-owned enterprises.

Marketing

Helping businesses find markets is a fairly new activity for state governments. By and large, they have concentrated on two areas: "procurement assistance," through which they help small firms sell to the state and the federal governments; and export assistance. Typically, they have approached both as a form of technical assistance to business, offered through local or state business assistance programs. They have also set up foreign offices to promote trade and foreign investment. A few states have gone further: Virginia has created the Helping Hand Program, through which corporations with overseas employees advise noncompeting firms on exporting; Wisconsin has linked large exporters with small companies through its Mentor Program; and at least fifteen states have created export finance programs, mostly to provide short-term guarantees for bank loans used to finance exports.[62]

Though helpful, most of these efforts are inadequate. Exporting is so difficult for small businesses that it requires more than capital or routine technical assistance. One estimate indicates that even though only 10 percent of small manufacturers export, 75 percent produce products or services that could be sold abroad.[63] "There are a minimum of 30,000 small businesses that have the know-how and ability to compete internationally," says Sam Beard, chairman of the National Commission on Jobs and Small Business. The problem is a shortage of organizations to connect these firms with foreign markets. "There's no mechanism either in the private sector or the public sector combined to stimulate that. What does the guy do if he has a product in Indianapolis? Is he going to leave Indianapolis and fly to 12 capitals and meet people and so forth?"[64]

In Japan and other countries, export trading companies play this role. Some buy goods from manufacturers and resell them overseas, through their extensive marketing networks. Others simply handle export sales for manufacturers and take a percentage of the profits. In 1982, Congress passed the Export Trading Company Act, which permits banks and other financial institutions to participate in trading companies and reduces the risk of antitrust suits. But export trading companies have been slow to develop in the United States.

Government might be able to speed up the process, using the same techniques state governments have employed to stimulate the creation of BIDCOs and seed funds: public investments and quid pro quos. The obvious problem is that most private trading companies would not want to limit themselves to contracting with firms in only one state. Hence a state that subsidized trading companies would find its investments helping neighboring states as well. This argues for a regional approach—as reflected in the New York-New Jersey Port Authority—or a federal program.

The Culture of Industry

One of the biggest surprises of the 1980s has been the trouble encountered by American manufacturers who have automated and retrained their workers, but who have not changed the hierarchical, adversarial cultures within their plants. Automated technologies not only require an educated, trained work force, it turns out; they also require a more democratic work place. The $40-billion investment in automation by General Motors, which bought little improvement in productivity and enormous frustration, is the example most often cited. But the same dynamic has occurred throughout American industry. When American managers began flocking to Japan to learn the secret of its success, the Japanese stressed the human side of the equation. Most Americans did not listen. "Our managers kept looking for the technological solution to the growing Japanese success," says George H. Kuper, who as director of the National Academy of Sciences Manufacturing Studies Board, led some of those tours. "The Japanese were trying to be honest with us, and we were too stupid to listen to them."[65]

Seventy years ago, when new technologies ushered in the assembly line, the culture of industry in America underwent a profound change. Corporate managers embraced "scientific management"—also known as Taylorism, after its principal proponent, Frederick Taylor. They broke every job down into hundreds of routine actions, each of which could be performed by one worker, over and over. Labor was reduced to one more input in the process of production. To maximize their control, managers created hundreds of different job classifications, each describing one of the routine functions. In the drive for ever greater efficiency, they sped up the assembly line and forced workers to perform their routine functions as rapidly as possible. Being humans rather than machines, workers responded by unionizing and demanding hundreds of specific work rules, delineating exactly what each worker could and could not be asked to do. The factory became a battleground, in which every attempt by management to squeeze out more productivity brought forth demands for more precise work rules. Inevitably, all flexibility—all capacity to respond to problems or changes on the factory floor in a creative manner—disappeared. American industry had created its own straightjacket.

For a time, we could afford to operate this way. When World War II ended, the United States had the world's only intact industrial economy. But once other nations recovered, our adversarial culture began to hurt us. In a 1983 survey done by Daniel Yankelovich and John Immerwahr for the Public Agenda Foundation, fewer than one of every four American workers said they were working at their full potential, and almost half said they put in only as much effort as was necessary to keep their job. They saw little reason to do more. Whereas 93 percent of Japanese workers believed that they would share in any profits achieved through improved productivity and harder work, only 10 percent of American workers agreed. Instead, the vast majority thought managers, stockholders, and consumers would benefit.[66]

When the problems on the factory floor became intolerable, American managers initiated a range of new techniques—"quality circles," work teams, even suggestion boxes—designed to increase communication and boost morale. Meanwhile, governments began to fund labor-management committees designed to improve cooperation in the plant and reduce the number of strikes. Pennsylvania, West Virginia, Kentucky, Ohio, Illinois, Minnesota, Michigan, and Texas all created small programs along these lines.[67] The federal government did the same.

As noted in chapter 2, most of these efforts proved to be superficial. Quality circles often simply substituted peer pressure for management coercion. Labor-management committees resolved the most obvious problems, but then tended to bog down. Of seven hundred participative labor-management initiatives surveyed by the U.S. Department of Labor, two hundred had failed.[68] The new islands of cooperation had little chance within the much larger sea of antagonism.

This antagonism can only be overcome through fundamental changes in the culture of industry. Just as the assembly line required a radical change in the organization of work, so do the microelectronic technologies of the postindustrial age. When factories are automated, machines become the "inputs" and workers must learn to run them—which means they must think, they must communicate, they must trouble-shoot.

Few workers are likely to buy into this new role unless their positions within the corporation change fundamentally. If they are given no power in decision making, they will take no responsibility for improvements. If they are left at the bottom of a hierarchy, they will act like foot soldiers, following orders and volunteering for nothing.

As discussed in chapter 2, corporations seeking to get the most out of automation have changed their cultures in several ways. They have replaced hierarchical organizations with relatively flat structures, in which layers of middle managers and supervisors disappear because so many judgments are left to the workers themselves. They have organized their workers into self-managed teams. They have narrowed pay differentials between management and labor, to reinforce the sense of teamwork. They have instituted gain sharing—through bonuses and profit-sharing plans—so their workers will reap the benefits of improved productivity and higher profits. And a few of them—including Ford and General Motors—have guaranteed their workers job security, so they know that automation will not cost them their jobs.

During the 1960s, this combination of flat structures, work teams, democracy, equality of reward, gain sharing, and job security went by the name of worker control. (The logical extension of this principle is of course worker ownership.) In the more conservative 1980s, business has come up with a new phrase: "sociotechnical systems." Whatever the label, firms that have adopted the new model have typically seen their productivity rise from 30 to 50 percent. These firms are in the minority, however. As *Business Week* said in late 1986, "The great wave of automation that has swept through offices and factories since 1980 is losing momentum, largely because not enough companies are adopting the innovative work practices that get the most out of automation."[69]

On the government side, things are moving even more slowly. A few states are beginning to grapple with the deeper issues, including Pennsylvania, Ohio, and Michigan. New York has taken an important step to spur worker ownership, with its Center for Employee Ownership and Participation. But by and large, state governments have not yet tackled the issue of industrial culture. Because it involves a fundamental restructuring of power and ownership in American industry, this is perhaps the most difficult challenge we face. It requires changes in *attitudes* and *values*, more than programmatic initiatives. Governors can help with this process, but the true bully pulpit in American society is the presidency. Hence we are unlikely to take up the challenge until a president leads the way.

Social Organization

Much of the economic development agenda—education, training, the culture of industry—boils down to better social organization. Our entire network of social programs was developed during the industrial era, for an economy in which stability was the norm. None of the major pieces of that system—unemployment insurance, welfare, and social security—stress the acquisition of new skills, the adjustment to new economic realities, or the process of helping people become self-sufficient. Quite the contrary:

our unemployment insurance system, which was designed for workers who lost their jobs temporarily, makes it impossible in most states to take retraining courses while collecting unemployment, on the outdated theory that the unemployed should be looking for new jobs in their old industry, rather than retraining. As a result, fewer than one-quarter of one percent of those collecting unemployment checks are enrolled in training programs.[70] Our welfare system was designed for widows with children, who were assumed to be incapable of working and therefore to need financial support, not training and job placement. Hence only one percent of our AFDC dollars are spent on employment or training programs.[71]

In the 1960s, we augmented this system with health care programs. Again, we assumed a rigid distinction between those outside the labor market, who were eligible for medicare and medicaid, and those with jobs, who were not. No thought was given to the process of transition. Upon discovering that we had large populations of poor people who appeared to be locked out of the economic mainstream, we augmented AFDC with other welfare programs, food stamps, a few job-training programs, and educational programs. But even the best of these, such as Head Start, were designed to help the poor get into what was assumed to be a stable mainstream economy. None was designed to help the average worker adjust to change.

Today, economic change is the norm. We have a safety net when we need a social adjustment system. To understand the difference, consider the one set of social programs created during the industrial era that focused on social adjustment: the GI bill, Veterans Administration mortgages, and related efforts to help GIs make the transition from war to peace. That strategy was an enormous success, demonstrating just how powerful an economic force social adjustment systems can be.

During the 1980s, states have created a few social adjustment programs, such as emergency response teams to provide counseling and to set up training programs after plant closings. But in most states, the effort stops there. We do little to help the affected company or industry move into new, more promising products or services. We do little to create new businesses where the plant has closed. We do little to create jobs for those who cannot find work. With a few exceptions, we do little to help people move to other regions to find jobs.

As a consequence, we lose many productive workers. Economist Bennett Harrison has studied the fate of almost 700,000 people who lost their jobs in New England mills between 1958 and 1975. He found that by 1975, the majority had not made it back into mainstream jobs. Roughly 40 percent had retired, died, or become disabled; another 22 percent remained unemployed (or were working in jobs not registered with Social Security). Only a third had found service, trade, or government jobs, and fewer than 3 percent were working in high-tech firms.[72]

In 1984, when the congressional Office of Technology Assessment traced what had happened to 11.5 million people who had lost jobs because of plant shutdowns or relocations in the five previous years, a similar picture emerged. Of the five million considered "displaced workers," meaning that they were not likely to find new jobs in the same industry, over a quarter were still unemployed in January 1984. Another 14 percent had left the work force. Of those who had previously worked as laborers, helpers, and equipment cleaners, only 42 percent had found new jobs—compared to 75 percent of those in managerial or professional positions. Of those who had found new jobs, nearly half had taken pay cuts, most of which totaled more than 20 percent.[73]

The Office of Technology Assessment estimated that JTPA was retraining only 5 percent of all dislocated workers. Separate state programs are retraining others, but the overall percentage is still quite low. According to Robert Kuttner, at the peak of the 1982 recession the United States spent roughly $30 billion a year to pay for the cost of unemployment, but only about $5 billion a year to retrain workers and create new jobs. In other words, we use 80 to 90 percent of our labor market outlays to subsidize idleness. In contrast, Sweden uses about the same proportion to subsidize reemployment.[74]

If we want our workers to embrace technology and change, these policies are backwards. Our unemployment insurance system should reward firms that retrain their workers and penalize those that frequently lay off workers. (The Japanese provide subsidies during recessions to firms that retrain surplus workers rather than laying them off.) It should create incentives for companies to give early warning of layoffs and plant closings, so workers can get into retraining programs as soon as possible, or explore options such as worker buy-outs. After someone is laid off, it should create incentives, not penalties, for retraining. Whenever possible, unemployment benefits should be used to finance retraining and reemployment, not idleness.

As noted earlier, most other developed nations—our competitors—have comprehensive adjustment systems. In addition to training systems, these include national plant closing laws, under which firms must work out plans for retraining, relocation, and job placement of employees before closing a plant. They include programs to help declining industries reduce excess capacity, retrain and relocate their workers, and invest in new technologies. And they include programs to help regions hit by industrial decline grow new industries. In Britain and France, for instance, industrial firms have invested heavily in incubators, in "enterprise centers" that operate as local development corporations, and in new businesses created by their former employees.[75] Britain and France even encourage the unemployed to become entrepreneurs, by allowing those who meet certain criteria to use their unemployment or welfare checks to start businesses. Over the first five years, nearly 200,000 people took advantage of these programs, which appeared quite successful upon early evaluation.[76] (In late 1988, Washington state will launch a demonstration project based on this model.)

Even Canada has a comprehensive adjustment program, called the Manpower Consultative Service. Under this program, a joint labor-management committee is set up to help all workers who request aid when a plant announces a closing. The government funds retraining efforts and provides 50 percent of moving expenses for workers who must relocate. The company, the union, and the provincial job service all work to find new jobs for those laid off. Under a joint project of the National Governors Association and the U.S. Department of Labor, six states are now experimenting with an American version of this model.[77]

If we followed the example of our competitors and set up a comprehensive adjustment system, we would benefit in several ways. First, our entire society—individual workers, communities, labor unions, and governments—would be more receptive to change, and thus more flexible and innovative. Second, our work force would be far more productive, because we would be wasting fewer of its talents and energies. Finally, by investing more in training and the other mechanisms of transition, we would spend far less on transfer payments and collect far more in taxes.

The other major area that cries out for better social organization is our support network for families. The new economy has radically changed the American family. In 1950, 12 percent of women with children under the age of six worked; by 1985, 54 percent did, and according to Pat Choate, child-care problems kept another 20 percent of women with preschool children out of the labor market.[78] The divorce rate has also increased dramatically, and roughly 12 million children now live in single-parent families. A majority of them are poor, many because their mothers cannot afford child care, and therefore cannot work.[79] Despite these obvious problems, the United States is one of the only industrialized nations that does not have a comprehensive child-care policy of some kind.

The states are beginning to respond. Nineteen states passed increases in child-care spending in 1986, and several states are beginning to tighten up their enforcement of child-support payments by divorced or separated fathers.[80] Wisconsin has even launched a program that will provide state child support when the father cannot pay at least $3,000 a year, for the first child.[81] Many states have also set up programs designed to deal with the intractable problem of teenage pregnancy, although none has found anything amounting to a solution.

All of these efforts are important, but they do not yet add up to a coherent family policy. We need child-care subsidies, enforcement of child-support payments, early childhood education programs, and a host of other efforts to help low- and moderate-income families remain productive participants in the new economy. By avoiding this challenge, we are undermining our own future as surely as when we fail to retrain a dislocated worker or invest in a new technology.

The Federal Role

What is Washington's role in making all of this happen? Many in Washington assume that the new state programs are important primarily because they will provide proven models for federal initiatives. They foresee new national programs in technology development, education, industrial restructuring, labor-management cooperation, job training, child care, and on down the list. In contrast, many in the state capitols fear this impulse. They argue that Congress can neither discriminate between the needs of different regions nor target aid to areas that need it most. They speak from bitter experience about what poor partners federal bureaucrats make, because they are so seldom willing to let local actors control programs.

This is clearly an important issue. If in a rush of enthusiasm for American "competitiveness" we simply round up the best state programs and legislate them into federal law, without a careful sorting of the appropriate level for each form of intervention, the results will inevitably be disappointing.

The experiments being conducted in America's laboratories of democracy do have enormous implications for the federal government. But as during the Progressive Era, the answer is not simply to replicate state programs at the national level. Nor is it simply to encourage the states to do more. It is to embrace the new *roles* state governments are learning to play, without necessarily bringing the specific programs to the national level. We need new federal initiatives in many areas, and we would be wise to construct them on the methodological principles of sound economic development: the use of government to change the marketplace; investment rather than spending; and the rest. But those initiatives should focus on problems the federal government is particularly suited to address, not on problems the states are already addressing with success. Our goal should be a new partnership between the state and federal governments, in which each level of government acts in ways that are appropriate to its capacities and responsibilities.

The reason for this dualism lies in the structure of our economy. As I have argued throughout this book, the American economy—indeed the world economy—is made up of a series of regional economies, each of which radiates out from a city or network of cities. Each regional economy is unique. Each has a different mix of industries, a different labor market, a different set of educational institutions, and different capital markets. In this country, the governmental unit that most closely matches the regional economy is the state.

Macroeconomic policy deals with questions that, for the most part, are national in scope: fiscal and monetary policy, tax policy, trade policy. Proper macroeconomic management is tremendously important, and must be the federal government's primary economic responsibility. But as I have argued, in today's economy microeconomic intervention is also critical. (If macroeconomic policy is handled well, microeconomic policy will be all the more important, because it will have far more impact in an economy whose fundamentals are sound.) Microeconomic policy deals with matters that vary a great deal from one regional economy to another. Indiana may have a severe shortage of risk capital, but California does not. Massachusetts may have a labor market in which employers will hire welfare recipients at $5.50 an hour, but Michigan does not. Pennsylvania may have strong engineering schools and research institutions, but Arkansas does not. Hence the design of most microeconomic programs should, ideally, be specific to one region. "Cookie cutter" models imported from one state to another—or crafted solely in Washington—will not do the job.

Past experience suggests that the federal government is not well equipped to develop different models for different regions of the country. Nor is it very good at limiting its efforts to those regions that need them most; when money is involved, every legislator seeks a share for his or her constituents. The Economic Development Administration was created to stimulate development in poor communities, yet 80 percent of the nation was soon eligible for EDA grants.[82] One recent study of federal grant programs found that in 1984, wealthier states actually received *more* federal money per capita than poor states.[83]

There are problems of scale as well. Federal programs, because of their size and scope, are normally more bureaucratic and less accountable to voters than state or local programs. Federal programs also tend not to generate the feelings of ownership at the state and local level that are necessary for careful, creative implementation and continued support. For years the EDA and the Appalachian Regional Commission, which were designed to be run as partnerships between federal, state, and local governments, have been virtually ignored by governors and state legislators, because they are seen as Washington's programs.

At the same time, there are clear limits to what can be achieved at the state level. States cannot deal with problems affecting entire industries, because industries cross state lines. Much regulation of capital markets is national in scope. International trade is beyond the control of state governments. Moreover, the states have resource problems. Because state governments feel that they are competing with one another for industry, there are severe pressures to keep taxes low. This makes it difficult for any state to come up with the funding necessary to deal with problems that require substantial investment, such as job training, or development in poor communities. In addition, regions that need the most investment have the least ability to make that investment. If we are to transfer resources from wealthy regions to poor regions, the federal government must be the agent of redistribution.

These realities suggest a relatively simple rule of thumb. When the appropriate model differs from one region to another, programs should be run by the states. The federal role should be to provide funds, particularly for poorer states; to create financial incentives for states to act; to evaluate state efforts; and, above all, to provide the leadership necessary to create nationwide support for reform. When problems transcend the capacities of individual states, on the other hand, or when they are rooted in national realities that do not vary from region to region, the federal government should administer the programs.

Looking back at an earlier period, one can see a similar duality. The progressives focused primarily on ending the worst abuses of the new industrial era: the use of child labor, the awesome powers of the new trusts, the corruption of the new urban political machines. They achieved a few systemic reforms, such as the creation of the Federal Reserve Board and the Federal Trade Commission. But it was not until the New Deal that government fashioned a new institutional framework for the industrial economy—something only the federal government could do. The Agricultural Adjustment Administration, the National Recovery Administration, the National Labor Relations Act, the array of new laws and institutions designed to stabilize the financial system—all of these had to be national in scope.

In parallel fashion, state governments today have addressed many of the new problems that have erupted during the transition to a postindustrial economy. But only the federal government can create the new institutional frameworks—at both the national and international levels—needed to accommodate the new economy.

Most of the initiatives states have taken should remain primarily in state hands. This category would include education, training, specific social adjustment programs, programs to stimulate entrepreneurship, efforts to improve regional capital markets, programs to stimulate interaction between academic and industrial researchers, and most technology deployment efforts. In these areas, conditions vary so sharply from one region to another that the actual administration of programs should be left to the states. But the federal government can play a critical role in providing funds and in creating incentives for states to act. This is the model the New Deal adopted for many of its social programs, including AFDC, unemployment compensation, and workmen's compensation.[84] (As noted earlier,

JTPA is built along similar lines.) This approach would not only allow for handcrafting at the regional level, it would increase the likelihood that specific programs would be integrated into comprehensive, decentralized development systems.

Areas in which the federal government must take the lead include international trade, national capital markets, labor-management relations, industrial modernization and restructuring, and strategic analysis. If we are to remain competitive, the next wave of federal economic activism will create a new framework for international trade, to accommodate the realities of today's global economy. It will create new institutional frameworks at home to accommodate rapid industrial change: to help emerging industries compete with those in other nations; to help mature industries restructure to survive in the new economy; and to promote social adjustment. It will create a new institutional framework that encourages cooperative labor-management systems, and it will do the same to encourage the creation of new financial structures for the new economy.

Consider international trade. Virtually all experts agree that the trading system set up after World War II has been rendered obsolete by the new realities of global capital markets, multinational corporations, and managed trade. The General Agreement on Tariffs and Trade (GATT), for instance, now covers less than 7 percent of world imports, exports, and capital flows.[85] Only the federal government can bring other nations to the bargaining table to hammer out a new framework for international trade.

Similarly, U.S. firms need new institutions through which to sell their goods abroad, to compete with foreign export trading companies. Because it would seldom make sense for such institutions to limit their services to firms in one state, state governments cannot be expected to play a leading role in their development.

Our banking system is decentralized, because interstate banking has historically been outlawed. (This is gradually changing, of course.) Hence the states have played important roles in improving statewide capital markets. But the federal government also plays a critical role in the regulation of banking, as well as in the regulation of equity markets, which are largely national and international in scope. For this reason, Washington has an important role to play in this arena as well.[86]

Labor-management relations are equally embedded in federal legislation and judicial interpretation. Many of the incentives that might change industrial behavior, such as the tax code and the unemployment insurance system, are primarily federal. Some national industries and unions do not allow enough flexibility to their local units to achieve a great deal through local bargaining. For all these reasons, it is largely up to Washington to create a new framework for labor-management relations—a framework that will encourage the redefinition of industrial culture.

When industries are national in scope, the states are often powerless to affect change. The states can create research consortia involving local universities and businesses, for instance. But they cannot be expected to play a role in industrywide research consortia, such as the Semiconductor Research Corporation, the Microelectronics and Computer Technology Corporation, and the proposed $250-million research effort in semiconductor manufacturing, known as Sematech. Because no state can capture all the benefits of an industrywide research project, and because these projects carry hefty price tags, states do not initiate them. To compete with Japan and Western Europe, the Pentagon has begun to finance industrywide research consortia, but Pentagon sponsorship brings myriad problems.[87] If we are to remain competitive, we need nondefense agencies capable of playing this role.

The states are equally powerless to help nationwide industries restructure to remain competitive, although they can play this role for regional industrial sectors. Michigan can work with local auto industry suppliers, or propose an innovative partnership in one auto plant, but it cannot address the overall problems of the auto industry. The United States has done little of this, although the Carter administration did help Chrysler restructure, and Carter's Commerce Department did experiment with a small modernization effort in the footwear industry.[88] Our trading partners routinely take on these tasks. "In the rest of the world," writes Lester Thurow, "it would be completely normal to ask the members of a sick industry—the firms, the unions, the suppliers, the banks, the communities—to sit down and determine what part of the industry could be saved and how the industry could work together to strengthen itself."[89]

Social adjustment is both a federal and a state task. Federal policies regarding taxes, welfare, unemployment compensation, education, training, student loans, and so on must be addressed if we are to transform the safety net into a social adjustment system. Some specific programs, such as a GI bill for training, would be national, because they would be equally available in every region of the country. Others, such as programs to respond to plant closings, would be administered by the states.

Finally, only the federal government can provide the strategic analysis and data collection necessary to help governments at all levels play intelligent roles in the economy. Federal data collection and analysis are hopelessly fragmented and out of date, and the capacity of the federal government to monitor the strategies of our trading partners and long-term trends in world markets barely exists. Viewed as a whole, the federal economic apparatus is a bundle of conflicting impulses, with no strategic vision.

The most fundamental task we face in adjusting to the postindustrial economy is not in the realm of policy and program, but in the realm of perception and ideology. It is the task of redefining our core problems. Governors such as Clinton and Blanchard and Babbitt have begun this process, in their own states. But governors do not have anything like the platform enjoyed by the president.

Ben Fischer, the Carnegie-Mellon economist, uses the analogy of Franklin Roosevelt's "Peace Bridge" speech, in which the president pushed America toward the commitment it would inevitably make to the war against fascism. "I am old enough that I remember that this was an isolationist country," Fischer says. "And I recall Roosevelt's 'Peace Bridge' speech very vividly. It wasn't just the speech, but the speech certainly touched off a whole change in the perceptions of the American people. Did they change 100 percent? No, we still have isolationists. But Roosevelt put us on a different road."

Today we need a national leader who will once again change the perceptions of the American people, one who will educate us about the new problems we face, the new solutions we must embrace, and the new partnerships we must fashion between government and business, between labor and management, between academia and industry, and between our federal, state, and local governments. We need a president who will put us on the road to a new agenda.

THE SECOND AGENDA: BRINGING THE POOR INTO THE GROWTH PROCESS

Creating economic growth and bringing the poor into that process are fundamentally different tasks. Even the best economic development system will not do a great deal for the poor. It will help some, but it will also hurt some, for it will speed up the transition from an industrial economy to a postindustrial economy. The better our social adjustment systems, the greater the number of people who will be able to make the transition. But even with the best of adjustment systems, some will be left behind, because most growth jobs today—particularly those that pay decent wages—require intellectual capacities. Secretaries must be able to read, write, and work with computers. Repair people must be able to deal with sophisticated machinery.

Three groups are caught in the mismatch between available jobs and available workers: dislocated industrial workers; the urban poor; and the rural poor. Increasingly, these three groups live in isolated communities that have lost their connections to the economic mainstream. These communities are caught in a downward spiral of disinvestment, increasing poverty, and further disinvestment. A few of their members successfully make the jump into the economic mainstream, but as communities, they grow ever more isolated.

Consider the urban ghettos. During and after World War II, a renewed wave of mechanization in agriculture pushed millions of blacks off southern farms, while America's industrial machine pulled them to the northern cities. Even as they arrived, however, American manufacturing was beginning its migration out of the cities. When foreign competition and automation brought on even further shrinkage in the 1970s and 1980s, the urban black population found itself stranded, with virtually no access to the industrial jobs that had enabled previous waves of rural migrants to climb the ladder of opportunity. In some cities, even the booming service sector has moved to the suburbs.

The effect of this isolation from the job market has been dramatic. In 1957, black teenage unemployment was 19 percent; by 1985, it was 40 percent.[1] In 1970, 46 percent of young black men still held craft and operative jobs; by 1984, the figure was down to 26 percent.[2] From 1959 through 1973, the real income of young black men, aged 20 to 24, rose by 68 percent. Between 1973 and 1984, it fell by 44 percent.[3]

The "culture of poverty" we hear so much about today existed on southern plantations. But in the northern ghettos, where young black men were increasingly cut off from the only kinds of jobs they could realistically get, it intensified. When the victories of the civil rights movement allowed the black middle class to escape the ghettos, the cultural norms that they and their social institutions had enforced began to crumble. Crime rates increased. The school dropout rate skyrocketed past 50 percent.[4] Marriage became the exception, rather than the rule. In 1964, roughly 25 percent of black babies were born out of wedlock. By 1985, 58 percent were.[5] Half of all black families were headed by women, and 70 percent of young black fathers were absent fathers.[6]

In the ghettos today, dropping out of school virtually guarantees unemployment. By 1980, a high school graduate had a 61 percent better chance of being employed than a dropout—double the figure from the late 1960s.[7] Only one out of every six poor young persons who had graduated from high school by 1970 remained poor ten years later.[8] Similarly, having children out of wedlock virtually dictates unemployment and welfare dependency. By 1985, more than half of all women who received AFDC were teenagers when they had their first baby, and half of all black children were supported by some form of welfare.[9] Overall, the level of dependence on public assistance among blacks had doubled in only 20 years.[10]

The culture of poverty—of teenage pregnancy, welfare, drugs, and crime—has become so strong that it is perhaps the major barrier facing black youths today. In Boston during the mid-1980s, jobs paying $5.00 an hour went begging and tens of thousands of illegal immigrants from Ireland found work. But Boston's native poor families—more than 60 percent of which were led by single mothers—actually lost ground. By 1985 nearly one of every five Boston families lived below the federal poverty line ($10,609 for a family of four). For blacks, the figure was roughly 28 percent; for Hispanics, 46 percent. Sixty percent of poor families in Boston were led by people who were not even looking for work.[11] These statistics no doubt overstate the case by ignoring the underground economy. Nevertheless, they provide powerful evidence that even in America's growing regions, the culture of poverty has created a world unto itself.

In some rural areas, the problems are almost as bad. Appalachian and southern poverty have been well publicized for decades. But even in a state such as Michigan, six of the seven counties with the highest dependence on public assistance are rural. (The seventh is of course Wayne County, which includes Detroit.)[12] Rural areas that do not have a strong agricultural or resource base, or significant tourism, are often completely isolated from the mainstream economy.

The problems are not as intense in our depressed industrial regions. These communities are caught in a downward spiral, but they have not hit bottom. Nor are they burdened by the cultural and social disadvantages bred by three hundred years of slavery and discrimination. Still, some deindustrialized communities are in danger of sinking into passivity and dependence.

When an entire community is trapped within a culture of poverty, or within a cycle of decline, barriers exist that make it very difficult to take advantage of opportunities. To help people over those barriers, and to interrupt those cycles, states such as Massachusetts and New York have begun to pioneer a second agenda.

This second agenda is necessary not only for social and economic reasons, but to ensure broad political support for the first agenda. (This is particularly true for the national Democratic party, in which minorities and industrial unions play an important role.) When politicians talk about technological innovation and industries of the future, blue-collar workers see automation and unemployment. To the poor, such messages are not so much threatening as irrelevant. To win support from these constituencies, a new agenda must appeal directly to their interests. Hence it must have two tracks. Without the first, the second may fail for lack of economic growth. But without the second, the first may fail for lack of political support.

Welfare Reform: Bringing Down the Barriers

Until the 1980s, there was no consensus that welfare even constituted a barrier to participation in the mainstream economy. Over the past five years, however, governors of both parties, in states as diverse as New York and California, have put aside the ideological debate and created programs designed to help people overcome the barriers.

The welfare debate, as we know it, began during the 1960s. Liberal activists, moved by the civil rights movement and the new awareness of poverty it created, saw welfare as part of the solution. The welfare rights movement forced benefits up and battered down the many barriers local and state governments had erected to keep people off public assistance. The rolls skyrocketed, and for a few years poverty rates fell.[13] In its most extreme form, this movement argued that the cure to poverty was simply more money.

As the welfare rolls ballooned, conservatives complained about fraud and abuse and charged that higher welfare benefits discouraged work and encouraged dependency. They fought to drive people off the rolls by making welfare less comfortable: by lowering welfare benefits, and by requiring that recipients work off their grants.

Both the liberal approach and the conservative approach failed. But in trying them, we have learned a great deal. Conservatives have learned that neither lower welfare checks nor workfare succeed in moving people into the mainstream economy. Welfare benefits have dropped by roughly a third since 1970, in real dollars, with no apparent impact on the rolls.[14] Workfare has proven administratively impractical in the cities and economically ineffective in rural areas. Creating enough workfare jobs to handle even a portion of urban welfare caseloads has proven impossible, because of the expense, the administrative difficulties, and the political opposition from organized labor (which fears that workfare jobs will gradually take the place of government jobs). In rural areas, with smaller welfare caseloads and fewer unions, workfare has been easier to administer, but it has failed to drive people off the rolls. The only genuine workfare program that has been thoroughly evaluated, in West Virginia, had absolutely no impact on the subsequent employment rate of participants—no doubt because few jobs were available.[15]

Liberals, in turn, have learned that redistributing income without redistributing opportunity leads to greater dependency. The rapid increase in welfare rolls and budgets during the 1960s and early 1970s, combined with the deindustrialization of the cities and the exodus of the black middle class, served only to intensify the culture of poverty.

The best glimpse of this reality is provided by the Panel Study of Income Dynamics (PSID), a University of Michigan survey that has tracked the incomes of a large group of families since 1968. Although initial interpretations of PSID data suggested that welfare was primarily a temporary expedient with which families made it through difficult times, closer examinations have painted a very different picture.[16] They have shown that most AFDC recipients fall into one of two groups. The first—women who have been married, have high school degrees, and first collect welfare after the age of 25—does use welfare as a temporary expedient. But the second—younger women who have not graduated from high school, have not married, and have had a child out of wedlock—tends to stay on welfare for long periods of time. In one analysis of the PSID sample, 64 percent of all unmarried AFDC recipients under 40 who lacked high school degrees were on AFDC for at least ten years.[17] A second analysis found that the average expected time for all women on welfare was 11.6 years, and an estimated 60 percent of every AFDC dollar went to women who collected welfare for at least ten years.[18]

This is a portrait of welfare dependency. Though welfare did not create the culture of poverty, it has clearly intensified it. The link shows up not only in the PSID data but in any number of other statistics, studies, and anecdotal reports. A study by the National Bureau of Economic Research found that black youths from welfare homes or public housing have done far worse in the job market than their counterparts—with equal family incomes and other attributes—from nonwelfare homes and nonpublic housing.[19] In Michigan, the AFDC population is so disconnected from the mainstream economy that AFDC caseloads neither soared during the 1982 recession nor dropped with the recovery. Over half of all AFDC recipients in the state have not worked in the past five years, and almost half of the rest have worked for less than one year out of the last five.[20] They are so removed from the world of work, in other words, that no matter how many jobs the economy creates, they will remain on welfare.

Once within the typical welfare system, virtually all the incentives are to remain dependent. In roughly half of the states AFDC discourages family stability, because women cannot collect it if a man lives in the house. In many states it discourages people from working, because a welfare mother who takes a low-wage job without medical coverage or a child-care subsidy *lowers* her family's standard of living. In most states it discourages people from investing in their own futures, because it cuts them off the minute their assets reach a minimal level. If they save enough money to buy a car to get to suburban job interviews, for instance, they automatically lose their welfare benefits.[21]

To borrow an analogy from the Corporation for Enterprise Development, which has led the effort to pioneer a second agenda at the state level, welfare is economic methadone. Like methadone, it is widely considered to be superior to its alternative: crime, prostitution, starvation, or poorhouses. It does make poverty more tolerable. But like methadone, it does not help people kick the habit.

The solution is not to eliminate welfare, for that would do nothing to cure the fundamental problem. It would not change three hundred years of history, or bring economic opportunity to the ghetto. Eliminating methadone sends people back to heroin; eliminating welfare would send them deeper into crime and social pathos. The solution is withdrawal from the fundamental addiction: poverty. To borrow again from the Corporation for Enterprise Development, the solution is a safety net that also operates as a ladder.[22]

The Emerging Consensus

As state governments have experimented with ways to turn the safety net into a ladder, a consensus has begun to emerge. It marries the liberal emphasis on training, employment, and child care with the conservative emphasis on requiring something in return for a welfare check. The most comprehensive expression of that marriage is California's Greater Avenues for INdependence (GAIN) program, a compromise between Republican Governor George Deukmajian and liberal Democrats in the legislature. GAIN is mandatory, but what it requires is participation in some effort that may lead to employment, such as remedial education, training, workfare, or a group job-search process. Like E.T. Choices, GAIN provides child-care subsidies.

This kind of approach has proven popular across the political spectrum. It has been embraced by Deukmajian, a conservative, and Cuomo, a liberal. Opinion polls find strong support for it. The National Governors Association (NGA) has endorsed it, and several bills in Congress built on the NGA proposal have achieved widespread support.

These proposals seek to do two things: to change the incentives built into welfare, and to provide the support necessary for people to overcome the barriers that keep them out of the mainstream economy. To accomplish the former, they would eliminate the marriage penalty; provide child-care subsidies and temporary medicaid extensions; and require that states withhold child-support payments from absent parents' paychecks. To accomplish the latter, they would create a menu of education, training, and job placement options, on the E.T. Choices model.

This menu approach is important, because it offers different paths to people with different needs. As noted earlier, AFDC recipients fall into at least two distinct camps: long-term dependents, many of whom need a great deal of help to surmount the barriers that keep them dependent; and those who use AFDC as a temporary cushion, who may simply need training or job placement. Between these extremes lie many subtle gradations. Outside AFDC are those on General Assistance, many of whom are young, single males, and those on AFDC-Unemployed Parent: two-parent families in which the major breadwinner is unemployed.

The choices offered by various state programs include direct job placement efforts; job clubs for those who need psychological support during the search process; career assessment and counseling for those who need help deciding which direction they want to take; remedial and vocational education; job training; supported work; workfare; public-sector jobs; the self-employment demonstration sponsored by CfED; and on-the-job training, subsidized by diverting welfare grants to employers.

Another option might be some form of community service. Lee Bowes, who worked closely with welfare recipients at Transitional Employment Enterprises (TEE), argues that many people on welfare provide valuable services in their communities. They take care of their own children, of course, but many also care for their neighbors' children, or for elderly relatives or neighbors. Others do work for their churches or other voluntary organizations in the neighborhood. If we were to use community organizations (particularly CDCs) to provide some of the training programs, self-employment programs, remedial education efforts, and workfare jobs for welfare recipients, as New York does, we could also use them to administer a community service program. They could provide the oversight and accountability, at the neighborhood level, necessary to make such an effort work.

Some people argue that programs like E.T. Choices and GAIN do not go far enough to overcome the culture of poverty. Politicians as diverse as Illinois Senator Paul Simon, a liberal Democratic presidential candidate in 1988, and former Delaware Governor Pierre du Pont, a conservative Republican candidate, have suggested that we replace welfare with a guaranteed public jobs program. This approach has a number of appealing features, including its emphasis on jobs and its insistence that we need nothing less than a radical overhaul of our welfare system. As one part of a comprehensive overhaul, a public jobs program would be extremely important. But if it were the *entire* program, it would suffer from the same flaws as workfare.

First, it would be impractical. If it were truly available to all the able-bodied poor, a public jobs program would be extremely expensive. Simon claims that his version would cost only $8 billion a year. But as even supporters of the concept have admitted, the true cost would be far higher.[23]

Second, and more fundamental, a public jobs program would turn the safety net, not into a ladder out of poverty, but into another trap: the make-work, dead-end job. Simon's bill would give people one day a week to look for better jobs, and it would require that participants without high school diplomas enroll in education programs at night or on weekends. But no poor adult could afford to enroll in a full-time education or training program, because there would be no welfare check to rely on. The group that uses welfare as a temporary expedient might be trapped by the new system, because they would be unable to go back to school or get job training. (Most of these people have children, so night school is not an option.) The second group would simply move from long-term dependency on welfare checks to long-term dependency on make-work jobs. It is instructive that only a third of those who held public jobs under CETA went on to find jobs in the regular labor market.[24]

Simon insists that the jobs would not be make-work. He argues that New Deal programs created *real* jobs. But in fact, the New Deal had its problems with make-work, and today they would be worse, because government workers are unionized.[25] The unions would force a new jobs program to keep anything resembling normal public-sector jobs to a minimum, just as they did with CETA, the federal jobs program in the 1970s.

The goal of providing jobs to all the poor is laudable, and public-sector jobs are one important element of a system that helps people make the transition to work. But simply substituting public-sector jobs for welfare, without building bridges to the mainstream economy, is a classic example of spending rather than investing.

The Difficult Issues

If the next wave of reform is to yield significant results, a number of more difficult issues must be resolved. The first is whether employment and training programs should be voluntary, like E.T. Choices, or mandatory, like California's GAIN. The NGA and the major congressional bills have opted for the mandatory approach: all able-bodied welfare recipients whose children are at least three years old would be required to sign a contract stipulating what they would do to achieve self-sufficiency. If they refused to participate in some effort, they would, at least theoretically, be dropped from the rolls.

The symbolism of this approach is correct: it forces people to earn their right to welfare by making a commitment to self-sufficiency. This is not only good politics, it is good policy. In any situation—in school, in the work place, or in the welfare system—people act according to the expectations set for them. If teachers expect little, students produce little. If a welfare system expects dependency, it produces dependency. But if it expects a commitment to self-sufficiency, it is likely to get that commitment. Welfare recipients have confounded liberals for years by telling pollsters and case workers that they enjoy workfare and that they feel they should be required to work off their grants. Our welfare system should reinforce these attitudes—not by providing make-work jobs, but by channeling people into education, training, and job placement programs.

The difficult question arises when the mandatory approach has to be put into practice. Is society willing to deny welfare to poor children if their mothers refuse to participate in an employment and training program? Will it make the mandatory requirement stick?

The solution lies in a two-tier system of welfare grants. Under this approach, if recipients refused to participate, or signed contracts but failed to follow through, they would receive lower grants. This policy could be articulated in the following way: "We will provide an income for every poor child in America, but we will provide an income only for those adults who make a commitment to self-sufficiency. Hence people who refuse to participate will keep the children's portion of their grant, but lose the adult portion." Children would obviously suffer under such a system, but children suffer under the current system, because it encourages long-term dependency.

The second issue is more practical: the sheer difficulty and expense of implementing a mandatory employment and training program. In its fifth year, E.T. Choices is still essentially under construction. Yet it is voluntary; it serves only about a third of the eligible population; and it has no workfare or public jobs component. To expect a state with far fewer resources to do far more, within the first year, is to guarantee chaos and failure.

A program that is mandatory from the start will also lose the advantage E.T. Choices has had in dealing only with motivated clients. As argued in chapter 6, this advantage was critical to the success of Massachusetts. It allowed the program to pile up early victories; it helped the welfare department convince the training system and the employment service to make serious efforts to train and place welfare recipients; and its early successes created hope for welfare recipients who had not yet volunteered.

Governor Cuomo's Task Force on Poverty and Welfare provided the right solution to this dilemma: it proposed that states put new systems in place piece by piece, as they can manage and afford them.[26] Under this approach, a state might start with a voluntary program similar to E.T. Choices. For those who failed to find jobs after moving through the education and training programs, it might add community service and public jobs components. Once this system was working adequately, the state would increase its investment until it met the demand from volunteers. (This entire process could easily take five years.) When that happened, the state might begin requiring that anyone receiving General Assistance participate in some component. Next, it could extend mandatory participation to all AFDC recipients except mothers with children under six. Finally, it could include mothers with younger children.[27]

This entire process might take close to a decade. But it is the only realistic approach. It would give states the time they needed, and it would make the reform effort more affordable, because savings from initial successes with voluntary participants could be channeled back into more intensive efforts for those who are harder to reach. Finally, it would help states cope with the law of unintended consequences, for it would give them time to address unforeseen problems as they emerged.

The third difficult issue is health care. Extending medicaid coverage for a year after a welfare recipient finds a job is helpful, but if the states want to *keep* people in the work force, they will have to do more. Without some form of health insurance for the working poor, many who pile up medical bills will be forced to quit their jobs and go onto welfare, simply to qualify for medicaid. This kind of negative incentive is precisely what makes our welfare system a trap.

The ideal solution might start with the experiment pioneered by Arizona and perfected by Wisconsin: an HMO-based medicaid system (in metropolitan areas). To give HMOs an incentive to participate, states could follow Wisconsin's example and include public employees in the system.

The state could then require private employers to offer health insurance, but allow them to do so by joining the state HMO system, at cost. If a state decided certain firms needed subsidies—very small firms or new firms—they could be offered lower rates. This kind of approach would solve three problems: it would build cost containment into the system; it would extend coverage to the working poor; and it would avoid a blanket subsidy for all firms not providing health coverage, while preserving the option of subsidizing new and small firms.[28]

The fourth difficult question involves wages: how do we deal with the fact that many jobs available to welfare recipients pay wages so low that they represent a *loss* of income? In Massachusetts, the solution is to place people only in jobs paying more than $5 an hour. But in much of Massachusetts, $5 an hour is the effective minimum wage.

Some experts have suggested various government subsidies for the working poor, including refundable tax credits and wage subsidies.[29] Increasing tax credits for the poor makes sense, but even this strategy would require a larger IRS bureaucracy to sort those who qualified for the tax credit from those who did not. Before taking this step, it would be wise to simply raise the minimum wage. If we raised the minimum wage to $4.65 by 1990, we would return it to about the level established in 1981, in real dollars. One can always argue that this would destroy some low-wage jobs, although careful analysis suggests that this effect is usually overstated.[30] If we continue to let inflation erode the value of the minimum wage, of course, there is no doubt that we will have more jobs. But they will be jobs that keep people poor, not jobs that offer them a ladder out of poverty.

The fifth difficult issue is the price tag of welfare reform. The leading congressional bills, which would provide between $2 and $5 billion over the program's first five years, duck this issue entirely. In Massachusetts, the entire system described above might pay for itself, by lowering welfare outlays. But in less affluent areas, the cost would be much higher. It could be kept manageable, to a degree, by implementing the program in steps. But eventually, the child-care bill, the training bill, and the public-jobs bill would add up to significant amounts. If done on the cheap, none of these components will yield the results we expect. If done well—for instance, if child care is augmented by Head Start-type programs—they will not be cheap. An employment and training system would not be as expensive as a guaranteed public jobs program, but it would cost far more than Congress appears ready to spend.

Unless we are willing to make a serious investment, however, we will be limited to tinkering. State experience has demonstrated a number of hard truths: that the most expensive interventions have the greatest long-term impact; that without higher starting wages, guaranteed health care, and child care for the working poor, welfare will remain more attractive than work; and that unless we invest enough in supervision and training to make public jobs true learning experiences, they will not serve as steps toward private-sector employment.

If we embark on the path laid out above, perhaps one day we will no longer have a welfare system. In an ideal world, we would have a training and employment system that offered temporary financial support to all adults who moved through it—because they had lost their jobs, because they had sought retraining on their own, or because they had been out of the labor market. In such a system, guaranteed public jobs would be a last resort used in hard times and in communities with high levels of unemployment. They would be funded, not by "welfare" offices, but by regional labor market boards. They would not be make-work jobs, but constructive investments in the capacities of our people and our communities.

In that ideal world, we would also have a health care system that offered coverage to all Americans, and a family support system that subsidized child care for low-income people and guaranteed a minimum level of financial support to all children. These systems would be available to every American. This last point is extremely important. As long as we keep the poor in a separate system, we tell them—and we tell the larger society— that we do not expect them to be productive members of society. Such messages are extremely powerful. They condition the behavior of poor people, and they condition society's entire response to human needs: the funds we provide, the programs we set up, the way we structure those programs, and the mind-set we encourage in case workers, who actually operate the programs. Today, the entire welfare system gives poor people a clear message: they are dependent, and we expect them to remain dependent.

We need a system that says just the opposite: all adults are productive members of society, and society will provide the transitional support, education, training, health care, and child care people need to remain productive. We will reward effort, not lack of effort; work, not lack of work. No able-bodied adult will have a right to an income without a responsibility to work for it. But no able-bodied adult will be left without a ladder he or she can use to climb out of poverty.

Creating a Development Process in Poor Communities

Would an employment and training program for welfare recipients work as well in Detroit as it does in Boston? Obviously not. Unless the private economy is expanding the supply of jobs, there are severe limits to a training strategy. In Detroit, the public jobs component would play a far greater role than in Boston.

For this reason, welfare reform efforts need to be linked to comprehensive development strategies. By asking corporations that receive state aid to hire welfare recipients, for instance, states can build links between economic development programs and welfare systems. And by nurturing a development process within poor communities, states can attack the problem at its roots.

Unfortunately, "community development," as this is known in bureaucratic circles, has remained a poor cousin of economic development in the 1980s. Even where governments have invested in community development, they have tended to focus more on the *appearance* of development than on the *process* of development. They have constructed new buildings, or rehabilitated older ones—as if the appearance of growth would somehow create the reality of growth. But development does not occur because new buildings pop up or because housing is renovated; it occurs because *people* begin creating something of economic value, earning income, and reinvesting in the creation of more value. The most attractive housing development or urban renewal project will create no real growth if it is filled with or surrounded by people who are unable to generate economic activity.

The underlying problem in poor communities is not poor housing, it is an absence of economic activity. Healthy communities, according to Robert Woodson of the National Center for Neighborhood Enterprise, generate roughly 250 new businesses a year for every 100,000 residents. Low-income black and Hispanic communities generate *three*.[31] Hence the primary goal of community development should not be to redistribute income or to improve housing, but to redistribute economic activity: ownership, investment, and employment.

Business start-ups are only one aspect of economic activity, of course. In urban ghettos, housing is often the greatest economic resource—after the untapped potential of community residents. In this sense, state programs that invest in developing the capacities of community organizations to build and rehabilitate housing—as in New York, Massachusetts, and other states—are an important step in the right direction. Looked at purely in terms of volume, they are still relatively insignificant. Looked at in terms of a model through which to build capacity in poor communities, they show promise. Their major flaw is their exclusive focus on housing. We need to stand current thinking on its head: rather than investing in community development organizations because they are effective vehicles with which to develop housing, we should invest in housing programs because they are (one of many) effective ways to build the capacities of community development organizations.

What would an intelligent development strategy in a poor community look like? The goal would be similar to that of economic development in general: the creation of an entrepreneurial process, a process that is generated from within and that can at some point become self-sustaining. That process would not unfold as development does in the larger economy, with heavy elements of traditional entrepreneurship and technological innovation. But an effective development strategy in a poor community would follow the same *methodological principles* as a development strategy for the broader society.

It would begin, for instance, with a careful study of the local economy. The appropriate strategy for the Mon Valley would be very different from that for the Philadelphia ghetto. Indeed, the appropriate strategy might differ from one Philadelphia ghetto to another. Some urban communities are so far gone that the best thing government can do may be to help people get out, as Nicholas Lemann argued about Chicago's South Side in his *Atlantic* series, "The Origins of the Underclass."[32] (Lemann failed to point out that such communities house a small minority of the poor.)[33] Other neighborhoods have enough social cohesion and community identity that an effective strategy might lift the entire community out of poverty. This is particularly true of ethnic neighborhoods, whose members tend to stay within the community as their lives improve, rather than departing for the suburbs. Other poor communities fall in between: they have the capacity for significant improvement, but many of those whose lives improve will inevitably leave. Communities like this function as transmission belts: they provide an inexpensive place to live while new immigrants (whether from foreign countries or from other areas of the United States) find jobs and save enough money to seek greener pastures. (When a "culture of poverty" takes over, the transmission belt breaks down.) In such communities, our expectations must be realistic. We cannot expect to lift the entire community out of poverty, for even as we succeed, the success stories will leave and be replaced by new, impoverished arrivals.

An effective development strategy would also seek to wholesale: to change the structure of the local economy. Retailing is obviously necessary in a poor community, because the private market is taking capital out of the community, not putting it in. To reverse the process, significant public investments are necessary. But government can make those investments in ways that also pull in private capital—through the use of public-private partnerships, tax incentives, regulatory power, and quid pro quos.

The integration of economic and social programs is particularly important in poor communities. An in-depth study of revitalization strategies undertaken by the American Enterprise Institute found that efforts which lacked this dual focus usually failed.[34] In healthy communities, social structures such as the family, churches, informal neighborhood networks, and voluntary organizations reinforce stability. They discourage crime and encourage marriage, education, and work. But in many poor communities, particularly the black ghettos, these structures have given way. In the Chicago neighborhoods Lemann profiled in the *Atlantic,* gangs had become the strongest force.

Most antipoverty programs are classic spending strategies: they provide income maintenance, or they construct buildings. Much more effective are *investments* in the capacities of poor people—to hold jobs, to create businesses, to improve the housing stock, and to build neighborhood organizations. Similarly, effective development efforts focus on building the capacity of local institutions and individuals. The principal actors in the development process must come from within the community. Outsiders can help, but unless local community members are in the driver's seat, little more than charity is possible.

While they must be local, effective development programs must also be comprehensive. In a community that is caught in a downward spiral, development strategies that attack only one or two problems—only drugs and crime, or only business formation and housing—will often be overwhelmed by a sea of other problems. Appropriate scale is equally critical—and often missing in antipoverty programs. Once viable local organizations are in place, the public sector must be prepared to make significant investments. In a poor community, government must create the minimal market conditions necessary to give local entrepreneurs and development organizations a chance to succeed.

Finally, effective development programs have market feedback mechanisms and operate with long-term perspectives. They are responsive to changing local market conditions; if one strategy fails, they have the flexibility to try another. At the same time, they have enough capital and enough commitment from government to try a series of approaches, until they find those that work. If government demands results within five years and pulls the financial plug when that does not happen, no development strategy will succeed.

In sum, then, the ideal community development strategy would build comprehensive development organizations, each tailored to the realities of the local community. These institutions would have significant resources. They would focus on both economic and social problems. Their goals would be investment, rather than spending. They would leverage as much private investment as possible. They would seek to build the capacity of local people and institutions. They would have built-in market feedback mechanisms. And they would have the capital and political commitment to remain in place for the long haul.

Community Development Corporations

In this country, the closest things to the model described above are the best of the community development corporations. Previous chapters have described a few of these: the North Side Civic Development Council, in Pittsburgh; the St. Nicholas Neighborhood Preservation Corporation, in Brooklyn; Chicanos por la Causa, in Arizona. Most CDCs are not comprehensive: they focus primarily on housing rehabilitation, tenant organizing, and related activities. Some add services such as job training, care for the elderly, and remedial education, usually on contract with state and local programs. But a few of the largest CDCs also do economic development work.

In Vermont, the Northern Community Investment Corporation has developed more than $13.5 million worth of real estate and invested in more than 165 businesses, including a once dormant shoe factory that by 1987 employed 240 workers.[35] In Mississippi, the Delta Foundation and its subsidiary organizations own for-profit manufacturing companies in the apparel, metalworking, and electronics industries; a farmers' cooperative; a radio station; and a restaurant. They operate a venture-capital fund that has invested in more than 35 firms; and in 1986 they opened an incubator for women entrepreneurs.[36]

In large urban areas, CDCs are normally based in one community, rather than the entire city. Because most urban residents assume that they will work outside their neighborhood, they build CDCs, not to create jobs, but to strengthen the community fabric—through housing rehabilitation, social service programs, and anticrime efforts. But occasionally even urban CDCs tackle economic development, particularly when they have access to significant government or private-sector funding. Perhaps the most famous urban CDC is the Bedford Stuyvesant Restoration Corporation, launched by Robert Kennedy and others in 1967. With federal funding of up to $4 million a year (until 1981, when the Reagan administration eliminated the Community Services Administration), the Restoration Corporation built a supermarket and a 200,000-square-foot retail and office complex; brought an IBM manufacturing facility to Bedford Stuyvesant; provided loans and technical assistance to 130 local businesses; created a recording company and an "Off Off Broadway" theater; produced a successful Broadway play; renovated thousands of units of housing; and hired thousands of youths.[37]

The most successful CDCs meet a number of the methodological principles laid out above: they are tailored to the needs of their community; they invest rather than spending; they integrate economic and social programs; they build local capacity; they invest with a long-term perspective; and their boards, which are typically made up of community residents and local business and community leaders, operate as effective feedback mechanisms. A few CDCs are also somewhat comprehensive: they work simultaneously in economic development, housing renovation, job training, and other areas.

There are two limits to the work of even the best CDCs, however. First, they do very little wholesaling. Rather than changing private investment patterns, they *substitute* for private-sector investment. Second, they seldom operate on the scale necessary to have a serious impact. Where they have begun to make progress, federal, state, and local governments have not followed through with the sizable investments necessary to take maximum advantage of the capacity they have built. The federal government has eliminated the Community Services Administration, which provided core funding to about 40 large CDCs. The budget of HUD, which once provided a great deal of project funding for CDCs, has been cut from $30 billion in 1980 to $9.4 billion in 1987.[38] Other federal agencies provide some project funding, and state and local governments have also begun to provide limited subsidies. But the amounts are still quite small. "In the eighties you've got a lot of organizations, a lot of capacity, and very little money," says Tom Miller, who directs a Ford Foundation unit that often invests in CDC projects.

Because of these limitations, even the best CDCs rarely have enough impact to kick off a development process that lifts their community into the economic mainstream (or helps a substantial segment of the population get into that mainstream and move out of the community). Most CDCs make a small but appreciable dent in the quality of life—particularly the quality of housing—in their communities. A few are successful enough to counteract the downward spiral and stabilize a poor community. But rarely do they create an upward spiral, in which the market begins investing in the community again.

CDCs, in sum, are valuable but imperfect resources. If we are to take full advantage of their capacities, we must begin to invest significant amounts in them, and we must find a way to move them into the wholesaling business.

To achieve these goals, the foundation world has begun to create a series of "intermediary" organizations, which raise money from corporations, foundations, and governments and invest it in CDCs and their projects. The largest of these is the Local Initiatives Support Corporation (LISC), launched by the Ford Foundation and six major corporations in 1980. LISC has created local intermediary organizations in 23 cities, two states, and two regions (Pennsylvania's Mon Valley and eastern North Carolina). These organizations, jointly financed by LISC and local foundations, corporations, and governments, provide technical assistance and grants to CDCs. In concert with local banks and other financial institutions, they also make loans. With assets of more than $100 million, LISC even has plans to create a subsidiary that would buy up CDC loans and resell them to institutional investors, to make more private capital available to CDCs.[39]

"LISC deals are a curious blend of social investment and business discipline," says Peter Goldmark, a former cabinet officer under Hugh Carey and an active member of the LISC board. "LISC builds the capacity of CDCs to structure their deals in business terms, and that makes corporations and bankers comfortable. The lender has the satisfaction of making a loan, getting repaid, and contributing to the community at the same time. LISC-sponsored deals provide a systematic way of linking corporate capital to neighborhood rebuilding."[40]

The Development Bank Model

As we try to take the CDC model up a dimension—to give it greater resources, more wholesaling capacity, and a more comprehensive development focus—we could learn a great deal from an experiment conducted by a small group of activists-turned-bankers in Chicago. This group, which in 1973 bought a bank on Chicago's South Side, has turned around a black ghetto that was headed for the bottom. Government has been only marginally involved in the effort, but it has an enormous amount to learn from the results.[41]

The story begins in the late 1960s, when a young banker named Ron Grzywinski ran a small bank in Hyde Park, home of the University of Chicago. Adlai Stevenson III, who went on to the U.S. Senate and two losing bids for the Illinois governorship, was state treasurer. Searching for a way to help the ghettos, Stevenson decided to deposit state funds in Illinois banks that agreed to create units specializing in minority business lending. (This was the first state "linked deposit" program.)[42] Because Grzywinski and his colleagues were serious about minority business lending, they outperformed Chicago's larger banks.

The experience led them to think further about what role a bank could play in urban revitalization. Grzywinski left the bank and put together a model for a new development institution. Now called the Shorebank Corporation, it has four pieces: a bank, a venture capital fund, a real estate development corporation, and a community organization much like a CDC.

Grzywinski recruited a group of investors—foundations and wealthy philanthropists—and bought a bank a few miles to the south of Hyde Park. The neighborhood, South Shore, had changed from a 98 percent white to 98 percent black community in the preceding decade. It was the perfect community for the experiment, because it was not yet too far gone to help. As a white neighborhood, it had been middle and upper-middle class, with

single-family homes of all sizes and gracious, red brick apartment buildings built in the 1920s. Despite the racial turnover, it was still perhaps one-
third middle class and one-third working class.[43]

For all its amenities, however, South Shore was clearly headed for the
bottom. "There were no loans being made," recalls James Lowell, community affairs manager for the Federal Reserve Board. "The neighborhood
was going to lose its park, because the city felt it was just going to be a
crime hazard. The shoreline was becoming a disaster area. A lot of those
old, beautiful buildings were just crumbling. And it looked like it was on
the steepest slide."

Grzywinski and his colleagues plunged ahead with a variety of aggressive lending programs: single-family mortgages, small-business loans, and
consumer loans. Even though no other bank or savings and loan would
offer a mortgage in the neighborhood, South Shore bank had no trouble
with its single-family mortgages. By 1980, it had not foreclosed on one
loan, and other banks and S&L's had decided to enter the market.

Most of the bank's other early efforts failed. Between 1974 and 1980, it
loaned $6.7 million and provided heavy technical support to small busi-
nesses. Outside of loans to McDonald's franchises, the results were dismal.[44] The bank survived its first five years primarily through the invention
of what it called "development deposits": large, market-rate deposits made
by institutions and wealthy individuals who shared the bank's social goals.
By 1981, this new money accounted for almost a quarter of the bank's
deposits.[45]

As the bank groped for a successful development strategy, it became
clear that the key to stabilizing the neighborhood was not offering single-
family mortgages or lending to black merchants, but rehabilitating the
apartment buildings that housed 70 percent of South Shore's 80,000 people. At the time, financial institutions were not offering mortgages on
apartment buildings in Chicago's poor, black neighborhoods. Encouraged
by their experience with single-family mortgages, South Shore Bank's
managers decided to try. Slowly, carefully, they began lending to neighborhood people who wanted to buy apartment buildings. They started
with three- and six-unit buildings, then gradually moved up. They made
loans only in South Shore, and only to landlords who agreed to rehabilitate
their buildings.

The strategy worked. When neighborhood residents began borrowing
to buy run-down buildings, it was a new, and often frightening, experience. But as they filled up one building with paying tenants, they often
bought another, and then another. Today South Shore has a core of perhaps 50 active housing entrepreneurs, some of whom own as many as ten
buildings. They have learned the trade; some have even taught themselves
Spanish to communicate with their low-cost crews; and they have invested

in the neighborhood's primary resource, its housing stock. In the process, they have kicked off a development process that has its own momentum, that needs no government subsidies or special programs.

By 1987, the bank had made more than $35 million in mortgage and rehab loans on more than two hundred buildings—close to a quarter of all apartment buildings in South Shore.[46] The impact has been dramatic. Driving the tree-lined streets, one sees elegant courtyard buildings that would fit well into the tonier North Side neighborhoods. The brick is freshly sandblasted; the grounds are immaculate; wrought-iron fences and gates lend the old buildings an air of grace. There are still pockets of decay, but the better blocks bring to mind a white, well-to-do community in the 1940s, not an all-black inner-city neighborhood in the 1980s.

Shorebank's other subsidiaries have also been successful. Using heavy government subsidies, the real estate development corporation put together the largest scattered-site rehab project in Illinois history, involving 20 buildings and 446 units of low- and moderate-income housing. It is also developing an eight-acre shopping center, with a well-known supermarket chain as an anchor.

Shorebank's Neighborhood Institute has done housing rehabilitation, job training and placement, remedial education, and a training program for women who want to go into business for themselves. In 1987, it began a radical experiment based on a model developed in Bangladesh, in which small loans are granted to low-income people to go into business for themselves—starting day-care operations, word-processing businesses, cleaning services, and so forth.[47] In 1988 the Neighborhood Institute plans to develop a small business incubator.

The South Shore story is not one of unqualified success. One or two pockets of the community have shown no improvement, and the problems of crime, drugs, and poor schools have always been beyond the reach of the bank. Shorebank has yet to prove that it can successfully do business development in the neighborhood, other than in real estate. All that said, its work remains one of the most dramatic inner-city success stories of the past 25 years. Fifteen years ago, crime in South Shore was skyrocketing, owners were walking away from their buildings, and nearly a third of the neighborhood's large apartment buildings were tax delinquent, on their way to abandonment.[48] Since then, the bank has made more than $90 million in loans, a good portion of them to people who had never before borrowed from a financial institution.[49] The bank's sister companies have channeled more than $50 million in other funds, public and private, into the community. A third of the neighborhood's apartment buildings have been rehabilitated, tax delinquencies have fallen sharply, and the real estate market is as active as in any other part of the city.

The Shorebank Corporation has succeeded in reversing the disinvestment process; whereas capital once flowed out of South Shore, it now flows in. It has kicked off a self-sustaining development process—at least in the housing market—by releasing the energies of the local people and supporting their entrepreneurial efforts. And it has done all this without gentrifying the neighborhood. These are stunning achievements, given the reality of black, inner-city America.

In Arkansas, Shorebank will try to adapt its model to a rural economy, drawing on the experience of the Grameen Bank in Bangladesh, entrepreneurial training programs in Europe, and several rural development efforts in this country.[50] One of the most successful of the latter is the Kentucky Highlands Investment Corporation (KHIC), which is remarkably similar in philosophy to Shorebank. Located in Harlan County, Kentucky, an area long famous for labor violence in its coal-mining towns, KHIC was launched during the late 1960s as a federally funded CDC. Tom Miller, who ran it (the same Tom Miller who now runs part of the Ford Foundation), decided to use the federal money primarily to create a for-profit venture capital corporation. Because most people in Appalachian Kentucky had long since given up on anything resembling entrepreneurship, Miller used venture capital to bring start-up companies into the region—companies that were ready to launch elsewhere, but could not raise the capital they needed. Kentucky Highlands provided equity investments, loans, and hands-on guidance to a series of small, labor-intensive businesses. One made kayaks, another sleeping bags, a third stuffed animals, a fourth bodies for coal trucks.[51]

Over the years, Miller and his colleagues added a Small Business Investment Company, a real estate development corporation, and a capital corporation that makes business loans. After 15 years of work and $11 million in federal dollars (a subsidy that came to an end in 1981), it finally became clear that the strategy worked. "If you look at the nature of the problem, I don't think it's surprising that it took that long," says Miller. "We're talking about a brute force strategy, and it takes a long time to get that rock moving uphill."

By 1986, KHIC was turning profits of about $1 million a year and launching roughly two new businesses each year. Firms backed by KHIC had created 1,250 jobs, a number that was growing by about 200 a year.[52] In 1980, before Kentucky Highlands began turning a profit, Miller calculated the "return on taxpayers' investment" from the federal subsidies. Miller's method calculated the corporate taxes paid by each KHIC-funded start-up, the personal taxes paid by employees who had previously been unemployed, and the savings in welfare spending on those who had previously collected welfare. It included no "soft" factors, such as the psychological impact of successful businesses in a region where welfare had become common. In 1980, the return was 18.7 percent, and in previous years it had gone as high as 25 percent.[53]

The Shorebank Corporation and Kentucky Highlands represent a conceptual breakthrough in the fight against poverty. They are among the first development vehicles ever created in this country that are truly appropriate to the needs—particularly the scale of needs—found in poor communities. Shorebank has both its deposit base and, because of its size and competence, access to significant public funds. Kentucky Highlands has $12 million in assets. Whereas CDCs must spend an enormous amount of time hustling grants, both Shorebank and KHIC can sustain themselves through their own profits. Because they have this capital base—and because they are *financial institutions*—they are also far better than CDCs at igniting community self-confidence and encouraging local investment.

KHIC and Shorebank are also at risk in the marketplace—hence driven to invest in winners—in a way that few CDCs are. Most CDCs invest in the people of their community, but without a great deal of thought to who might be the most successful entrepreneurs. A bank or venture capital firm takes an entirely different attitude. Because it will go out of business if it loses money, it seeks out those in the community who have the skills and toughness to succeed in the marketplace—to build a business, to turn a profit, and to reinvest. Similarly, those with entrepreneurial drive seek out the bank or venture capital operation, in a way they would never seek out a CDC.

"Our competitors in other areas [other federally funded CDCs] had their hearts in exactly the right places and wanted it just as badly as we did, but they were coming at it from the wrong perspective," says Fred Beste, a venture capitalist who spent close to a decade at KHIC. "They were coming at it from the social and the emotional perspective, and we were coming at it from the cold, calculating, venture capital investment perspective. Tom Miller felt that business talent was more important than the desire to save the world, and that's where the dividing line was. If anything, the other CDCs were more noble than we, but they didn't have much of a chance. They would launch something, which is very easy to do—all it takes is money—and delude themselves with the fact that there were 50 jobs created. But the company never made a profit, and eventually the money ran out."

"If you want to make loans," adds Mary Houghton, one of Shorebank's officers, "you've got to make loans where the borrowers are really going to be able to take advantage of markets. Most CDCs have an ideology—it may be a very good ideology—but they really do have an overlay of social objectives that they want to achieve. And they have a relatively open process, so that people can express that ideology and make sure it's getting achieved. And it just won't work. The decision making has got to be based on how the market works, not what's good and right. Because if you let what's good and right add into it you'll have high loss rates."

By investing in local entrepreneurs, Shorebank and Kentucky Highlands also have the advantage of building capacity throughout the community. Most CDCs build primarily their own capacity. They become the entrepreneurs, the housing developers, the investors. With the exception of those that spin off or invest in businesses, like the Delta Foundation, they do not help other individuals and groups become entrepreneurs.

Finally, a private financial institution has a far greater capacity to wholesale—to change the capital flows into the community from the larger economy—than a CDC. Unlike a CDC, Shorebank can go to the private financial community as a peer, to propose a joint project or an investment.

Some readers may take this line of reasoning as an argument for the supremacy of for-profit, private businesses over nonprofit or public-sector institutions. This is the traditional conservative line: the private sector can do it better. But Shorebank Corporation and Kentucky Highlands are *not* traditional private businesses, and the traditional private sector is incapable of doing what they have done. They are classic *third-sector* institutions. They do not exist to make a profit; they exist to solve social problems. They use the methodology of the private sector to achieve public goals. Their funding base comes from government, in the case of Kentucky Highlands, or philanthropy, in the case of Shorebank. It is the creative tension between their social goals and the bottom line that makes them so effective. If they did not have the social goals, they would not be investing in South Shore or Appalachian Kentucky; if they did not have a bottom line, they would not be driven to find the potential entrepreneurs within their communities.

The important distinction is not between for-profit and nonprofit institutions; it is between institutions that are at risk in the marketplace—and that must therefore make successful investments to survive—and those that operate on subsidies and grants, and therefore will survive regardless of their investment performance. One of Shorebank's subsidiaries is a nonprofit, and parts of the new Southern Development Bancorporation, in Arkansas, will be nonprofit. But these institutions still operate with a bottom line; like a nonprofit hospital or university, they must balance revenues and expenditures to stay alive.

Were Shorebank and KHIC traditional private-sector businesses, they would not be in South Shore or Appalachia. When Grzywinski and his investors bought South Shore Bank, they thought they could make enough profit to lure other private entrepreneurs to follow their lead and buy ghetto banks. Fifteen years later, they know better. "I think we've learned what the limits are, what a traditional commercial bank can and cannot do," says Houghton. "Increasingly, we realize that if you want to do this kind of activity, you have to be specialized professionals, and the operation has to be subsidized at some level. Since most commercial banks are owned by people who are maximizing profits, it's unlikely that they're going to run crack professional units doing this kind of stuff. They could, but it's got to be a profound commitment. If not, they'd get it all wrong. They just wouldn't be able to make the qualitative judgments, they wouldn't have the local knowledge, they wouldn't get their hands dirty. Everything would have to be by the book."

Similarly, government cannot do what Shorebank and Kentucky Highlands have done. Government might have occasional successes if it created public development banks on the Shorebank and Kentucky Highlands models, but the norm would be far different. Government institutions do not have the same bottom line: they can always ask for more capital if they lose money (as many federally funded CDCs constantly did). Hence they are less driven to find those entrepreneurs who have a real chance of surviving in the marketplace.

Another factor is credibility. "One of the problems we faced was the whole taint of being a federal grantee," explains Beste. "We were dealing with bankers and lawyers and people who stood to benefit our ventures, and if they saw us as just another federal program, we'd be instantly labeled incompetent, unbusinesslike, people who think with their hearts, and they'd be sure they were going to lose their money. It was death. So we had our pitch down to a tee. We never used the terms *grantee, nonprofit, federal agency,* or *Appalachia.*"

Private financial institutions also inspire more confidence among the poor. More important, people look at banks and venture funds, not as programs designed to do something *for them,* as they might look at government programs, but as sources of credit as they try to do something for themselves.

Another issue is government's inability to pay people enough to compete with the private sector for talent and expertise. Michigan's Treasury Department and Strategic Fund, for instance, have been plagued by this problem. "It would be a terrific mistake—and a lot of people have fallen into this trap—to hire on the cheap," says Beste. "Because you get what you pay for."

Finally, government institutions, like all monopolies, are simply more bureaucratic, less flexible, and less efficient than institutions that operate in a competitive marketplace. Government would be likely to take a "cookie cutter" approach, using the same model in all poor communities. If past experience is any indicator, public development banks would also be tempted to focus on the large-scale investments that catch the public eye, such as big housing complexes or shopping centers. These are important, and Shorebank's officers believe their model cannot succeed without large infusions of public capital to make such projects feasible. But public development banks would be less likely to do the small-scale, piece-by-piece investing that is also important—the kind of investing that led to the emergence of a core of real estate entrepreneurs in South Shore.

If we are to pursue an effective development strategy in poor communities, neither the public nor the private sector is the best vehicle. We need a new creature here, a creature that lives between the public and private sectors. We have created thousands of CDCs; we have created third-sector financial institutions in many states; if we are to learn from South Shore Bank and Kentucky Highlands, we need to add yet another third-sector model, the community development bank.

Government's Role in Creating Community Development Banks

The role of government is not to run community development banks, but to act as a catalyst in their creation and survival. The greatest difficulty will be finding enough people with the combination of expertise and commitment necessary to make such institutions work. Hence, government's most important role might be to issue a call to arms to legitimize such work, as John F. Kennedy did with the Peace Corps. But governments could also provide start-up capital, as Pennsylvania and Michigan did with seed funds and BIDCOs, to get community development banks off the ground. They could provide subsidies along the way, to allow these institutions to invest in segments of the market that would otherwise not generate profits. And they could use their tax and regulatory powers to steer private capital into community development banks, as Massachusetts did to get the life insurance industry to create a development institution.[54]

The base on which to build already exists: CDCs and their intermediary organizations. If state government has to choose which communities get development banks, we will start with half a dozen in each major city, all of them with too little capital. Inevitably, most will fail, and the experiment will be discredited. State governments would be wiser to broker deals with existing intermediary organizations: the state might provide partial grants to create several development banks, if the intermediary agreed to match the funds and shift its focus from housing to more comprehensive strategies. The intermediaries might solicit applications from CDCs to launch development banks, either by buying an existing bank or by creating a new institution.

The specific model would vary from community to community. In particular, urban communities, rural areas, and depressed industrial regions would require very different vehicles. But overall, the ideal institution would be something like a holding company with a series of subsidiaries. In addition to a bank, the options would include a venture capital fund; a BIDCO or other business lending institution; a business assistance staff; a commercial real estate development firm; a housing development corporation; a CDC; a job-training corporation; and an entrepreneurial training subsidiary.

The CDC would concentrate primarily on "social" programs: job training, remedial education, crime prevention, tenant organizing, elderly care, and youth programs such as conservation corps, school-to-work programs, and pregnancy prevention efforts. A CDC might even work with the tenants of local public housing complexes to organize self-management and self-repair systems.[55]

Job-training corporations might be modeled on Great Britain's Information and Technology Centers, which offer training in high-technology careers to unemployed youths aged 16 to 18. These centers, which were developed by two teachers who had given up on the public schools, offer practical training in basic computing, microelectronics (including repair and maintenance), and office work. They boast job placement rates of 76 percent, and some have even set up viable service and repair businesses.[56]

For the entrepreneurial training component, the model might be the Hawaii Entrepreneurship Training and Development Institute (HETADI), another third-sector organization. The idea of training low-income people to start businesses often elicits skepticism. But as this country's history has demonstrated, entrepreneurs often spring from the bottom rungs of society. George Kanahele, chairman of HETADI, puts it this way: "Entrepreneurs do not usually come from the cradles of soft, rich living; they often come from the pits of disaffection, rebellion, and struggle. They are people who have lost their jobs, or are in a low-paying, dead-end job; or who have had so many jobs that they never want to work for anybody again. . . .

"This same type of person is often found among the unemployed or underemployed. . . . The unemployment situation ought to be viewed as a breeding ground, rather than a burial site, of entrepreneurial motivations and ambitions."[57]

Kanahele's program recruits people through advertising and local employment offices, then screens them with tests and interviews to pick out the potential entrepreneurs. About a third of those who apply are selected for the program's eight- to twelve-week workshops, during which they receive training, develop their own business plans, and do market research. Some graduates go right into business; others serve internships with mentor firms, which help them get started; still others are placed in transitional jobs with established businesses, to gain the experience and skills they will need when they go out on their own. In all cases a trainer from HETADI continues to work with the person for anywhere from one to three years.[58]

Another model is the Women's Economic Development Corporation (WEDCO), a private, nonprofit operation in Minneapolis-St. Paul. Like Shorebank, Kentucky Highlands, and HETADI, WEDCO is a third-sector institution that operates with a marketplace perspective. Of the more than 2,500 people it has counseled since 1983, it has offered its training services to only half. Under the training program, women write their own business plans, loan proposals, two-year cash flow projections, and marketing strategies. WEDCO has nurtured close relationships with three local banks, and when a woman is ready, WEDCO sends her to the banks to apply for a loan. The result is a parade of low-income women receiving bank loans (which average about $10,000) to go into business. WEDCO also has its own small seed capital fund, plus a growth fund for successful businesses that are ready to expand.[59]

Close to half of WEDCO's clients have entered the program with annual incomes of less than $7,000, and almost a quarter have been on welfare or food stamps. Yet every client signs a contract and pays a fee, from $5 an hour up to $50. "We have them all pay because it establishes a business relationship," says WEDCO President Kathryn Keeley. "Especially for women who've been on welfare, we must be seen as peers and consultants in a business relationship—rather than being their welfare workers." Besides, when women are paying for the time, they appear on time, don't miss appointments, and don't come in unless their homework is finished.

"There's a stereotype that people on welfare are not creative or entrepreneurs," Keeley adds. "It's just not true. We find many do have ideas; all they need is support and a little leeway in the system."[60]

There are many other successful models that could be integrated into comprehensive local development institutions. All of these programs could of course be set up independently, by state and local governments, foundations, and community organizations. Where they have cropped up so far, that has been the pattern. But when they are done piecemeal—when an entrepreneurial training program exists in one community, a housing rehabilitation effort in another—there is no synergy. The positive strides made in housing or small-business development are often overwhelmed by the negative movement in other areas.

With a comprehensive development institution, virtually all problems in a community can be attacked at once. When that happens, each step forward reinforces all others, and the entire task becomes far less overwhelming. If a neighborhood watch lowers the crime rate, people will be more willing to invest in property; hence a mortgage-lending operation will succeed. If youths begin repairing computers rather than loitering on street corners, and a shopping center opens, community members will shop in the neighborhood—and new retail stores will survive.

Comprehensive local institutions also give governments at all levels a common vehicle through which to channel their programs. It is far easier to create integrated local development institutions than to integrate a dozen different government bureaucracies.

This may all have the ring of utopia. But as Ron Grzywinski and his colleagues have demonstrated, it can be done. The third sector exists; we simply need to learn how to make better use of it. "Some time in the last century or before, we figured out ways to create universities and hospitals as major not-for-profit organizations that were capitalized either with public funds or private funds, to achieve a public purpose," says Grzywinski. "We created them in a way that they would be substantial, permanent, and in the marketplace. They have to be managed like businesses. One could ask, why don't we create development institutions the same way?"

The Federal Role

Community development and welfare reform are fundamentally local tasks. Because conditions vary radically from one poor community to another, solutions must vary as well. Yet most of the money in both of these arenas must come from the federal government, particularly if we are to make any progress in the poorest states. Hence community development and welfare reform are classic examples of arenas in which programs should be run at the state and local level, but with significant federal funding.

During the New Deal, federal social programs such as AFDC, unemployment insurance, and workmen's compensation were typically set up to be administered by the states.[61] But during the 1960s, Great Society activists, citing what they called the George Wallace syndrome, bridled at the thought of giving governors and state legislators more money or power. As a result, they created hundreds of new "categorical grant" programs, which required states and localities to spend federal money in precise ways. With lengthy, detailed regulations, they sought to hem in the state and local officials they viewed with such suspicion.[62] This approach led to intense frustration on the part of state and local officials, who had to deal with nightmarishly complex regulations and paper work. It also drove them to create narrow programs according to federal standards, rather than comprehensive programs that responded to local priorities and needs.

Conservatives responded by advocating that categorical grants be consolidated into broad block grants, and Presidents Nixon and Reagan succeeded in pushing a few block grants through a grudging Congress. But as liberals were quick to point out, block grants had their own problem: they came with *no* strings attached. State government has changed dramatically since the 1960s, thanks to the Supreme Court's "one man, one vote" rule in 1962 and the growth and professionalization of state governments during the 1960s and 1970s.[63] But the capacities of different state governments still vary widely. With block grants, wasteful, ineffective state programs get the same priority as sophisticated, innovative strategies.

Clearly, we need a new model. Perhaps the most promising approach is the "challenge grant" model used by Pennsylvania's Ben Franklin Partnership (and MITI's Technopolis program). Under this approach, state and local governments would have to compete with one another for block grants, based largely on the quality of their programs. The federal government would set up broad criteria by which to judge state and local applications. These criteria would include several factors: the degree of need (the unemployment rate, the poverty rate, the median income, and so on); the principles upon which state programs were built (whether they whole-saled, whether they favored investment over spending, whether they created comprehensive but decentralized development institutions, etc.); and their performance (placement rates, leveraging of private capital, number of jobs created, etc.).

This kind of model might work in a number of arenas. One challenge grant would be for community development, another for comprehensive employment and training programs for welfare recipients. But a third might focus on economic development, a fourth on job training (a broadened, better-funded JTPA program), and a fifth on social adjustment systems. (Some challenge grants, particularly the community development grant, might go to both state and local governments.) The federal share of funding could vary, depending upon the difficulty of leveraging private capital in a particular arena and region. For instance, Washington might finance far more of the total costs of community development programs than of economic development programs. It might also provide a greater proportion of the total funding for poor states than for affluent states.

Broad challenge grants of this kind would create incentives for states to act, but they would leave the job of designing and running programs to the states. By building performance criteria into the funding formula, the federal government could exercise some quality control, as the Ben Franklin Partnership does, without dictating program structure and content. And by making the states compete based on rational criteria, Washington could drive them toward the creation of comprehensive, sophisticated strategies, as MITI did with its Technopolis program. These challenge grants would constitute the heart of a new partnership between the federal government and state and local governments.

PART III

THE POLITICS

10
THE EMERGING POLITICAL PARADIGM

When the dust settled after the Reagan landslide in 1984, a paradox emerged. Although the president had won 49 of 50 states, his party counted only sixteen of the nation's fifty governors among its ranks. Stranger still, in Reagan's strongest areas—the South and the Rocky Mountain states—Democratic governors outnumbered Republicans by sixteen to three. Democrats even dominated state legislative houses and mayors' offices by two-to-one margins.

This contrast between a thriving grass-roots party and its national counterpart was too much for the Democratic governors. One after another they rose to demand that the party turn away from its traditional path, so obviously repudiated by voters, and look to the states for a new direction. A handful of the most prominent Democratic governors waged a two-month campaign to name the next Democratic National Committee chairman—and failing that, created their own group, the Democratic Leadership Council.

Two years later, something similar happened in the Republican party. Frustrated by his party's meager numbers, Tennessee's Republican Governor Lamar Alexander invited a handful of his gubernatorial colleagues, a few Republican congressmen, and several campaign strategists to his retreat in the Smoky Mountains, to come up with an agenda for the future of the Republican party. The Reagan revolution had focused largely on a negative agenda, at least on the domestic side: tax cuts, spending cuts, and the elimination of unnecessary regulations. Alexander and his colleagues, who included Richard Thornburgh, wanted to come up with part two of the Reagan revolution: a positive agenda that focused on the creative use of government, particularly at the state level. "If Reagan Stage I was an end to the smothering excesses of government from Washington," they said, "Reagan Stage II is a new beginning for creative excellence in government close to the people."[1]

The national party ignored their efforts. But with a campaign committee led by Thornburgh and New Hampshire Governor John Sununu, the Republican Governors Association built its entire 1986 strategy around the new theme. They asked Republican governors to submit examples of their best programs, then put them together in a glossy brochure that depicted Republicans as innovative activists in education reform, economic development, welfare reform, even environmental protection. They also raised a significant war chest for Republican challengers. Many of those challengers used the innovation theme, and when the dust had cleared, the Republicans had picked up eight governors' seats. In the Senate, where Republican candidates were inevitably tied to the Reagan administration, the party lost seven seats—and control of the Senate.

"It didn't happen by accident," says Thornburgh. "The issues and the programs—the ideology, if you will—that these Republicans presented to the electorate at the state level in 1986 were vastly different from those put out by the Reagan administration and the senatorial candidates."

When they let their guard down, a few governors will admit that they feel philosophically closer to their gubernatorial colleagues from the other side of the aisle than to their Republican or Democratic colleagues in the national party. When I have asked governors in both parties why they have been successful, they have virtually all talked about the same things: fiscal responsibility; the clear priority they have placed on economic growth and opportunity, particularly through new forms of cooperation among government, business, labor, and the education community; their independence from special-interest groups; and their commitment to reform of basic systems such as education, health care, and welfare, regardless of opposition from those interest groups.

Two months after the Mondale debacle, Bill Clinton and Richard Lamm, then governor of Colorado, wrote an op-ed piece that summed up the views of many Democratic governors. "The struggle to reshape the Democratic party must begin in earnest, if the party is to survive," they warned. The swing voters who decide every national election—"hardworking, open-minded, middle-class Americans—increasingly see the Democratic party as a party without credible programs to promote economic growth at home and peace abroad; a party concerned about equally dividing the economic pie through taxing and spending rather than expanding economic opportunity for everyone; a party unable or unwilling to say no to its particular interest groups, even when the public interest demands it."

Clinton and Lamm offered three basic principles on which the party should be rebuilt. "Our No. 1 priority in the 1980s, as in the 1930s, should be to get America's economy growing again. The social agenda must remain strong, but we must put a creative economic agenda first. . . . Second, the Democratic party must learn what New York Mayor Fiorello La-Guardia called the most important lesson of politics: how to say no to your friends. . . . Third, the Democratic party should take the lead in reforming the very systems it had the foresight to initiate. Clearly, many of these systems cannot be sustained as they now exist. Medicare officials project astronomical deficits; health care costs are soaring; farm programs are unsustainable."[2]

On the Republican side, governors such as Thornburgh and New Jersey's Thomas Kean have been saying remarkably similar things. It is no surprise when a Republican talks about fiscal responsibility and economic growth. But they also talk about public-private partnerships, innovative uses of government, and education reform. Kean identified the three priorities of his second term as jobs, environmental protection, and education reform.[3] When I asked Thornburgh what the next president's priorities should be, he talked about our international trade problem, education reform, job training, new partnerships between the federal government and state governments, and new partnerships between the federal government and business.

What we may be seeing in the laboratories of democracy is the emergence of a new political paradigm, tailored to the realities of the new economy. Neither of the two reigning ideologies—traditional liberalism and Reagan conservatism—speaks to the problems of the postindustrial era. Peter Drucker put it bluntly several years ago, speaking about politics not only in the United States but throughout the industrialized world. The "basic issues ahead of us," he said, "don't fit the political alignment of the nineteenth and early twentieth centuries. They do not fit liberal and conservative and socialist. The traditional parties make absolutely no sense whatever to anybody of age 30."[4]

The Demise of the New Deal Paradigm

The traditional liberal and conservative ideologies that competed within the New Deal paradigm did not fail; they simply outlived their usefulness. They evolved in response to the realities of the industrial age, and that era is over. Indeed, few political ideologies have ever experienced such enormous success as New Deal liberalism. Propelled by the global expansion of American power during and after World War II, New Deal liberalism stabilized the economy, unleashed three decades of furious growth, and turned a nation that had been two-thirds poor into a nation that was two-thirds middle class. It took a century and a half for per capita income in the United States to reach $3,500 (in 1984 dollars). It took just 25 more years, after World War II, for that figure to double. Meanwhile, under an international economic system created largely by American liberals, Western Europe and Japan grew at an even faster clip, while much of the Third World also began to develop.

By its success, New Deal liberalism ensured its own demise. It so fundamentally changed both American society and the international economy that it unleashed a host of new forces with which it was ill prepared to cope: Third World nationalism and economic competition abroad; racial unrest and profound cultural changes at home.

From the 1930s through the 1950s, American politics revolved around one axis: the economic issue. The Democrats stood for big spending, Keynesian financing, and active government management of the macroeconomic aggregates; the Republicans fought to stuff big government back in the bottle. On social issues, both parties took traditional, conservative positions.

In the 1960s, another axis opened up, around race and culture. Beginning with the civil rights movement, a steady drumbeat of new issues entered the mainstream of American politics: school busing, affirmative action, sexual behavior, women's rights, the "family," abortion, the environment. This new polarity did not divide America along the same lines as the economic issue had, however. Since cultural and racial liberalism are so often the products of background and education, the fissure occurred along class, not party, lines. It split the ruling Democratic majority down the middle, and the Vietnam War widened the gap.

The sudden collapse of the Democratic presidential majority was not solely a function of the new cultural axis within American politics. Had it been, the decline would have been more gradual. The other factor was Johnson's Great Society, which delivered on neither of its promises: peace in Vietnam and a solution to our social problems at home. In 1966, two years after Johnson's landslide, the Democrats lost 46 seats in the House. In 1968, Hubert Humphrey received only 43 percent of the vote—12 million fewer votes than Johnson had in 1964.[5] In 1972, George McGovern received only 38 percent. Had it not been for Watergate, Republican domination would clearly have continued throughout the 1970s.

At the congressional level, the Democrats were able to maintain their majority—in part because of Watergate, in part through their skillful use of interest-group politics. With generous entitlements and other spending programs—one for the elderly, another for blacks, a third for college students—the Democrats continued to knit together a coalition that included the poor and the middle class, the black and the white, the young and the old. When their politics had to be embodied in one candidate, the contradictions showed. But when they could run different campaigns in different districts—when John Stennis could run as a conservative and Ted Kennedy could run as a liberal—they could keep the coalition together. All they needed was enough public money to dispense.

To a significant degree, interest-group politics was a new phenomenon. During the New Deal, FDR had sought to restructure society: he had given labor the right to organize, restructured the marketplace in agriculture, and attempted to rationalize, under the ill-fated National Recovery Administration, the nation's business. His entitlement programs had primarily been universal, not focused on one or two constituencies. Social security and unemployment compensation were available to virtually anyone who worked.

During the Great Society, restructuring was out, programs for specific interest groups were in. Once the pattern was established, there was no going back. Spending for social programs grew more than twice as fast during Nixon's first five years as it had during Johnson's five years.[6] Revenue sharing was created. The food stamp budget exploded. Social security benefits were increased and indexed to inflation. Medicaid was extended to millions of new beneficiaries. Eligibility rules for welfare were relaxed. Grants and loans were extended to middle-income college students. The process had begun as an effort to help the poor. But gradually, the elderly and the middle class, who had the greatest political clout, secured more and more of the benefits.

By the early 1970s, liberalism had become a kind of caricature of itself, in the eyes of many voters. Ted Van Dyk, a former speechwriter for Hubert Humphrey and George McGovern, summed it up perfectly at a National Democratic Issues Forum in 1975, where Democratic activists gathered to discuss the future of their party. As quoted by *The Washington Monthly*, Van Dyk summarized the liberal *modus operandi* this way: "Once a social and/or economic problem is perceived, a new federal program or agency should be established to solve it. If the problem becomes intractable, the program or the agency should be given additional funding and personnel. . . . If the problem still exists, it should be studied through grants to former colleagues in the agency. If, at last, the problem begins to be solved, nonetheless leave the agency or program, its budget, and its personnel in place."[7]

Interest-group liberalism kept the congressional party together, for a time. But when inflation heated up and the public trough went dry, the glue that held the disparate Democratic constituencies together melted. While inflation ate away at people's real incomes, bracket creep and increasing payroll taxes (to finance medicare, medicaid, and higher social security benefits) sharply increased the tax burden on middle-income Americans.[8] The result was predictable: a tax revolt and a shift to the antigovernment party. Thus was the Democratic coalition finally torn asunder.

The Carter Years

Beginning in the mid-1960s, opinion polls reflected a steady deterioration of confidence in the nation's institutions, particularly its political institutions.[9] By 1973, the Vietnam War and inflation had severely undermined the faith Americans had once had in their government and their political parties. Watergate drove the final nail in the coffin.

Watergate also brought a post–New Deal, post–Great Society Democrat to the White House. After 40 years of big government, Jimmy Carter campaigned against Washington, against the federal bureaucracy, and against big spending and deficits. He understood that the voters no longer wanted traditional liberalism. That insight—combined with his southern heritage and his exploitation of the post-Watergate mood ("I will never lie to you")—earned him a narrow victory in an essentially Republican electorate.

Carter's pollster, Patrick Caddell, understood that without a new paradigm to replace New Deal liberalism, Carter would have difficulty against the Republicans' traditional free-market ideology. "I think it can be argued clearly that we are at one of those points in time when—as Marx or Hegel would have argued—neither the thesis nor the antithesis really works," Caddell wrote in a long memo to Carter before his inauguration. "To borrow from the philosophy of science, we desperately need an ideological 'paradigm' to replace the 'free market capitalist model' that we don't really want. American society does not need another 'patch-up' job; it needs some kind of direction."[10]

Caddell and Carter may have known that they needed a new paradigm, but they had no idea what it should be. They settled for a new style. In the same memo, Caddell urged that as Carter sought to work out "the new ideology," he use symbolic actions to make it clear to the public that he was "different from other politicians, not part of the establishment." Caddell recommended cutting back on "imperial frills and perks," using "fireside chats" and "town meetings" to build a sense of "intimacy with the people." Carter did all of these things, and they all worked. But what his pollster could not provide him was the new substance that eventually had to go with the new style. Carter had to deal with a Congress still dominated by interest-group liberals, yet he had to face problems interest-group liberalism could never address: double-digit inflation, stagnant productivity, an energy crisis, and, in 1979, the Iranian revolution. He failed, and that failure doomed his presidency.

Confidence in government fell to new lows. In 1967, 76 percent of the American electorate had given one of the two parties a "highly favorable" rating. By 1980, the figure had plummeted to 45 percent.[11] Only 43 percent of the electorate felt there was "an important difference in what the Republican party and the Democratic party stand for."[12] In this climate, voters swung wildly from one party to the other, or, within the parties, from one candidate to another.[13]

Meanwhile, surveys measuring public attitudes swung barely at all.

The volatility lay not in the electorate's values or opinions, but in its dissatisfaction with the candidates offered by its two political parties. As Martin Wattenberg documents in *The Decline of Political Parties,* the two parties' particular positions and images became almost irrelevant to a large majority of voters.[14] Beginning in 1968, an increasing percentage of voters held their noses and picked the lesser of two evils.

All the while, voters were abandoning the two parties in droves, shifting into the independent camp. Millions more were giving up on voting altogether. By 1980, it was as if the entire nation were searching desperately for a new face, a new answer—a new ideology. "All the anchors are being raised at the same moment in American politics, and the electoral ship is drifting as never before," said political scientist Everett Carll Ladd.[15]

The Rise of Reagan Conservatism

The only realistic alternative offered to Americans, in 1980, was the conservatism of Ronald Reagan. Reagan had been elected governor of California chiefly by posing as a man who would stand up to the ghetto and student uprisings of the midsixties. As his philosophy evolved, Reagan became almost a mirror image of the new brand of liberalism ascendant within the Democratic party, variously known as the "new politics," or McGovernism. Lulled by the boom years of the 1960s, many liberal Democrats had begun to take economic growth for granted; their causes were redistribution of income, equal opportunity, and environmental protection. Reagan embraced economic expansion, promised to roll back affirmative action and environmental regulation, and actually advocated redistributing income back *toward* the wealthy through tax cuts. Whereas many liberals had come to see government as the solution to every problem, Reagan saw government's *removal* as the solution to every problem. Whereas liberals used federal spending as the glue to hold their coalition together, Reagan used tax cuts. Whereas liberals fought to curtail America's military adventures and define a new role in the Third World, Reagan wanted to win the Vietnam War, keep the Panama Canal, and use force against Third World revolutions. On the social front, Reagan conservatives embraced "traditional values," passionately resisting the tides of change championed by the "new politics" liberals.

Reagan won the 1980 election because he offered the only serious alternative to Jimmy Carter, and the nation desperately wanted a change of course. For a time, some commentators predicted that he would transform the Republican party into the new majority party. But Reagan's brand of conservatism was a reaction to liberalism, not a program relevant to the realities of the postindustrial economy. His agenda—tax cuts, spending cuts, a regulatory rollback, and a military build-up—could only go so far before it became irrelevant. He accomplished most of what the American people wanted during his first year, and a stalemate then ensued. By 1984, his only agenda was preservation of the new status quo. In that year, 60 percent of those sampled told pollsters that Reagan's election in 1980 had been important because the country needed a new direction, but 60 percent also said that Reagan was not the person who would lead us into the future.[16]

Major party realignments have occurred regularly every 28 to 36 years throughout American history. Today, it has become clear that Reagan's election did not mark the beginning of a realignment, as some had thought, but simply one phase in a period of ideological interregnum. Political analyst Kevin Phillips, who in the late 1960s wrote *The Emerging Republican Majority*, argues that the realignment occurred when it was due, in 1968, but Watergate so muddied the waters that the Republicans never extended their presidential majority to Congress. "The five realignment periods [in American history] all shared a common pattern: in each case, the party newly ascending to power invariably controlled the White House for at least 16 of the 20 years following the watershed, and such 16- to 20-year party hegemonies have occurred only in these circumstances," Phillips writes. "By January 1989, the Republicans will have controlled the Presidency for 16 of the previous 20 years."[17]

Had Phillips compared the current period to the Progressive Era, he might have explained why the realignment was so shallow, and why it involved no consistently dominant ideology. Like the 1970s and 1980s, the Progressive Era was a time of adjustment to rapid change, in which several ideologies competed but no ruling ideology emerged. It was an era in which a new generation of political leaders emerged—the progressives— but failed to create a majority and an ideology that dominated their age.[18] Underlying their failure was the fundamental economic change that was so rapidly remaking the face of America. The Progressive Era was a time of transition, marked by rapid immigration, explosive urbanization, the growth of huge new economic entities, and shifting class alignments. It was the process of adjustment—the search for order, as one historian put it—that gave the era its distinctive character.[19] That same process, and that same search, mark our own time.

The Emerging Paradigm

If traditional liberalism was the thesis and Reagan conservatism was its antithesis, the developments in America's state capitols offer the glimmerings of a new synthesis—a paradigm that may foreshadow the *next* realignment of American politics, as progressivism foreshadowed New Deal liberalism. The thesis, in its purist form, viewed the private sector as the problem and government as the solution. The antithesis, again in its extreme form, viewed government as the problem and the private sector as the solution. The synthesis redefines the nature of both the problem and its solution. It defines the problem as our changing role in the international marketplace. It defines the solution as new roles for and new relationships between our national institutions—public sector and private, labor and management, education and business. The fundamental goal is no longer to create—or eliminate—government programs; it is to use government to change the nature of the marketplace. To boil it down to a slogan, if the thesis was government as solution and the antithesis was government as problem, the synthesis is government as partner.

The new paradigm can be described as a series of interdependent assumptions about political reality, which together form a coherent way of thinking about our problems. The first assumption is that economic growth must be our major priority, but that it can be combined with equity, environmental protection, and other social goals. Whereas interest-group liberals put their social goals first, and Reagan conservatives put growth first, many governors are beginning to understand that in the new economy, growth *requires* equity and environmental protection.

Second, and perhaps most important, the new breed of governor assumes that the real solutions lie in changing the structure of the marketplace. By the late 1960s, many liberals had come to view the market as the problem; often they saw government as a way to overcome or replace the market. If the market would not build low-income housing, government would. If the market would not bring capital into Appalachia, government would. Reagan conservatives, in contrast, wanted government out of the marketplace—a logical contradiction, given that government sets the rules that allow the marketplace to operate. Today both Democratic and Republican governors understand that the market is far more powerful than government—that government cannot "overcome" or "replace" it. But they also understand that government *shapes* the market. To solve problems, they change the rules of the marketplace, or they use government to channel the market in new directions.

A related assumption has to do with attitudes toward government bureaucracies. Today's governors search for nonbureaucratic solutions to problems; if reshaping the marketplace will not suffice, they turn to third-sector organizations. They believe that many of the large, centralized government programs created in the past—medicaid, medicare, welfare, housing programs—have been inefficient and wasteful (often because government had to buy off the private sector, as in the case of medicare and medicaid). Health care provides a good example: many traditional liberals have favored some kind of national health care system. When new paradigm governors look to expand health coverage, however, they are more inclined to turn to health maintenance organizations, so as to inject decentralization and competition, rather than new government bureaucracies, into the system.

The fourth assumption is that in the newly competitive global economy, our governments have in a sense bumped up against their fiscal limits. Every governor portrayed in this book has taken great pains to make it clear to the electorate that he is not a big spender. Even Mario Cuomo, who is portrayed by the media as a New Deal liberal, has cut taxes in every year since 1984. In 1985, the National Governors Association, which had 34 Democratic and 16 Republican members, voted in favor of a balanced budget amendment to the U.S. Constitution.[20]

Yet few of the governors are tax cutters in the Reagan mold. "We've gone beyond both where the Democrats have been and where Reagan is," says Bill Clinton. "People are not necessarily blindly antitax. What they want is the assurance that they have some opportunity to buy into the tax, to make a judgment about whether the investment is appropriate. Historically, Arkansas is a fairly antitax state. The sales tax was raised for the first time in 26 years, in 1984, and we had 350 local school millage [property tax] elections in March of '84 and March of '85. Seventy percent of them passed. During that entire time we had an unemployment rate higher than the national average, but people perceived that it was worth it to fight for better education because it would lead to better economic growth."

The fifth assumption flows from the fiscal climate: if public resources are relatively scarce, they must be *invested*, not merely spent. Interest-group liberals responded to many problems, as Ronald Reagan likes to say, by "throwing money at them." If people were poor, the solution was higher welfare grants, more food stamps, greater housing subsidies. Reagan and his followers responded to the same problems by taking money away. The failure of both approaches has created a deep ambivalence within the American public, and a desire for a third path. When public opinion polls ask voters if welfare spending should be increased, they overwhelmingly say no. When polls ask if we have a responsibility to improve the plight of the poor, they overwhelmingly say yes. [21] This seeming contradiction actually has a compelling logic: voters want solutions, but not the ones the two parties have traditionally offered.

The governors are gradually working out new ways to address these problems, by investing in the capacities of poor people and poor communities. "I think the American people don't want to simply break with our commitment to improve the lives of the poor; they don't want to throw all that away," says Art Hamilton, the black minority leader of the Arizona House. "But they don't want to have to pay for all the Great Society madness. People don't believe that the welfare system is designed to put itself out of business; that's what bothers a lot of the people I talk to. If the system were designed to lift people from where they are to where their potential can take them, I think people would gladly support that system."

The new paradigm governors also focus on broadening opportunity, rather than redistributing income. Doug Ross, the former grass-roots activist who now runs Governor Blanchard's Commerce Department, puts it well. "During the New Deal," he argues, "the Democrats were able to combine their fights for social justice with increased opportunities for individual Americans to succeed. For example, the Wagner Act that gave unions the right to organize said to millions of people, we're going to give you an opportunity to organize so that you have a better chance of getting your fair share. Those New Deal reforms were piece-of-the-action reforms, by and large, not piece-of-the-pie guarantees." During the 1960s, however, "we became concerned that offering people a piece of the action might not be a real fair test of how just the system was. And so we began to buy into the notion, somewhat understandably, that output was the real measure of the system's justice.

"I think we then began to lose our focus on the proper balance, which says, 'We will offer real opportunities—we can't ensure that people succeed—but we will make available the resources so that a person who's willing to make the effort can succeed.' As we moved to try to assure outcomes, we lost the center of the American electorate, because that's not what they ever bought into. They began to see government as an obstacle, rather than a source of opportunity. They began to see government redistributing their income to people who they were not so certain were always the deserving poor. They began to see jobs and college admissions distributed in ways that seemed to be other than merit. That's why I think you can sell people scholarships, but you cannot sell them affirmative action quotas. And that enabled Reagan to finally come in and say, 'Government is the problem.'"

The new paradigm also involves new assumptions about the proper roles of federal, state, and local governments. The New Deal was a time in which America finally accepted bigness: big business, big labor, and big government. An economy dominated by large, stable, mass-production industries required large, centralized institutions in all three areas. Today, however, our economy is decentralizing. Mass production is moving offshore, and smaller, more automated, more flexible manufacturing operations are thriving in the United States. In the service sector small businesses are proliferating, and in both sectors the entrepreneurial process is accelerating. In 1985, seven times as many new businesses were formed as in 1950.[22]

Great Society liberalism pushed the centralization of government to new levels. In reaction, Reagan tried to push government back to the state and local level. To the surprise of many commentators, however, the governors resisted Reagan's New Federalism. Almost to a person they favored greater decentralization, but they insisted upon an intelligent sorting-out of the appropriate state and federal roles. They wanted a New Federalism that made sense. "We need a more decentralized system, the same kind of decentralized system that businesses have been moving toward since the early seventies," explained Jim Blanchard. "At the same time, we need stronger national direction. We're in a global economy, facing global challenges. Whether it's energy, or trade, or the need for a policy of cooperation between business and labor, we need a more coherent and stronger national policy."

If current state trends do foreshadow national politics, these principles—growth with equity, a focus on market solutions, a search for nonbureaucratic methods, fiscal moderation, investment rather than spending, redistribution of opportunity rather than outcomes, and a new federalism—provide a rough outline of the next political paradigm. They do not represent a new liberalism, or a new conservatism, but a new context within which the two parties will compete for ascendance. If historical patterns repeat themselves, the party that fully embraces the new paradigm will win a realigning election and dominate the following decades.

The media often describes politicians who fit this paradigm as "moderates." They are clearly not liberals, in the sense that Ted Kennedy and Walter Mondale are liberals. Nor are they conservatives, in the sense that Ronald Reagan and Gerald Ford are conservatives. Lacking any other category, reporters put them in the middle. But this description is simply not useful. Within the new paradigm there is a left, a right, and a center, but they have little to do with the left, right, and center to which we are accustomed. They have less to do with questions of spending and taxing, for instance, than with how aggressive government should be in reshaping the marketplace, and whose interests should be protected in the process. Those on the left want to actively plan patterns of economic growth, whereas conservatives try simply to perfect flaws in the marketplace. The left seeks to protect the poor and disadvantaged in the process; the right puts the interests of bankers and business people first.

When traditional liberal or conservative standards are applied to a politician like Babbitt or Dukakis or Thornburgh, they shed no light. Traditional liberals in Massachusetts attack Dukakis for not raising welfare benefits to the poverty line. Dukakis responds that such a move would destroy incentives to work, and that the better path is more investment in education, training, job placement, and low-income housing. Does this put Dukakis to the left or right of his critics? The answer is that it puts him within a different paradigm.

Those most often described as moderates by the media are the Democratic governors who are working hardest to reshape their national party—

the Bruce Babbitts, Bill Clintons, and Chuck Robbs. These governors may have moved right on some issues, compared to a Mondale or a Kennedy, but they have moved left on others. More to the point, they have moved to *different* issues altogether. Babbitt built his presidential campaign on four basic themes. Two of them—work place democracy and the creation of a new international trading system—are not even on the old spectrum.

Consider as well Chuck Robb, the former governor of Virginia and a leader of the Democratic Leadership Council, described by the media as a group of Democratic moderates. In 1987, Robb gave a speech in which he called for "a profound change in our capitalist culture, a fundamental change in the way our entire society is organized to do business. Just as we did in the New Deal, the time has come for Americans to negotiate a new social contract, to insist on economic growth with economic equity. . . . This new emphasis on resourceful and versatile workers, on teamwork and innovative capacity . . . means the end of an aristocracy of management and the beginning of a democratic capitalism characterized by a new egalitarian ethic in the American work place."[23]

These are not the words of a moderate. If anything, they are radical. The simple truth is that they do not fit the old categories. One can only make sense of them, in ideological terms, by placing them within a new paradigm.

Some of the Republican governors are also beginning to experience this problem. In 1986, the editors of the *Ripon Forum*, the publication of the "moderate" Ripon Society, interviewed New Jersey Governor Tom Kean. They asked him, "What should the leadership of the GOP do to capture the middle?"

"I reject the word 'middle,' just as I reject the words 'conservative' and 'liberal,'" Kean responded. "'Aggressive' is a word I like to use. If you follow the kinds of policies that I'm talking about, you're talking about a pro-growth philosophy. You create a sense of excitement and understanding about the country's direction."[24]

Kean's emphasis on "the country's direction" is revealing, for the new politics, at this stage, are more about transition than anything else. The old paradigm operated in a relatively static system, in which rapid economic growth was a given and the nation's social structure was remarkably stable. Today the governors are focusing on social and economic adjustment to a new set of circumstances. Although they represent the broad middle classes, they are not class-based politicians, in the sense of fighting for a larger share of the pie for their constituents. Their mission is to remold our political and economic institutions to adapt to the new economy. In this respect, they are again similar to the progressives, who clearly sprang from what historian Richard Hofstadter called "the new middle class," but who—unlike the populists—were not pushing the interests of one class so much as they were pushing the entire society to adapt to the industrial era.[25] The Progressive Era was a period of adjustment to rapid change; redistribution would come later. In the same way, the issues of today are those of adjustment; battles over distribution and power will await a more stable time.

The Race for the High Ground

Leaders such as Kean and Thornburgh, on the Republican side, and Babbitt and Clinton and Blanchard, on the Democratic side, understand that the party which first embraces the new paradigm will command the high ground of American politics. "Today you have Democrats running around the country talking about economic growth and the virtues of the free enterprise system and the need to balance budgets and reduce deficits," Thornburgh told me in 1987. "These are sound Republican principles. What an irony it would be if, by preoccupation with all these sideshow issues [the gold standard, New Right social issues], we were to let shrewd, competent Democrats come in and steal that birthright of the Republican party."

Babbitt described the same threat from the other side. "There are some disquieting signs," he warned, "that the Republicans will succeed in stealing our clothes while we are in the swimming hole."

Both the Babbitts and the Thornburghs face significant hurdles in taking their politics to the national level. Most new-paradigm Democrats come from educated, middle-class backgrounds and political bases. Although they strive to include industrial workers and minorities in their visions and their solutions, a class divide separates them. In part the problem is style: middle-class professionals do not speak the language of the party's traditional labor and minority constituencies. Moreover, a new paradigm is often pioneered by the most intellectual of politicians, so its early advocates tend to be too cerebral and technocratic to stir the political juices. But the problem goes deeper, just as it did during the Progressive Era. New-paradigm Democrats advocate economic change—and in our system, economic change is a threat to industrial workers and irrelevant to the poor. This problem showed up graphically in 1984: Gary Hart raised the hackles of blue-collar workers and industrial unions, while leaving black and Hispanic voters cold. The Democratic party split into three distinct constituencies: the educated middle class, which voted for Hart; the working class, Humphrey Democrats, who voted for Mondale; and blacks, who voted for Jackson. (Hispanics, interestingly, are moored to none of these constituencies; perhaps a third of them voted for Reagan.)

The Democratic governors I have spoken with acknowledge that uniting these constituencies will be their toughest task. Some in the party's left wing have argued that they can be brought together with share-the-wealth, anti-big-business populism. But the truth is that there are no significant constituencies demanding such policies. In 1976, Oklahoma Senator Fred Harris mounted a presidential campaign on anti-big-business themes, but went nowhere. The populist Citizens Action groups (Massachusetts Fair Share, the Ohio Public Interest Campaign, the Illinois Public Action Council, and others) have never reached the critical mass necessary to become major players in their states. Even mildly antibusiness politics in the first Dukakis administration, and again under New Mexico's Toney Anaya from 1983 to 1987, led to rejection by the electorate. Only in depressed rural areas and depressed industrial areas has economic populism had any resonance, and there the enemy is more often Toyota than General Motors.

Big business in America is simply not viewed as all-powerful anymore. Instead, it is seen as bloodied by foreign competition and in need of all the help we can give it. For the past decade, voters' antiestablishment sentiments have been aimed at government, not business. Their aspirations are for greater opportunity, not a redistribution of wealth. The few constituencies that do respond to populist economic themes tend to be culturally conservative. They mix with the party's educated middle-class voters like oil and water.

The only hope the Democrats have of uniting the Hart, Mondale, and Jackson constituencies lies, not in punishing big business, but in reshaping the marketplace so it works for blue-collar workers and minorities, rather than against them. This is precisely the strategy the New Deal used to unite its working and middle-class bases. FDR gave labor the right to organize; created a socialized savings fund (social security) so even the working poor could look forward to old-age pensions; reorganized the agricultural market so it worked for farmers again; created an unemployment insurance system; and used government investments in public works to create jobs for the unemployed. These efforts brought a huge wave of new working-class voters into the electorate and into the Democratic camp.

Franklin Roosevelt learned how to bring middle-class progressives and working-class Democratic machines together under one umbrella from his predecessor as governor of New York, Al Smith. Smith was a Tammany Hall Democrat, but as governor he brought progressive leaders into his inner circle and pushed much of the progressive social and economic agenda through the legislature. In similar fashion, some of the Democratic governors today are learning how to bridge the gaps between their middle-class, working-class, and minority constituencies.

Dukakis, for instance, is a middle-class politician who—after suffering the massive defection of working-class voters in 1978—has learned to reach out. Though he lacks the inspirational quality we often associate with champions of the disadvantaged, Dukakis has pleased the Massachusetts labor movement and minority communities by creating jobs in depressed areas, retraining dislocated workers and providing them with supplemental unemployment checks, moving welfare recipients into jobs, and investing in poor communities. Dukakis has been able to do this, without triggering worries about excessive spending and giveaways among his middle-class supporters, because he has also embraced economic growth and fiscal moderation. (Much of his success in both areas must of course be attributed to the booming economy.) "There are certain thresholds for the public, in terms of how they view candidates," Dukakis's former campaign manager and chief of staff, John Sasso, told me in 1985. "Maintaining trust and credibility on the economy is a very important threshold. People trust Michael Dukakis with the economy, and they trust us to spend their money wisely. Having developed this reputation, people trust us to spend their tax dollars on the needy and on other things that we as Democrats feel are important and are consistent with our values and principles."

Mario Cuomo is a bridge candidate from the other side—the Al Smith of the 1980s. He comes out of the outer boroughs of New York City, and he speaks the language of the party's traditional constituencies. But as governor, Cuomo has also shown an ability to reach out to the middle class. He has cut taxes, built prisons, and managed state finances well.

Bill Clinton may be the party's most natural bridge candidate. Clinton appeals equally to blacks and whites, to rural voters, blue-collar workers, and the educated middle class. He is an innovator, a passionate advocate of new ideas and new approaches, but he can speak the language of the poor and raise the rafters of a black church. This ability stems in part from the force of his personality, but Clinton has also put the classic bridge issues—education and economic growth—at the top of his agenda. Significantly, he has pulled together his diverse constituencies even in a time of economic pain and severe fiscal constraints, something Dukakis failed to do during his first term and Cuomo has not had to do since his first year in office.

If the Democrats will have difficulty embracing the new paradigm, the Republicans face even greater obstacles: the antigovernment principles of Reagan conservatism and the social values of the New Right. Kevin Phillips, who urged Republicans to embrace an activist economic agenda in his 1984 book, *Staying on Top,* underlines the first problem.[26] "Modern conservatism's ability to manage a new round of governmental innovation— not the previous bureaucratic overintervention, but *new* involvements and objectives focused by today's changed requirements—is anything but clear," he writes. "Pragmatism may be strong in the business community and among elected officeholders, but there is a strong counterforce. Ideologically committed people who finally obtain real power after being spurned for decades have a tendency to excess. . . ."[27]

Even if pragmatic Republicans can overcome their party's bias against activist government, the social and cultural issues will be a problem. The New Right represents a solid and well-organized minority of Republican voters. Demographically, these are the less-educated Republicans, those whose occupations are outside the growing information and knowledge-based sectors of the postindustrial economy. According to Phillips, they tend to be small business people, farmers, blue-collar artisans such as plumbers and electricians, retirees, and service workers.[28] They are generally people whose cultural horizons have not been broadened by higher education, and whose way of life seems threatened by the cultural and economic changes that have swept through postindustrial America.

Phillips estimates that these "conservative populists" make up 20 to 25 percent of the electorate—enough to impose their values on the Republican party, but not on the nation.[29] Unless the economy suffers a collapse, these groups will decline in significance as knowledge-intensive industries and the information sector expand.

As this happens, our politics will almost inevitably be dominated by the educated middle class—what some academics call the "new class." The "tremendous growth of [the] white-collar and professional-technical work force," "the rise of the knowledge and information sectors of the economy," and "the unprecedented expansion of higher education" have created "a new 'social class,' differing from what we have known historically," explains Everett Carll Ladd. "Classes need not be defined simply by income or type of job; they can emerge just as naturally around levels of education. And in this new class division, the 'top' is consistently more 'liberal' than is the 'bottom.'"[30]

The "new class" is particularly concentrated among those born since World War II. In 1968, baby boomers constituted 10 percent of the electorate; in 1988, for the first time, they are a majority. Since not all baby boomers are middle class, analysts usually estimate the new class at about a third of the electorate. It is the core growth constituency that could cement a new majority, if its members are pulled more fully into the active electorate. In this sense, it is in the same electoral position the industrial working class found itself in during the 1920s. It does not have a party, but its numbers are now so large that when it finds one, it will have a majority. "It is this group that has been looking for a replacement of the old Democratic ideology and looking for a candidate who comes up with a new formulation," says Curtis Gans, director of the Committee for the Study of the American Electorate and an astute analyst of voting behavior. "Because they constitute probably the largest single outlook and tendency in the country, but are a majority tendency in neither political party, they are frustrated."

In 1984, when the new class propelled Gary Hart suddenly to the top of the Democratic heap, the media tagged them with the label young urban

professional, or "yuppie." But not all members of the new class are professional, and even fewer are affluent. Political scientist Ralph Whitehead,
another of the nation's most perceptive political analysts, more accurately
described the majority of baby boomers with the term *new collar*, by which
he meant to distinguish them from traditional blue-collar workers and
white-collar professionals. New-collar workers work largely in service industries, in jobs that require some education but fall short of professional
status. They are nurses, technicians, and office workers. Whereas young
blue-collar workers have experienced extreme difficulties during the 1980s
and white-collar professionals have generally done well, new-collar workers have struggled to buy their first homes, to find adequate child care, and
to make ends meet, even with two incomes.

New-class baby boomers are generally liberal on social and cultural
issues, but the economic problems of the past decade have made them
skeptics of government. "I think there's a sense that the affluence we grew
up in and took for granted has not worked out quite the way we thought it
would," says pollster Paul Maslin. "My parents, who were born in the
depression and came out of the war experience, felt there was nowhere to
go but up. They took it as a matter of course that they could buy a house,
have the best schools, bequeath a better life to their children. Our generation doesn't feel that way. Part of the way this cuts on economic issues is
that this generation now has become much less trusting of the government. Hart appealed to them because he tapped into the sense that there
was a different way: the government has certain obligations, but by the
same token, we have to be entrepreneurial. We have to grow beyond what
we've managed so far—not the unbridled growth of the past, but growth
into new industries, new technologies. People don't know quite what the
new package is yet, but they know they want it."

The race for the high ground is, in demographic terms, a race for the
allegiance of the new class. This group is socially liberal; economically
pragmatic; skeptical of big government, big labor, and big business; supportive of entrepreneurship; extremely change-oriented; environmentalist;
and very individualistic.[31] Many of its members, especially those touched
by the 1960s, want to see American society once again attack its glaring
social inequities. But they are skeptical of the abilities of both existing
parties to do so with any success. Almost literally, the new class is looking
for a "third way." It is the core constituency out of which the new paradigm will grow.

Packaging the New Paradigm

In 1983, Pat Caddell took a poll. It concerned one Senator Smith, a
moderate liberal in his early forties who had served a decade in the Senate.
As described by Sidney Blumenthal in *The New Republic*, Smith rejected the

policies of the past, offered bold new solutions for the future, and promised a new generation of leadership that would rise above the special interests in Washington.[32] Senator Smith, in other words, was a new-paradigm candidate. In Caddell's poll, he beat Walter Mondale and John Glenn, then the Democratic front-runners, hands down.

The only problem was that Senator Smith did not exist. So in early 1984, Caddell signed on with Gary Hart, who shared many of Smith's attributes but was finding it difficult to project them. Soon Hart was using Senator Smith's slogans. His was a candidacy of "new ideas" and "a new generation of leadership." The 1984 race was a contest between "the future and the past." Walter Mondale was a candidate of the "special interests."

In the space of three weeks after Hart first unveiled his new slogans, he shot from 7 percent in New Hampshire polls to 37 percent, his winning number on primary day.[33] Nationally, he strode from virtual invisibility to the front of the pack, leaving pollsters to mutter about the most volatile electorate they had ever measured.

Gary Hart was never able to flesh out the vision behind his "new ideas" theme. In addition, the American people never felt comfortable with this cool intellectual from Colorado, this man who had changed his name and birth date and could not explain why in any convincing fashion.

Hart's character flaws were real, as the world discovered in 1987. But the thematic problems he experienced—the difficulty he had answering Walter Mondale's question, "Where's the beef?"—are common to new-paradigm candidates. Hart was successful in overcoming the media's tendency to stereotype him as a moderate, because his "new ideas" and "new generation" themes framed the debate in a new way: not left versus center, but the future against the past. This appealed to new-class voters, but when they took a closer look, they were not sure what they saw. Too often, new-paradigm candidates frustrate voters, because they do not offer a clear enough philosophy, a vision that makes sense of their different positions and proposals. Voters cannot find a consistent pattern, a sense of the candidate's bottom line—what he stands for and who he stands with. Hence they cannot bring him into sharp focus. The problem is magnified in presidential campaigns, when so many messages must be delivered in thirty-second bites.

To overcome this problem, the new-paradigm candidates will have to weave their politics into a compelling whole, in which each "new idea" relates to the larger vision of where they want to move the nation. They will have to do more than break the old mold, as Hart did; they will have to create a new one. This is a difficult task, requiring far more than a series of new programs.

Doug Ross gets at this issue in describing what Blanchard and his administration learned during their first term. "When we started out," he says, "we started with the old model, what the national Democratic platform had become—a list of programs. We had a 15-point plan for small business, a 20-point plan for this. We wanted to show people how active we were, how concerned we were. But we gradually became aware that people are not very interested in programs, per se. They need some sense of what kind of community it is that you want to see evolve. They're interested in seeing whether they share the basic notion of what you want the state to become."

In essence, Ross is talking about what Robert Kuttner calls "one big idea"—a central theme about the role of government, which unifies an array of more specific positions and offers the central definition of a party or candidate.[34]

To some extent Blanchard has used the idea that by "getting smart," Michigan can once again become the best place in the world to manufacture products—with the most skilled workers, the most innovative industries, the best universities. Clinton has done the same thing in Arkansas, by talking about the importance of a world-class education system if Arkansas is to compete in the global economy. Those who would bring the new paradigm to Washington will have to do the same. They will have to tell the American people a new story about where we, as a society, are heading. That story must deal with the new realities of the global economy and the new roles necessary for government, business, labor, and the American people. It must resonate with the experience of the average voter. It must weave the candidate's campaign themes and slogans into a seamless vision of the future. And it must come together in one big idea. That idea will probably have to do with government as a partner, working with the private sector—creating new partnerships to keep America competitive.

It may still be too early for the new-paradigm candidates. "My fear is that we really haven't stirred this stuff deeply enough, that it's not time for the image makers to show up and make the phrases, because this stuff hasn't been pushed far enough," Bruce Babbitt told me in 1985. "There's kind of an unfinished quality about all of this that does not lend it to labels, and really requires that you relentlessly try to push the thinking and the programmatic side of it forward."

One day, a politician will run for president—a Democrat or a Republican—who combines a commitment to the new agenda with a sense of vision, a knack for telling stories, and a silver tongue. Then, and probably only then, that agenda will be woven into a set of coherent symbols and themes, a compelling vision. Perhaps it will happen in 1988. Perhaps it will happen in 1992, or 1996. Or perhaps it will not happen until after a presidential campaign, when a more traditional liberal or conservative is searching for some way to respond in a period of crisis, as Franklin Roosevelt was when he fashioned the New Deal. Given the stirrings in America's laboratories of democracy, however, it is hard not to believe that it *will* happen.

NOTES _____

Note on Sources: Most of the research for this book was done through interviews. All quotes that are not footnoted are from interviews with the author. When information about a particular program comes from interviews with those involved in the program—state officials, business people, and others—I have not generally footnoted that information. Were I to do so, the footnotes would become extremely cumbersome. When information comes from other sources, such as documents or articles or books, I have generally provided footnotes.

Introduction

1. Arthur M. Schlesinger, Jr., *The Age of Roosevelt. Vol. III: The Politics of Upheaval* (Boston: Houghton Mifflin, 1960), p. 520.

2. See Arthur M. Schlesinger, Jr., *The Age of Roosevelt, Vol. II: The Coming of the New Deal* (Boston: Houghton Mifflin, Sentry Edition, 1958), pp. 297–315; Clarke A. Chambers, *Seedtime of Reform: American Social Service and Social Action 1918–1933* (Minneapolis: University of Minnesota Press, 1963); John R. Commons et al., *History of Labor in the United States, Vol. III* (Fairfield, N.J.: Augustus M. Kelley, Reprint of 1918 edition, 1966); and Robert A. Caro, *The Power Broker: Robert Moses and the Fall of New York* (New York: Vintage Books, 1975), particularly pp. 261, 265, 294, and 344.

3. Jack Russell, *On Base Modernization: The Contribution of a State-Sponsored Extension Service*, Michigan Modernization Service, 1986, p. 6.

4. David Birch, "The Atomization of America," *Inc.*, March 1987, p. 22.

5. Roger J. Vaughan, Robert Pollard, and Barbara Dyer, *The Wealth of States: The Political Economy of State Development* (Washington, D.C.: Council of State Planning Agencies, 1985), p. 41. Vaughan, Pollard, and Dyer report that one-sixth (17 percent) of those in the work force run a business or are self-employed. According to the Bureau of Labor Statistics, 17.5 percent of the work force belonged to a union in 1986.

6. David Birch, interview with author, June 1987.

7. Twenty percent: Allegheny Conference on Community Development, *A Strategy for Growth: An Economic Development Program for the Pittsburgh Region* (Pittsburgh: Allegheny Conference on Community Development, 1984), Vol. 1, p. 14. Seventy percent: Robert B. Reich, *The Next American Frontier* (New York: Penguin Books, 1984), p. 121.

8. Reich, *The Next American Frontier*, p. 121.

9. John O. Wilson, *The Power Economy: Building an Economy That Works* (Boston: Little, Brown, 1985), p. 234.

10. Robert W. Coy, Jr., *The Pennsylvania Economy: Past, Present and Future* (Harrisburg: MILRITE Council, 1984), p. 2.

11. "Management Discovers the Human Side of Automation," *Business Week*, Sept. 29, 1986.

12. *Statistical Abstract of the United States 1985* (Washington, D.C.: U.S. Department of Commerce, 1984), p. 135. (Source: U.S. Bureau of the Census, *1980 Census of Population*, Vol. 1, chapter C.)

13. John Kasarda, "The Regional and Urban Redistribution of People and Jobs in the U.S.," prepared for the National Research Council Committee on National Urban Policy, October 1986.

14. James M. Howell, "The Lesson of Massachusetts," *Mass High Tech*, July 6–19, 1987, p. 12.

15. Corporation for Enterprise Development, *Taken for Granted: How Grant Thornton's Business Climate Index Leads States Astray* (Washington, D.C.: Corporation for Enterprise Development, 1986), p. 69.

16. See for instance Roger Schmenner, "Location Decisions of Large Firms: Implications for Public Policy," *Commentary* (journal of the Center for Urban Economic Development, in Washington, D.C.), January 1981; Roger Schmenner, *Making Business Location Decisions* (Englewood Cliffs, N.J.: Prentice-Hall, 1982); and Patricia L. Barden and Susan R. Rideout, "Location Decision-Making in Export-Oriented Business and Industry," Ann Arbor: University of Michigan Graduate School of Business Administration, Division of Research, 1978, p. III-13.

17. See for instance Data Resources Inc., *The Macroeconomic Impacts of Federal Pollution Control Programs: 1981 Assessment*, Report for the U.S. Environmental Protection Agency, 1981; Henry Peskin, Paul Portnoy, and Allen Kneese, *Environmental Regulation in the U.S. Economy* (Baltimore: Johns Hopkins University Press, 1981); U.S. Congress, Joint Economic Committee, *Environmental and Health/Safety Regulations, Productivity, Growth and Economic Performance: An Assessment*, Report prepared by Robert Haveman et al., Joint Committee Print, 1981; The Conservation Foundation, *Environmental Regulation of Industrial Plant Siting* (Washington, D.C.: The Conservation Foundation, 1983); Howard Stafford, "Environmental Protection and Industrial Location," *Annals of the Association of American Geographers*, November 1985.

18. See Richard H. Nelson, ed., *Government and Technical Progress: Cross Industry Analysis* (Elmsford, N.Y.: Pergamon Press, 1982).

19. "A Conversation with Robert B. Reich: The Challenge of Changing America's Future," *Labor Relations Today* (newsletter of the U.S. Department of Labor), Vol. II., No. 2 (March–April, 1987), p. 5.

20. See Industry Policy Study Group, *Restoring American Competitiveness: Proposals for an Industry Policy* (Washington, D.C.: Center for National Policy, 1984).

21. See Robert Kuttner, *The Economic Illusion* (Boston: Houghton Mifflin, 1984).

22. Thomas Chmura, James Gollub, and Steven Waldhorn, *Redesigning Social and Economic Problem-Solving* (Menlo Park, Calif.: Stanford Research Institute International, 1985), p. 13.

Chapter 1: The Class of '74: The Roots of a New Paradigm

1. Diane Granat, "Whatever Happened to the Watergate Babies?", *Congressional Quarterly*, March 3, 1984, p. 499.

2. Alan Ehrenhalt, "Last Hurrahs for the New Deal," *The Washington Monthly*, January 1976, p. 57.

3. David Osborne, "The Democrats' Chameleon Politics," *Inquiry*, Dec. 25, 1978, pp. 8–10.

4. Office of State Planning, *The Massachusetts Economic Development Program: A Progress Report*, Commonwealth of Massachusetts, 1978, p. 8.

5. Paul Henning, Wang Public Relations Office, interview with author, 1985.

6. Neal R. Peirce, Jerry Hagstrom, and Carol Steinbach, *Economic Development: The Challenge of the 1980s* (Washington, D.C.: Council of State Planning Agencies, 1979), pp. 32–33.

7. Ronald F. Ferguson and Helen F. Ladd, "Massachusetts," in *The New Economic Role of American States*, ed. by R. Scott Fosler (New York: Oxford University Press, 1988), p. 48.

8. Office of State Planning, *An Economic Development Program for Massachusetts,* Commonwealth of Massachusetts, 1976, p. 2.

9. Ferguson and Ladd, "Massachusetts," p. 42.

10. Spiro Mitrokostas, Communications Director, Massachusetts Industrial Finance Agency, interview with author, April 1987. MIFA has issued more than $3 billion in tax-exempt bonds since its creation, and it claims to have created more than 70,000 jobs. In reality, most of these projects would have gone forward without MIFA. Tax-exempt industrial development bonds simply provide a public subsidy for loans that would normally be made by banks at a slightly higher interest rate. Banks still make and service the loans, bond agencies such as MIFA simply provide the tax exemption. This allows banks to lend to businesses without paying federal taxes on the interest they earn, which enables them to offer lower interest rates to businesses.

The drawback is that industrial development bonds cost the federal government billions of dollars in lost revenue. As state governments scrambled to create jobs in the wake of the 1975 recession, the use of industrial development bonds rose from $4.9 billion, in 1975, to $41.6 billion, in 1982. (Advisory Commission on Intergovernmental Relations, *The States and Distressed Communities: The Final Report* [Washington, D.C.: Advisory Commission on Intergovernmental Relations, 1985], p. 108.) Beginning in 1984, when the revenue drain reached an estimated $3.5 billion a year, Congress restricted the use of industrial development bonds—at least partially in the belief that most were public subsidies for businesses that could afford to pay market rates.

In this new context, MIFA has been one of the more innovative bond agencies in the country. Perhaps its most important innovation has been the development of taxable umbrella bonds, which are used to bring the cost of capital down for a large group of loans to small and medium-sized companies. MIFA pays a fee to have the bonds guaranteed by banks, to limit the risk. By tapping overseas banks, it has pulled foreign capital into Massachusetts and given small and medium-sized manufacturers the kind of access to the bond markets normally limited to large firms. See Charles A. Radin, "Beefed-Up Industrial Bond Agency Quietly OK'd," *Boston Globe,* July 20, 1987, and David C. Isgur, "Winning the Tax-Reform War," *Boston Globe,* Feb. 8, 1987.

11. Massachusetts Technology Development Corporation, *Annual Report,* 1986, p. 5. MTDC's profits included over $4 million in stockholdings from companies that had gone public. These were technically considered "unrealized gains" as of 1986, because of MTDC's accounting procedures.

12. Ferguson and Ladd, "Massachusetts," p. 44.

13. Foster Aborn, interview with author, 1986.

14. John Wilke, "New England Computer Firms Hiring Again," *Boston Globe,* April 28, 1987.

15. Ibid., and Martin Miller, Wang Laboratories, interview with author, April 1986.

16. William Torpey, President, Massachusetts Capital Resource Company, interview with author, December 1987.

17. Massachusetts Capital Resource Company, *Annual Report,* 1985, and Ferguson and Ladd, "Massachusetts," p. 334.

18. *Boston Globe,* March 17, 1978, p. 13.

19. Roger J. Vaughan, *State Taxation and Economic Development* (Washington, D.C.: Council of State Planning Agencies, 1979).

20. Michael Kieschnick, *Taxes and Growth: Business Incentives and Economic Development* (Washington, D.C.: Council of State Planning Agencies, 1981).

21. Douglas Henton and Steven A. Waldhorn, "California," in *The New Economic Role of American States,* p. 214.

22. Joel Kotkin and Paul Grabowicz, *California INC.* (New York: Rawson and Wade, 1982), p. 80.

23. Terence Smith, "Democrats Agree Defeat May Help in Reformulating Social Programs," *New York Times,* Nov. 26, 1980.

24. C. R. Viswanathan, chairman, MICRO, interview with author, December 1987.

25. Catherine Lyons, President, California Capital (a San Francisco-based BIDCO), interview with author, September 1985.

26. "California's New Pension Investments," *National Journal,* Aug. 21, 1982, p. 1468. For an overview, see California Pension Investment Unit, *Annual Report: Targeting Investment for Economic Development,* State of California, 1982.

27. Sid McCausland, Executive Officer, California Public Employees Retirement System, interview with author, September 1985.

28. For more information on Indiana, see Charles R. Warren, "Indiana," in *The New Economic Role of American States,* pp. 269–290.

29. Quoted in "State Strategies for Success," speech delivered by Gov. Michael Dukakis, Feb. 11, 1987.

30. For more on North Carolina, see Randall Rothenberg, *The Neoliberals: Creating the New American Politics* (New York: Simon and Schuster, 1984), pp. 181–196.

31. Robert Freidman and William Schweke, eds., *Expanding the Opportunity to Produce: Revitalizing the American Economy through New Enterprise Development* (Washington, D.C.: Corporation for Enterprise Development, 1981).

Chapter 2: Pennsylvania: The Economic Development Model

1. "Profile of an Incubator Company: PMI and Plasma Coating," *Network: A Newsmagazine of the North East Tier Ben Franklin Advanced Technology Center,* Vol. 1, No. 1 (Winter 1985), pp. 6–9; and interviews with the author.

2. Robert Bittenbender, Secretary of the Budget and Administration in the Thornburgh administration, interview with author, June 1986.

3. Total expenditures for AFDC and General Assistance increased by only 3 percent between 1978–1979 and 1984–1985, according to data from the Pennsylvania Department of Public Welfare. The consumer price index rose from 195.4 in 1978 to 322.2 in 1985.

4. Coy, *The Pennsylvania Economy: Past, Present and Future,* p. 4 (see chap. 1, n. 10).

5. Pennsylvania Business Roundtable, *Partnership for Pennsylvania's Development* (Harrisburg: Pennsylvania Business Roundtable, 1986), p. 7.

6. Harold Miller, "Economic Revitalization in Pennsylvania and Michigan," memorandum, Pennsylvania Governor's Office of Policy and Planning, Aug. 15, 1986.

7. Walt Plosila, interviews with author.

8. "Metro Report: Hot Spots," *Inc.,* April 1987, pp. 50–51.

9. Robert Goodman, *The Last Entrepreneurs: America's Regional Wars for Jobs and Dollars* (New York: Simon and Schuster, 1979), pp. 2–3.

10. Chet Bond, Volkswagen of America, interview with author, July 1987. Shapp's prediction: Goodman, *The Last Entrepreneurs,* p. 2.

11. Howard J. Grossman, "The Ben Franklin Partnership: Linking Higher Education, Government and Business for Economic Growth," *Information Service,* No.

34 (published by the National Council for Urban Economic Development), November 1985, p. 3.

12. As told by Walt Plosila, in interview with author.

13. Ben Franklin Partnership Board, *Ben Franklin Partnership Challenge Grant Program for Technological Innovation: 48 Month Progress Report*, May 1987, pp 1–3.

14. William K. Stevens, "Economy Tops Pennsylvania Agenda," *New York Times*, Jan. 21, 1987.

15. Will Lepkowski, "Lehigh: One University's Approach to Rejuvenating U.S. Industry," *Chemical and Engineering News*, May 14, 1984, p. 40.

16. Emory Zimmers, interview with author, May 1987.

17. Wendy Zeliner, "High-tech Firms Lead Job Growth, Study Says," *Pittsburgh Post-Gazette*, Dec. 9, 1986. The survey was conducted by the University of Pittsburgh's University Center for Social and Urban Research. It was released by the Pittsburgh High Technology Council.

18. Ben Franklin Partnership Board, *Ben Franklin Partnership Challenge Grant Program for Technological Innovation: 42 Month Progress Report*, December 1986, and other program documents.

19. Ben Franklin Partnership Board, *48 Month Progress Report*.

20. Frederick Cusick, "A State Agency Takes Credit for Job-Creating Relocations," *Philadelphia Inquirer*, Nov. 25, 1984.

21. Garfield Schwartz Associates, Inc., "Challenges to Pennsylvania: An Overview of Economic Prospects," *House Democratic Economic Studies Report*, Vol. 1, No. 1 (April 1983).

22. DeWitt John, *Shifting Responsibilities: Federalism in Economic Development* (Washington, D.C.: National Governors Association, 1988), p. 55.

23. Robert Benko, interview with author, May 1987.

24. Allegheny Conference on Community Development, *A Strategy for Growth*, pp. 13, 18 (see Introduction, n. 7).

25. By 1984: Allegheny Conference on Community Development, *A Strategy for Growth*, p. 25; more people: Neal R. Peirce and Jerry Hagstrom, *The Book of America: Inside 50 States Today* (New York: Warner Books, 1984), p. 117.

26. Pennsylvania Department of Commerce, *Forging Revival and Renaissance: An Action Program for the Revitalization of the Mon Valley*, January 1986, p. 8.

27. Ibid., Technical Supplement, p. 5.

28. Robert Coy, interview with author, May 1987.

29. For more on the Gaines Pet Food plant, see David Jenkins, *Job Power: Blue and White Collar Democracy* (Garden City, N.Y.: Doubleday, 1973); *Interim Report on New Plant Organization at Gaines Pet Food Plant, Topeka, Kansas*, General Foods, Dec. 23, 1971; Trevor Armbrister, "Beating Those Blue-Collar Blues," *Reader's Digest*, April 1973; and Michael Putney, "Job Enrichment Plans Let Workers Shape Own Job; Bosses Smile as Happier Employees Produce More," *National Observer*, March 17, 1973.

30. *Interim Report on New Plant Organization*, General Foods, p. 10.

31. "Reexamining In-Plant Labor-Management Committees," *QWL Report* (published by the Center for Quality of Working Life at Pennsylvania State University, Harrisburg, and the MILRITE Council), Vol. 4, No. 3 (January-February 1987), p. 1.

32. John Hoerr, "Getting Man and Machine to Live Happily Ever After," *Business Week*, April 30, 1987, pp. 61–62.

33. Ibid.

34. Karen Nicely, State Employees Retirement Fund, and Michael Grubick,

Public School Employees Retirement System, interviews with author, October 1987.

35. Harold Miller, "Economic Revitalization in Pennsylvania and Michigan."

36. Dun & Bradstreet Corp., Economic Analysis Department, "New Business Incorporations by States and Geographic Regions," Vol. 28, No. 12 (December 1986).

37. Richard L. Thornburgh, "State Strategies and Incentives for Economic Development," *Journal of Law and Commerce*, Vol. 4, No. 1, p. 1.

Chapter 3: Arkansas: The Education Model

1. National Advisory Board of First Commercial Bank, N.A., *Capital: The Missing Link* (Little Rock: First Commercial Bank, N.A., 1984), p. 9.

2. Barry Ballard, interview with author, November 1986.

3. Jim McKenzie, *An Agenda for Tax Reform in Arkansas* (Little Rock: Winthrop Rockefeller Foundation, 1986), p. 4.

4. Hastings Wyman, Jr., "A Southern Governor Warily Eyes the National Stage," *The Wall Street Journal*, March 26, 1986.

5. David Broder, *The Changing of the Guard: Power and Leadership in America* (New York: Penguin Books, 1981), p. 381.

6. Frank Fellone, "45 RPM Reporter and a 78 RPM Governor," *Arkansas Democrat*, Nov. 4, 1984.

7. "Arkansas Moves to Revamp Its Schools," *Washington Post*, Nov. 13, 1983; Mark Shields, "Testing Time for the Teachers," *Washington Post*, Dec. 23, 1983.

8. William Bowen, Chairman, First Commercial Bank, N.A., interview with author, April 1985.

9. Kern Alexander and James Hale, *Educational Equity, Improving School Finance in Arkansas*, Report to Advisory Committee of the Special School Formula Project of the Joint Interim Committee on Education, 1978, p. 11. Cited in Diane D. Blair, *Arkansas Politics and Government: Do the People Rule?* (Lincoln: University of Nebraska Press, in press).

10. For Clinton's first term, see Phyllis Finton Johnston, *Bill Clinton's Public Policy for Arkansas: 1979–1980* (Little Rock: August House, 1982).

11. Ibid., and Steve Smith, interview with author, November 1986.

12. See Johnston, *Bill Clinton's Public Policy for Arkansas*.

13. Robert Johnston, "The 1980 Election in Arkansas," *Arkansas Political Science Association*, February 1981, p. 3.

14. Maria Henson, "Clinton Says He's Learned from the Past," *Arkansas Gazette*, May 18, 1986.

15. Hastings Wyman, Jr., "A Southern Governor Warily Eyes the National Stage."

16. Learn from GOP's Victory, Clinton Urges Florida Party," *Arkansas Gazette*, Oct. 11, 1981.

17. Johnston, *Bill Clinton's Public Policy for Arkansas*, p. 16.

18. "State's Distinction Subject of Debate," *Arkansas Gazette*, Sept. 11, 1983. School districts with fewer than 500 students: Forest Kile, Superintendent of Schools, Saratoga, Ark., interview with author, April 1986.

19. " 'Opportunity' Not Motto for Students," *Arkansas Gazette*, Sept. 11, 1983.

20. "Test Links Colleges, Teachers," *Arkansas Democrat*, Oct. 20, 1986.

21. Ellie McGrath, "No More Dragging Up the Rear," *Time*, Dec. 26, 1983.

22. Statistics from Arkansas Department of Education.

23. "Test Links Colleges, Teachers," *Arkansas Democrat*, and Lloyd Hackley, interview with author, April 1985.

24. Diane Blair, interview with author, April 1986.

25. Arkansas Department of Education, *A Report to the People: The State of Education in Arkansas*, February 1986, p. 8.

26. C. Emily Feistritzer, *The Condition of Teaching: A State by State Analysis, 1985* (Princeton, N.J.: The Carnegie Foundation for the Advancement of Teaching, 1985).

27. Blair, *Arkansas Politics and Government*.

28. Arkansas Department of Education.

29. William Ernst, interview with author, April 1986.

30. Statistics from Wanda Miles-Bell, letter to author, Dec. 17, 1986.

31. *Statistical Abstract of the United States 1987* (Washington, D.C.: U.S. Department of Commerce, 1986), p. 126, chart 207.

32. Test scores from the Arkansas Department of Education. By 1987 fourth graders were at the 62d percentile in reading and the 68th in math; seventh graders were at the 53d and 57th percentiles, and tenth graders were at the 49th and 51st percentiles, respectively.

33. Arkansas Department of Education, *A Report of the Southern Regional Education Board (SREB) Assessment of Educational Progress*, 1986.

34. Winthrop Rockefeller Foundation, *Twelve Obstacles to Economic Development in the Land of Opportunity*, July 1983.

35. Barry Ballard, interview with author, November 1986.

36. Thomas McRae, "Winthrop Rockefeller Foundation: Context for the Economic Development and Banking Activities," in *Southern Development Bancorporation: An Arkansas Development Bank Holding Company Model, Supplemental Report* (Little Rock: Winthrop Rockefeller Foundation, 1986), p. 49.

37. Winthrop Rockefeller Foundation, *Eleven Obstacles to Economic Development in the Land of Opportunity*, 1982.

38. Arkansas State Bank Department.

39. William Bowen, interview with author, April 1985.

40. See David Osborne, "Bootstrap Banking," *Inc.*, August 1987, pp. 69–72.

41. For a review of Arkansas corporate tax incentives, see Jim McKenzie, *An Agenda for Tax Reform in Arkansas*; HISTECON Associates, Inc., *Analysis of Arkansas Sales Tax Exemptions* (Little Rock: Arkansas Public Policy Project, 1986); and Tynan and Associates, *Responsible Choices in Taxation: The Corporate Contribution* (Little Rock: Winthrop Rockefeller Foundation, 1984).

42. McKenzie, *An Agenda for Tax Reform in Arkansas*, p. 7; and HISTECON Associates, *Analysis of Arkansas Sales Tax Exemptions*, Appendix.

43. Bill Clinton, "Arkansans Must Commit and Compete to Achieve Potential," *Arkansas Gazette*, June 19, 1986.

44. Guy Reel, "Clinton Calls Northeast Arkansas Victim," *Memphis Commercial Appeal*, May 21, 1986.

Chapter 4: Arizona: Protecting the Environment, Rethinking Social Services

1. Barbara Rose, "Commercial Market Mixed in '86, Study of Valley Suggests," *Arizona Republic*, Jan. 23, 1987.

2. Ioanna Morfessis, Executive Director, Phoenix Economic Growth Corporation, interview with author, January 1987.

3. Keven Ann Willey, "Take-Charge Governor," *Arizona Republic,* Dec. 28, 1986.

4. Patrick Yack, "The Democratic Gospel according to Babbitt," *Denver Post Empire Magazine,* April 14, 1985.

5. Ronald Brownstein, "Babbitt's New Politics," *National Journal,* March 9, 1985, p. 518.

6. Ibid.

7. Ibid.

8. Willey, "Take-Charge Governor."

9. Brownstein, "Babbitt's New Politics," p. 519.

10. Don Harris, "Making Things Happen," *Arizona Republic,* Dec. 28, 1986.

11. Irene Sege, "Census Bureau Has America's Numbers," *Boston Globe,* April 12, 1987.

12. Mary A. M. Gindhart, "The Babbitt Legacy—Water Management," *Arizona Waterline* (published by Salt River Project), Summer 1986, pp. 1–2.

13. Desmond D. Connall, Jr., "A History of the Arizona Groundwater Management Act," *Arizona State Law Journal,* 1982, No. 2, p. 314.

14. Ibid., p. 318.

15. Ibid.

16. For more on the history of groundwater management regulation in Arizona, see Connall, "A History of the Arizona Groundwater Management Act."

17. Ibid., pp. 324–325.

18. Ibid., p. 325.

19. T. R. Reid, "Babbitt Delights in the Details," *Washington Post,* June 23, 1986.

20. For a detailed description of the Groundwater Management Act, see Connall, "A History of the Arizona Groundwater Management Act"; and Arizona Groundwater Management Study Commission, *Final Report,* June 1980.

21. Connall, "A History of the Arizona Groundwater Management Act"; and Kathleen Ferris, interviews with author.

22. See Gindhart, "The Babbitt Legacy—Water Management."

23. For more on the Environmental Quality Act, see *Arizona Waterline,* Winter 1986.

24. Gindhart, "The Babbitt Legacy—Water Management," p. 2.

25. Pete Garcia, interview with author, January 1987.

26. Alan Flory, interview with author, January 1987.

27. Democratic Policy Commission, *Investing in America's Future: Bruce Babbitt's Initiatives for Children* (Washington, D.C.: Democratic National Committee, 1986), p. 3.

28. Howard E. Freeman and Bradford L. Kirkman-Liff, "Health Care under AHCCCS: An Examination of Arizona's Alternative to Medicaid," *Health Services Research,* Vol. 20, No. 3 (August 1985), p. 246; and *Arizona: The Babbitt Years,* Babbitt campaign committee, p. 22.

29. Bradford Kirkman-Liff, Frank G. Williams, and L. A. Wilson II, "Medicaid and Capitated Competitive Contracting: The Arizona Experiment," *New England Journal of Human Services,* Summer 1985, p. 31.

30. Ibid., pp. 32–33; and *Arizona: The Babbitt Years,* p. 23.

31. John Dacey, interview with author, January 1987.

32. Kirkman-Liff, Williams, and Wilson, "Medicaid and Capitated Competitive Contracting," p. 34.

33. Bradford Kirkman-Liff, interviews with author.

34. Ibid.

35. John Dacey and Bradford Kirkman-Liff, interviews with author.
36. Freeman and Kirkman-Liff, "Health Care under AHCCCS."
37. Richard Trujillo, interview with author, January 1987.
38. Freeman and Kirkman-Liff, "Health Care under AHCCCS."
39. Bradford Kirkman-Liff, interviews with author.
40. See Kirkman-Liff, Williams, and Wilson, "Medicaid and Capitated Competitive Contracting;" and Diane G. Hillman and Jon B. Christianson, "Health Care Expenditure Containment in the United States: Strategies at the State and Local Level," *Social Science and Medicine*, Vol. 20, No. 12, pp. 1319–1330.
41. Larry Landry, "Arizona," in *The New Economic Role of American States*, p. 260 (see chap. 1, n. 7).
42. Dean Roland Haden, interview with author, May 1985; and *Engineering Excellence*, Arizona State University.
43. Haden, interview with author, May 1985; and *Engineering Excellence*, Arizona State University.
44. Bill Tompkin, Director, New Business Development, Arizona Department of Commerce, interview with author, January 1987.
45. Willey, "Take-Charge Governor."
46. Maria Recio, "Bruce Babbitt: Out to Save the Democrats from Themselves," *Business Week*, Jan. 21, 1985, p. 86.

Chapter 5: Michigan: Creating the Factory of the Future

1. Maralyn Edid, "The Wall Street Pro Who Got Michigan off the Rocks," *Business Week*, Jan. 14, 1985, p. 118.
2. Sen. Harry DeMaso, interview with author, May 1985; and Charles Press and Kenneth Verburg, "Gubernatorial Transition in Michigan, 1982–83," in *Gubernatorial Transitions: The 1982 Election*, ed. by Thad Beyle (Durham, N.C.: Duke University Press, 1985), p. 216.
3. Phil Power, Chairman, Governor's Commission on Job Training, interview with author, May 1985.
4. Statistics from Robert Naftaly, former Budget Director, interviews with author.
5. Ibid.; Robert Bowman, interviews with author; and Michigan Governor's Office, "Fiscal Recovery Plan," February 1983.
6. Robert Bowman, interview with author, May 1985.
7. Statistics from Robert Naftaly, interviews with author.
8. Harold Miller, "Economic Revitalization in Pennsylvania and Michigan," Tables 2, 4 (see chap. 2, n. 6).
9. Ibid., Table 6.
10. Ibid., Table 11.
11. Ibid., Table 1.
12. Charles Bartsch, *Reaching for Recovery: New Economic Initiative in Michigan* (Washington, D.C.: Northeast-Midwest Institute, 1985), p. 58.
13. Ibid., and Cabinet Council on Jobs and Economic Development, *Breaking New Ground* (Annual Report), December 1985, p. 9.
14. Cabinet Council, *Breaking New Ground*, p. 9.
15. Task Force for a Long-Term Economic Strategy for Michigan, *The Path to Prosperity*, Michigan Governor's Office, 1984.
16. Michigan Governor's Office, *Michigan: The Primary Source of Industrial Technology*, p. 7.

17. Michigan Treasury Department.

18. Memorandum dated Sept. 10, 1987, from Steve Rohde and Lawrence Schrauben of the Michigan Strategic Fund staff to MSF Board of Directors.

19. Memorandum dated Feb. 21, 1986, from James Kenworthy of the Michigan Strategic Fund staff to MSF Board of Directors.

20. See Industrial Technology Institute, *A Program of Manufacturing Technology Development and Deployment*, May 15, 1987.

21. Ibid. See also Bartsch, *Reaching for Recovery;* Marietta L. Baba and Stuart L. Hart, "Portrait of a New State Initiative in Industrial Innovation: Michigan's Industrial Technology Institute," in *Technological Innovation*, ed. by Denis D. Gray, Trudy Solom, and William Hetzner (Amsterdam: North-Holland Press, 1986), pp. 89–110.

22. For more on these projects, see Industrial Technology Institute, *A Program of Manufacturing Technology Development and Deployment*, Appendix; and Industrial Technology Institute, *A Program of Manufacturing Technology Development and Deployment*, Addendum, July 15, 1987.

23. Jack Russell, *On Base Modernization*, p. 1 (see Introduction, n. 3).

24. John E. Jackson, "Michigan," in *The New Economic Role of American States*, p. 98 (see chap. 1, n. 7).

25. Muriel Converse, Ann Thomas, and John Jackson, *Financing Small Manufacturers of Metalworking Machinery and Equipment* (Ann Arbor: Institute for Social Research, 1984), cited in Jackson, "Michigan," pp. 98–99.

26. Statistics from Jack Russell, "First Annual Report to the Michigan Legislature," Michigan Technology Deployment Service.

27. "First Annual Report," Office for New Enterprise Services, Sept. 26, 1986.

28. One Market Deployment Service effort is called "Crosswalks." It "identifies, through progressively finer screens of several hundred 5-digit SIC final use product markets, a manageable number (30) of high-growth markets. After identifying the machine tool endowments of the firms known to supply these markets with direct or indirect inputs, we search for Michigan firms with comparable capacities. We believe these firms may find sales opportunities where demand is growing at rates that extend existing suppliers. The analysis can also be reversed, beginning with the capacities of foundation firms, and inverted, yielding early warning to able firms whose markets have begun to shrink." Jack Russell, "Manufacturing Base Modernization," unpublished draft, October 1987, p. 9.

29. Statistics from Jack Russell, Michigan Modernization Service, interview with author, October 1987.

30. Jackson, "Michigan," p. 125.

31. Ibid., p. 126.

32. *Memorandum of Agreement between Saturn Corporation and UAW*, June 28, 1985.

33. The information on Michigan's Saturn proposal is drawn from the proposal itself, an internal Blanchard administration document titled "Manufacturing Innovation Partnership: A Partnership, Not Just a Bid." This document was never released or published.

34. Michigan Strategic Fund, "The Michigan Fund for Strategic Human Investments," proposal, September 1987, p. 1.

Chapter 6: Massachusetts: Redistributing Economic Growth

1. Charles Kenney and Robert L. Turner, "The Contented Technocrat," *Boston Globe Magazine*, March 17, 1985, p. 46.

2. Ben Bradlee, Jr., "Taking the Measure of Michael Dukakis, *Boston Globe*, March 17, 1987, p. 13.

3. *Economic Strength, Fiscal Stability: The Governor's Budget Recommendations for Fiscal Year 1986*, Vol. 1 *Narrative*, "The Economy," Commonwealth of Massachusetts, 1985, pp. 3–4.

4. James Botkin, Dan Dimancescu, and Ray Stata, *The Innovators* (New York: Harper and Row, 1984), p. 135.

5. There is great debate about the precise impact of Reagan's defense buildup on growth rates in Massachusetts. Sorting out the precise impact is extremely difficult. Two things are clear, however: first, increases in defense spending have made an important contribution to the state's boom; and second, growth would have been rapid even if defense spending had not risen as fast as it did during the 1980s. Massachusetts benefits from rising defense spending for precisely the same reason it does well in general in the new economy: its world-class intellectual infrastructure. The current boom began in 1976; the Reagan defense budget simply made a hot economy even hotter.

6. Allan E. Alter, "The Making of the 'Massachusetts Miracle': Does the Duke Deserve the Credit?", *Mass High Tech*, Aug. 17–30, 1987, p. 12.

7. Ibid., p. 1.

8. John Judge, Governor's Office of Economic Development, interviews with author; and Anthony J. Yudis, "Another Try for Mount Greylock," *Boston Globe*, July 26, 1987.

9. John Judge, interviews with author; and Jean Caldwell, "'World Class' Museum Planned," *Boston Globe*, June 2, 1987.

10. Richard Johnson, "Taunton Is Also a High-Tech Area," *Boston Globe*, Jan. 16, 1987.

11. For background on CDCs, see Stewart E. Perry, *Communities on the Way* (Albany: State University of New York Press, 1987); Neal R. Peirce and Carol F. Steinbach, *Corrective Capitalism: The Rise of Community Development Corporations* (New York: Ford Foundation, 1987); and Robin J. Erdmann, Harlan Gradin, and Robert O. Zdenek, *Community Development Corporation Profile Book* (Washington, D.C.: National Congress for Community Economic Development, 1985). Peirce and Steinbach estimate that there are 3,000 to 5,000 CDCs, broadly defined, in the United States. Robert Zdenek, president of the National Congress for Community Economic Development, estimates that there are between 2,000 and 3,000.

12. Carl Sussman, interview with author, June 1985; and Nancy Nye, "Six Years Later: The Experience of the Massachusetts CDFC," *The Entrepreneurial Economy* (newsletter of the Corporation for Enterprise Development, in Washington, D.C.), March 1984, p. 12.

13. Charles Grigsby, interviews with author.

14. In addition to interviews with participants, this summary of CDFC's problems draws on Belden Daniels, Beth Siegel, and Steven Klein, *The Community Development Finance Corporation: A Review and Action Plan* (Cambridge, Mass.: Counsel for Community Development, 1982).

15. Daniels, Siegel, and Klein, *The Community Development Finance Corporation*.

16. In addition to interviews with participants, the discussion of Arnold Print Works draws on Margaret Pantridge, "Anatomy of a Bailout," *The Review*, Jan. 25, 1985; Howard Baker-Smith, Lucy Gorham, and Lindsay French, "Draft Case Study: Adams Print Works," prepared for the John F. Kennedy School of Government, March 23, 1984; and interview transcripts provided by Gorham.

17. Baker-Smith, Gorham, and French, "Draft Case Study," p. 13.

18. Ibid., p. 21.

19. "It is the only bank . . . :" from Douglas M. Bailey, "Banking Turn-around," *Boston Globe*, Aug. 4, 1987.

20. Government Land Bank, *1975–1985: The Massachusetts Government Land Bank Tenth Anniversary Report*, 1985.

21. Statistics from Timothy Bassett, interview with author, December 1986.

22. "Nonprofit Groups Take Housing Initiative," *Boston Globe*, Aug. 16, 1987.

23. Ferguson and Ladd, "Massachusetts," p. 65 (see chap. 1, n. 7).

24. Massachusetts Executive Office of Labor, internal memorandum.

25. Ibid.

26. For a comprehensive treatment of the Commission on the Future of Mature Industries, see Samuel Leiken, "The Governor's Commission on the Future of Mature Industries: A Study of Public Governance," paper prepared for the John F. Kennedy School of Government (available from Samuel Leiken, Director, Massachusetts Product Development Corporation).

27. Tom Gallagher, "Mature Industries Law Quietly Crumbling in Mass.", *Boston Globe*, July 14, 1987.

28. Leiken, "The Governor's Commission on the Future of Mature Industries," p. 18.

29. Evelyn Murphy, "Bay State Success Story: Helping Ailing Industries," *Boston Globe*, Aug. 18, 1987.

30. Massachusetts Industrial Services Program.

31. Murphy, "Bay State Success Story."

32. Massachusetts Industrial Services Program, "Report on the Activities of the Massachusetts Industrial Services Program," Nov. 14, 1986, p. 7.

33. In addition to interviews with those involved, this account draws upon Lucien Rhodes, "Against All Odds," *Inc.*, November 1986, pp. 102–108; Michael Kranish, "A New Twist in New Bedford," *Boston Globe*, May 19, 1987; and other *Boston Globe* reports.

34. Alter, "The Making of the 'Massachusetts Miracle.' " The 4.8 percent figure applies to five targets of opportunity, not including Roxbury, Boston's black community.

35. John Aloysius Farrell, "Varied, Flourishing Economy Fuels Manchester, N.H. Rebirth," *Boston Globe*, Feb. 1, 1987.

36. Mary McGrory, "Welfare Success Story," *Washington Post*, Feb. 9, 1986.

37. "The Old Ruby Is Dead": *ibid.*; "Being able. . .": interview with author, March 1987.

38. See Hugh O'Neill, *Creating Opportunity* (Washington, D.C.: Council of State Planning Agencies, 1986), pp. 17–18, 157–161.

39. Peter Cove, Lee Bowes, interviews with author.

40. Department of Public Welfare, Office of Research, Planning, and Evaluation, *An Evaluation of the Massachusetts Employment and Training Choices Program: Interim Findings on Participation and Outcomes, FY84–FY85*, January 1986, p. 8.

41. Massachusetts Department of Public Welfare, Office of Research, Planning, and Evaluation.

42. Ibid.

43. Department of Public Welfare, *An Evaluation of the Massachusetts Employment and Training Choices Program*; Department of Public Welfare, Office of Research, Planning, and Evaluation, *Follow-Up Survey of the First 25,000 ET Placements*, August 1986; and Department of Public Welfare, Office of Research, Planning, and Evaluation, *An Analysis of the First 25,000 ET Placements*, August 1986.

44. Department of Public Welfare, *An Analysis of the First 25,000 ET Placements*.
45. Department of Public Welfare, *Follow-Up Survey of the First 25,000 ET Placements*.
46. Department of Public Welfare, *An Analysis of the First 25,000 ET Placements*.
47. Comptroller General of the United States, *An Overview of the WIN Program: Its Objectives, Accomplishments, and Problems* (Washington, D.C.: U.S. General Accounting Office, 1982).
48. Department of Public Welfare, *An Evaluation of the Massachusetts Employment and Training Choices Program*.
49. Department of Public Welfare, *Follow-Up Survey of the First 25,000 ET Placements*.
50. Department of Public Welfare, Office of Research, Planning, and Evaluation.
51. Ibid.
52. Ibid.
53. Irene Sege, "Merit of Welfare-to-Work Program in Dispute," *Boston Globe*, Feb. 2, 1987.
54. For this data and an excellent study of family poverty in Massachusetts, see Andrew Sum, Paul Harrington, Neal Fogg, and William Goedicke, *Family Poverty in the New Boston Economy: Recent Trends in the Size and Composition of Family Poverty Problems in the City of Boston* (Boston: Northeastern University Center for Labor Market Studies, 1987).
55. Massachusetts Taxpayers Foundation, *Training People to Live without Welfare: Executive Summary* (Boston: Massachusetts Taxpayers Foundation, 1987).
56. Massachusetts Department of Public Welfare, Office of Research, Planning, and Evaluation.
57. Bay State Skills Corporation, *The Bay State Skills Corporation: 1981–1986, Evolution and Innovation*, 1986.
58. Massachusetts Department of Revenue, "Voluntary Compliance: The $564 Million Story," December 1985.
59. Ibid., and John Sasso, interview with author, February 1985.
60. Anne Swardson, "States Test Idea of Tax Amnesty," *Washington Post*, March 4, 1986.
61. Bob Kuttner, "Fiscally Prudent Dukakis Must Also Meet the Needs of Citizens," *Boston Globe*, March 30, 1987.
62. "How the Governors See It: A Newsweek Poll," *Newsweek*, March 24, 1986, p. 32.
63. Ben Bradlee, Jr., "Taking the Measure of Michael Dukakis," p. 13.
64. Ibid.
65. Ibid., p. 12.
66. Ibid.

Chapter 7: New York: Housing the Poor

1. Robert H. Connery and Gerald Benjamin, *Rockefeller of New York: Executive Power in the Statehouse* (Ithaca: Cornell University Press, 1979), pp. 190–191.
2. Ibid., p. 191.
3. Peirce and Hagstrom, *The Book of America*, p. 64 (see chap. 2, n. 25).
4. Michael Kramer and Sam Roberts, *I Never Wanted to Be Vice President of*

Anything: An Investigative Biography of Nelson Rockefeller (New York: Basic Books, 1976), pp. 145–146; and Peirce and Hagstrom, *The Book of America*, p. 64.

5. Connery and Benjamin, *Rockefeller of New York*, p. 231; and Gerald Benjamin, interviews with author.

6. Thirteen years: Ken Auletta, "Governor, Part 1," *The New Yorker*, April 9, 1984, p. 89. The cost of $1.7 billion: Elaine Ryan, Assistant to the Director of State Operations and Policy Management, New York, interviews with author.

7. Peirce and Hagstrom, *The Book of America*, p. 65.

8. Connery and Benjamin, *Rockefeller of New York*, pp. 236–237.

9. Gerald Benjamin, interview with author, May 1986.

10. Nearly 20,000: Interview with Gov. Hugh Carey, in Gerald Benjamin and T. Norman Hurd, eds., *Making Experience Count: Managing Modern New York in the Carey Era* (Albany: Rockefeller Institute, 1985), p. 13. Tax cut: Wayne Diesel, New York State Budget Director, interview with author, May 1986.

11. Gerald Benjamin, interview with author, May 1986; and New York Senate Office of Fiscal Studies, *Analysis of the 1986–87 Executive Budget: Staff Report to the Chairman of the New York State Senate Finance Committee*, January 1986, p. 13.

12. New York State Assembly Program Development Group, *Economic Growth and Revitalization: A Review of the Assembly Record 1979 to 1985*, April 1986, Appendix A, p. 2.

13. Peirce and Hagstrom, *The Book of America*, p. 60.

14. New York State Assembly Program Development Group, *Economic Growth and Revitalization*, Appendix A, p. 2.

15. For more on economic development legislation initiated by the Assembly, see ibid.

16. For more on the Science and Technology Foundation, see ibid., pp. 21–24, and Appendix K; Science and Technology Foundation annual reports; and other publications from the New York State Science and Technology Foundation.

17. Mario Cuomo, "Address to New Democratic Coalition," May 11, 1974 (available from New York Governor's Office).

18. Auletta, "Governor, Part 1," p. 76.

19. Gerald Benjamin, "The Gubernatorial Transition in New York," in *Gubernatorial Transitions: The 1982 Election*, ed. by Thad Beyle, pp. 347–348 (see chap. 5, n. 2).

20. Registration edge: ibid., p. 349; 180,000 votes: "Voter Poll Shows Big Cuomo Margin," *New York Times*, Nov. 6, 1986.

21. Benjamin, "The Gubernatorial Transition in New York," p. 367.

22. Elaine Ryan, interviews with author.

23. Gerald Benjamin, "The Carey Governorship," in *Making Experience Count*, p. 250.

24. New York Senate Office of Fiscal Studies, *Analysis of the 1986–87 Executive Budget*, p. 13.

25. Scott Christianson, Executive Assistant to the Director of Criminal Justice, New York, interview with author, May 1986.

26. Miriam Pawel, "Cuomo and the Cost of Crime-Fighting," *Newsday*, March 3, 1986.

27. Joe Mahoney, "New York Hopes Program Will Ease Prison Crowding," *Boston Globe*, Aug. 31, 1987.

28. See Mary K. Nenno, *New Money and New Methods: A Catalog of State and Local Initiatives in Housing and Community Development* (Washington, D.C.: National Association of Housing and Redevelopment Officials, 1986); John Sidor, *State Housing*

Initiatives: A Compendium (Washington, D.C.: Council of State Community Affairs Agencies, 1986); National Governors Association, *Decent and Affordable Housing for All: A Challenge to the States* (Washington, D.C.: National Governors Association, 1986); Citizens Housing and Planning Council, *On Its Own: New York City Approaches Affordable Housing* (New York: Citizens Housing and Planning Council, 1985); and Mary Jordan, "A Place to Call Home: Local Governments and Nonprofit Groups Are Changing the Way We Are Housing Our Poor," *Washington Post, National Weekly Edition,* April 20, 1987.

29. Bill Eimicke, interviews with author.

30. Housing Partnership Development Corporation, "The Housing Partnership New Homes Program: A Public/Private Financing Model Designed to Stimulate Production of Affordable Owner-Occupied Housing," p. 1.

31. Bill Eimicke, interview with author, October 1987.

32. Michael Dowling, Deputy Commissioner, New York Department of Social Services, interview with author, October 1987.

33. Some estimates go as high as $2 billion a year; the $1.5-billion estimate was provided by Bill Eimicke, in an interview with the author.

34. Citizens Housing and Planning Council, *On Its Own,* p. 1.

35. Kathryn Wylde, President, Housing Partnership Development Corporation, interview with author, August 1986.

36. By 1987, Governor Cuomo had delivered $25 million per year for the Low Income Housing Trust Fund, $25 million per year for the Affordable Home Ownership Development Program, $20 million per year for the Homeless Housing Assistance Program, and $200 million in Battery Park City bonds, for affordable housing in New York City. The projected ten-year total had grown to $1.8 billion.

37. Bill Eimicke, interview with author, October 1987.

38. See Citizens Housing and Planning Council, *On Its Own,* chap. 2.

39. Ibid., p. 22.

40. Bill Eimicke, interview with author, October 1987.

41. Gary Sam Hattem, interview with author, July 1986, citing 1980 census.

42. *Ten Years of Change: Saint Nicholas Neighborhood Preservation Corporation, 1985 Annual Report.*

43. See O'Neill, *Creating Opportunity,* p. 98 (see chap. 6, n. 38).

44. Gary Sam Hattem, interview with author, October 1986.

45. *Ten Years of Change,* p. 17.

46. New York State Division of Housing and Community Renewal, *Annual Report 1985–1986: Housing New York, Progress and Commitment,* pp. 14–15, 20, 52.

47. Ibid.

48. See Nenno, *New Money and New Methods;* Citizens Housing and Planning Council, *On Its Own,* chap. 2; and Peirce and Steinbach, *Corrective Capitalism* (see chap. 6, n. 11).

49. Thomas Brock, *Strengthening an Education/Work Initiative: The Second Year of New York State's School-to-Employment Program* (New York: Manpower Demonstration Research Corporation, 1986); and report dated Feb. 13, 1986, to Governor Cuomo from Lillian Roberts, Commissioner of Labor.

50. *Statistical Abstract of the United States, 1987,* p. xxii.

51. New York State Department of Social Services, *Statistical Supplement to the 1985 Annual Report.*

52. Office of Program Planning, Analysis, and Development and Division of Income Maintenance, New York State Department of Social Services, *Evaluation of*

the *Employment Assistance Program*, March 1984. See also O'Neill, *Creating Opportunity*, pp. 153–154.

53. Herb Ouida, interview with author, August 1987.

54.. "What Makes Mario Run?", *Newsweek*, March 24, 1986, p. 26.

55. "America As a Family: An Interview with New York Governor Mario Cuomo," *New Perspectives* (published by the Institute for National Strategy, Los Angeles), Summer 1985, p. 7.

56. Brock, *Strengthening an Education/Work Initiative*.

57. Auletta, "Governor, Part 1," p. 84; and "Governor, Part 2," *The New Yorker*, April 16, 1984, p. 121.

58. Jeffrey Schmalz, "Second Inaugural by Cuomo Sums up Accomplishments," *New York Times*, Jan. 2, 1987.

Chapter 8: The First Agenda: Creating Economic Growth

1. See Kent C. Redmond and Thomas M. Smith, *Project Whirlwind: The History of a Pioneer Computer* (Bedford, Mass.: Digital Press, 1980).

2. Botkin, Dimancescu, and Stata, *The Innovators*, p. 134 (see chap. 6, n. 4).

3. Howell, "The Lesson of Massachusetts," p. 12 (see Introduction, n. 14).

4. Ibid.

5. Jane Jacobs, *Cities and the Wealth of Nations: Principles of Economic Life* (New York: Vintage Books, 1985), p. 221. Although this quote appears in her 1984 book, it offers a good summary of the central thesis of her 1969 book: *The Economy of Cities* (New York: Random House, 1970).

6. See, for instance, Ronald Rosenberg, "U.S. Losing Monopoly on Software," *Boston Globe*, Feb. 8, 1987.

7. Robert B. Reich, *Tales of a New America* (New York: Times Books, 1987), pp. 121–123.

8. Jacobs, *The Economy of Cities*, pp. 71–74.

9. Counsel for Community Development, *Small Business and Capital Markets* (Washington, D.C.: U.S. Department of Commerce, Economic Development Administration, 1981), p. 11.

10. David Birch, "Matters of Fact" (interview), *Inc.*, April 1985, p. 32.

11. Jacobs, *The Economy of Cities*, p. 77.

12. The employment figures are from Pat Choate and J. K. Linger, *The High-Flex Society: Shaping America's Economic Future* (New York: Alfred A. Knopf, 1986), p. 93.

13. Ibid.

14. U.S. Department of Commerce, Bureau of Economic Analysis, personal communication.

15. Reich, *Tales of a New America*, pp. 122–123.

16. Choate and Linger, *The High-Flex Society*, p. 14.

17. Ibid.

18. Allegheny Conference on Community Development, *A Strategy for Growth*, Vol. 1, p. 14 (see Introduction, n. 7).

19. Reich, *The Next American Frontier*, pp. 128–130 (see Introduction, n. 7).

20. Henton and Waldhorn, "California," p. 214 (see chap. 1, n. 21).

21. Task Force for a Long-Term Economic Strategy for Michigan, *The Path to Prosperity*, p. 35 (see chap. 5, n. 15). This report cites Janet Wolfe and John Yinger, "Shift-Share Analysis," unpublished, which relies on data from the U.S. Department of Commerce, Bureau of Economic Analysis, Regional Economic Information System, 1958–1982 detailed components of personal income and employment, revised, 1983.

22. David Birch, "The Q Factor," *Inc.*, April 1987, p. 53.

23. Jacobs, *The Economy of Cities*, pp. 201–202.

24. Paul Taylor, "The People and the Economy," *Washington Post*, May 19, 1986; Taylor cites the Southern Growth Policies Board.

25. See Jacobs, *The Economy of Cities*; and Jacobs, *Cities and the Wealth of Nations*.

26. For the closest thing to such a methodology, see the Council of State Planning Agencies books referred to in chapter 1, and publications from the Corporation for Enterprise Development, including David Jones, ed., *Building the New Economy: States in the Lead* (Washington, D.C.: Corporation for Enterprise Development, 1986); Robert Friedman and William Schweke, eds., *Expanding the Opportunity to Produce* (see chap. 1, n. 31); and *Making the Grade: The Development Report Card for the States* (Washington, D.C.: Corporation for Enterprise Development, 1987).

27. Marianne K. Clarke, *Revitalizing State Economies* (Washington, D.C.: National Governors Association, 1986), p. 40.

28. Jacobs, *Cities and the Wealth of Nations*, pp. 221–230.

29. Battelle Columbus Laboratories, *A Strategy for the Development of High Technology Activities in New York State* (Albany: New York State Science and Technology Foundation, 1982), pp. VI-48–52.

30. Interview with author, January 1987.

31. Task Force on Technological Innovation, *Technology and Growth: State Initiatives in Technological Innovation* (Washington, D.C.: National Governors Association, 1983), p. 64.

32. David Birch, "The Q Factor," p. 53.

33. See for instance Dan Dimancescu and James Botkin, *The New Alliance: America's R&D Consortia* (Cambridge, Mass.: Ballinger, 1986), pp. 38–40.

34. See Sheridan Tatsuno, *The Technopolis Strategy* (New York: Prentice Hall Press, 1986); and Sheridan Tatsuno, "Building a Japanese Techno-State: MITI's Technopolis Program Underway," *Dataquest Research Newsletter*, 1987, No. 3.

35. Quoted in Peter Behr, "Economic Weaknesses Seen Hurting U.S. Industry in Global Competition," *Washington Post*, Feb. 17, 1985.

36. "High Tech to the Rescue," *Business Week*, June 16, 1987, pp. 100–101.

37. Choate and Linger, *The High-Flex Society*, p. 29.

38. Jacques Koppel, "Manufacturers Must Face the Music," *High Technology*, March 1986, p. 12.

39. Cited in John Cleveland, "Common Ground . . . Mutual Gains: A Business Plan for Fostering Productive Work Relations in Michigan," Michigan Modernization Service, June 5, 1987.

40. Choate and Linger, *The High-Flex Society*, p. 7.

41. Barbara Vobejda, "Before They Can Learn Robotics, They Have to Learn the Three R's," *Washington Post*, National Weekly Edition, April 20, 1987, p. 36.

42. Paula Duggan, *Literacy at Work* (Washington, D.C.: Northeast-Midwest Institute, 1985).

43. Choate and Linger, *The High-Flex Society*, p. 207.

44. Edward Morrison, testimony before a Subcommittee of the House Committee on Government Operations, in *Federal and State Roles in Economic Development* (Washington, D.C.: U.S. Government Printing Office, 1986), p. 310.

45. Reich, *Next American Frontier*, p. 220.

46. Barbara Dyer, in *Federal and State Roles in Economic Development*, p. 307.

47. Information based on documents from the Minnesota Department of Jobs and Training.

48. For more information, see documents from the Prairie State 2000 Authority, State of Illinois Center, Suite 4–800, 100 W. Randolph St., Chicago, Ill., 60601.

49. See Kuttner, *The Economic Illusion*, pp. 150–151 (see Introduction, n. 21), and Robert Kuttner, *The Life of the Party: Democratic Prospects in 1988 and Beyond* (New York: Viking, 1987), pp. 226–228.

50. See, for instance, New Enterprise Institute, *Final Report to the W. K. Kellogg Foundation: New Enterprise Institute Program Grant* (Portland: University of Southern Maine, 1982); and Mary Ann Scheirer et al., *Innovation and Enterprise: A Study of NSF's Innovation Centers Program* (Washington, D.C.: Westat Inc., 1986). The NSF found that among the ten Innovation Centers it funded between 1973 and 1982, the most successful "worked extensively with start-up businesses, rather than existing businesses, offered intensive services, especially in business and marketing, and worked with a comparatively limited number of clients."

51. SRI International, *Innovations in Industrial Competitiveness at the State Level: Report to the President's Commission on Industrial Competitiveness*, December 1984, p. 64.

52. New Enterprise Institute, *Final Report*.

53. David Ahlen, Pennsylvania State University, Secretary of National Business Incubation Association, speech to the Council of State Community Affairs Agencies conference, Key West, Florida, September 1987.

54. Nell Henderson, "'Incubators': A Small-Business Case Study," *Washington Post*, June 30, 1986, citing National Business Incubation Association.

55. Kibre Damit and Robert Friedman, "Myths of Small Business Failure," *The Entrepreneurial Economy*, July 1982, p. 5.

56. "Thinking about the Future of Business Incubators: An Interview with Randall Whaley," *NBIA* (National Business Incubation Association) *Review*, Vol. 1, No. 2, p. 3.

57. Corporation for Enterprise Development, *Eight Lessons from Europe: Report of the American Study Tour on Local Employment Initiatives* (Washington, D.C.: Corporation for Enterprise Development, 1984), pp. 29–37.

58. Ibid., pp. 37–38.

59. See David P. Ellerman, "Entrepreneurship in the Mondragon Cooperatives," *Review of Social Economy*, Vol. 42, No. 3, pp. 272–294; and Industrial Cooperatives Association, "Mondragon: An English Language Bibliography," Somerville, Mass., 1985.

60. See Jones, ed., *Building the New Economy*, pp. 2–4.

61. Choate and Linger, *The High-Flex Society*, p. 104.

62. See U.S. Small Business Administration, *State Export Promotion Activities* (Washington, D.C.: Small Business Administration, 1984); and Clarke, *Revitalizing State Economies*, p. 79.

63. John, *Shifting Responsibilities*, p. 27 (see chap. 2, n. 22).

64. Mark Potts, "Smaller Firms Speak out on Trade," *Washington Post*, National Weekly Edition, Feb. 23, 1987.

65. "Management Discovers the Human Side of Automation," *Business Week*, Sept. 29, 1986.

66. Choate and Linger, *The High-Flex Society*, pp. 121–122.

67. See John R. Stepp and John L. Bonner, "States Tie Economic Development to Improved Labor Relations Climates," *Journal of State Government* (published by the Council of State Governments), January–February 1987, pp. 40–43.

68. Choate and Linger, *The High-Flex Society*, p. 137.

69. "Management Discovers the Human Side of Automation," *Business Week*.

70. Choate and Linger, *The High-Flex Society*, p. 162.

71. Charles M. Atkins, Massachusetts Commissioner of Public Welfare, quoted in John Robinson, "States Seek Wide Shifts in Policies on Welfare," *Boston Globe*, Nov. 25, 1986.

72. Botkin, Dimancescu, and Stata, *The Innovators*, p. 130.

73. Office of Technology Assessment, *The Displaced Worker* (Washington, D.C.: U.S. Government Printing Office, 1986).

74. Robert Kuttner, quoted in "Beyond Recession," *World Policy Journal*, Fall 1985, p. 758.

75. Corporation for Enterprise Development, *Eight Lessons from Europe*, pp. 22–28.

76. Ibid., pp. 15–21; and Robert Friedman, "63,000 Entrepreneurs," *Inc.*, May 1984.

77. National Governors Association, *Making America Work: Productive People, Productive Policies* (Washington, D.C.: National Governors Association, 1987), p. 65.

78. Choate and Linger, *The High-Flex Society*, pp. 8, 39.

79. Judy Mann, "Child Care: A Wise Investment," *Washington Post*, Jan. 3, 1986.

80. Neal R. Peirce, "State Investments in Children," *Washington Post Writers Group*, Nov. 23, 1986.

81. Robert I. Lerman, "Helping the Poor outside the Welfare System: A Proposal for Restructuring Antipoverty Policy," testimony before the Subcommittee on Social Security and Family Policy of the Senate Finance Committee, Feb. 23, 1987.

82. Reich, *Next American Frontier*, p. 212.

83. Paul Peterson et al., *When Federalism Works* (Washington, D.C.: Brookings Institution, 1986), pp. 107–108.

84. See Schlesinger, *The Coming of the New Deal*, pp. 301–315 (see Introduction, n. 2).

85. Choate and Linger, *The High-Flex Society*, p. 7.

86. For interesting treatments of this issue, see Lester C. Thurow, *The Zero Sum Solution* (New York: Touchstone, 1986); Susan Friedman and S. M. Miller, "The Reconstruction of Finance: Implications of Industrial Policy," in *Beyond Reagan: Alternatives for the '80s*, ed. by Alan Gartner, Colin Greer, and Frank Riessman (New York: Harper and Row, 1984); and Michael Kieschnick, "Do We Really Need a Reconstruction Finance Corporation?", *Politics and Markets* (newsletter of the Gallatin Institute), Nov. 28, 1983.

87. For a useful discussion of the problems, see Robert B. Reich, "Bread and Circuits," *The New Republic*, Aug. 3, 1987, pp. 29–36.

88. On the Chrysler bail-out, see Robert B. Reich and John D. Donahue, *New Deals: The Chrysler Revival and the American System* (New York: Penguin Books, 1986); on the Footwear Revitalization Program, see Michael J. Piore and Charles F. Sabel, *The Second Industrial Divide* (New York: Basic Books, 1984), pp. 303–305.

89. Thurow, *The Zero Sum Solution*, pp. 281–282.

Chapter 9: The Second Agenda: Bringing the Poor into the Growth Process

1. Choate and Linger, *The High-Flex Society*, p. 209.

2. John, *Shifting Responsibilities*, p. 62 (see chap. 2, n. 22).

3. Ibid.

4. MAGI Educational Services, Inc., *Project AVE: Final Evaluation Report 1985* (Albany: New York State Department of Labor, 1985), p. 5.

5. Ann Hulbert, "Children as Parents," *The New Republic*, Sept. 10, 1984, p. 15; and Spencer Rich, "While Most Gain, Millions Suffer," *Washington Post*, Jan. 20, 1986.

6. Half of all black families: Rich, "While Most Gain;" Young black fathers: Robert Lerman, "Who Are the Young Absent Fathers?", *Youth and Society*, Vol. 18, No. 1 (September 1986), pp. 23–24.

7. MAGI Educational Services, Inc., *Project AVE*, p. 6, citing G. Berlin, "Youth Unemployment: Will the Past Be Prologue?", paper presented at the National Neighborhood Coalition Conference, 1985.

8. Charles Murray, with Deborah Laren, "According to Age: Longitudinal Profiles of AFDC Recipients and the Poor by Age Group," Working Seminar on the Family and American Welfare Policy, American Enterprise Institute, Washington, D.C., September 1986, p. 76. By "young persons," Murray means those aged 20 to 34.

9. More than half of all women: Hulbert, "Children as Parents," p. 19; half of all black children: Glenn C. Loury, "A New American Dilemma," *The New Republic*, Dec. 31, 1984, p. 15.

10. Loury, "A New American Dilemma," p. 15.

11. Andrew Sum et al., *Family Poverty in the New Boston Economy* (see chap. 6, n. 54).

12. Governor's Blue Ribbon Commission on Welfare Reform, *Redefining Independence in a Changing Economy*, Michigan Cabinet Council on Human Investment, 1987, p. 23.

13. Frances Fox Piven and Richard Cloward, in *The New Class War: Reagan's Attack on the Welfare State and Its Consequences* (New York: Pantheon, 1982), p. 14, report that the welfare rolls increased fourfold between 1960 and the early 1970s. David Kirp, in "The California Work/Welfare Scheme," *Public Interest*, No. 83 (Spring 1986), p. 39, reports an eightfold increase between 1960 and 1970.

14. Task Force on Poverty and Welfare, *A New Social Contract: Rethinking the Nature and Purpose of Public Assistance* (Albany: New York Governor's Office, 1986), p. 30; and Robert Kuttner, "The Welfare Strait," *The New Republic*, July 6, 1987, p. 21.

15. Daniel Friedlander, Marjorie Erickson, Gayle Hamilton, and Virginia Knox, *West Virginia: Final Report on the Community Work Experience Demonstrations* (New York: Manpower Research Demonstration Corporation, 1986).

16. For an initial interpretation, see Greg J. Duncan with Richard D. Coe, Mary E. Corcoran, Martha S. Hill, Saul D. Hoffman, and James N. Morgan, *Years of Poverty, Years of Plenty: The Changing Fortunes of American Workers and Families* (Ann Arbor, Mich.: Institute for Social Research, 1984). For later examinations see Murray, "According to Age," and David Ellwood, "Targetting 'Would-Be' Long-Term Recipients," paper prepared for the U.S. Department of Health and Human Services by Mathematica Policy Research Inc., Princeton, N.J., January 1986. Charles Murray is of course best known for his 1984 book, *Losing Ground*, which was quite justifiably criticized for dispensing its facts selectively to prove an ideological point. "According to Age" is a far more careful document. Murray sticks to the facts, and as a result his analysis is far more convincing. Ellwood, who is regarded as one of the most authoritative experts on this subject, comes to very similar conclusions. His 1986 paper substantially altered the conclusions he had reached in a 1983 study with Mary Jo Bane, which had reinforced the notion that most of those on welfare used it as a temporary expedient.

17. Murray, "According to Age," p. 62.

18. Ellwood, "Targetting "Would-Be' Long-Term Recipients," pp. 4–6.

19. Richard B. Freeman, "Cutting Black Youth Unemployment: Create Jobs That Pay as Well as Crime," *New York Times*, July 20, 1986.

20. Governor's Blue Ribbon Commission on Welfare Reform, *Redefining Independence in a Changing Economy*, p. 18.

21. Ibid., p. 27.

22. Robert Friedman, *The Safety Net as Ladder* (Washington, D.C.: Council of State Planning Agencies, 1988); and Steve Quick and Robert Friedman, *The Safety Net as Ladder: Transfer Payments and Economic Development* (Washington, D.C.: Corporation for Enterprise Development, 1985).

23. See for instance Mickey Kaus, Review of *Let's Put America back to Work*, by Sen. Paul Simon, *The Washington Monthly*, March 1987, p. 59.

24. Rep. Sander M. Levin, letter to the editor, *The New Republic*, Sept. 1, 1986, p. 6.

25. See Robert A. Caro, *The Power Broker*, pp. 363–372 (see Introduction, n. 2), on the Civil Works Administration.

26. Task Force on Poverty and Welfare, *A New Social Contract*.

27. The NGA proposal and most congressional proposals would not require women to participate if they had children under the age of three. This is a difficult issue; some experts argue that all women with children should be required to participate. If a state chose to require participation by all women, it might consider making the work requirement half time for those with very young children. According to David Ellwood, less than 30 percent of married American mothers work full time, all year. See David Ellwood, "Outside the Ghetto," *The New Republic*, Oct. 6, 1986, p. 20.

For mothers who have not completed high school, a requirement that they return to school might be wiser than a work requirement. In all cases, quality child care is extremely important, and programs such as Head Start should be expanded and extended to younger children.

28. If government extends health coverage to the working poor, it would be using taxpayers' money to subsidize those corporations that fail to provide health insurance to their employees. This would create exactly the wrong incentives, for it would encourage firms *not* to provide health insurance. The other extreme—requiring all firms to provide insurance—creates different problems. It would place severe financial burdens on some new, small, and marginal firms. The best option is clearly to require that all corporations provide coverage, then to offer low-cost, subsidized rates under an HMO system to certain classes of firms judged unable to afford coverage on their own. Rates could be linked, on a sliding scale, to corporate size, age, and profitability.

29. See Task Force on Poverty and Welfare, *A New Social Contract*; and Robert I. Lerman, "Separating Income Support from Income Supplementation," *Journal of the Institute for Socioeconomic Studies*, Autumn 1985, pp. 101–124.

30. See F. Gerard Adams, *Increasing the Minimum Wage: The Macroeconomic Impacts* (Washington, D.C.: Economic Policy Institute, 1987).

31. Robert Woodson, quoted in *Creating Opportunity: Strategies for Increasing the Self-Sufficiency of Americans through Economic Development, Proceedings of the National Symposium and Showcase of Promising Policies and Programs for Public and Private Decision-Makers* (Washington, D.C.: Council of State Planning Agencies, 1985), pp. 44–45.

32. Nicholas Lemann, "The Origins of the Underclass," *The Atlantic*, June 1986, pp. 31–55, and July 1986, pp. 54–68.

33. Residents of concentrated poverty areas in the 100 largest central cities constituted only 6.7 percent of the nation's poor in 1980, according to the New York Task Force on Poverty and Welfare, *A New Social Contract*, p. 21. Another source— Mary Jo Bane, Julie Wilson, and Lauren Young, "Poverty and Welfare in America," paper prepared for the Task Force on Poverty and Welfare, 1986—estimates that only 20 percent of the statistical poor are "chronically poor residents of urban ghettos or rural poverty pockets who are dissociated from the labor market and dependent on welfare." Charles Murray, in "According to Age," also demonstrates that a minority of the statistical poor are in fact chronically poor. If these analyses are correct, most of the poor are not long-term, chronic poor, and most of the chronic poor are not residents of urban ghettos. Add to these observations the obvious fact that most urban ghettos are not in as bad shape as those Lemann described, and one must conclude that Lemann was describing a very small minority of America's poor. This is not to denigrate his description of the worst urban ghettos, but it *is* to remind readers that the worst urban ghettos, though presenting enormous problems, are not representative of American poverty—or even of America's urban ghettos in general.

34. Cicero Wilson, "Neighborhood-Based Groups: A Key Ingredient in Reviving Distressed Areas," *The Entrepreneurial Economy*, March 1984, pp. 4–5.

35. See Peirce and Steinbach, *Corrective Capitalism*, p. 31 (see chap. 6, n. 11).

36. See Ibid., p. 40; O'Neill, *Creating Opportunity*, p. 95 (see chap. 6, n. 38).

37. Peirce and Steinbach, *Corrective Capitalism*, p. 19; and O'Neill, *Creating Opportunity*, p. 94.

38. Yvonne Brooks, "House to Consider $17 Billion Housing Bill," *Boston Globe*, June 10, 1987.

39. See Peirce and Steinbach, *Corrective Capitalism*, p. 77.

40. Ibid., p. 76.

41. For a comprehensive treatment of the Shorebank Corporation's first decade, see Richard P. Taub, *Community Capitalism* (Boston: Harvard Business School Press, 1988).

42. Ron Grzywinski, interview with author, October 1987.

43. Milton Davis, Chairman, South Shore Bank, interview with author, October 1986.

44. Woodstock Institute, *Evaluation of the Illinois Neighborhood Development Corporation* (Chicago: Woodstock Institute, 1982), pp. v, 11; Richard Taub, *Community Capitalism*, pp. 61–65; and interviews with Ron Grzywinski, Mary Houghton, and others at Shorebank Corporation.

45. Joan Shapiro, South Shore Bank, interview with author, December 1981.

46. James Bringley, South Shore Bank, interviews with author.

47. See Osborne, "Bootstrap Banking" (see chap. 3, n. 40).

48. Richard Taub, interview with author, October 1986.

49. Ron Grzywinski and others, South Shore Bank, interviews with author.

50. See Osborne, "Bootstrap Banking."

51. For more information on Kentucky Highlands Investment Corporation, see Peirce and Steinbach, *Corrective Capitalism*, p. 42; Perry, *Communities on the Way* (see chap. 6, n. 11); and Thomas P. Murphy, "The Right Way to Do It?", *Forbes*, March 20, 1978, p. 108.

52. Peirce and Steinbach, *Corrective Capitalism*, p. 42; and Tom Miller, interview with author, August 1986.

53. Perry, *Communities on the Way*, pp. 184, 242.

54. For more on how government could support the creation and maintenance of third-sector development banks, see Ronald Grzywinski, "The Role of Banks in

Neighborhood-Based Development Strategies, *The Entrepreneurial Economy*, March 1984, pp. 7–9; and Ronald A. Grzywinski and Dennis R. Marino, "Public Policy, Private Banks and Economic Development," in Friedman and Schweke, eds., *Expanding the Opportunity to Produce*, pp. 243–256 (see chap. 1, n. 31).

55. The few public housing projects that have allowed tenant management have shown dramatic results: rent collections have increased, vacancy rates have fallen, crime has been reduced, and teenage pregnancies have declined. Some tenant-managed projects have even created businesses and day-care centers, run rehab projects through which they have trained residents for construction work, and set up programs to help residents go to college. See Arthur S. Brisbane, "Public Housing Tenants Try out Self-Government," *Washington Post*, May 20, 1985; Robert L. Woodson, "Self-Help, Not Big Daddy, Must Rescue the Black Underclass," *Washington Post*, May 12, 1985; "Running Public Housing," *Washington Post*, May 23, 1985; and Kitty Krause, "Hammers and Nails in Mt. Winans," *The Washington Monthly*, April 1986, pp. 21–26.

56. Corporation for Enterprise Development, *Investing in Poor Communities* (Washington, D.C.: Corporation for Enterprise Development, 1985), p. 58; and Corporation for Enterprise Development, *Eight Lessons from Europe*, pp. 46–48 (see chap. 8, n. 57).

57. George Kanahele, "Entrepreneurship Development as a Tool of Employment Policy," in Friedman and Schweke, eds., *Expanding the Opportunity to Produce*, p. 418.

58. Ibid., p. 423. For more on HETADI, see Kanahele's essay; O'Neill, *Creating Opportunity*, pp. 114–115; and publications from HETADI.

59. Kathryn S. Keeley, "Women's Economic Development Corporation," *The Entrepreneurial Economy*, October 1984, pp. 11–12; and Neal R. Peirce, "Welfare to Entrepreneurship," Washington Post Writers Group, Dec. 23, 1984.

60. Peirce, "Welfare to Entrepreneurship."

61. See Schlesinger, *The Coming of the New Deal*, pp. 301–315 (see Introduction, n. 2).

62. Between 1960 and 1970, Congress expanded the number of federal grant programs from 45 to 430. The watershed Great Society Congress, the 89th, created 21 new health programs, 17 new education programs, 15 new economic development programs, 12 new urban aid programs, and four new job-training programs. By 1969, the Department of Health, Education, and Welfare operated 209 separate grant programs. Connery and Benjamin, *Rockefeller of New York*, p. 216 (see chap. 7, n. 1). See also John E. Chubb, "Federalism and the Bias for Centralization," in *The New Direction in American Politics*, ed. by John E. Chubb and Paul E. Peterson (Washington, D.C.: Brookings Institution, 1985), pp. 273–306.

63. See Chubb, "Federalism and the Bias for Centralization," pp. 295–301.

Chapter 10: The Emerging Political Paradigm

1. David S. Broder, "State Officials Becoming Innovative in Domestic Policy-Making," *Washington Post*, Dec. 8, 1985.

2. Richard D. Lamm and Bill Clinton, "Democrats' Future: Priorities, Discipline," *Christian Science Monitor*, Jan. 15, 1985.

3. "Profiles and Perspectives: A Conversation with Thomas Kean," *Ripon Forum*, April 1986, p. 6.

4. Peter Drucker, "The Entrepreneurial Mystique" (interview), *Inc.*, October 1985, p. 56.

5. Alan J. Matusow, *The Unraveling of America* (New York: Harper and Row, 1984), p. 438.

6. David E. Rosenbaum, "LBJ's Great Society Scores High, Low Marks in History," *Austin American-Statesman* (originally published by the *New York Times*), April 18, 1985.

7. Ehrenhalt, "Last Hurrahs for the New Deal," p. 58 (see chap. 1, n. 2).

8. See Joseph A. Pechman, *Who Paid the Taxes, 1966–85?* (Washington, D.C.: Brookings Institution, 1985); Joseph J. Minarik, *Making Tax Choices* (Washington, D.C.: Urban Institute Press, 1985); and Frank S. Levy and Richard C. Michel, "An Economic Bust for the Baby Boom," *Challenge*, March–April 1986, pp. 33–39.

9. See Seymour Martin Lipset and William Schneider, *The Confidence Gap: Business, Labor, and Government in the Public Mind* (New York: Free Press, 1983); and Seymour Martin Lipset and William Schneider, "Confidence in Confidence Measures," *Public Opinion*, August–September 1983, pp. 42–44.

10. Sidney Blumenthal, *The Permanent Campaign* (New York: Simon and Schuster, 1982), p. 58.

11. Everett C. Ladd, "Realignment? No. Dealignment? Yes," *Public Opinion*, October–November 1980, p. 54.

12. Ibid.

13. See "The Last Lap," *Public Opinion*, October–November 1980, p. 21; and Everett Carll Ladd, "Public Opinion: Questions at the Quinquennial," *Public Opinion*, April–May 1983, pp. 20–41.

14. Martin Wattenberg, *The Decline of Political Parties, 1982–1984* (Cambridge, Mass.: Harvard University Press, 1984).

15. Ladd, "Realignment? No. Dealignment? Yes," p. 55.

16. Patrick Caddell, "Will Republicans Lower the Baby Boom on Democrats?," *Economic Democrat* (newspaper of the Campaign for Economic Democracy), March 1985, p. 5. According to Robert Kuttner, "Warren Miller, using data from the University of Michigan's National Election Surveys, calculated that the 1984 election was mainly an affirmative vote for the country's positive condition, and that Reagan's ideology substantially *detracted* from his electoral appeal." Kuttner, *The Life of the Party*, pp. 114–116 (see chap. 8, n. 49).

17. Kevin Phillips, "Hubris on the Right," *New York Times Magazine*, May 12, 1985, p. 60.

18. Richard Hofstadter, in *The Age of Reform: From Bryan to F.D.R.* (New York: Vintage Books, 1955), p. 167, writes: "The ascension of Theodore Roosevelt to the presidency, the youngest man ever to occupy the White House, was no more than symbolic of the coming-of-age of a generation whose perspectives were sharply demarcated from those of their fathers and who felt the need of a new philosophy and a new politics. T. R. himself had been thirty-two in 1890, Byran only thirty, La Follette thirty-five, Wilson thirty-four."

19. Robert H. Wiebe, *The Search for Order, 1877–1920* (New York: Hill and Wang, 1967). Even voter participation dropped steadily between 1898 and 1928, just as it has between 1960 and 1986. See Kuttner, *The Life of the Party*, p. 136.

20. Milton Coleman, "Governors Would Freeze Defense, Social Security," *Washington Post*, Feb. 27, 1985.

21. William Schneider, interview with author, April 1984.

22. David L. Birch, "The Atomization of America," *Inc.*, March 1987, p. 21.

23. Charles S. Robb, "Democratic Capitalism: A New Response to Economic Change," speech to the Detroit Economic Club, March 2, 1987, available from the Democratic Leadership Council, Washington, D.C.

24. "Profiles and Perspectives: A Conversation with Thomas Kean," p. 5.

25. Hofstadter, *The Age of Reform*, p. 217.

26. Kevin Phillips, *Staying on Top: Winning the Trade War* (New York: Vintage Books, 1986).

27. Phillips, "Hubris on the Right," p. 57.

28. Kevin Phillips, *Post-Conservative America: People, Politics and Ideology in a Time of Crisis* (New York: Random House, 1982), p. 197.

29. Ibid.

30. Ladd, "Realignment? No. Dealignment? Yes," p. 15.

31. See Caddell, "Will Republicans Lower the Baby Boom on Democrats?"

32. Sidney Blumenthal, "Mr. Smith Goes to Washington," *The New Republic*, Feb. 6, 1984, pp. 17–20.

33. James R. Dickenson, "Campaign Trail Littered with Predictions," *Washington Post*, April 2, 1984.

34. See Kuttner, *The Life of the Party*, particularly pp. 190–191.

LIST OF ABBREVIATIONS

ADFA	Arkansas Development Finance Authority
AFDC	Aid to Families with Dependent Children
AHCCCS	Arizona Health Care Cost Containment System
AIDC	Arkansas Industrial Development Commission
ARC	Appalachian Regional Commission
ASTA	Arkansas Science and Technology Authority
ATC	Advanced Technology Centers (Pennsylvania)
BID	Business Improvement District (New York)
BIDCO	Business and industrial development corporation
BSSC	Bay State Skills Corporation (Massachusetts)
CAP	Central Arizona Project
CDC	Community development corporation
CDFC	Community Development Finance Corporation (Massachusetts)
CED	Campaign for Economic Democracy (California)
CEDAC	Community Economic Development Assistance Corporation (Massachusetts)
CfED	Corporation for Enterprise Development (Washington, D.C.)
CLT	Citizens for Limited Taxation (Massachusetts)
CODAMA	Community Organization for Drug Abuse, Mental Health and Alcoholism Services, Inc. (Arizona)
CPLC	Chicanos por la Causa (Arizona)
CSPA	Council of State Planning Agencies (Washington, D.C.)
DEQ	Department of Environmental Quality (Arizona)
EDA	Economic Development Administration
ERIM	Environmental Research Institute of Michigan
EST	Economic Stabilization Trust (Massachusetts)
ET Choices	Employment and Training Choices (Massachusetts)
GAAP	Generally Accepted Accounting Procedures
GAIN	Greater Avenues for INdependence (California)
GED	General (high school) equivalency degree
HETADI	Hawaii Entrepreneurship Training and Development Institute

HHAP	Homeless Housing Assistance Program (New York)
HMO	Health maintenance organization
ICC	Industrial Cooperation Council (New York)
IDB	Industrial development bond
INVENT	Institute for Ventures in New Technology (Texas)
IPA	Independent practice association
ISP	Industrial Services Program (Massachusetts)
ITI	Industrial Technology Institute (Michigan)
JTPA	Job Training Partnership Act
KHIC	Kentucky Highlands Investment Corporation
LDD	Local development district
LISC	Local Initiatives Support Corporation
MAP	Manufacturing Automation Protocol
MBI	Michigan Biotechnology Institute
MCHT	Metropolitan Center for High Technology (Michigan)
MCRC	Massachusetts Capital Resource Company
MEDA	Michigan Economic Development Authority
MEED	Minnesota Employment and Economic Development program
MESBIC	Minority enterprise small business investment company
MICRO	Microelectronics Innovation and Computer Research Opportunities Program (California)
MIFA	Massachusetts Industrial Finance Authority
MIP	Manufacturing Innovation Partnership (Michigan)
MIT	Massachusetts Institute of Technology
MMS	Michigan Modernization Service
MPDC	Massachusetts Product Development Corporation
MTDC	Massachusetts Technology Development Corporation
NGA	National Governors Association
OEO	Office of Economic Opportunity
ONES	Office for New Enterprise Services (Michigan)
PennPRIDE	Pennsylvania Program for Recovery, Investment, Development, and Education
PERF	Pennsylvania Economic Revitalization Fund
PHTC	Pittsburgh High Technology Council
PIC	Private industry council
PIDA	Pennsylvania Industrial Development Authority
REAP	Revenue Enforcement and Protection Program (Massachusetts)
RFC	Reconstruction Finance Corporation
SBA	Small Business Administration
SBIR	Small Business Innovation Research Program
STEP	School-to-Employment Program (New York)

STF	Science and Technology Foundation (New York)
TDS	Technology Deployment Service (Michigan)
TEAP	Temporary Employment Assistance Program (New York)
TEE	Transitional Employment Enterprises (Massachusetts)
TMC	Technology Management Center (Pennsylvania)
UDC	Urban Development Corporation (New York)
WEDCO	Women's Economic Development Corporation

Index

A

Aborn, Foster, 30, 31
Absenteeism, 72
Accelerated cost recovery system (ACRS), 106
Achievement tests, 98–99, 100
ACRS. See Accelerated cost recovery system
Adams, Massachusetts, 178–179, 182–184
ADFA. See Arkansas Development Finance Authority
Adjustment teams, 21–22, 37
Adopt-a-School program, 40
Advanced manufacturing, 152–153, 162, 169, 171, 255. See also Computer technology; Industrial modernization
Advanced Technology Centers (Pennsylvania), 49–51, 58–59, 261, 266, 316; North East Tier, 51–54; Western Pennsylvania, 54–56. See also Ben Franklin Partnership
AEA. See Arkansas Education Association
AFDC. See Aid to Families with Dependent Children
Affordable Home Ownership Development Program (New York), 228, 233
AHCCCS. See Arizona Health Care Cost Containment System
Ahlen, John, 103
AIDC. See Arkansas Industrial Development Commission
Aid to Families with Dependent Children (AFDC): employment and training and, 197, 280; and welfare dependency, 292–293. See also Welfare reform
Alaska Renewable Resources Corporation, 193
Alexander, Lamar, 41, 319
Al Tech Fund (New York), 60
Alternative energy technology, 38–39
Alviani, Joseph, 195
American Federation of Teachers, 96
American Research and Development, 250
America Works, 200
Anderson, Barbara, 208
Antipoverty programs, 302
Appalachian Regional Commission (ARC), 60, 284
Applied research: business and, 37–38, 138, 273–274; industry and, 48–51, 52, 56, 58, 162, 171, 264, 285. See also Advanced Technology Centers; Ben Franklin Partnership; Research consortia; Research institutes; Research parks
ARC. See Appalachian Regional Commission
Arizona, 111–144; Department of Economic Security, 122; Department of Environmental Quality, 121; education reform in, 138–140; environmental protection in, 116–122; Office of New Business Development, 138; social services in, 122–135
Arizona Health Care Cost Containment System (AHCCCS), 129–135
Arizona Horizons, 137

Arizona Innovation Network, 137–138
Arizona State University, 135–136
Arizona Water Commission (AWC), 118–120
Arkansas, 83–110; community development bank in, 308; economic development in, 41, 102–108; education reform in, 83–85, 92–102; political-economic context in, 85–88
Arkansas Development Finance Authority (ADFA), 103–104
Arkansas Education Association (AEA), 94–96
Arkansas Industrial Development Commission (AIDC), 88–89
Arkansas Science and Technology Authority (ASTA), 102, 104
Arnold, David, 47
Arnold Print Works, 182–184
ASTA. See Arkansas Science and Technology Authority
ASU. See Arizona State University
ATC. See Advanced Technology Centers
Atkins, Charles, 197–198, 202
Auletta, Ken, 243
Austen, Al, 53–54
Auto industry, 169, 171. See also General Motors Saturn plant
Automated manufacturing. See Advanced manufacturing; Computer technology; Industrial modernization
Automation, 152–153, 162, 165–167, 278–279. See also Advanced manufacturing; Computer technology; Industrial modernization
AWC. See Arizona Water Commission

B

Babbitt, Bruce, 112–116, 140–144, 330, 331, 332, 338; economic development and, 135–138; education reform and, 138–140; entrepreneurial initiative and, 136–138; environmental protection and, 116–122; health care programs of, 129–135; social services and, 122–135
Baby boomers, 269, 335–336
Bacera, Gloria, 128
Baird, Doug, 209
Banana Kelly Community Improvement Association, 234
Barker, Michael, 24, 33, 34, 89, 137
Barr, Burton, 121
Barrett, Jim, 161
Bassett, Timothy, 179, 187, 189
Battelle Columbus Laboratories, 264
Battery Park City (New York), 227–228
Bay State Skills Corporation (Massachusetts), 206–207, 260, 270
Beard, Sam, 276
Bedford Stuyvesant Restoration Corporation, 234, 303

Ben Franklin Partnership (Pennsylvania), 43, 48–51, 260, 261, 266, 316; advanced technology centers of, 51–56; basic research and, 58, 59; evaluation of, 56–60, 78
Bennis, Warren, 75
Beste, Fred, 309
BID. *See* Business Improvement Districts
BIDCOs. *See* Business and Industrial Development Corporations
Big business, 253–254. *See also* Mature industries
Birch, David, 33–34, 47, 89, 137, 252–253, 254, 256
Bishop, Elbert, 25
Blacks, urban poverty and, 289–290, 293, 302, 308
Blair, Diane, 96, 97, 99
Blanchard, James, 15, 146–147, 170–174, 330, 337; Michigan budget crisis and, 147–149; Michigan Strategic Fund and, 158–161; and modernization of manufacturing, 165–167; recruitment strategies of, 167
Block grants, 315–316
Bolles, Don, 115
Boston, Massachusetts, 23–25, 290
Bowes, Lee, 294
Bowman, Bob, 145–146, 147, 155, 156, 157
Braly, Mark, 38–39
Brandeis, Louis, 2–3
Branfman, Fred, 35, 37
Breslin, Jimmy, 217, 218
Broder, David, 87
Brophy, David, 156–158
Brown, Jerry, 35
Brown, Pat, 35, 256
BSSC. *See* Bay State Skills Corporation
Budget deficit. *See under specific states*
Bullington, Ed, 95
Bumpers, Dale, 83, 86–87
Bund, Ian, 155–156
Bureaucracy: small business and, 151; social services and, 123–124, 126, 327–328
Business and Industrial Development Corporations (BIDCOs), 38–39, 160–161
Business Improvement Districts (New York), 232
Business-labor-government cooperation, 71–76, 104, 169–170, 213–214. *See also* Public-private partnership

C

Cabe, Gloria, 92
Cabinet Council on Economic Development (Michigan), 150
Cabinet Council on Human Investment (Michigan), 172
Caddell, Patrick, 324, 336–337
California, 35–42, 134, 256
California Commission on Industrial Innovation, 39–40
Campaign for Economic Democracy (California), 35
Canfield, Thomas, 55, 56
Cantelme, Pat, 140
CAP. *See* Central Arizona Project
Capacity building, 58, 59, 65–71, 104–105, 229–235, 261, 262, 302, 310. *See also* Ben Franklin Partnership; Kentucky Highlands Investment Corporation; Shorebank Corporation; Regional Enterprise Development Program
Capital. *See* Capital gaps; Private-sector investment; Risk capital; Seed capital; Venture capital
Capital Access Program (Michigan), 159–160, 260
Capital gaps, 28; pension funds and, 77; private investment and, 29–32; regional development and, 60–62; third-sector model and, 32; wholesaling and, 32, 158–161
Capital markets: federal government and, 286; state governments and, 7
Capital Resource Company (Massachusetts), 29, 32, 260, 263
Career ladder programs (Arizona), 139
Carey, Hugh, 213–214, 216, 218–219, 232, 238
Carey, Sister Maureen, 225
Carlson, Dwight, 154–155, 157
Carnegie-Mellon University, 56, 57
Carrick, Roger, 37
Carter, James Earl, 323–325
Castro, Raul, 115, 118
Categorical grants, 315
Catholic Charities of Brooklyn, 225
CDCs. *See* Community development corporations
CDFC. *See* Community Development Finance Corporation
CED. *See* Campaign for Economic Democracy
CEDAC. *See* Community Economic Development Assistance Corporation
Center for Employee Ownership and Participation (New York), 240–241, 279
Centers for Advanced Technology (New York), 215, 216
Centers of excellence, 265
Centers of Excellence program (Massachusetts), 180, 195
Central Arizona Project (CAP), 120
CfED. *See* Corporation for Enterprise Development
Challenge grants, 48–50, 57, 316
Chance, Britten, 49
Chicago, Illinois. *See* South Shore
Chicanos por la Causa (Arizona), 123–124, 303
Child care, 127–128, 168, 282; welfare reform and, 9, 201, 203, 237, 293, 294, 299, 359n27
Children: social services for, 89, 127–128, 134, 235; welfare reform and, 235–236, 296, 359n27
Choate, Pat, 33, 34, 63, 269, 282
Choices for Pennsylvanians, 46, 47, 48
CIM Lab. *See* Computer Integrated Manufacturing Laboratory
Citizens Action groups, 333
Citizens for Limited Taxation (Massachusetts), 208, 209
Class of '74, 21–42, 146
Clinton, Bill, 41, 83, 87–91, 319, 328, 334
Clinton, Hillary, 92–95, 105, 108
CLT. *See* Citizens for Limited Taxation
CNC machines. *See under Computer technology*
CODAMA. *See* Community Organization for Drug Abuse, Mental Health and Alcoholism Services, Inc.

Collective entrepreneurialism, 252, 273
Community-based organizations. *See* Community development banks; Community development corporations; Community development network; Community organizations
Community colleges, 64
Community development: comprehensive program for, 180–188, 302, 304, 312–315; economic development and, 89, 168, 299–302; federal funding for, 315–316; market feedback mechanisms and, 262–263, 302; third-sector institutions and, 303–315; in urban areas, 23–25, 303, 305–308. *See also* Community development banks; Community development corporations
Community development banks, 305–312; community development corporations and, 309–310; government role with, 312–316; needs of poor communities and, 309; Shorebank Corporation and, 305–308, 309–312; as third-sector institutions, 310–312. *See also* Kentucky Highlands Investment Corporation; Shorebank Corporation
Community development corporations (CDCs), 13, 26, 349n11; community development banks and, 309–310; economic development and, 303–312; limitations of, 304; methodological principles behind, 303–304; New York Neighborhood Preservation Program and, 234–235. *See also* Chicanos por la Causa; Community development banks; Community development network; North Side Civic Development Council; St. Nicholas Neighborhood Preservation corporation
Community Development Finance Corporation (Massachusetts), 26, 28, 180–188, 260
Community development network (Massachusetts), 180–188
Community Economic Development Assistance Corporation (Massachusetts), 181
Community Legal Services (Arizona), 131
Community Organization for Drug Abuse, Mental Health and Alcoholism Services, Inc. (Arizona), 124–128
Community organizations: administration of social services and, 124–126; delivery of social services and, 122–135; housing and, 221–224, 228–235, 300; welfare reform and, 294–295
Community service, 294–295, 297
Competency testing, 102. *See also* Teacher competency testing
Competition. *See* Global competition
Comprehensive development systems: community development and, 302, 304, 312–315; for economic development, 261–262, 273, 286; specific programs and, 259; training and, 270–273; welfare reform and, 293–296, 299–302. *See also* Advanced Technology Centers; Ben Franklin Partnership; Regional Enterprise Development Program
Comprehensive social adjustment systems, 281–282
Computer Integrated Manufacturing Laboratory (Lehigh University), 52, 268
Computer technology: computer-based produc-

tion technologies, 165–167, 267–268; computer integrated manufacturing, 164, 165, 167; computer numerically controlled (CNC) machines, 165; computerized machining centers, 152–153, 269. *See also* Microelectronic revolution
Conference on Alternative State and Local Policies, 35
Confidence in government, 323–325
Consensus politics, 208–209
Conservation Corps, 36, 151, 172
Conservation technology, 38–39
Conservative populists, 335
Conte, Silvio, 183
Continuous innovation, 4–11, 252–253
Conviser, Daniel, 229–230
Cooperation. *See* Business-labor-government cooperation; Labor-management committees; Public-private partnership
Cooperative Regional Industrial Laboratories program (Massachusetts), 195
Corporation for Enterprise Development (Washington, D.C.), 41–42, 150, 159, 239, 293
Corporation for Innovation Development (California), 39
Council of State Planning Agencies (Washington, D.C.), 33–35, 40, 41, 47, 89, 137, 150
Cove, Peter, 199–200
Cox, Tom, 56, 67
Coy, Robert, 74, 75, 80
CPLC. *See* Chicanos por la Causa
CRIL. *See* Cooperative Regional Industrial Laboratories program
Crosswalks, 348n28
CSPA. *See* Council of State Planning Agencies
Cultural issues, 322
Culture of industry, 8, 71–76, 277–279, 286
Culture of poverty, 290–293
Cuomo, Andrew, 226–227
Cuomo, Mario, 211–212, 328; as bridge candidate, 334; economic development and, 240, 242–243; emergence of, 216–221; housing and, 221–230; politics of, 243–246; welfare reform and, 235–240
Currier, William, 190–193
Customized job-training programs, 77, 270. *See also* Governor's Office of Job Training

D

Dacey, John, 131
Daniels, Belden, 25–27, 28, 29, 33, 103, 181–182
Day care. *See* Child care
Decentralization: of development systems, 59, 261; of economy, 329–330; of social services, 122–135, 271, 327–328; of training systems, 271
Defense spending, 154, 176–177, 256, 349n5
Delta Foundation (Mississippi), 303, 310
Demand-driven programs, 206–207
DeMaso, Harry, 148, 149
Demers, Richard, 182–184
Democratic constituencies, 96, 172–173, 291, 332–334
Democratic party, 320–323, 332–334
DEQ. *See* Arizona, Department of Environmental Quality

Deregulation. *See* Regulatory policy
Deukmajian, George, 294
Development cabinet (Massachusetts), 23, 27
Development deposits, 306
Development programs. *See* Community development; Comprehensive development systems; Economic development; Regional development
Digital Equipment Corporation, 250
Dislocated workers, 104, 270, 272, 281
Dislocated Worker Task Force (Arizona), 104
Distressed communities: community development organizations and, 230–235; development process for, 299–303; enterprise zones and, 65–66; programs for, 68–71; real estate development and, 186–188. *See also* Community development; Regional development
Donovan, John, 176
Doriot, Georges, 250
Dow Chemical Company, 36
Dowling, Michael, 236–238, 239
Drucker, Peter, 321
Dukakis, Michael: community development networks and, 180–188; economic development and, 25–32, 177–196; first administration of, 22–32; housing development and, 206; mature industries and, 188–193; politics of, 208–210, 333; record of, 193–196; targets of opportunity and, 177–180; tax amnesty and, 207–208; training programs and, 206–207; welfare reform and, 196–208
Dulworth, Ed, 71–73
Dumas, Ernest, 86, 87, 90
Du Pont, Pierre, 295
Durable goods manufacturers, 162–164, 171
Dyer, Barbara, 150

E

East Williamsburg (New York City), 230–234
Economic base, 152, 257–258
Economic development: creation of, 4–11; intellectual revolution and, 32–35; local market economy and, 152, 257–258; long-term perspectives and, 262; manufacturing vs. services and, 254–255; methodology of, 258–263; politics of, 79–80, 89–91, 192, 327; poverty and, 11–13, 80, 127, 172, 177, 240, 289–316, 328–329; process of, 249–252; social organization and, 8–9, 108, 260, 268–273, 279–283 (*see also* Education; Industrial culture; Job-training programs); technological innovation and, 3–4, 34, 176, 251–252. *See also under specific states*
Economic Development Administration (EDA), 33, 60, 89, 284
Economic Development Committee of the Cabinet (Pennsylvania), 47–48
An Economic Development Program for Massachusetts, 24–25
Economic Stabilization Trust (Massachusetts), 190–193, 268
The Economy of Cities (Jacobs), 251, 252–253
EDA. *See* Economic Development Administration
Education, 148, 269; attitudes toward, 99–100;

economic growth rates and, 5–6; economic participation and, 12; in factories, 102; high-tech growth and, 135–156; teacher salaries and, 138–139; welfare system and, 236–240. *See also* Higher education
Education reform: in Arizona, 138–140; in Arkansas, 88, 92–102; in California, 37; in Pennsylvania, 77; in the South, 40, 41
Eimicke, Bill, 222–224, 226, 229, 235
Elderly. *See* Senior citizens
Electorate, 328, 333, 336–338. *See also* Democratic constituencies
Ellwood, David, 358n16
Emergency Assistance Rehousing Program (New York), 225
Employee buy-out programs, 64, 281
Employee ownership, 8, 77, 166, 240–241, 275, 279
Employment. *See* Job creation; Job-training programs
Employment and Training Choices program (Massachusetts), 197, 200–206, 294, 296–297
Employment Opportunities Pilot (New York), 237–238
Employment security, 8–9, 75–79, 279
Employment Training Panel (California), 37, 270, 272
Enterprise Corporation (Pittsburgh), 54–55, 273
Enterprise forums, 49, 55
Enterprise zones, 65–67, 78, 259
Entrepreneurial climate, 7, 171, 273–275
Entrepreneurial initiative, 136–138, 309
Entrepreneurial training, 105, 185, 195, 274, 313
Entrepreneurs: low-income, 307, 313–314; services for, 138, 166–167. *See also* Entrepreneurial climate; Entrepreneurial initiative; Entrepreneurial training; Management assistance; Risk capital
Environmental protection, 6, 89, 116–122, 148
Environmental Quality Act (Arizona), 121
Environmental Research Institute of Michigan (ERIM), 154
ERIM. *See* Environmental Research Institute of Michigan
Ernst, William, 97–98
EST. *See* Economic Stabilization Trust
ET Choices. *See* Employment and Training Choices program
Ethnic neighborhoods, community development and, 301
ETP. *See* Employment Training Panel
Executive Corps (Michigan), 151
Expanding the Opportunity to Produce (CfED), 41
Export trading companies, 241–242, 276–277, 286

F

Factories, education in, 102
Factory of the future, 145–174. *See also* Advanced manufacturing
Fallone, Frank, 87
Fall River, Massachusetts, 195
Family policy, 282–283, 293, 299. *See also* Single-parent families

Faubus, Orval, 86
Faust, William, 146, 147
Federal government: budget cuts and, 304; defense spending of, 154, 176–177, 256, 349n5; macroeconomic policy and, 9, 284–285, 286–287; microeconomic policy and, 9–10, 288, 315–316; political paradigm and, 3. See also Government
Feistritzer, Emily, 97
Ferris, Kathleen, 118, 119
Financial institutions, community development and, 309–313. See also Community development banks; Kentucky Highlands Investment Corporation; Private-sector investment; Shorebank Corporation
Fink, Stanley, 214–215, 216
First agenda, 4–11, 249–288
Fiscal crises. See under specific states
Fischer, Ben, 76, 288
Flanders, Ralph, 250
Flexible manufacturing, 74–75, 153, 255
Flory, Alan, 124–126
Foley, Howard, 208
Ford Foundation, 198, 304
Foreign capital, 341n10
Forrester, Jay, 250
Foundation firms, 165–167
Foundations, 198, 227, 304
France, entrepreneurial training in, 274
Franchise law, 151
Fraser, Doug, 150
Freeman, Howard, 133
Free-trade zone, 214
Friedman, Bob, 41–42, 150, 205, 206
Friedman, Gen. Robert, 191
Frucher, Meyer (Sandy), 227–228

G

GAAP. See Generally Accepted Accounting Procedures
GAIN. See Greater Avenues for INdependence program
Gaines Pet Food, 72
Gain sharing. See Profit sharing
Gans, Curtis, 335
Garcia, Pete, 123–124
Gardels, Nathan, 35, 36, 37, 39
GATT. See General Agreement on Tariffs and Trade
GED. See General equivalency degree
General Agreement on Tariffs and Trade (GATT), 286
General equivalency degree (GED), 102
General Foods, 72
Generally Accepted Accounting Procedures (GAAP), 148, 220
General Motors Saturn plant, 168–169
Ghettos, 78, 164–165, 289–290, 305–308, 360n33
Glazer, Lou, 151, 159
Global competition, 3–4, 83–84, 286; innovation and, 3–4, 251–252; wages and, 11, 256
Glynn, Thomas, 204
Godfathers, 185. See also Mentor Program

Goldmark, Peter, 305
Government: confidence in, 323–325; marketplace and, 11, 14, 39, 327, 333; private-sector investment patterns and, 57, 79, 137, 152, 157, 158–161, 259–260 (see also Wholesaling); role of, 11, 80, 127, 152, 249, 327; third-sector institutions and, 13, 311–315. See also Business-labor-government cooperation; Federal government
Government Land Bank (Massachusetts), 186–187, 260
Governor's Office of Job Training (Michigan), 166
Grabowicz, Paul, 35
Great Britain, entrepreneurial training in, 274
Greater Avenues for INdependence program (California), 293–294
Great Society, 217, 315, 322, 323, 329
Greenfield, Massachusetts, 195
Grigsby, Charles, 184–186, 188
Groundwater Management Act (Arizona), 120
Grzywinski, Ron, 305–306, 310, 315. See also Shorebank Corporation
Gutierrez, Alfredo, 113, 116, 139

H

Hackley, Lloyd, 96
Haggerty, Pat, 135
Hamilton, Art, 114–115, 141, 143, 144, 328–329
Hammerschmidt, John Paul, 87
Hansen, Derek (Pete), 38, 159
Harlan County, Kentucky, 308–312
Harper, Lou, 131, 132
Harrington, Michael, 205–206
Harris, Fred, 333
Harrison, Bennett, 280
Hart, Gary, 15, 21, 332, 333, 337
Hattem, Gary Sam, 231–234
Hawaii Entrepreneurship Training and Development Institute (HETADI), 313
Hayes, Robert, 225, 243
Health care: long-term, 133, 135; national system for, 299, 327, 359n28; welfare reform and, 108, 130–135, 203, 297–298; for working poor, 133–134, 297–298, 359n28
Health maintenance organizations (HMOs), 129–135, 297. See also Arizona Health Care Cost Containment System
HELP. See Homeless Emergency Leverage Program
Helping Hand Program (Virginia), 276
Heritage Parks, 24, 178
HETADI. See Hawaii Entrepreneurship Training and Development Institute
HHAP. See Homeless Housing Assistance Program
Higher education, 5–6, 135–136
High technology. See Advanced manufacturing; Advanced Technology Centers; Computer technology; Microelectronic revolution; Technological innovation
HMOs. See Health maintenance organizations
Hofstadter, Richard, 331
Homeless Emergency Leverage Program (HELP), 226–227

Homeless Housing Assistance Program (New York), 224–225
Homeless programs, 222–227
Houghton, Mary, 309, 310–311
Housing cooperatives, 187, 231
Housing Partnership Development Corporation (New York), 228
Housing programs: affordable, 187, 222, 224, 225, 227, 228–230; community development organizations and, 185, 221–224, 230–235, 300; in Massachusetts, 206; in New York, 221–235, 353n36; South Shore, 306–307; tenant management and, 361n55. *See also* Homeless programs
Housing trust funds, 228
Howell, James, 6
Hull, Jane, 140
Human capital, 152, 268–273, 328–329. *See also* Welfare reform; Work force
Hunt, James, 40–41

I

Iacocca, Lee, 147, 150
ICC. *See* Industrial Cooperation Council
IDB. *See* Industrial development bond
Ideological interregnum, 14, 318–321. *See also* Political paradigm, emerging
Illiteracy, 12, 40, 100–101, 269
Immerwahr, John, 278
Incubators. *See* Product development incubators; Small-business incubators
Independent practice associations (IPAs), 130
Indiana, economic development in, 42
Industrial Cooperation Council (New York), 240–241
Industrial culture, 8, 71–76, 168, 277–279, 286
Industrial development bond (IDB), 28, 275
Industrial Effectiveness Program (New York), 240
Industrial era, 2, 9–10, 68, 251–252, 280
Industrial extension services, 8, 166–167, 260. *See also* Industrial modernization
Industrial modernization, 7–8, 49, 51–52, 267–268, 286; industrial culture and, 74–76, 278–279, 286; small manufacturing firms and, 165–167, 267–268, 286; training and, 269–273. *See also* Advanced manufacturing; Computer technology
Industrial parks, 232–233
Industrial policy, 10–11, 39
Industrial recruitment, 6, 89, 167–170, 193, 256–257. *See also* Smokestack chasing
Industrial sectors. *See* Sectoral policy
Industrial Services Program (Massachusetts), 190–193
Industrial Technology Institute (Michigan), 162–164, 167, 268
Industrywide research consortia, 287
Inflation, 10, 298, 323
Infrastructure, 34, 148; intellectual, 4, 5, 48, 56, 257, 261, 263–267, 349n5; physical, 4, 5, 64, 151, 178, 221, 256, 263
Innovare, Inc., 53–54
Innovation, 3–11, 249–258; in culture of industry, 71–76. *See also* Technological innovation

Institute for Ventures in New Technology (INVENT), 273–274
Interest deferrals, 64
Interest groups, 94–96, 320, 322–323
Intermediary institutions, 61–62, 235, 261–262, 304–305, 312. *See also* Advanced Technology Centers; Local development districts; Local Initiatives Support Corporation; Massachusetts Housing Partnership
International banking, 214
International trade, 286, 327. *See also* Global competition
"Intrapreneurship," 273
INVENT. *See* Institute for Ventures in New Technology
Investment. *See* Private-sector investment; Venture capital
Investment vs. spending, 260–261, 272, 283, 302, 303, 328
IPAs. *See* Independent practice associations
ISP. *See* Industrial Services Program
ITI. *See* Industrial Technology Institute

J

Jackson, Ira, 207
Jackson, Jesse, 332–333
Jackson, Marlin, 88
Jacobs, Jane, 251, 252–253, 258, 261–262
Japan, 164, 266–267, 268–269, 276–277. *See also* Global competition
Jarmin, Beth, 137
Job clubs, 294
Job Creation Equity Program (New York), 239
"The Job Generation Process" (Birch), 33–34, 252
Job placement programs, 199, 200, 201, 202–203. *See also* Employment and Training Choices program
Jobs, Steve, 39
Job security. *See* Employment security
Job-training corporations, 313
Job Training Partnership Act (JTPA), 61, 201, 270, 271, 281
Job-training programs: cost of, 298–299; customized, 77, 270; demand-driven, 206–207; development of system of, 268–273; entrepreneurial training and, 313–314; in Massachusetts, 206–207; in Michigan, 171–172; performance-based contracts with, 201; welfare system and, 37, 127, 236–240, 260, 271, 281, 293–296. *See also* America Works; Bay State Skills Corporation; Employment and Training Choices program; Employment Training Panel; Governor's Office of Job Training; Temporary Employment Assistance Program; Transitional Employment Enterprises
Johnson, Richard, 180
Jones, Graham, 216
JTPA. *See* Job Training Partnership Act
Just-in-time delivery systems, 165, 168

K

Kanahele, George, 313
Kane, Michael, 194

Kean, Thomas, 321, 331
Keefe, Frank, 22–25, 207
Keeley, Kathryn, 314
Kemp, Jack, 65
Kennedy, Robert, 303
Kentucky Highlands Investment Corporation
  (KHIC), 308–312
Keverian, George, 175
KHIC. See Kentucky Highlands Investment
  Corporation
Kieschnick, Michael, 33, 34, 37, 137, 150
King, Ed, 32, 175, 200–201, 206
King, Mel, 25–26
Kirkman-Liff, Bradford, 133, 134–135
Koch, Ed, 219
Koppel, Jacques, 267–268
Kotkin, Joel, 35
Kuper, George H., 277
Kuttner, Robert, 281, 338

L

Labor. See Unions; Work force
Laboratories of democracy, 2–3, 283
Labor-management committees, 71–76, 282; local,
  8, 61, 71–73, 74, 166; state, 61, 74, 278
Labor-management relations, 71, 153, 166, 170,
  286; cooperative systems and, 8, 169–170, 260.
  See also Labor-management committees; Partici-
  pative management
Ladd, Everett Carll, 325, 335
LaGuardia, Fiorello, 320
Lamm, Richard, 320
Landry, Larry, 137
Laser instruments, 152, 153
Lawrence, Massachusetts, 193–194
Lay-offs, 281
LDDs. See Local Development Districts
Lehigh University, 51–54
Lehrman, Lew, 219
Lemann, Nicholas, 301, 302
Life insurance industry, investment by, 29–31
Likins, Peter, 57, 58, 59
Lindemann, Anne, 112, 113, 129
Linked deposit programs, 305
LISC. See Local Initiatives Support Corporation
Literacy programs, 12, 100–101
Litvak, Lawrence, 33
Loan guarantees, 64
Loan insurance, 159–160
Local Development Districts (Pennsylvania), 60–
  62, 64, 73, 89
Local Initiatives Support Corporation (LISC), 304–
  305
Local market economy, 152, 257–258
Local Ownership Development Corporations, 241
Long-term debt, 7, 28, 30–31, 76, 77, 105
Long-term perspectives: community development
  and, 302, 303; economic development and, 262;
  regional development and, 193–196; in training
  system, 271–272
Lowell, James, 306
Lowell, Massachusetts, 23–24
Low-income housing, 222, 224

Low Income Housing Trust Fund (New York),
  228, 230, 235
Low-interest loans, 60–62
Low-wage competition, 11, 256–257
Lundine, Stan, 74

M

McAuto Systems Groups, Inc. (MSGI), 131–132
McFadden, Deborah, 182
McGovern, George, 87, 217–218
McRae, Tom, 90, 100, 101, 106
Machine tool industry, innovation in, 165
Machine Trades Action Project (Massachusetts),
  195
Machine-vision systems, 152, 153, 154
Macroeconomic policy, 9–10, 214, 284–285, 286–
  287
Mahony, Jodie, 90–91, 96
Mallett, Conrad, Jr., 172
Management assistance, 48, 54–55, 61, 138, 273–
  276
Management consultants, 274
Manpower Consultative Service (Canada), 282
Manpower Demonstration Research Corporation
  (MDRC), 198
Manufacturing automation protocol (MAP), 163
Manufacturing frontier, 152–153. See also Ad-
  vanced manufacturing; Industrial moderniza-
  tion
Manufacturing Innovation Partnership (Michi-
  gan), 168
MAP. See Manufacturing automation protocol
Market Deployment Service, 348n28
Market feedback mechanisms, 262–263, 302
Marketing, 7, 61, 166, 276–277
Marketplace, government and, 10–11, 14, 39, 327,
  333
Market solutions, 14, 26, 327. See also Wholesaling
Maslin, Paul, 336
Massachusetts, 22–32, 175–210; budget deficit in,
  22–23; economic development in, 23–32, 176–
  196; Employment and Training Choices pro-
  gram in, 200–206; under first Dukakis adminis-
  tration, 22–32; housing development in, 206;
  industry revitalization in, 188–193; regional
  development in, 177–188; tax amnesty program
  in, 207–208; tax policy in, 22–23; training
  programs in, 206–207; turnarounds in, 190–193;
  welfare reform in, 196–208
Massachusetts Capital Resource Company
  (MCRC), 29–32, 260, 263
Massachusetts High Technology Council, 28
Massachusetts Housing Partnership, 206
Massachusetts Industrial Development Authority
  (MIDA), 28
Massachusetts Industrial Finance Authority
  (MIFA), 28, 341n10
Massachusetts Institute of Technology, 176, 250
Massachusetts Metalworking Partnership, 195
Massachusetts Product Development Corporation
  (MPDC), 190
Massachusetts Technology Development Corpora-
  tion (MTDC), 28, 29, 39, 262

Matching grant programs, 48, 67, 71, 180, 206, 265–266, 272. *See also* Block grants; Challenge grants
Mature industries: industrial culture and, 74–76, 278–279, 286; modernization of, 7–8, 49, 51–52, 188–193, 267–268, 286–287
Mauro, Frank, 215–216
Mazda plant, 167
MBI. *See* Michigan Biotechnology Institute
MCRC. *See* Massachusetts Capital Resource Company
MDRC. *See* Manpower Research Demonstration Corporation
Mecham, Evan, 143
MEDA. *See* Michigan Economic Development Authority
Medicaid, 129–135, 201, 237, 297–298
MEED. *See* Minnesota Employment and Economic Development program
Meltzer, Allan, 78
Mentor Program (Wisconsin), 276
Merchant, David, 269
Merit pay, 138–139
MESBICs. *See* Minority Enterprise Small Business Investment Companies
Metropolitan Center for High Technology (Michigan), 164–165
Mezzanine financing, 160
Michigan, 145–174; budget deficit in, 145–148; industrial modernization in, 165–167; industrial recruitment strategies in, 167–170; *The Path to Prosperity*, 151–153, 171; private-sector investment in, 158–161; public pension funds in, 154–158; research in, 161–165; rural poverty and, 290; welfare culture in, 293
Michigan Biotechnology Institute (MBI), 162, 164–165
Michigan Economic Development Authority (MEDA), 159, 161
Michigan Education Trust, 171–172
Michigan Modernization Service (MMS), 165–167, 170, 260, 268
Michigan Strategic Fund, 158–161, 163–164, 170, 311
Michigan Venture Capital Fund, 154–158
MICRO. *See* Microelectronics Innovation and Computer Research Opportunities
Microeconomic policy, 9–10, 284–285, 287
Microelectronic revolution, 3–4, 7, 251–252, 254–255
Microelectronics Innovation and Computer Research Opportunities (California), 37–38
MIDA. *See* Massachusetts Industrial Development Authority
Mid Bronx Desperadoes Community Housing Corporation, 234
Middleton, Rob, 89
MIFA. *See* Massachusetts Industrial Finance Authority
Miles-Bell, Wanda, 98–99
Miller, Martin, 30–31
Miller, Tom, 304, 308, 309
Milliken, William, 40, 146, 148, 149–150, 162
MILRITE Council (Pennsylvania), 71–77

Minimum wage, 298
Minnesota, 42, 256
Minnesota Employment and Economic Development program, 272
Minorities, urban poverty and, 283, 289–290, 302
Minority Business Development Authority (Pennsylvania), 64
Minority Business Loan Fund (Michigan), 161
Minority Enterprise Small Business Investment Companies (MESBICs), 184
Minority lending, 64, 161, 184, 305
Minority-owned business, 184–186, 306–307
MIP. *See* Manufacturing Innovation Partnership
Mississippi, 41
MIT. *See* Massachusetts Institute of Technology
MMS. *See* Michigan Modernization Service
Mogan, Pat, 23–24
Mondragon Movement (Spain), 275
Monongahela Valley (Pennsylvania), 68–71
Morfessis, Ioanna, 136
Morse Cutting Tool Company, 192
MPDC. *See* Massachusetts Product Development Corporation
MSGI. *See* McAuto Systems Group, Inc.
MTAP. *See* Machine Trades Action Project
MTDC. *See* Massachusetts Technology Development Corporation
Murphy, Tom, 55, 79
Murray, Charles, 358n16, 360n33
Mutz, John, 40

N

Nash, Robert, 103
National Business Incubation Association, 274
National Center for Neighborhood Enterprise, 300
National Education Association, 96, 150
National Governors Association, 34, 40, 89, 260, 294, 328
National politics, future of, 15. *See also* Political paradigm, emerging
National Science Foundation, 171
Neighborhood Preservation Companies (New York), 230–235
Neighborhood Preservation Program (New York), 234–235
Neoliberalism, 15
Neoprogressivism, 15
New business: in Arkansas, 102–105, 106, 107; economic growth and, 152, 153, 252–253; job creation and, 33–34; tax incentives and, 65
New class, 335–336
New-collar workers, 336
New Deal, 285, 295, 329, 333
New Deal liberalism, 14, 321–323
New economy. *See* Postindustrial economy
New Enterprise Institute (Maine), 274
New Federalism, 329–330
New Left, 35
New paradigm politicians, 15–17; Democratic, 108–110, 320–321, 332–334; as moderates, 330–332; Republican, 16, 319–320, 321, 331, 334–335. *See also* Babbitt; Blanchard; Clinton; Cuomo; Dukakis; Kean; Thornburgh

New Right, 335
New York City, 214, 222; community development organizations in, 230–235; homeless programs and, 223–227; housing programs in, 227–230
New York-New Jersey Port Authority, 241, 277
New York (state), 211–246; community development in, 230–235; economic development in, 40, 240; housing programs in, 221–231, 235; welfare reform in, 235–240
The Next American Frontier (Reich), 252
NGA. See National Governors Association
Nonprofit institutions. See Not-for-profit institutions
North Adams, Massachusetts, 178–179
North Carolina, 40–41
North East Tier Advanced Technology Center (Pennsylvania), 51–54
Northern Berkshire County, Massachusetts, 178–179
Northern Berkshire Regional Industrial Development Authority (Massachusetts), 179
Northern Community Investment Corporation (Vermont), 303
The Northern Tier Economy: A Strategic Analysis (Mt. Auburn Associates), 194
North Side Civic Development Council (Pittsburgh), 66–67, 303
Notch group, 133–134
Not-for-profit institutions, 13, 122–129, 310

O

OEO. See Office of Economic Opportunity
Office for New Enterprise Services (Michigan), 166
Office of Economic Opportunity (OEO), 26, 180. See also Community development corporations
Office of Program Development (New York), 215
Ohio, 42
Olsen, Ken, 250
Olver, John, 194
O'Neill, Hugh, 214, 239
ONES. See Office for New Enterprise Services
Organized labor. See Unions
Ouida, Herb, 242
Owens, Reginald, 137–138, 264
Ozark Regional Commission, 89

P

Packard, David, 39
Palomino, Fabian, 219
Panel Study of Income Dynamics (University of Michigan), 292
Paradigm. See Political paradigm, emerging
Parks, Tim, 56
Participative management, 71–76, 168, 277–279. See also Culture of industry; Labor-management committees; Labor-management relations
The Path to Prosperity, 151–153, 171
Patiño, Douglas, 122–123, 127, 128
PennPRIDE. See Pennsylvania Program for Recovery, Investment, Development, and Education

Pennsylvania, 43–81; advanced technology centers in, 51–56; Ben Franklin Partnership and, 48–60; economic crises in, 45–51; Economic Revitalization Fund in, 62–65; enterprise zones in, 65–67; entrepreneurial climate of, 7; HMO-based medicaid program in, 134; industrial culture in, 71–76; MILRITE Council and, 71–77; public pension fund reform in, 76–77; Regional Enterprise Development Program in, 60–62; Renaissance Communities in, 68–71
Pennsylvania Capital Loan Fund, 60
Pennsylvania Economic Revitalization Fund (PERF), 62–65
Pennsylvania Industrial Development Authority (PIDA), 48
Pennsylvania Program for Recovery, Investment, Development, and Education (PennPRIDE), 63–65
PENNTAP, 57
Pension Fund Investment Unit (California), 39
Pension funds. See Public pension funds
Peoples, Bill, 250
Perceptron, 154–155, 157
PERF. See Pennsylvania Economic Revitalization Fund
Performance-based contracts, 238
Pfister, Jack, 112, 116, 119
Phelps, Dodge Corporation, 140–141
Phillips, Kevin, 326, 334, 335
Phoenix, Arizona, 111, 116–117
Phospho-Energetics, Inc., 49
PHTC. See Pittsburgh High Technology Council
PIC. See Private industry council
Picking winners, 10, 153
PIDA. See Pennsylvania Industrial Development Authority
Pittsburgh, Pennsylvania, 7, 54–56, 68
Pittsburgh High Technology Council (PHTC), 55
Pittsburgh Seed Fund, 55
Plant closings: labor and, 188–189, 282; legislation and, 77, 188–193, 281; responses to, 37, 104, 182–184, 241, 270–271, 280; re-use of facilities and, 70
Plastrik, Pete, 150–151, 158–159, 168
Plosila, Walt, 46–50, 57–58, 59, 60, 63, 69–71
Polar Materials, Inc., 43–44
Political paradigm, emerging, 318–338; assumptions underlying, 326–330; and Babbitt, 141–144; and Blanchard, 172–174; Carter administration and, 323–325; and Clinton, 108–110; and Cuomo, 243–246; and Dukakis, 209–210; new class and, 335–336; New Deal liberalism and, 321–323; packaging of, 336–338; political parties and, 319–321, 332–336; principles of, 326–330; Reagan conservatism and, 325–326; roots of, 21–42; and Thornburgh, 80–81
Political parties: dogma of, 109; labor-management cooperation and, 170; partisan conflict and, 62–65, 79; realignments in, 326; social issues and, 322. See also Democratic party; Republican party
Politics of economic development, 79–80, 89–91, 192, 327
Pollution control, 169

Populism, 332
Port Authority of New York and New Jersey, 241, 277
Postindustrial economy, 1–4, 7–8, 278, 283–288, 289, 321
Post-Watergate Democrats, 22, 141. *See also* Class of '74
Poverty: culture of, 290–293, 301; growth process and, 11–13, 172, 177, 240, 289–316, 328–329; health care programs and, 129–135, 297–298, 299. *See also* Welfare reform
Power, Phil, 150
Pragmatic progressivism, 108, 245
Prairie State *2000* Authority (Illinois), 272
Pratt, Stan, 156
President's Commission on Industrial Competitiveness, 267
Prisons, 148, 220–221
Private industry councils (PICs), 272
Private placement separate account, 77
Private-sector investment, 29–31, 32, 79, 260, 301; affordable housing and, 227; community development and, 302, 304; public-sector role and, 57, 79, 137, 152, 157, 158–161, 259–260. *See also* Wholesaling
Privatization of social services, 123, 128–129. *See also* Not-for-profit institutions
Procurement assistance, 61, 276
Product Development Fund (Michigan), 161
Product development incubators, 53
Productivity, 73, 75–76, 127, 279
Profit sharing, 278, 279
Progressive Era, 2–3, 15, 285, 326, 332
PSID. *See* Panel Study of Income Dynamics
Public investments. *See* Public pension funds; Public-private partnership; Wholesaling
Public pension funds, 39, 76–77, 103, 155–158. *See also* Michigan Venture Capital Fund
Public-private partnership, 32, 56, 260, 301; banks and, 186; coinvestment strategy and, 157; enterprise zones and, 65–67; HELP and, 226–227; Renaissance Communities program and, 69–71. *See also* Ben Franklin Partnership
Public sector jobs programs, 249, 272, 295–296, 298, 299

Q

Quality circles, 278
Quality of life, 6, 304
Quasi-public institutions: community development network and, 180–188; in Massachusetts, 26–29, 180–193, 262–263; mature industries and, 188–193
Quid pro quos, 30, 260, 277, 301

R

Racial issues, 12, 322; teacher testing and, 95–96; urban poverty and, 289–290
Radical centrism, 142
Raine, Alden, 177, 178, 194
Raines, Martin, 226
Reagan, Ronald, 325–326, 328
Reaganism, 80–81

Real estate development, 67, 186, 207. *See also* Housing programs
REAP. *See* Revenue Enforcement and Protection Program
Recession of *1975*, 21–22
Recession of *1982*, 41–42, 149–150, 175
Reconstruction Finance Corporation, 10
Redesigning Social and Economic Problem-solving (Stanford Research Institute), 13
Regional development: community development network and, 180–188; long-term strategy and, 193–196; in Pennsylvania, 60–62, 68–71; state vs. federal role and, 283–288; targeted regions and, 177–180
Regional Enterprise Development Program (Pennsylvania), 60–63
Regional Financial Enterprises (RFE), 156
Regulatory policy: access to marketplace and, 12; banking and, 214; federal role and, 284, 286; industrial recruitment and, 169; long-term debt and, 105; private investment and, 34, 259, 301; securities and, 39, 152
Reich, Robert, 8, 252, 253
Reilly, Edward, 209
Renaissance Communities program (Pennsylvania), 68–71, 78
Republican party, 318–319, 334–335
Research and development, 34, 37, 39, 263–268; academic domination of research and, 58, 265; in Arkansas, 102–103; manufacturing process and, 162–165; regional development and, 180; tax credit and, 106. *See also* Applied research
Research consortia, 163, 171, 265, 287
Research institutes, 161–165, 265, 268
Research parks, 136, 264–265
Research Triangle Park (North Carolina), 264–265
Retailing, 158, 259–260, 275, 301
Retention rates, 101, 199, 200, 202–203
Retraining programs, 8, 37, 166, 168, 270, 281
Revenue Enforcement and Protection Program (Massachusetts), 207–208
RFC. *See* Reconstruction Finance Corporation
RFE. *See* Regional Financial Enterprises
Rhodes, James, 27
Riley, Richard, 41
Risk capital, 7, 31, 159–160, 261, 275–276. *See also* Seed capital; Venture capital
Robb, Chuck, 330, 331
Robinson, Priscilla, 115, 118, 121
Robots, 152, 153, 269
Rockefeller, David, 228
Rockefeller, Nelson, 212–213
Rockefeller, Winthrop, 86
Roosevelt, Franklin Delano, 1, 322–323, 333. *See also* New Deal
Ross, Doug, 151–153, 170, 173–174, 329, 337–338
Rosston Swine Cooperative, 101
RPC. *See* Rural Preservation Companies
Rubinstein, Sidney, 75
Rural areas: culture of poverty in, 289, 290–291; development in, 92, 97, 104–105, 258; health care and, 89, 134
Rural Development Action Team (Arkansas), 104–105

Rural Preservation Companies (New York), 234
Russell, Jack, 3, 168

S

SAFE-BIDCO, 38
St. Nicholas Neighborhood Preservation Corpora-
    tion (New York City), 230–234, 303
Sampson, Ruby, 196–197
Sasso, John, 334
Savage Arms, 191
SBA. *See* Small Business Administration
SBA-insured loans, 160, 161
SBIR grants. *See* Small Business Innovation
    Research grants
Schaller, Donald, 132–133
Schippani, Michael, 195
Schlesinger, Steve, 246
School-to-Employment Program (New York), 235,
    242–243
Schucolsky, Jim, 70
Schuler, Raymond, 214, 244
Schumpeter, Joseph, 214
Schwartz, Gail Garfield, 63
Schweke, William, 41, 150, 159
Science and Technology Foundation (New York),
    215–216
Scientific management, 277
Scranton, Pennsylvania, 71
SEBCO Development, Inc., 234
Second agenda, 11–13, 289–316
Sectoral policy, 7, 195, 241, 268, 287
Securities law, 39, 152
Seed capital, 7, 39, 51, 52, 55, 64, 160. *See also*
    Venture capital
Self-Employment Demonstration project (New
    York), 239
Senior citizens, 89, 231, 232
Service economy, 254–255
Shapp, Milton, 44
Shared work, 104
Shorebank Corporation, 105, 305, 309
Simon, Paul, 295
Single-parent families, 204, 223, 236, 282, 290
Small Business Administration (SBA): and Arnold
    Print Works rescue, 183; loans and, 38, 160,
    161; Local Development Districts and, 61; Small
    Business Development Centers and, 48, 273
Small Business Development Centers, 48, 273
Small businesses: continual innovation and, 252–
    253; government bureaucracy and, 48, 151;
    growth of, 3; job creation and, 33–34, 47, 254;
    low-interest loans and, 60–62; tax policy and,
    48, 106, 151. *See also* Entrepreneurial initiative;
    Entrepreneurial training; Management assis-
    tance; Risk capital
Small-business incubators, 274, 307; in Arkansas,
    104; in Massachusetts, 187, 250; in Michigan,
    151, 168; in Pennsylvania, 43–44, 50, 52–54, 56,
    64, 261
Small Business Innovation Research grants (New
    York), 215–216
Small manufacturing firms, 165–167, 267–268, 286
Smith, Al, 333

Smith, Craig, 101
Smith, David, 25, 28
Smith, Howard, 27–28
Smith, Jerome, 162, 163
Smith, Roger, 169
Smith, Steve, 89, 90
Smokestack chasing, 27, 34, 41, 46, 48, 62, 88,
    105. *See also* Industrial recruitment
Social adjustment systems, 280–283, 285, 287, 289
Social organization, and economic growth, 8–9,
    12, 108, 260, 279–283, 301–302, 327. *See also*
    Education; Industrial culture; Job training
Social services: alternative delivery systems, 124–
    129; decentralization of, 122–135, 271, 327–328;
    expansion of federal programs for, 361n62;
    New Deal liberalism and, 321–323; productivity
    and, 127. *See also* Child care; Health care;
    Welfare reform
Sociotechnical systems, 279
South Carolina, 41
Southeastern Massachusetts Partnership, 179
Southern Development Bancorporation, 105
South Shore (Chicago neighborhood), 305–308
Southwest Corridor, 25, 26
Spain, entrepreneurial training in, 275
Special interests. *See* Interest groups
Spending vs. investment, 260–261, 272, 283, 302,
    303, 328
Spinoffs, 254, 264
Sprague Electric, 179
Stanford Research Institute, public policy center,
    13
Start-ups, 157, 160–161, 165
State economic strategy documents: *Arizona
    Horizons*, 137; *Choices for Pennsylvanians*, 46, 47,
    48; *An Economic Development Program for Pennsyl-
    vania*, 24–25; *The Path to Prosperity* (Michigan),
    151–153, 171
Steiner, Wesley, 122
STEP. *See* School-to-Employment Program
Stern, Leonard, 226
Stern, William, 240
Stevenson, Adlai, III, 305
STF. *See* Science and Technology Foundation
Strategic audits, 259. *See also Choices for Pennsylva-
    nians; The Path to Prosperity*
Summer jobs programs, 151, 172
Sununu, John, 318
Supported work, 198–200, 201. *See also* Employ-
    ment and Training Choices program
Surety bonds, 64, 185
Sussman, Carl, 181, 187
Sweden, labor market system in, 272–273

T

Tales of a New America (Reich), 252
Targeted industries, 10–11, 39, 49, 153
Task Force on Capital Formation (Massachusetts),
    25–32, 33
Task Force on High Technology (Michigan), 149–
    150, 152, 162
Task Force on Poverty and Welfare (New York),
    297

Taunton, Massachusetts, 179-100
Tax amnesty program, 207–208
Tax-exempt bonds, 28, 314n10
Tax incentives, 69, 169, 301; in Arkansas, 106–107; enterprise zones and, 65–67; industrial recruitment and, 169; job creation and, 106; tax credits and, 199–200, 298. *See also* Tax policy
Tax policy, 34, 39, 255–256; budget deficits and, 147–149; middle-income Americans and, 323; small business and, 106, 151; social programs and, 328–329
Tax revolt, 323
Taylor, Frederick, 277
Taylorism, 277
TDS. *See* Technology Deployment Service
Teacher competency testing, 84, 93, 94–96, 138
Teacher salaries, 138–139
TEAP. *See* Temporary Employment Assistance Program
Technology deployment, 162–164, 267–268, 285
Technological innovation: basic industry and, 255; business assistance programs and, 54–55; as continuous process, 4–11, 252; development vs. deployment of, 161–165, 267–268; durable goods manufacturers and, 162–164, 171; economic growth and, 3–4, 34, 176, 251–252; environment for, 4–11, 261; manufacturing problems and, 71; training and, 269, 270
Technology Assessment Program (Pennsylvania), 57
Technology Deployment Service (Michigan), 166
Technology Development Corporation (Massachusetts), 28, 29, 39, 262
Technology Management Center (Pennsylvania), 267
Technopolis program (Japan), 266–267, 316
TEE. *See* Transitional Employment Enterprises
Teenage unemployment, 235, 289–290
Temporary Employment Assistance Program (New York), 238–239
Tennessee, 41
Third-sector institutions: community development and, 34, 310–312; economic development and, 26, 32, 38–39; employment and training and, 200, 313–314; social service delivery and, 122–129. *See also* Community development banks; Community development corporations
Thodis, John, 147, 173
Thomas, Allison, 37, 39
Thomas, Ron, 43–44, 54, 58–59
Thornburgh, Richard, 44–50, 57, 318, 319, 321, 332; impact of programs of, 77–79; and PERF, 62–65; Reaganism and, 80–81; Renaissance Communities program and, 69–71
Thurow, Lester, 287
Tishman Speyer, 226
TMC. *See* Technology Management Center
Tompkin, Bill, 138
Topps Chewing Gum, 71, 73
Toward a Blueprint for Economic Survival (Mauro), 215
Traded sector. *See* Economic base
Training. *See* Job training
Training vouchers, 272

Transfer payment reinvestment. *See* Employment and Training Choices program; Self-Employment Demonstration project; Supported work; Temporary Employment Assistance Program; Welfare reform, comprehensive approach to
Transitional Employment Enterprises (Massachusetts), 198–200, 294
Trujillo, Richard, 130–131
Tucson, Arizona, 116, 120
Turley, Stan, 119
Turnarounds, 190–193
Turner, Curtis, Jr., 99
Tylawsky, Ivan, 60, 61, 70

U

UAPB. *See* University of Arkansas at Pine Bluff
UAW. *See* United Auto Workers
UDC. *See* Urban Development Corporation
Uehlein, Julius, 45
Umbrella bonds, 341n10
Umbrella organizations, 124–129
Unemployment benefits, 104, 188–189
Unemployment insurance, 8, 280, 281
Unemployment taxes, 37, 169
Unions: culture of industry and, 8, 73, 74, 75; plant closings and, 188–189, 192, 282; workfare and, 238, 292, 295. *See also* Labor-management committees; Work force; *specific unions*
United Auto Workers, 168
United Steel Workers, 75
University City Science Center (Philadelphia), 274
University of Arkansas at Pine Bluff (UAPB), 95–96
University of Pittsburgh, 56
Urban areas: community development in, 23–25, 230–235, 303, 305–308; HMO-based health care in, 134. *See also specific cities*
Urban Development Corporation (New York), 213, 221, 240
Urban poor, 289–290
Urban vs. rural development, 258
Usury law, 104, 105–106

V

Van Dyk, Ted, 323
Vaughan, Roger, 34, 40, 137, 150, 214, 272
Venture capital, 7, 38, 250–251; Ben Franklin Partnership and, 51, 57–58; community development corporations and, 308; private sources of, 29, 57–58, 156–158; public funds for, 28, 76, 155–158. *See also* Risk capital; Seed capital
Vermont, 303
Vocational-technical education, 9, 64, 100–102

W

Wages, competition and, 11, 256–257
Wage subsidies, 272, 273, 298
Walter, Susan, 34
Wang Laboratories, 24, 30–31
Ward, John, 86, 108, 109
War on Poverty, 113–114, 180, 229

Warren, Earl, 256
Water management, 116–121
Wattenberg, Martin, 325
Waverly Fabrics, 183–184
WEDCO. *See* Women's Economic Development
　Corporation
Wednesday Morning Breakfast Group, 25–28, 181
Welfare hotels, 223
Welfare reform: attitudes toward recipients and,
　201–202, 299; comprehensive approach to, 293–
　299; cost of, 298–299; demand-driven programs
　and, 200–206; dependency and, 290, 291–293,
　296, 299; employment or training subsidies and,
　127, 198–200, 239, 281, 293–296; federal fund-
　ing for, 315–316; health care and, 108, 130–
　135, 203, 297–298; mandatory approach to, 296–
　297; in Massachusetts, 196–208; in New York,
　235–240; public jobs programs and, 295–296;
　single-parent families and, 204, 236; social
　adjustment systems and, 8, 270–271, 299
Werner, Alan, 202
Western Pennsylvania Advanced Technology
　Center, 54–56
Whaley, Randall, 274
Wheatley, Roger, 49
Whirlwind I, 176, 250
White, Frank, 91, 102
Whitehead, Ralph, 208, 336
Wholesaling: capital gaps and, 32, 158–161;
　community development corporations and, 304,
　310; real estate development and, 186–187;
　training and, 271; vs. retailing, 259–260, 275–
　276, 301
Williams, Bob, 156, 157
Wilson, John, 4
Wilson, Malcolm, 213
WIN program, 201, 203
Winter, William, 41

Winthrop Rockefeller Foundation, 100, 101, 105
Wirth, Tim, 20
Wisconsin, 134, 297–298
Wise, Robert, 33, 89, 137
Women: as entrepreneurs, 303, 307, 314; welfare
　reform and, 196–197, 204, 236, 292, 305. *See also*
　Child care
Women's Economic Development Corporation
　(Minnesota), 314
Woodson, Robert, 300
Worker buy-outs, 64, 281
Worker ownership, 8, 77, 166, 240–241, 275, 279
Workfare, 197–198, 200–201, 205, 237, 296; orga-
　nized labor and, 238, 295; problems with, 292
Work force: culture of industry and, 3–4, 8, 11–
　12, 73–76, 188–189, 277–279; education and, 3–
　6, 256–257; in industrial era, 8–9; as resource,
　152, 268–273, 328–329
Workforce Development Service (Michigan), 166
Working poor, 298, 299, 359; health care for, 133–
　134, 297–298, 359n28
Workplace democracy. *See* Participative manage-
　ment
Work teams, 72, 278, 279
Wylde, Kathryn, 228, 229, 234, 235

Y

Yankelovich, Daniel, 278
Young urban professionals, 230, 335–336
Youth Conservation Corps, 64
Youth employment, 242

Z

Zelkus, Gregory, 164
Zimmers, Emory, 52, 58